Carving WIZARDS with Tom Wolfe

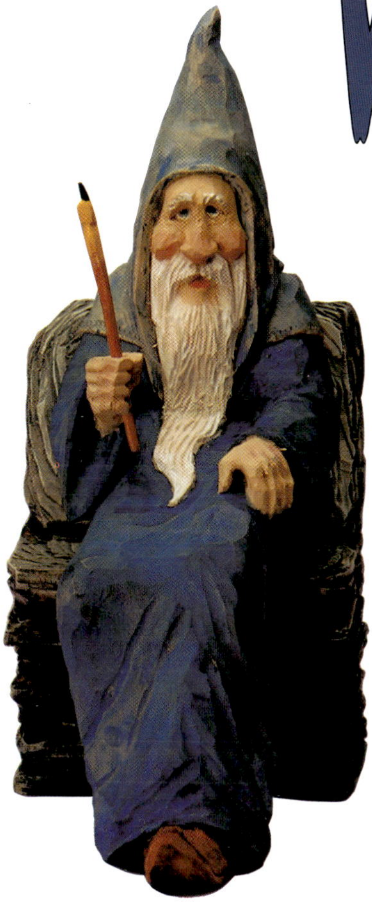

Text written with and photography by Douglas Congdon-Martin

Schiffer Publishing Ltd

77 Lower Valley Road, Atglen, PA 19310

I0805671

Acknowledgment

Thanks to Jody Garrett and the good folks at Woodcraft Supply Corp., Parkersburg, West Virginia for supplying some of the tools used in this book.

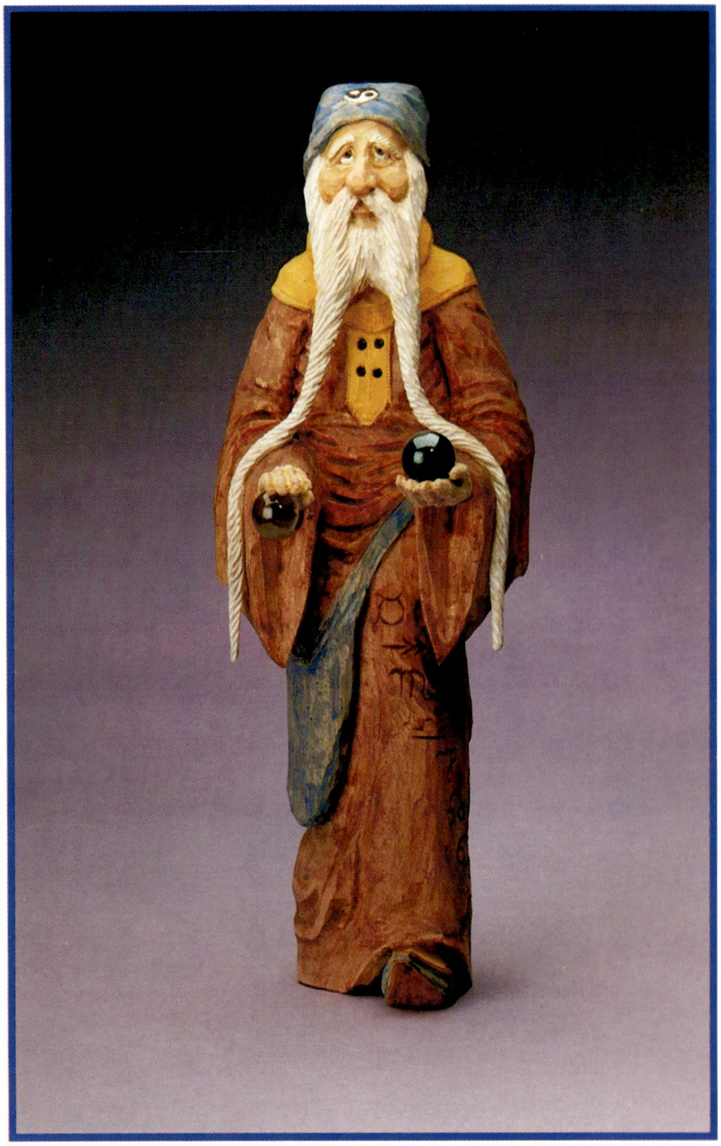

Library of Congress Cataloging-in-Publication Data

Wolfe, Tom (Tom James)
Carving wizards with Tom Wolfe / text written with and photography by Douglas Congdon-Martin.
p. cm. -- A Schiffer book for woodcarvers)
ISBN 0-88740-712-9
1. Wood-carving. 2. Wood-carved figurines. 3. Wizards in art
I. Congdon-Martin, Douglas. II. Title. III. Series.
TT199.7.W6388 1995
731.4'62--dc20 94-23251
CIP

Printed in China.
ISBN: 0-88740-712-9

Published by Schiffer Publishing, Ltd.
77 Lower Valley Road
Atglen, PA 19310
Please write for a free catalog.
This book may be purchased from the publisher.
Please include $2.95 postage.
Try your bookstore first.

We are interested in hearing from authors with book ideas on related subjects.

Contents

Introduction

Wizards have always had a fascination for me. They carry a lot of character and allow me to take off in flights of fancy...and they are popular with my customers. I have carved them for years, and in fact one Wizard made a guest appearance in the gallery of my first Christmas carving book, *Santa and His Friends.*

Wizard really means "wise one," and in fact one early English bible translation talks about the "wizards" that followed the star to the baby Jesus. For most of us today, though, a Wizard is one who has magical powers and knowledge of the astrological sciences. We think of Merlin, probably the most famous Wizard of all time. Through his knowledge and magic he was able to mold Arthur into the king of England and the subject of hundreds of years of myth and legend.

The popularity of Wizards today is chiefly among the young. From *Dungeons and Dragons* to many of the popular video games, some of the chief characters are Wizards of great power. In comic books, fantasy reigns and Wizards are among the heroes and villains.

Whatever your interest, I think you will find these carvings fun and challenging. I've tried to give you a basic approach to Wizard carving, along with some patterns. But it isn't difficult to take those as starting points and create your own Wizards from your imagination.

As always, I hope you enjoy the carvings!

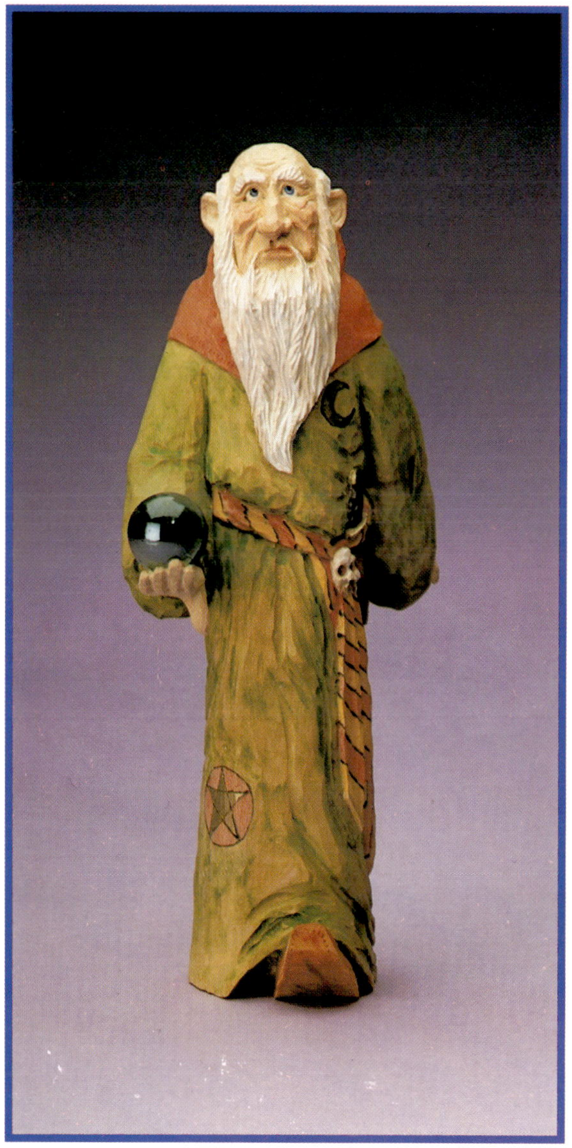

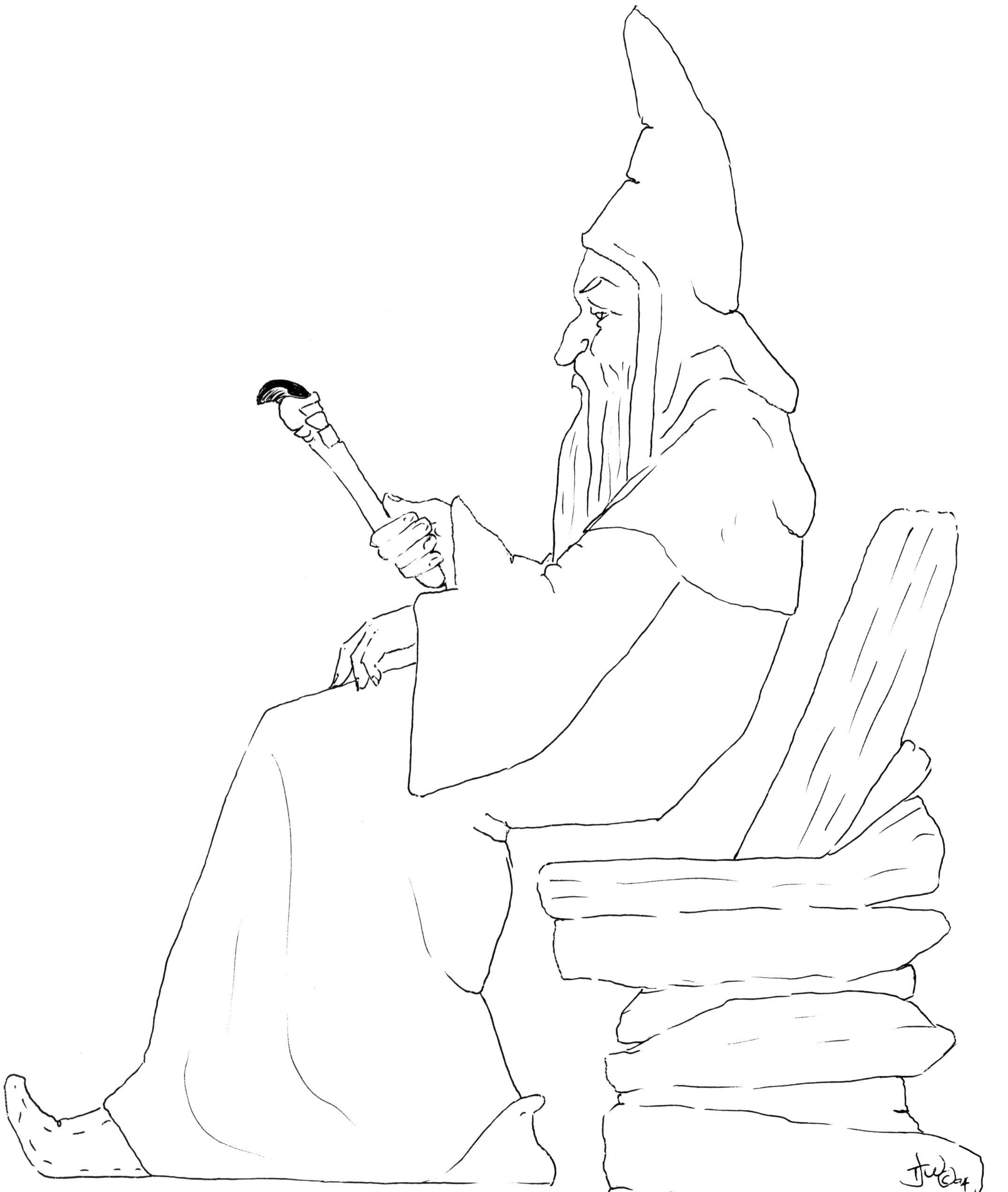

Carving the Wizard

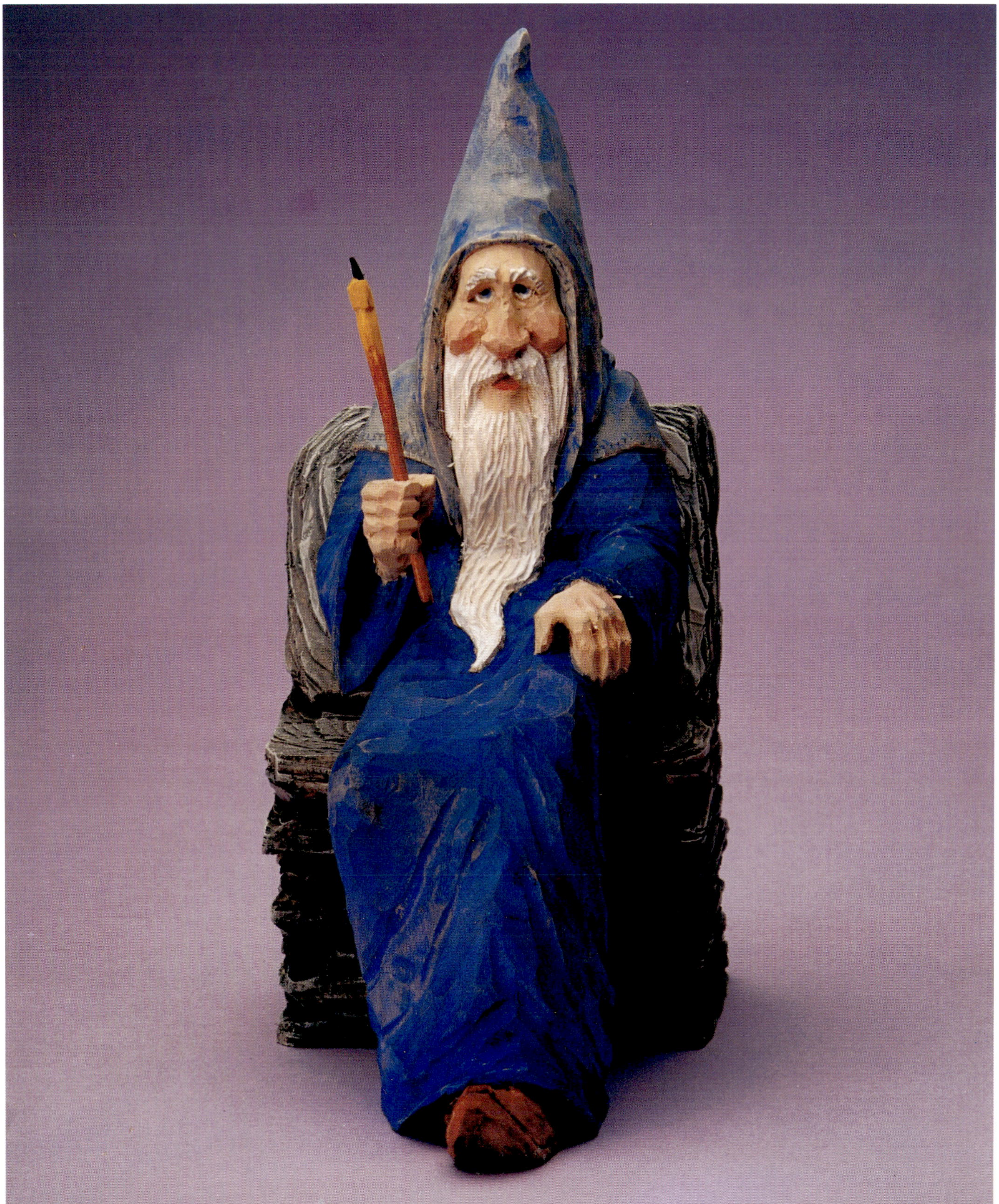

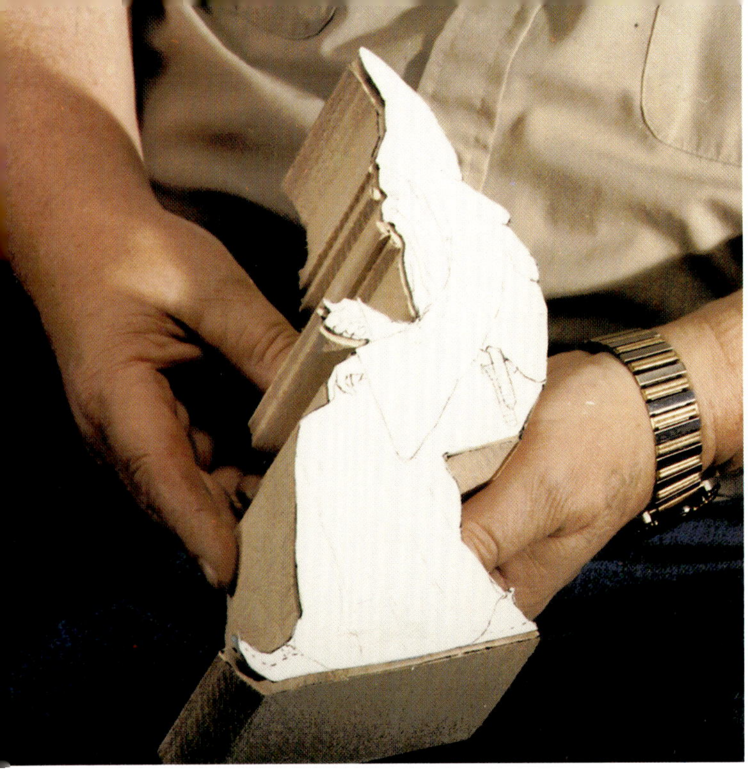

Cut the Wizard blank out of piece of 4" bass wood. Narrow it down to 3". When I do this I try to cut off the weathered surface of the wood. This rough surface will dull your knife, so it is good to get rid of it when you can.

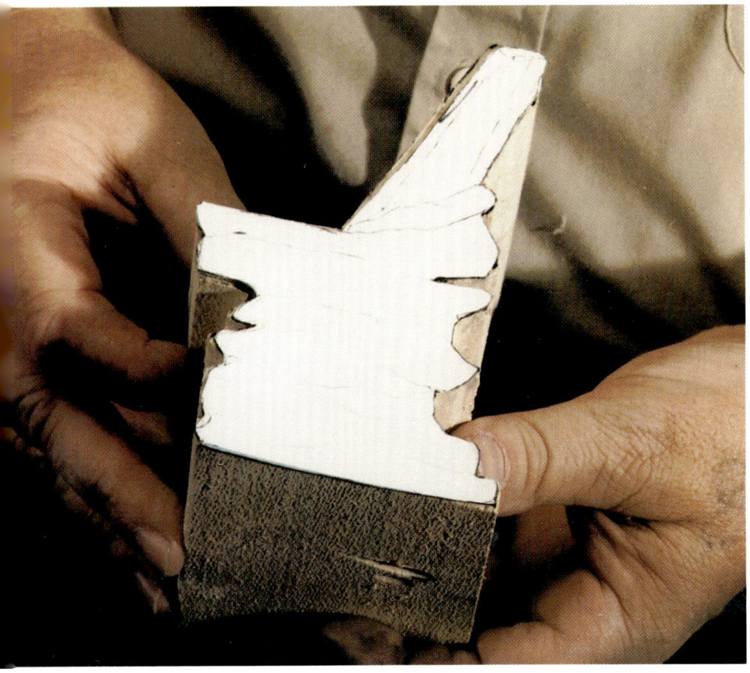

Cut the stone chair out of a full 4 " thick piece of basswood.

Draw a center line all around.

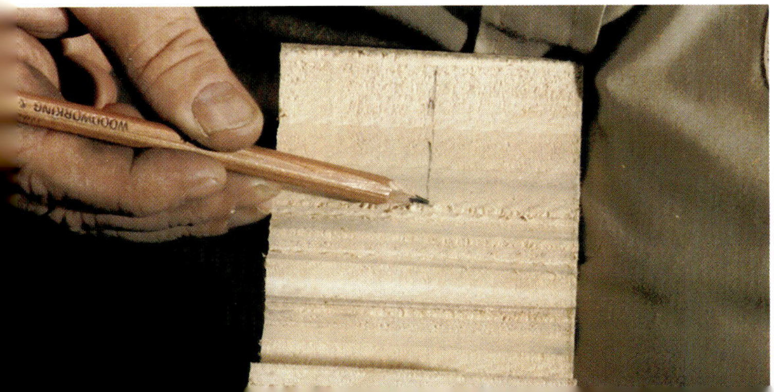

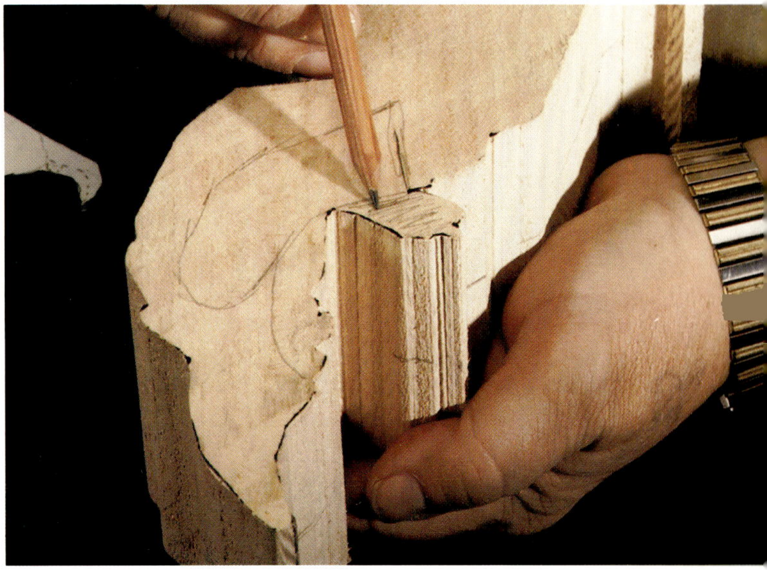

Refer to the pattern and draw in some of the profile details. This will help you get things right in your head before carving. With arm lower on this side, I know that this upper hand will removed on this side.

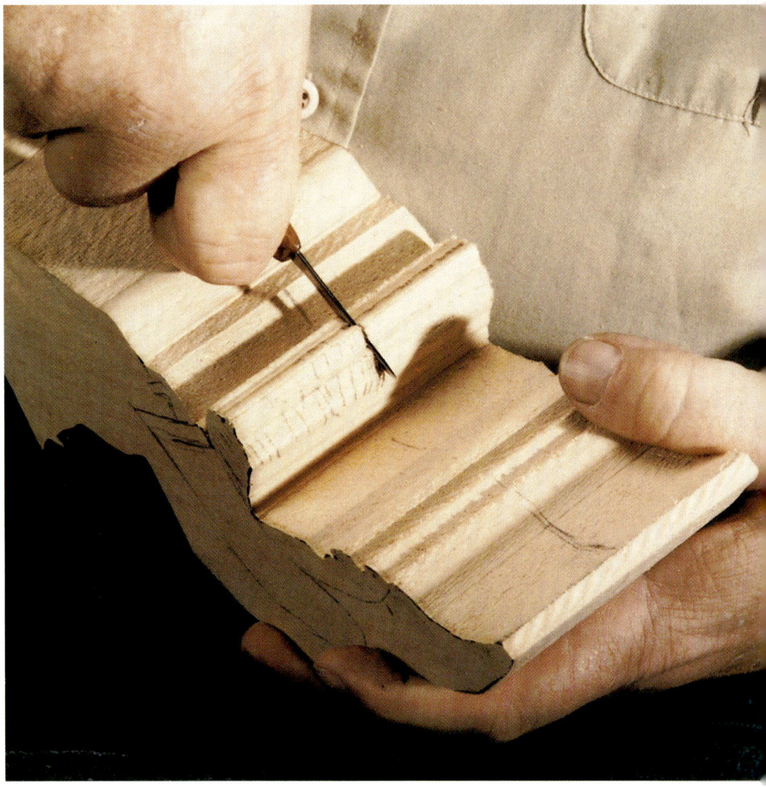

Cut on the center line between the hands.

Cut back to the line from the hand to be removed.

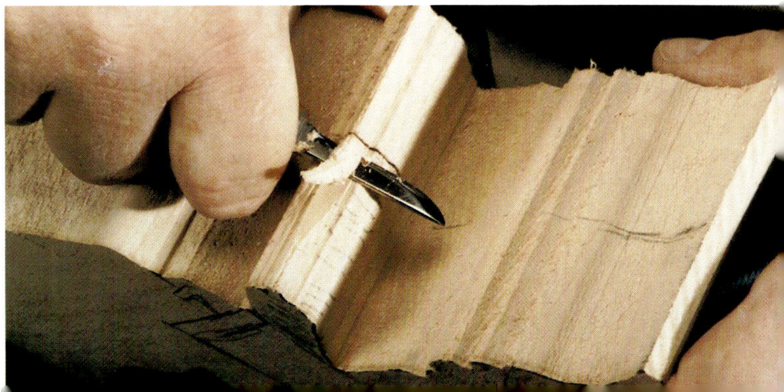

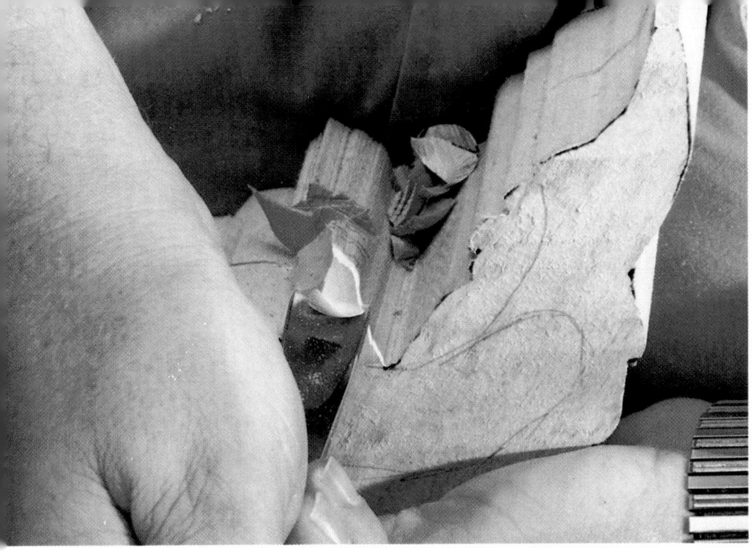

A gouge will remove a lot of this material easily.

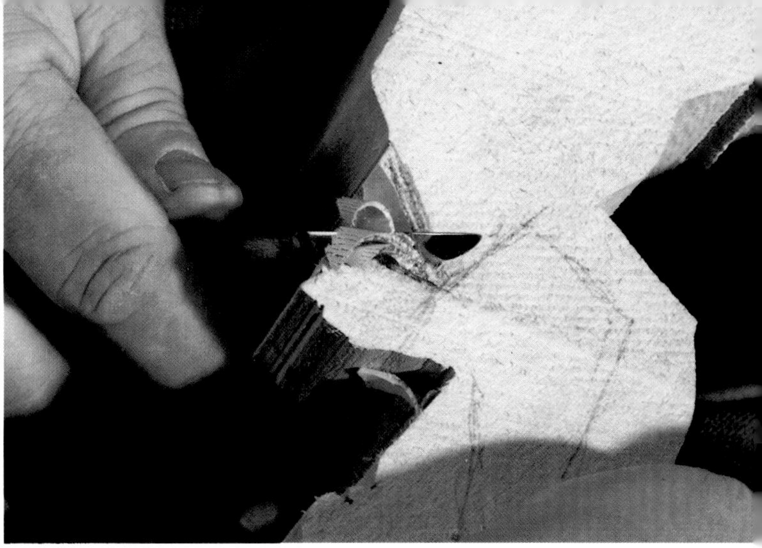

Cut a stop under the hand and come back to it from the leg.

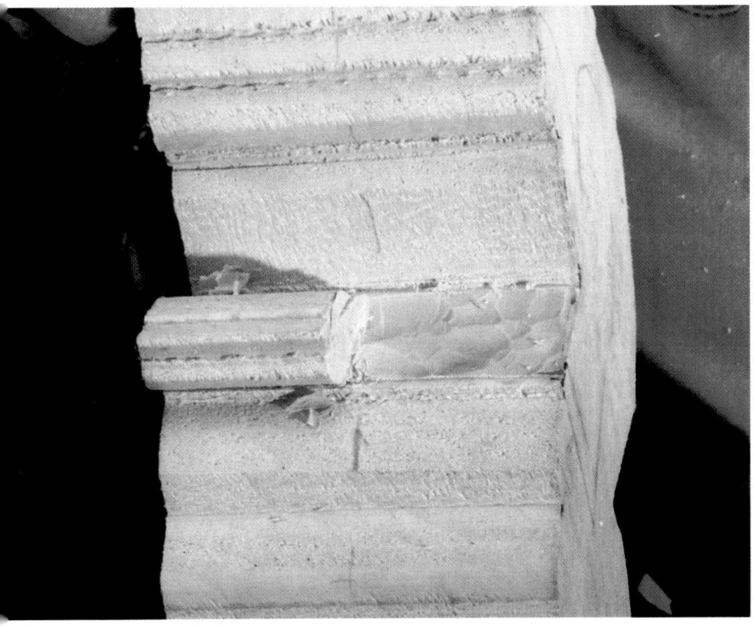

Progress.

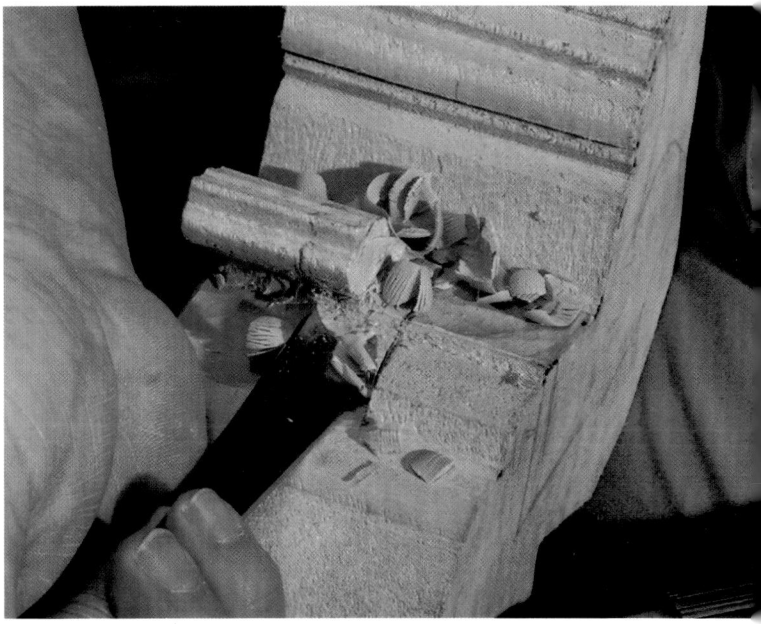

Because of the grain, it is easier to come up the lap beside the center line stop cut using a gouge.

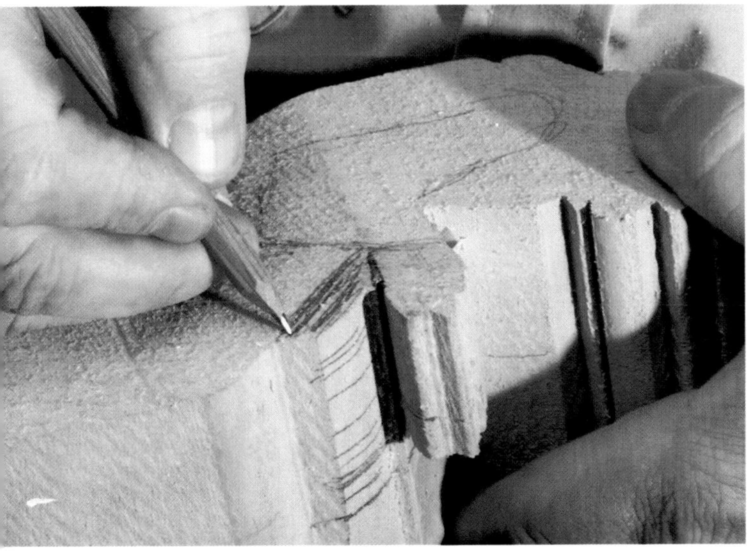

Below the raised hand I need to remove this area above the leg, back to the center line.

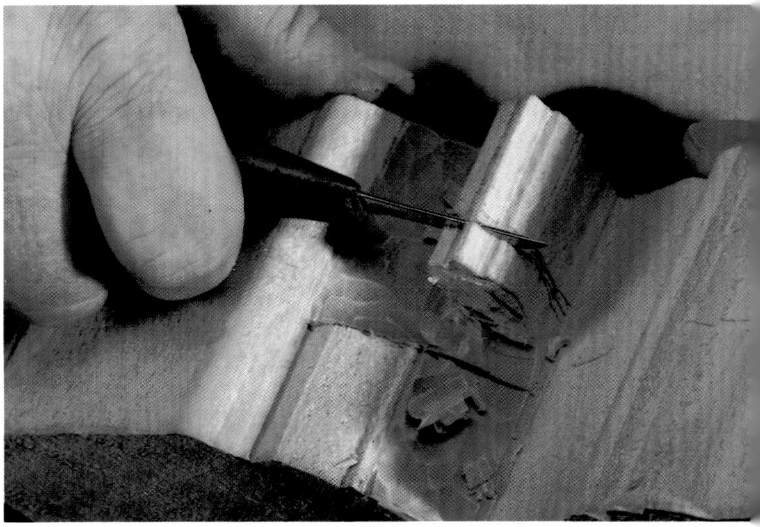

I'm going to thin the raised hand by cutting a stop on the inside edge...

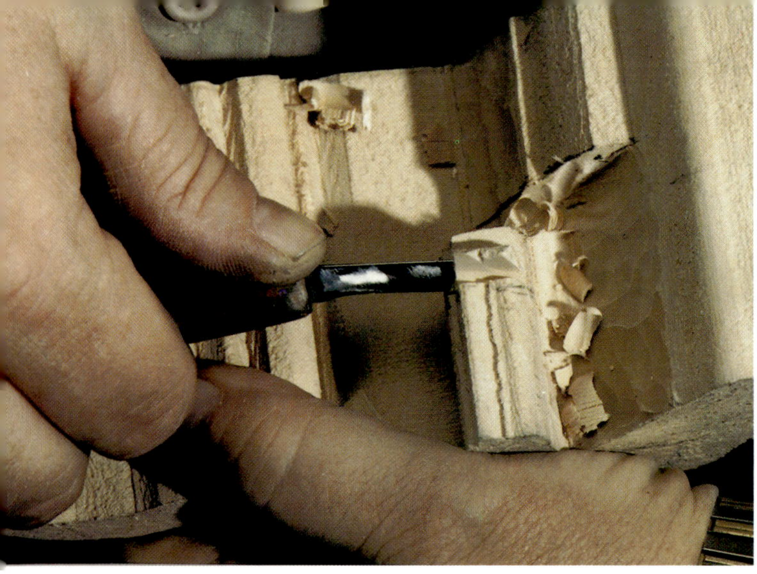

and cutting back to it.

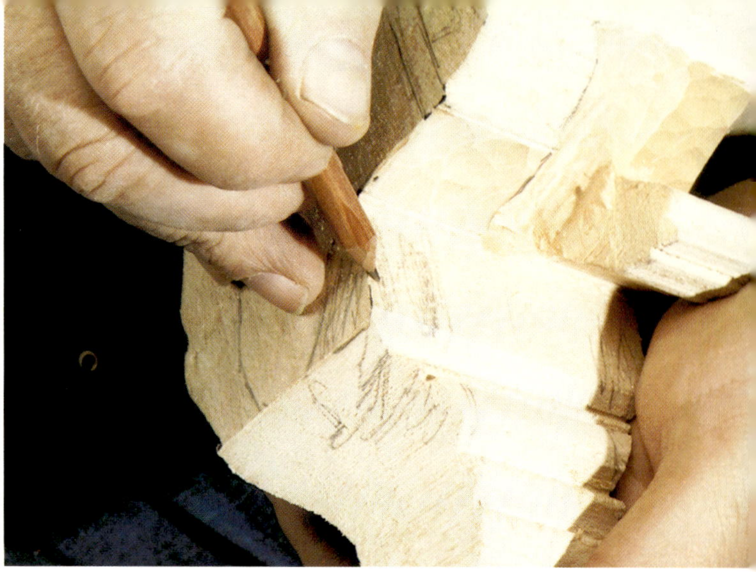

I want to knock off the corner between the shoulder and the face, bringing the face line straight down into the chest.

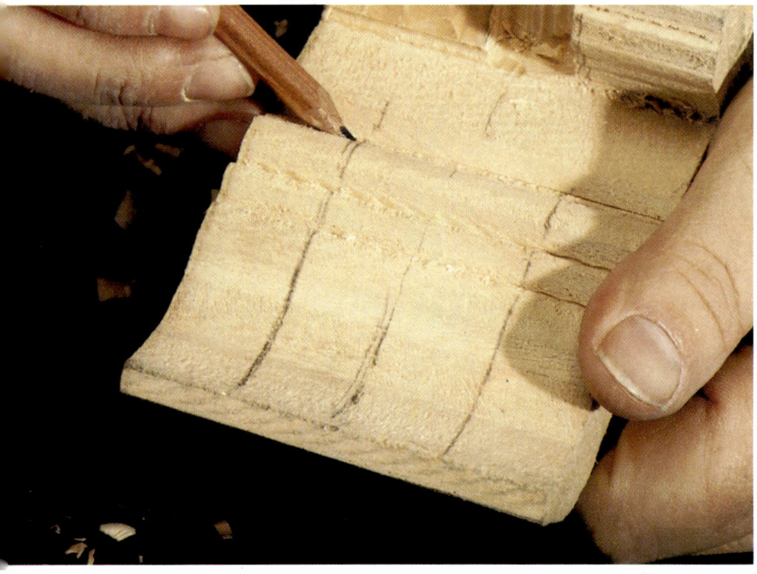

Draw in the width of the head.

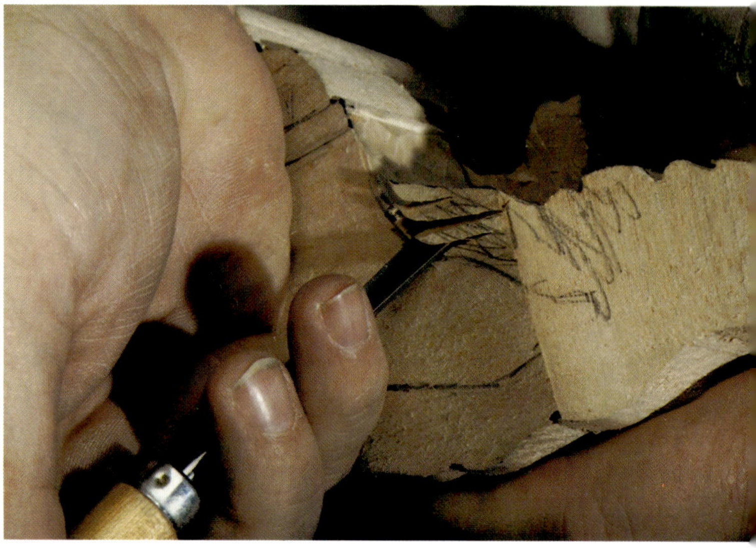

Come in from the shoulder with a gouge.

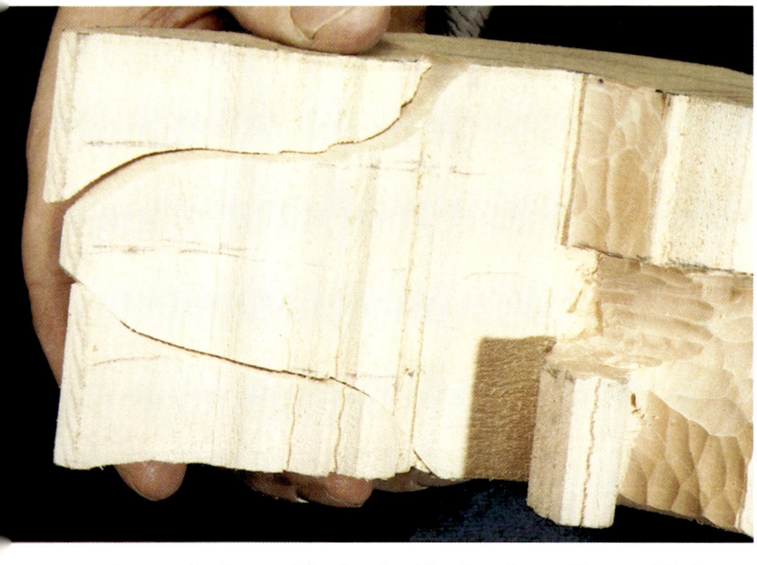

I've cut the lines of the head with a bandsaw. You could also use a coping saw or simply carve away the excess. The hat is pointed, so I've curved it in a little at the top.

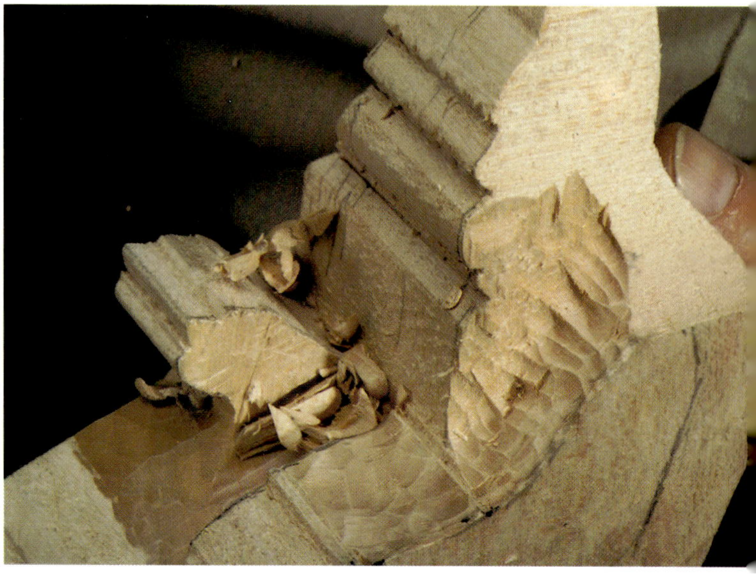

A scooping gouge cut eliminates the need for a stop. The result.

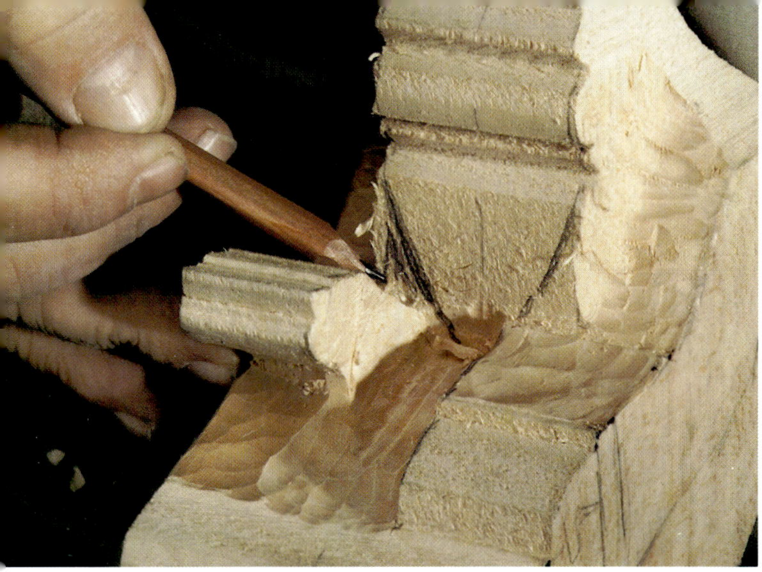

The beard will taper at the bottom into the chest...

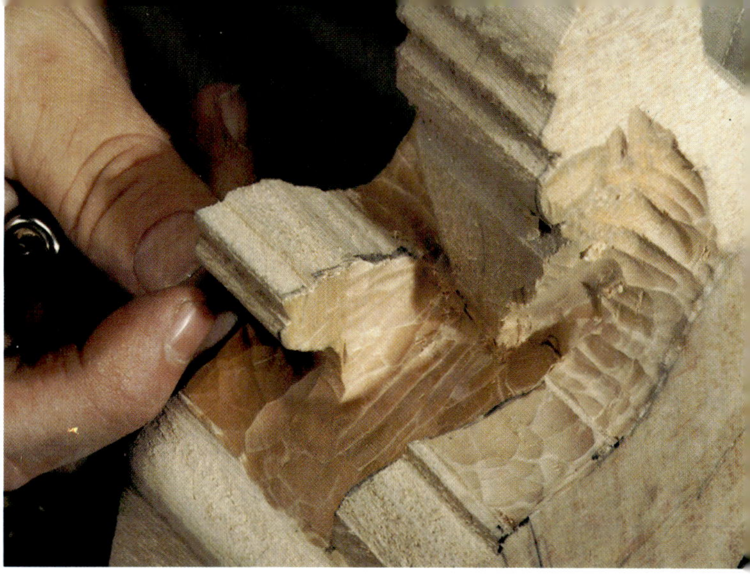

Progress.

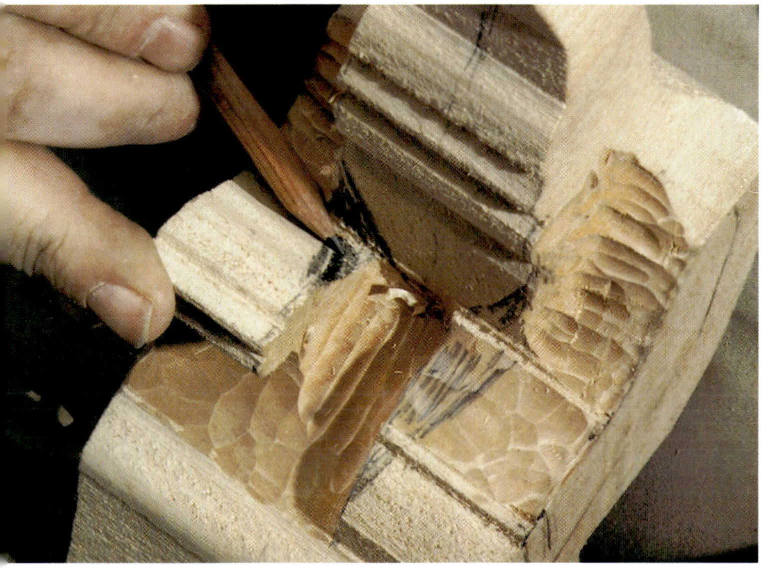

and, while I'm marking, we need to reduce the inside of the arms.

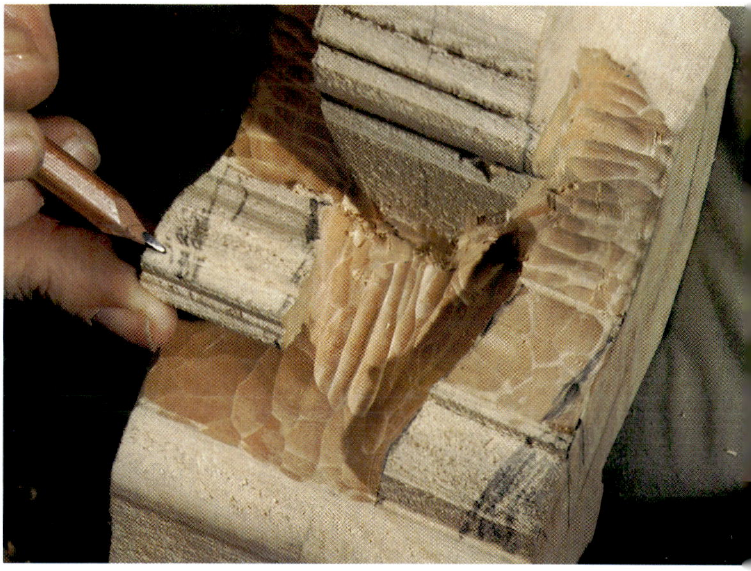

Mark the outside of the arms.

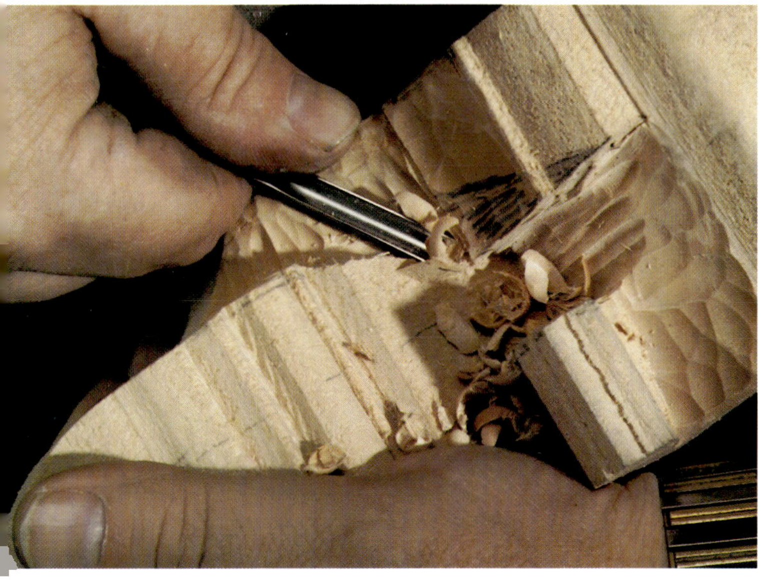

Clean the area with a gouge.

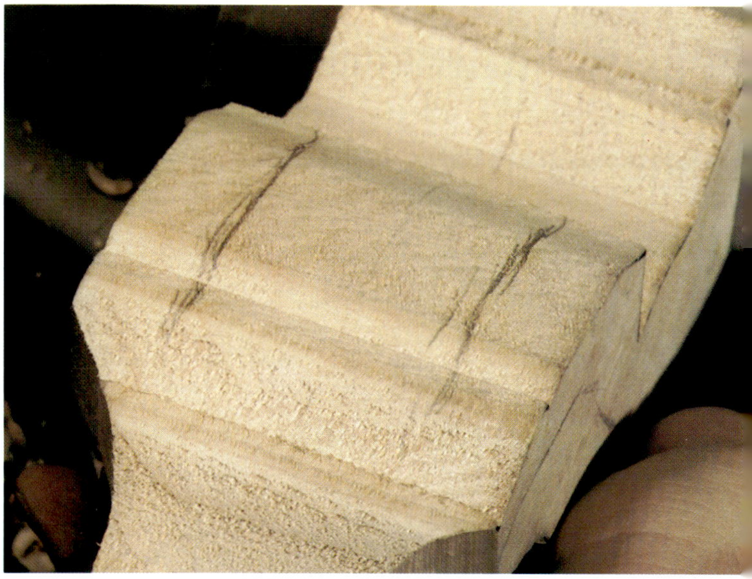

Mark the width of the back between the arms. This is an area that needs to be left untouched.

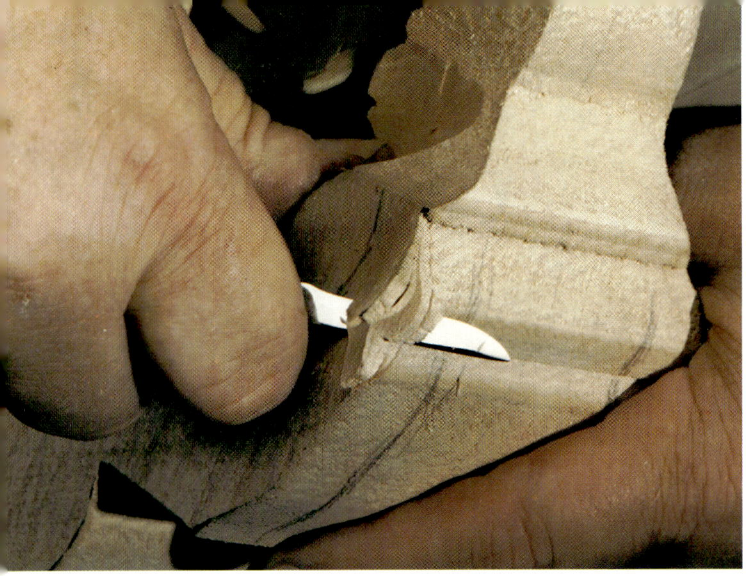

Pop off the corners on the back of the figure.

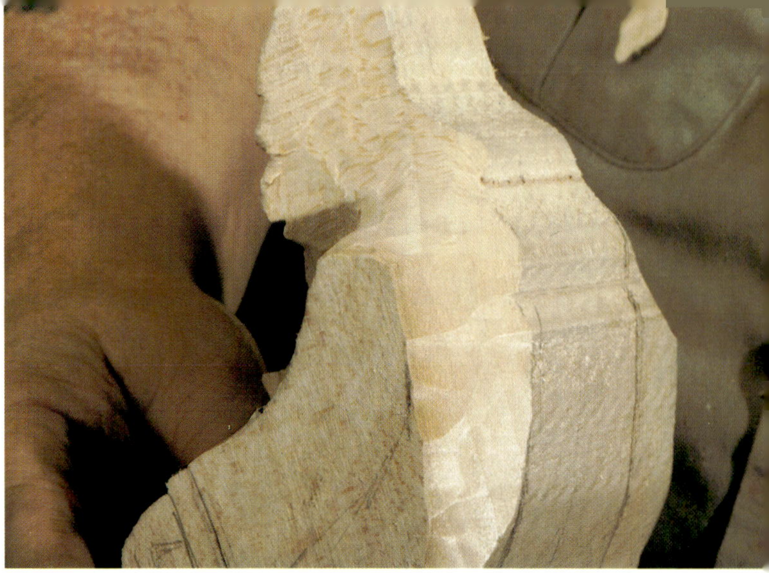

and back.

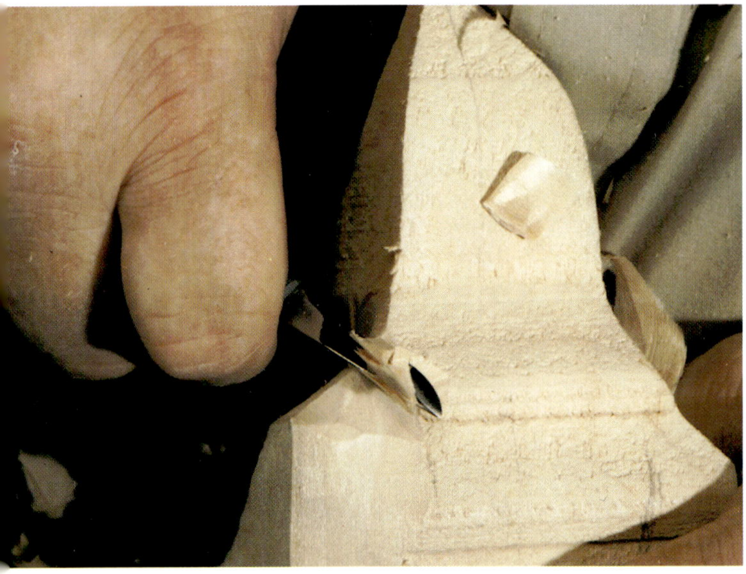

At the shoulder, round it over.

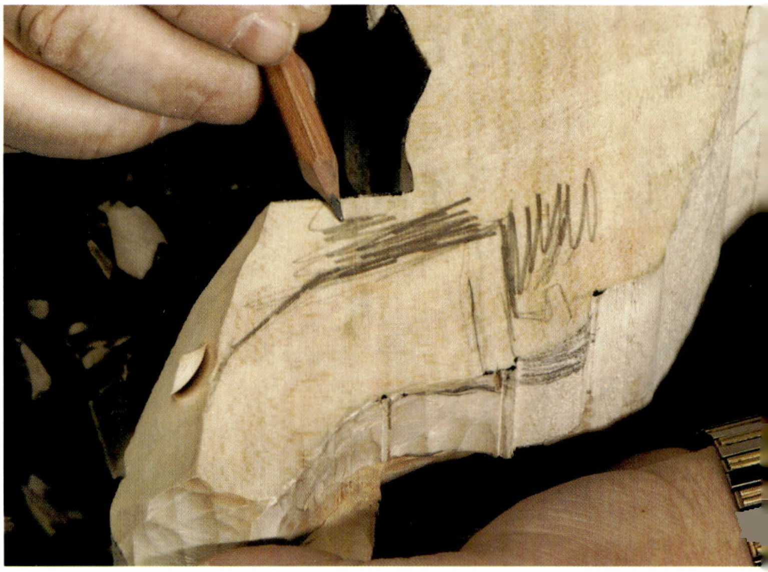

Mark the areas under the arms to be removed.

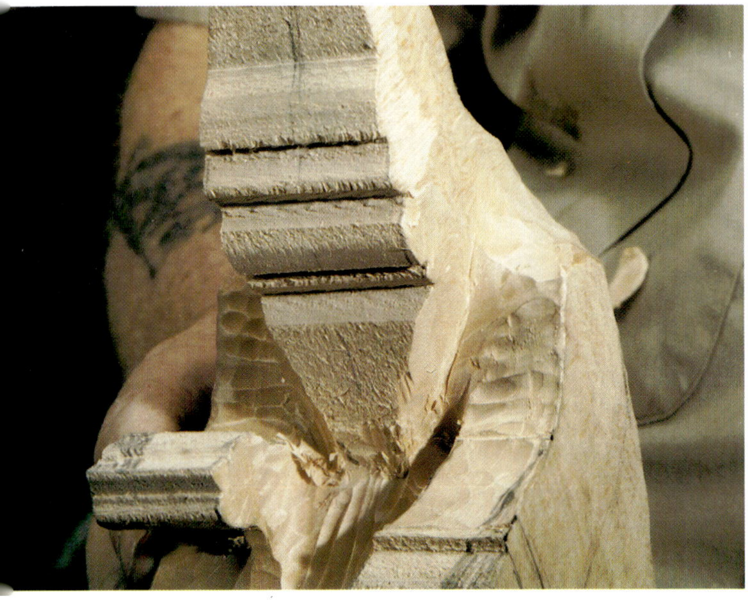

Progress, front...

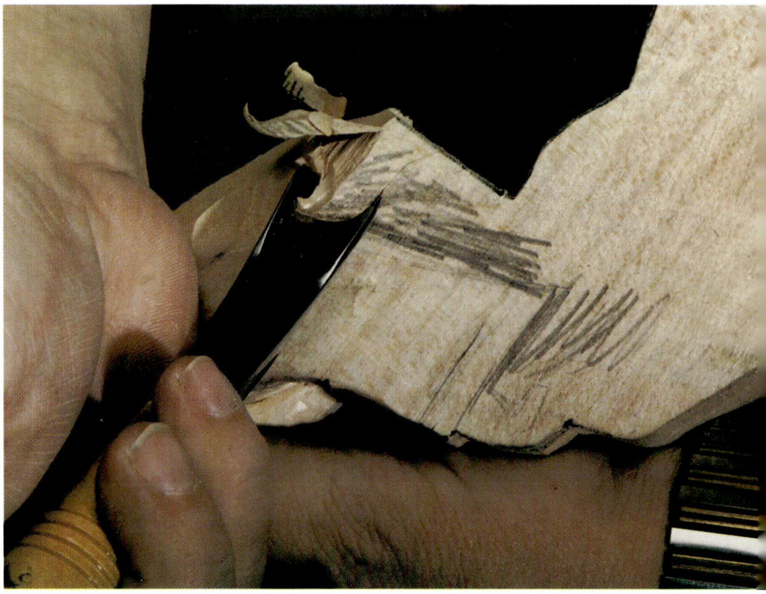

Cut them away with a gouge.

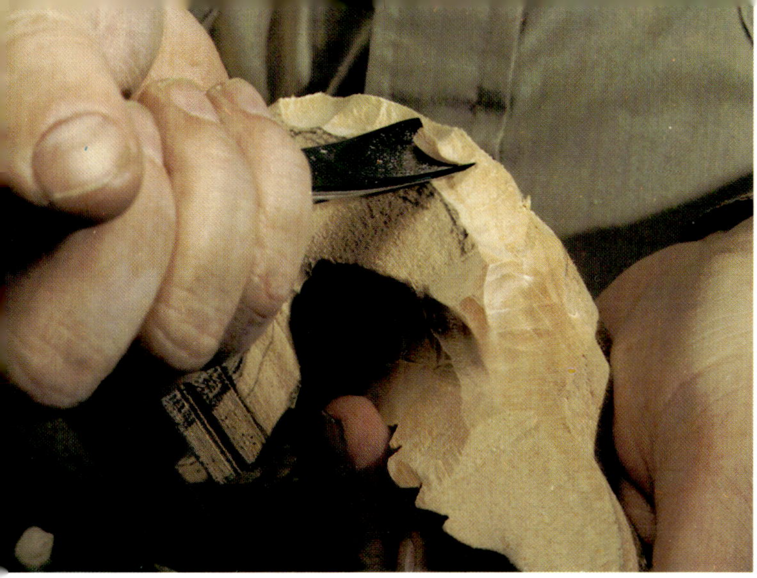

Repeat on the other side.

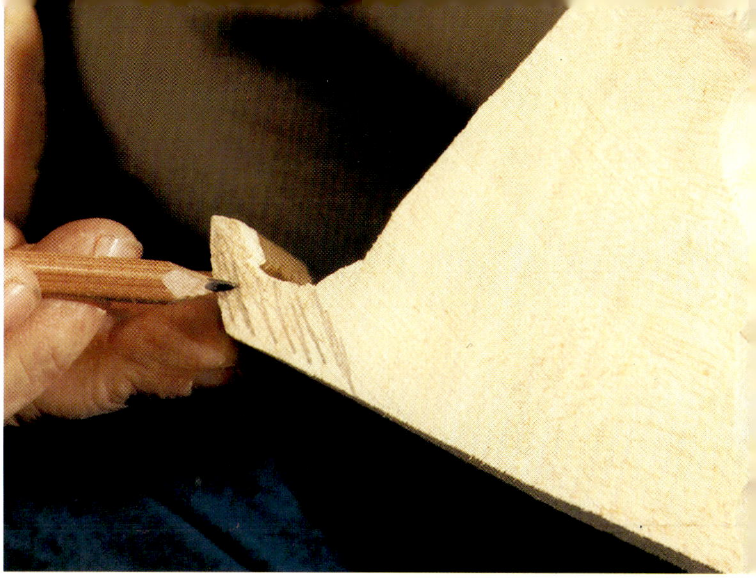

back to the line of the robe.

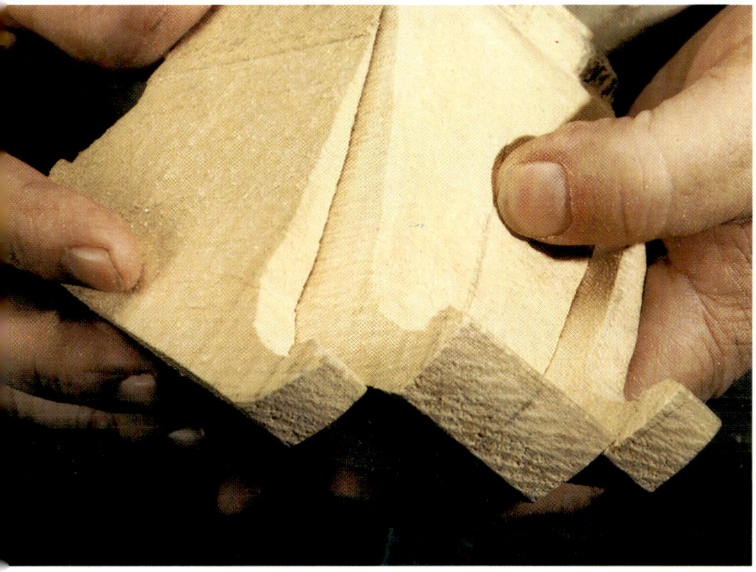

I cut the sides off the legs with the bandsaw. One foot will be behind the other, so the easiest way to take off this excess is the best way.

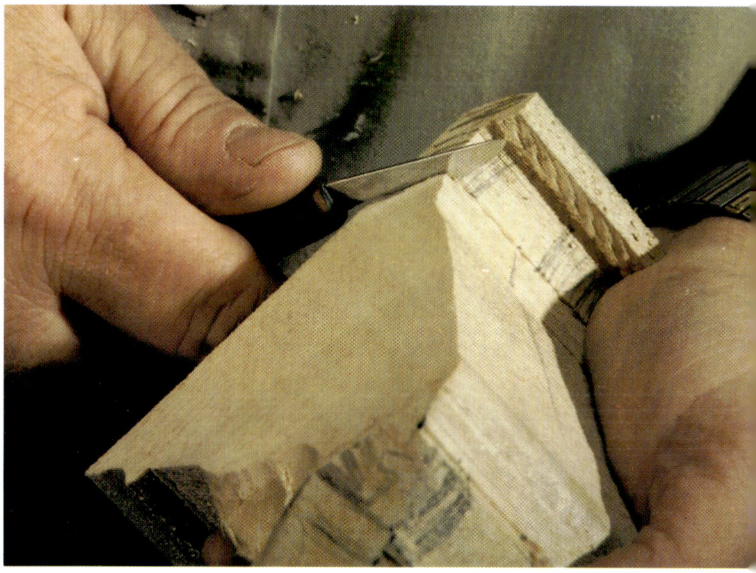

Cut a stop in the line of the robe...

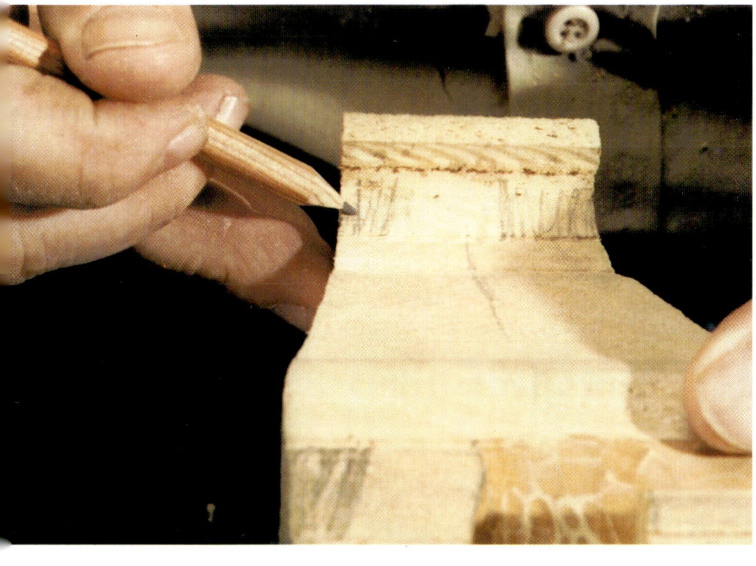

Mark the sides of the foot for removal...

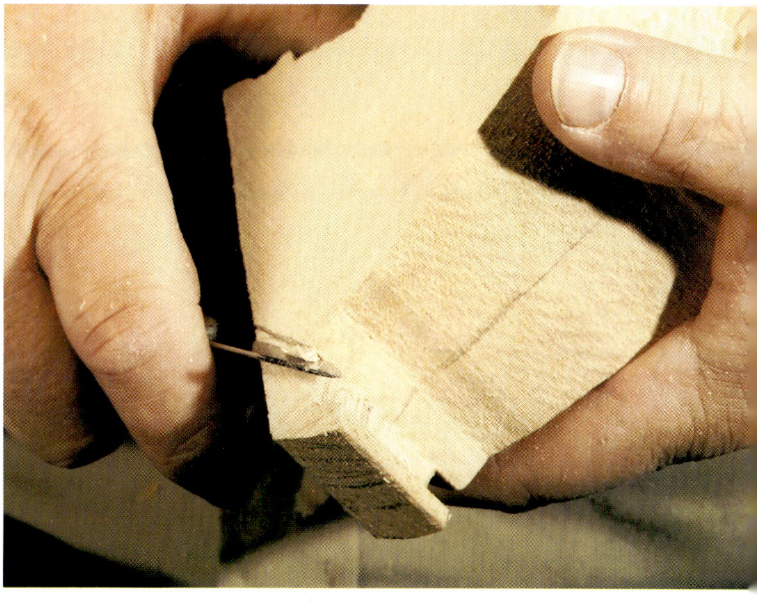

and back to it from the side of the foot.

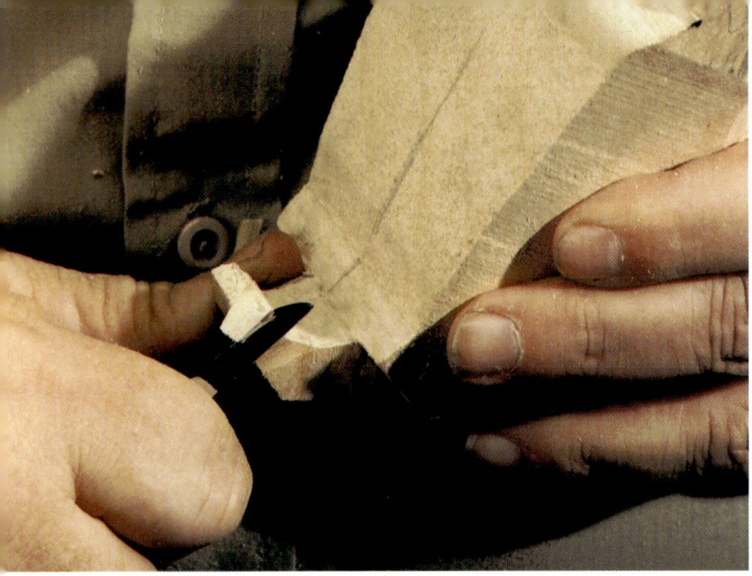

Do the other side the same way.

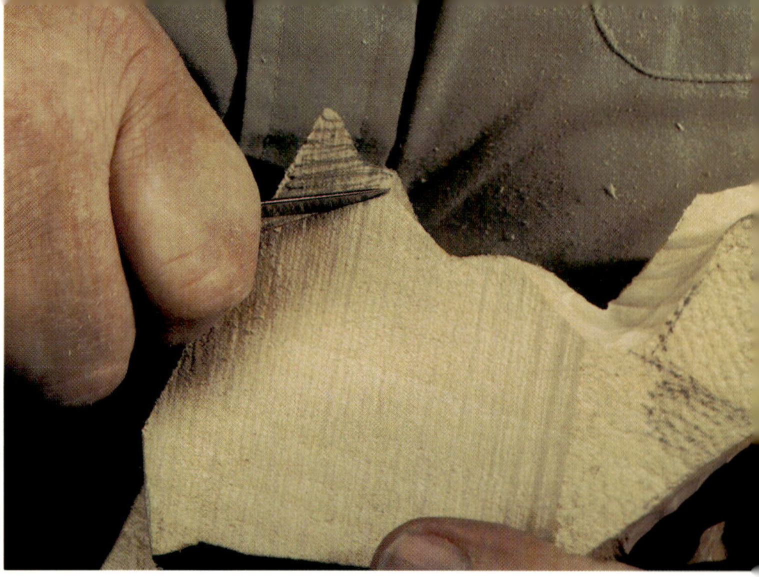

Remove this in the same way; cut a stop at the robe line...

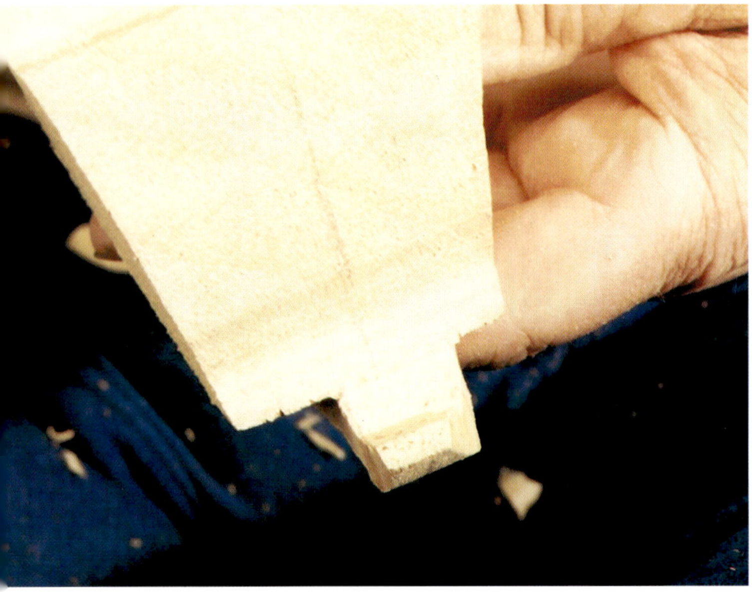

Shape the toe so it begins to look like a foot. Eventually this will be pointed, but for now I will leave it blunt.

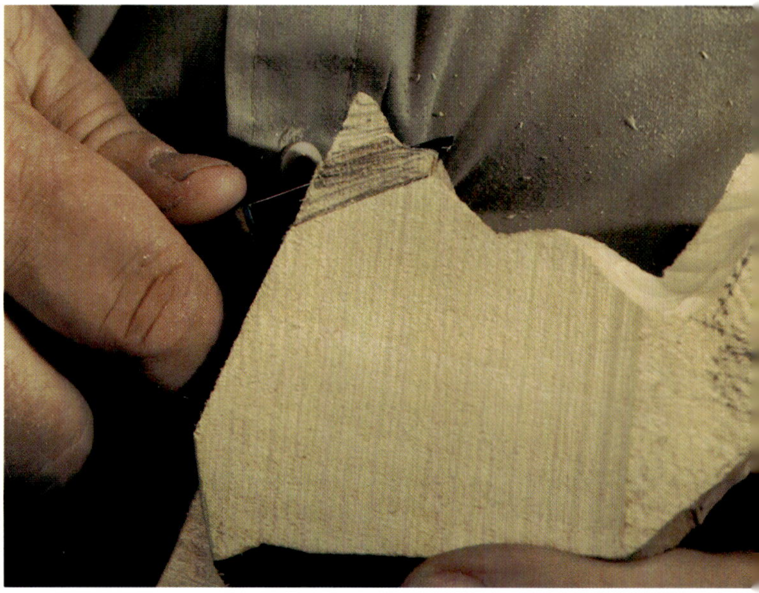

and cut back to it beside the foot.

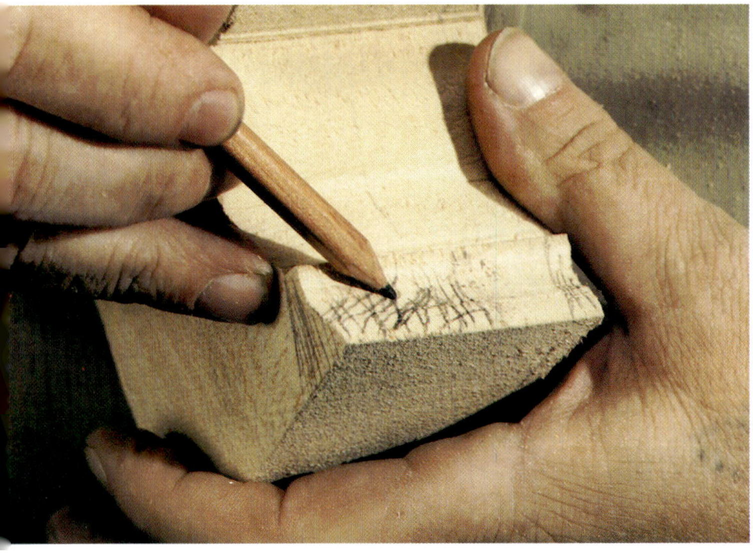

Mark the areas to be removed beside the hind foot.

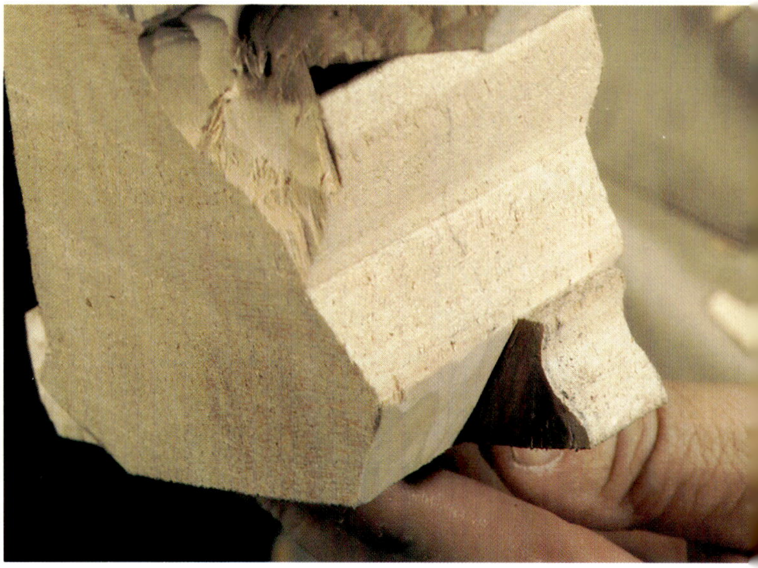

The result.

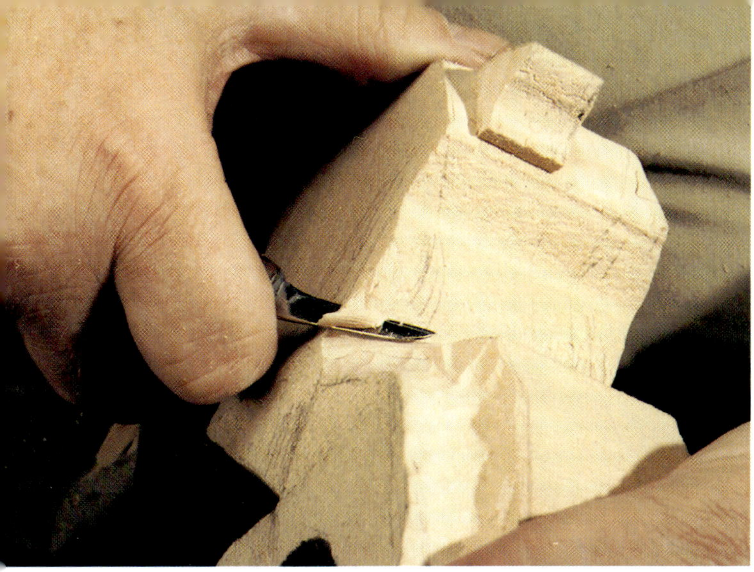

Knock off the back corner of the skirt of the robe so it begins to look like it is tucked under the chair.

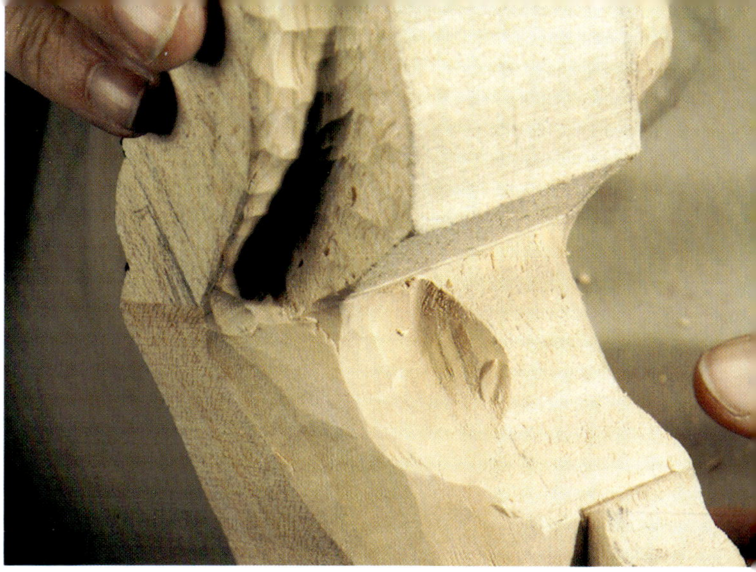

Progress.

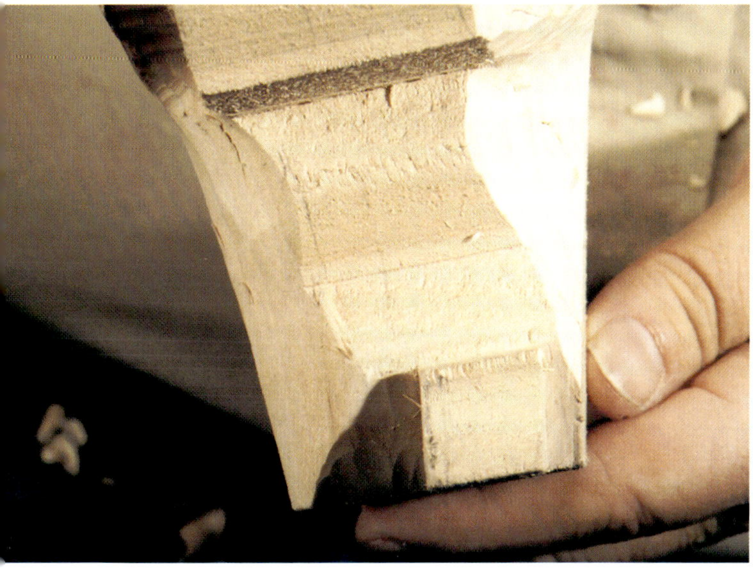

Progress. I need to reduce some on the left side of the right leg, to establish its shape.

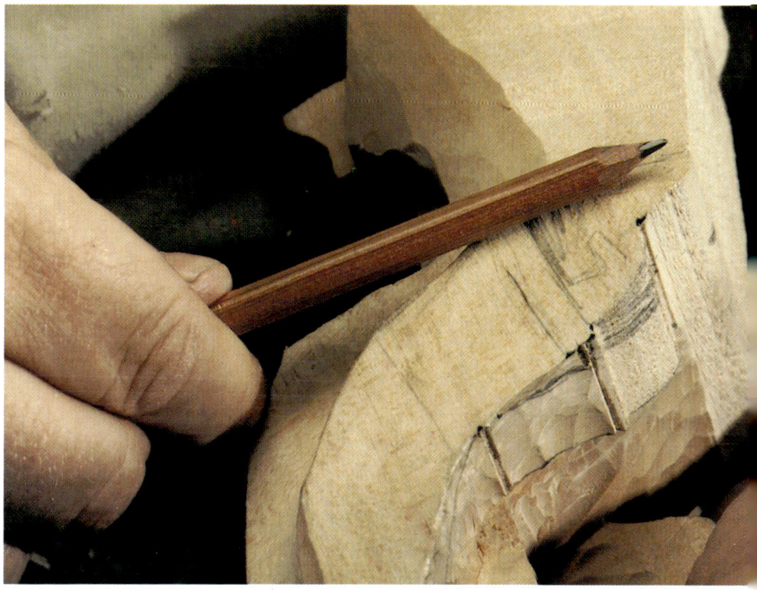

The leg is roughly divided into two equal lengths, from the back of the hip to the knee, and from the knee to the heel. To establish the location of the knee use a pencil as a depth gauge. Measure from the hip to the knee...

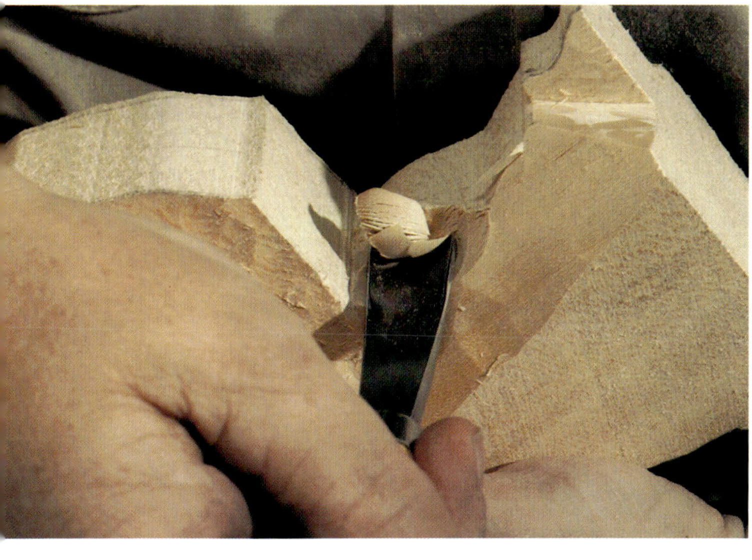

Take away the wood with a gouge from the side.

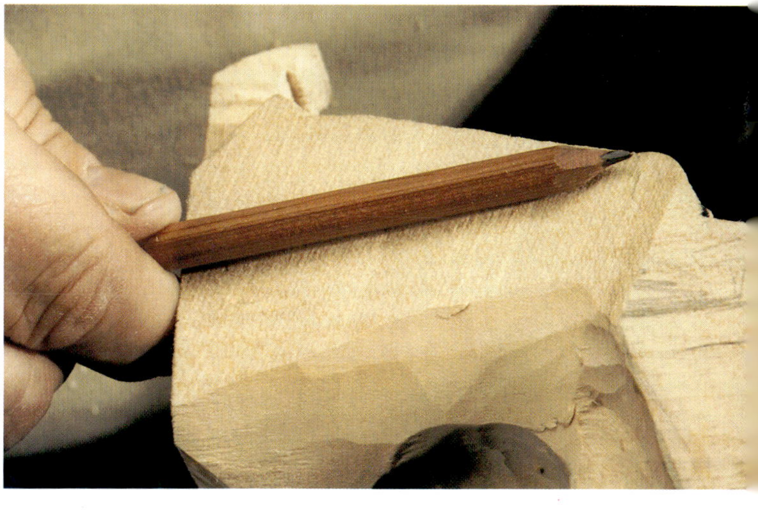

and from the knee to the heel.

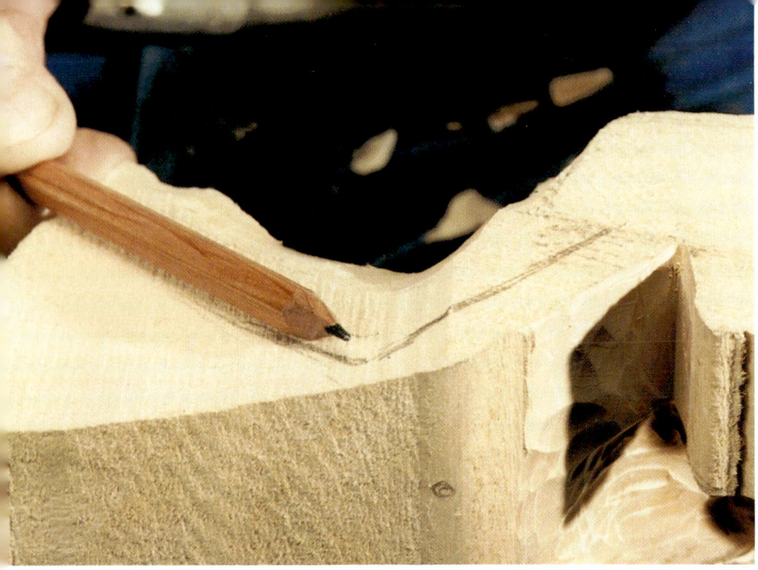

On the knee that is bent back, the knee is lowered because of the angle of the leg. Measure from the heel to the knee...

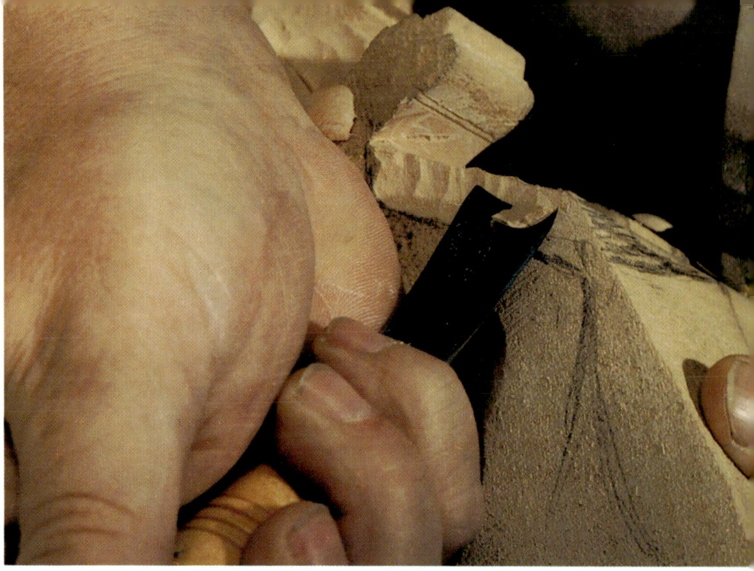

Establish the plane with a gouge.

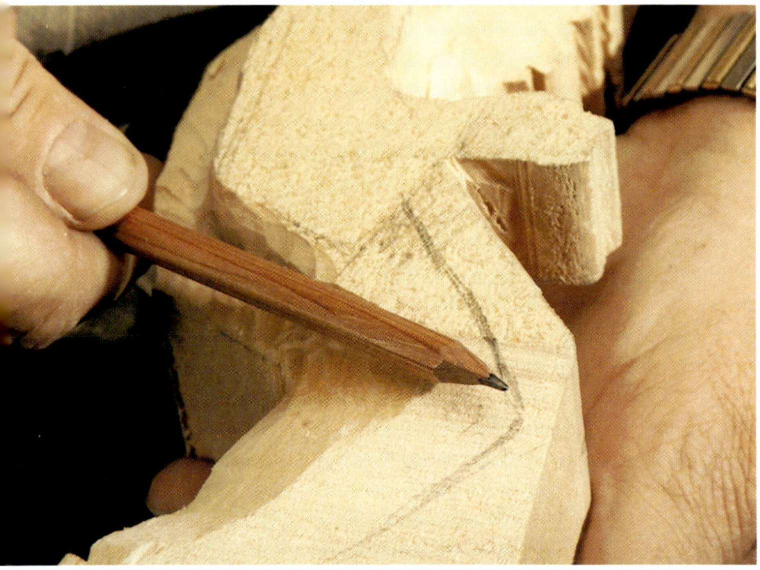

and from the hip to the knee. Where the lines intersect is the position of the knee.

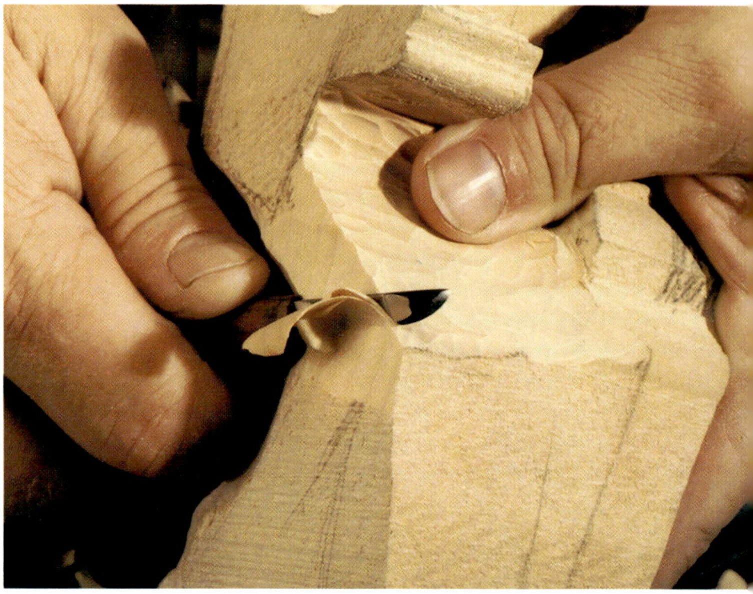

Bring the knee in a little bit by trimming the outside surface.

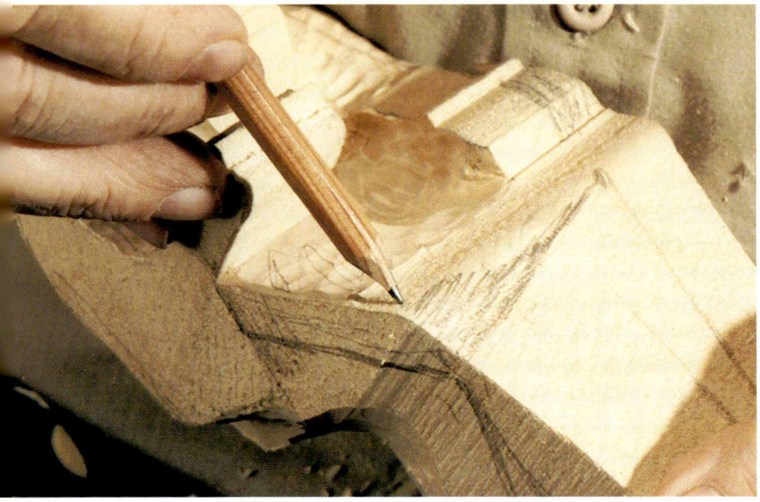

The area above the thigh of the right leg needs to be taken away. Since it will stretch to the left knee the fabric needs to taper up to it.

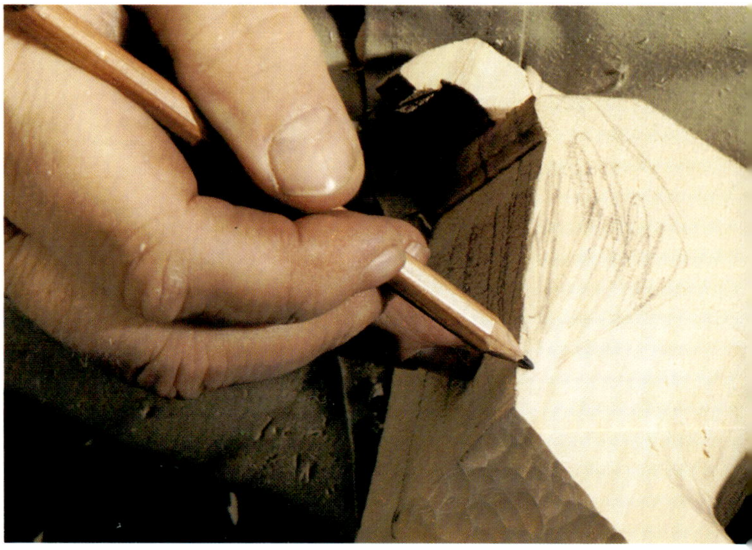

This area in front of the right leg will be scooped out. The fabric will, of course, flow around the forward left leg.

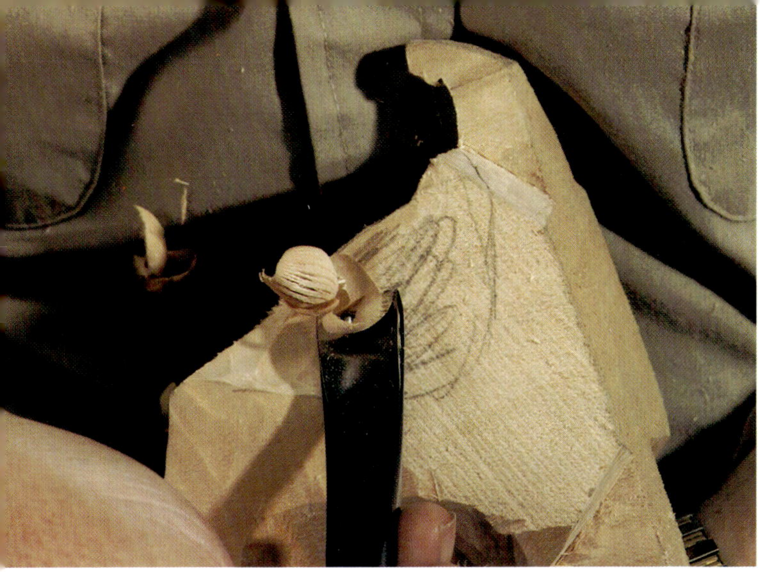

A curved cut with the gouge does well at this.

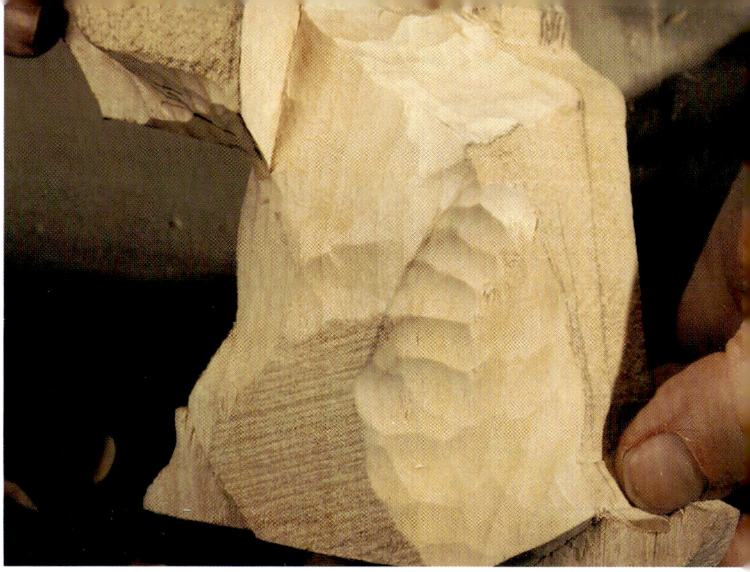

The right leg is taking shape.

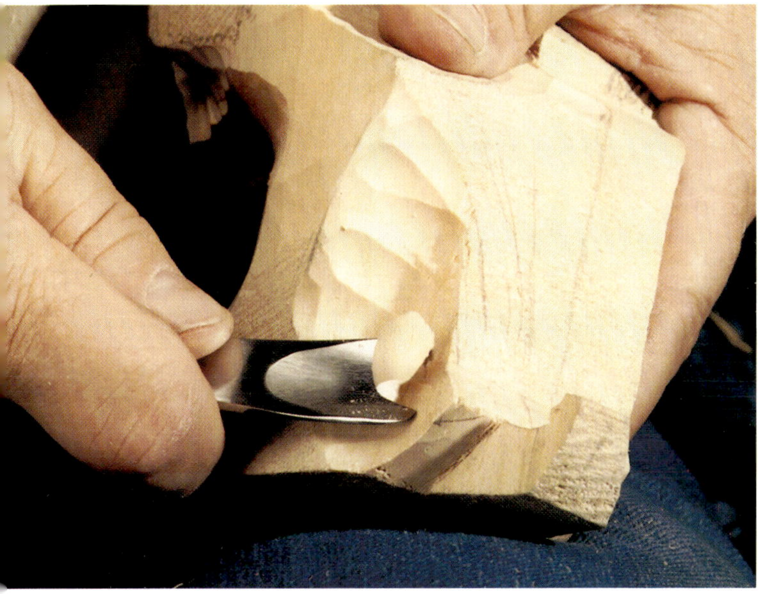

Continue down to the foot.

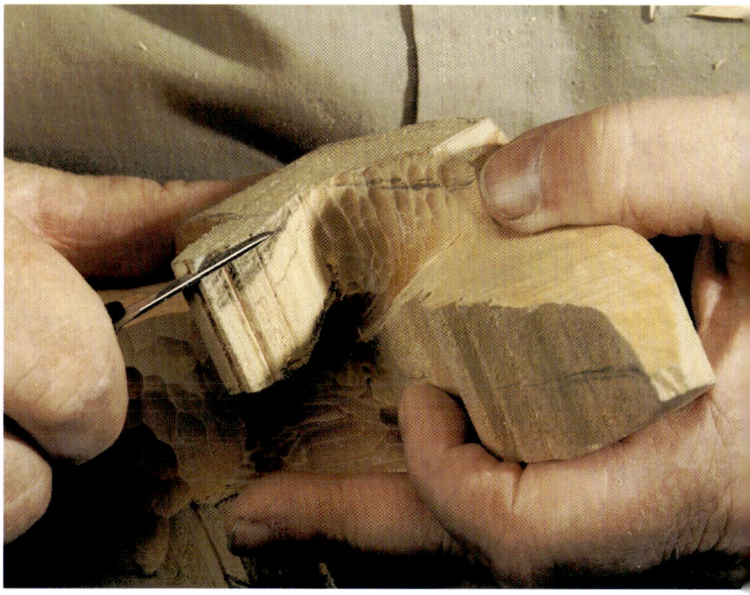

Trim away the outside surface of the hand.

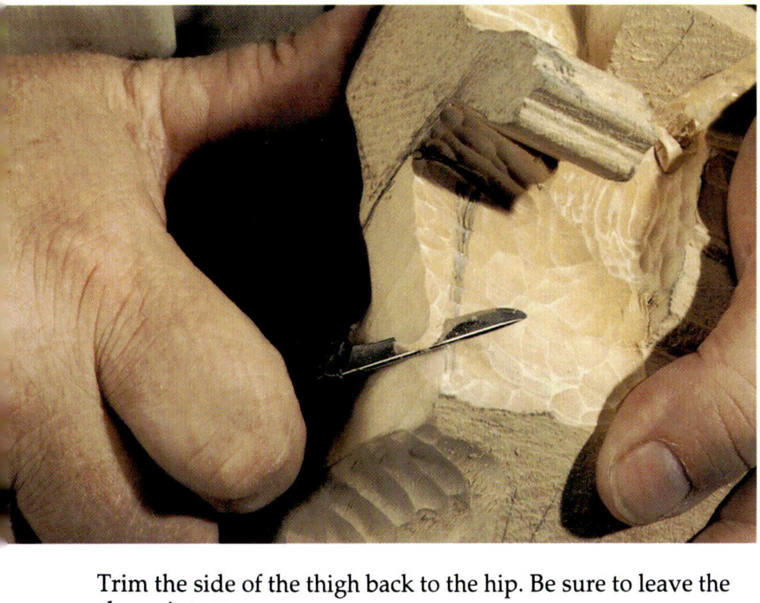

Trim the side of the thigh back to the hip. Be sure to leave the sleeve intact.

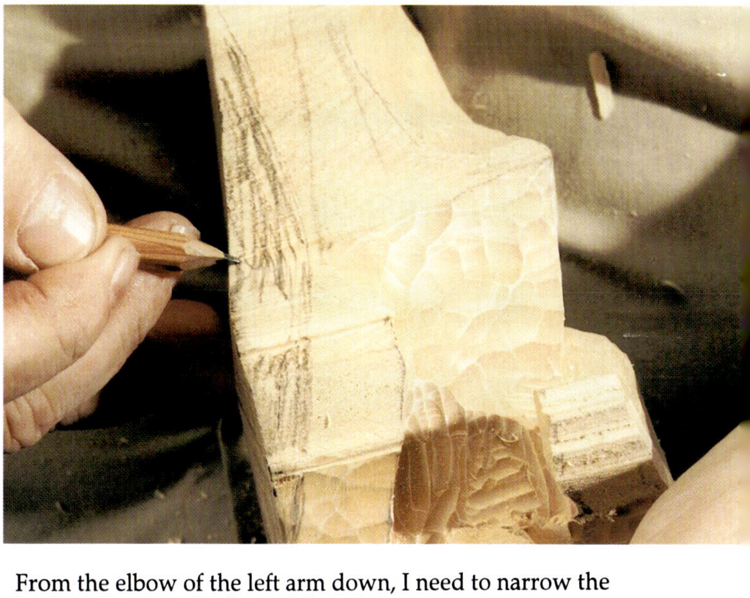

From the elbow of the left arm down, I need to narrow the body, following the flow of the robe.

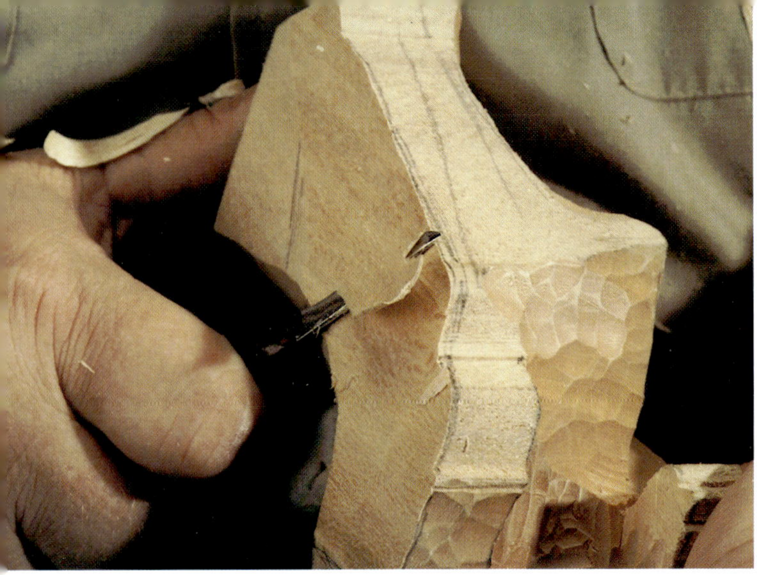

Trim it away.

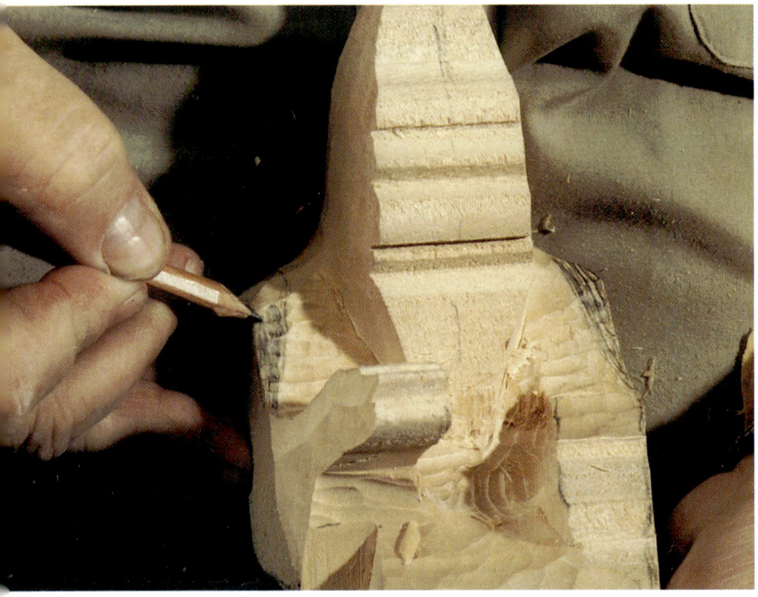

Slope the shoulders in from the elbows.

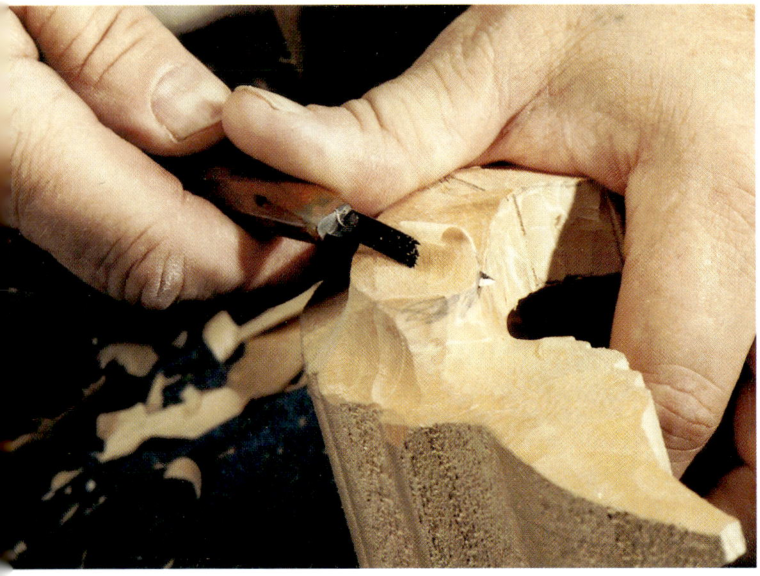

Trim 'em down.

Progress.

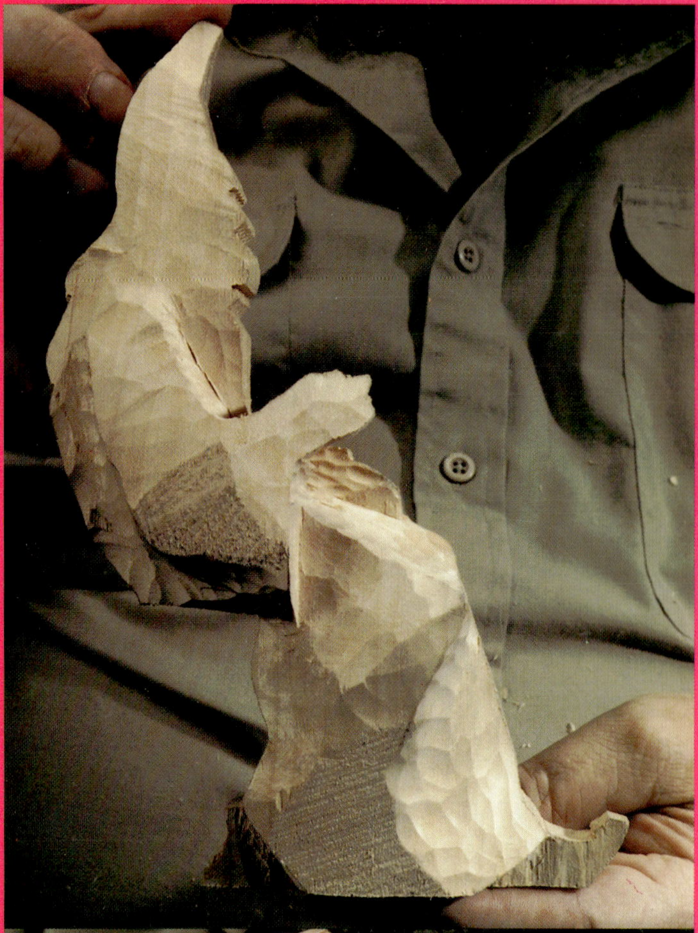

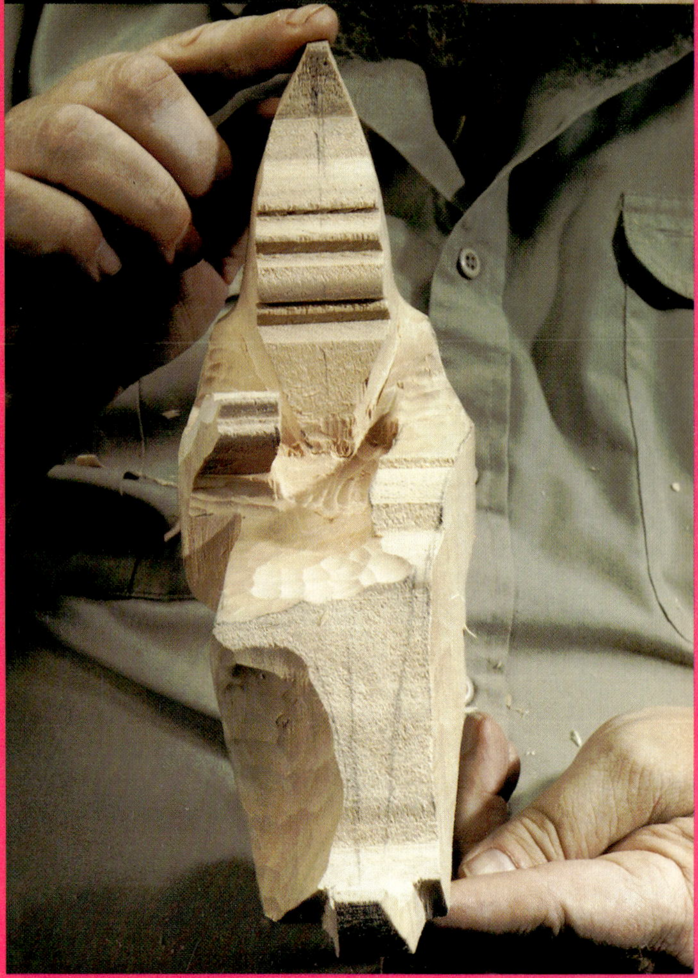

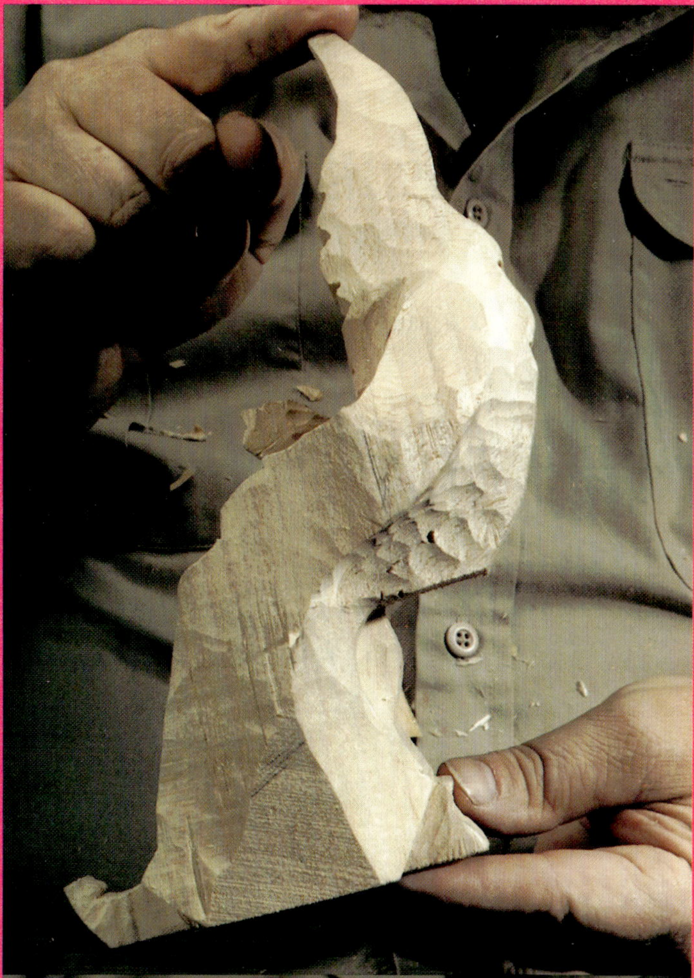

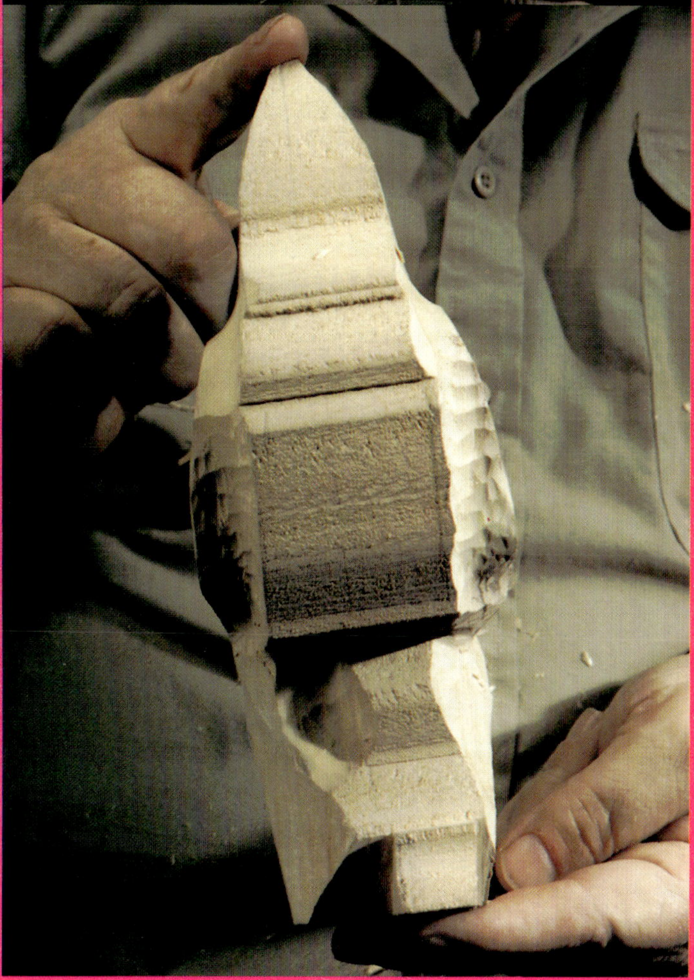

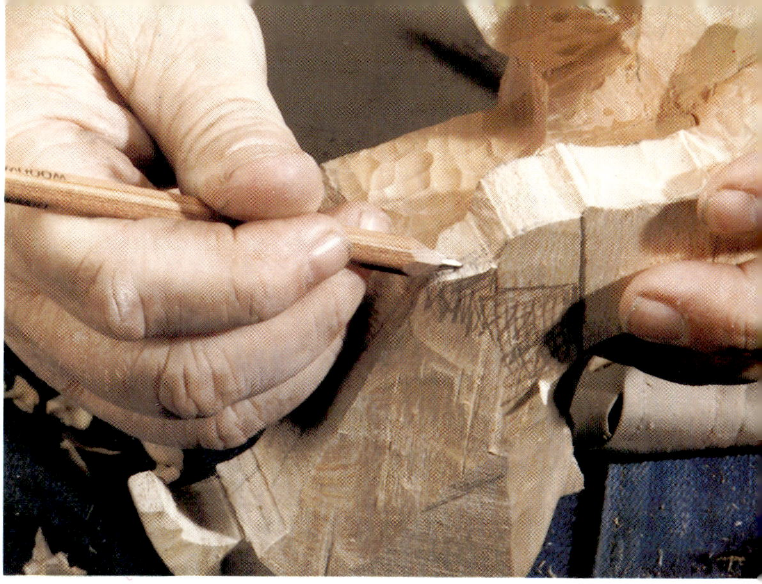

I need to bring the left hand out by cutting under it. The hand will be resting on the robe so don't cut too deeply.

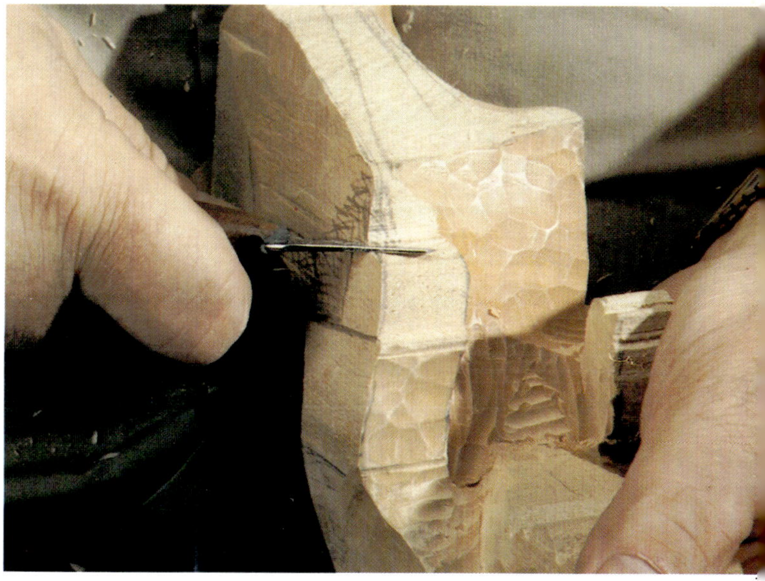

Cut a stop in the front edge of the hand...

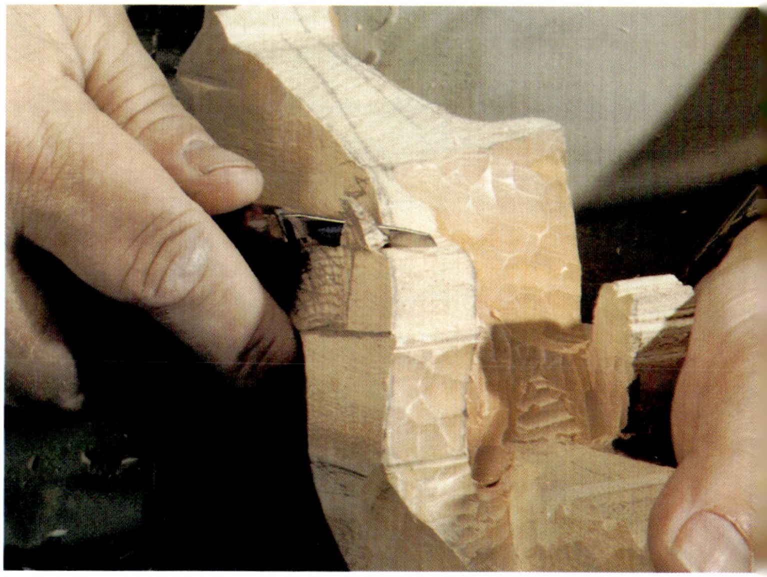

and trim back to it from the knee.

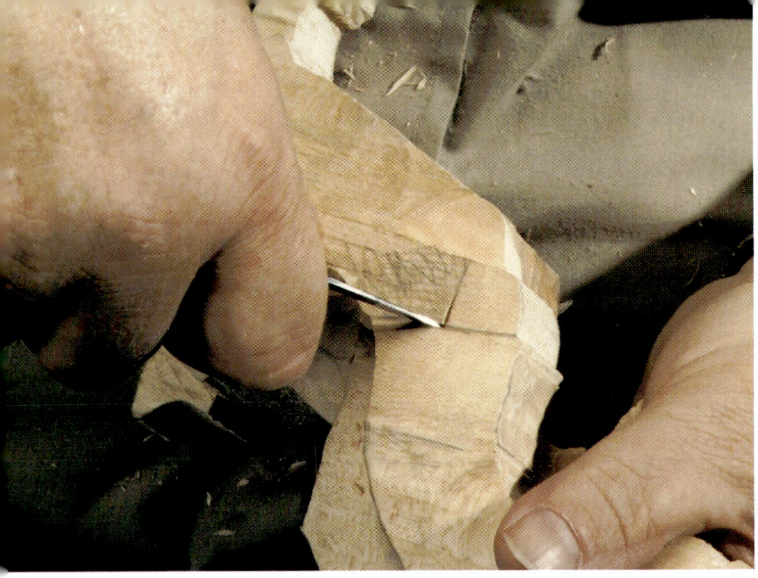

Cut another stop in the corner of the sleeve and the hand, along the front edge of the sleeve...

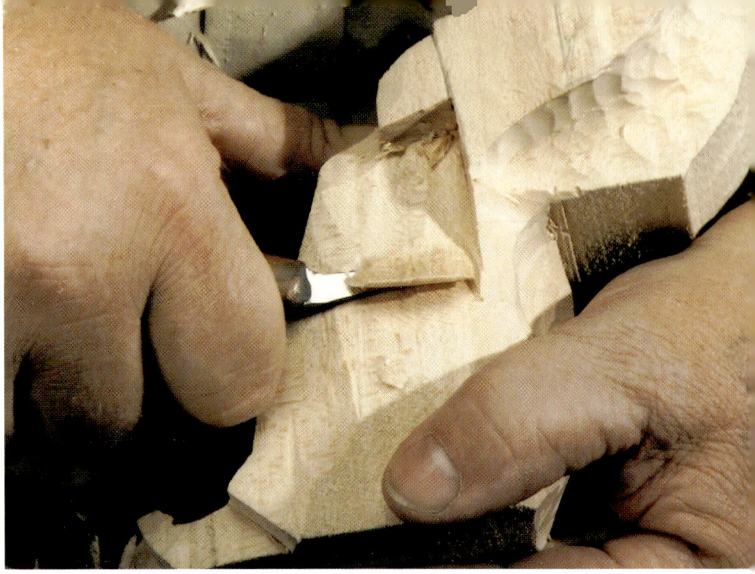

Continue to deepen the cut and thin the leg.

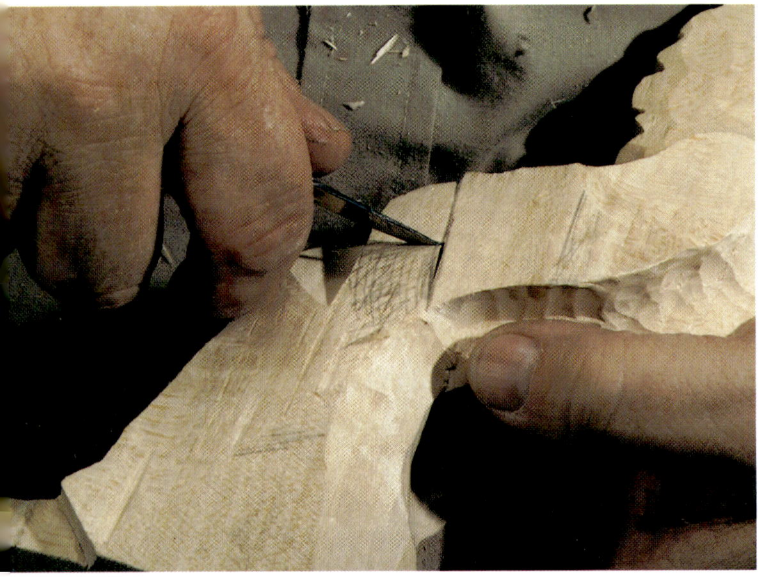

and the bottom edge of the hand.

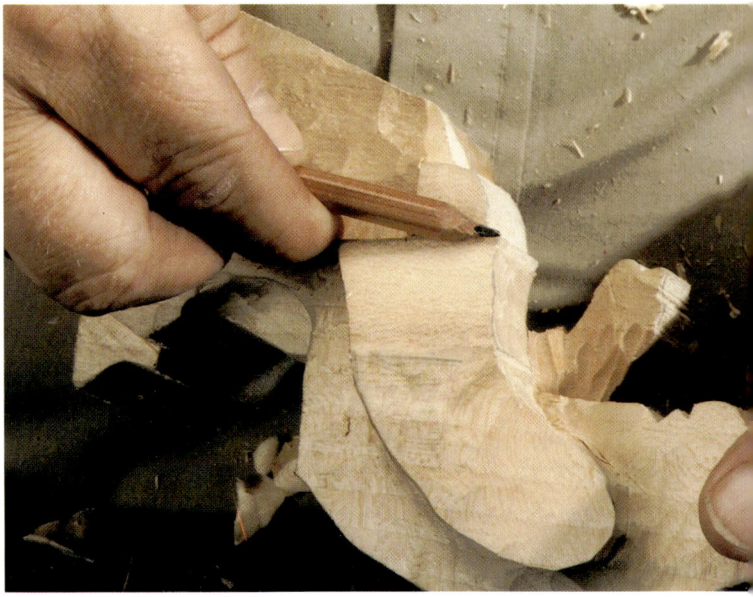

Transfer the measure of the sleeve opening from one arm...

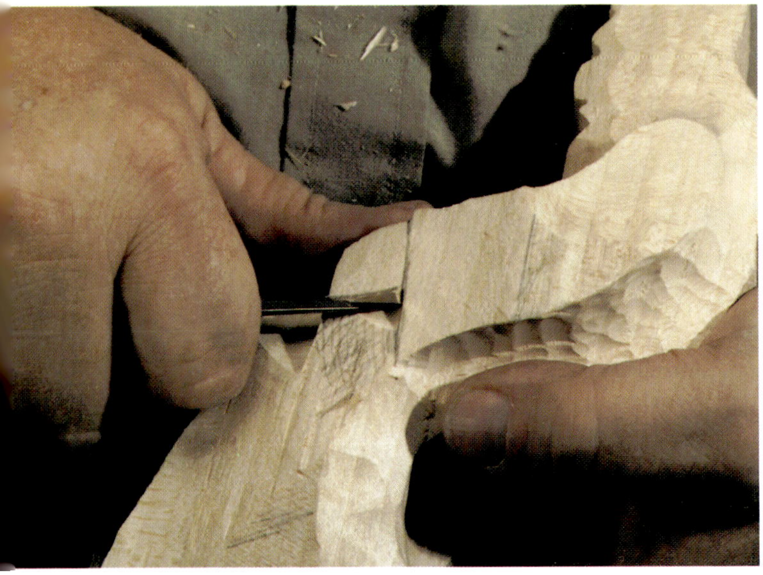

Come back to it from the side of the leg.

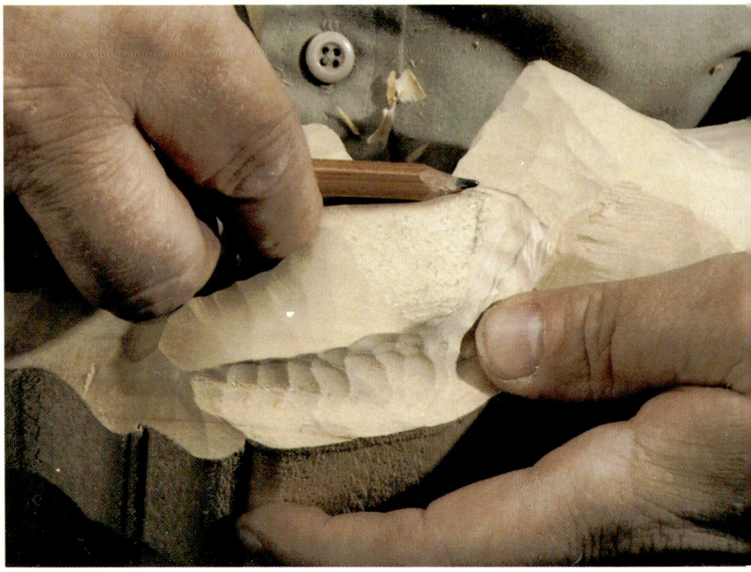

to the other and mark.

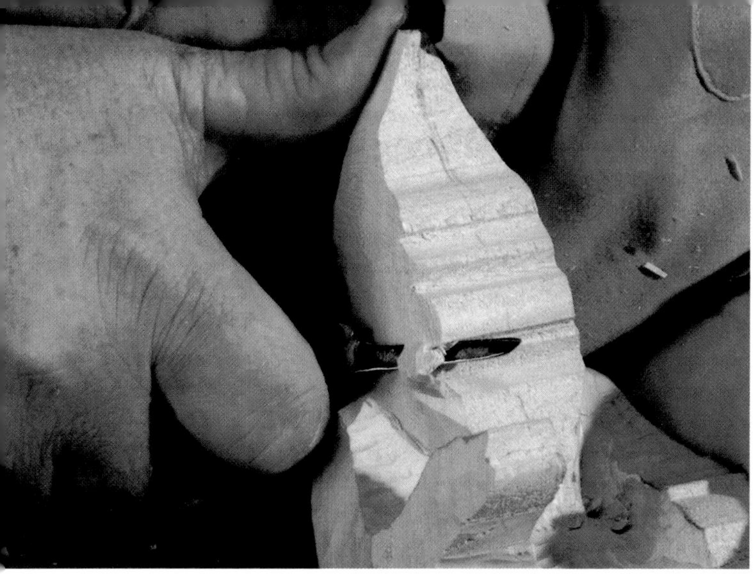

Knock off the corners of the face, taking it to octagonal.

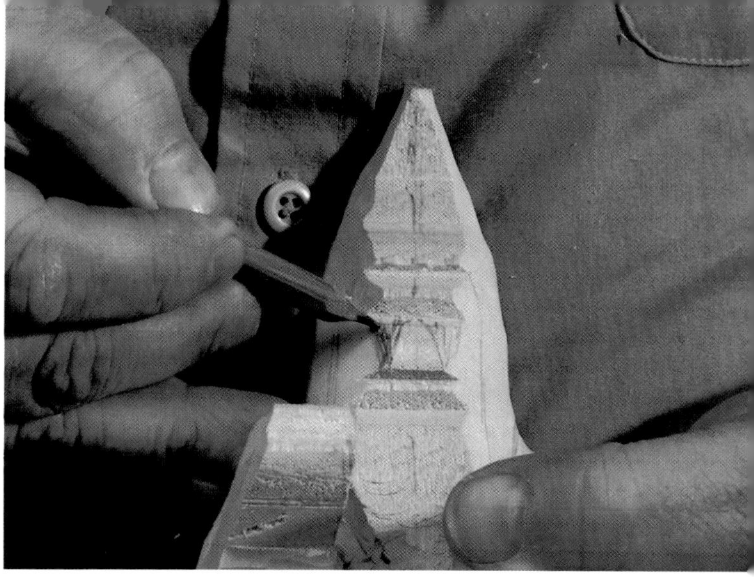

Mark the area to be removed beside the nose.

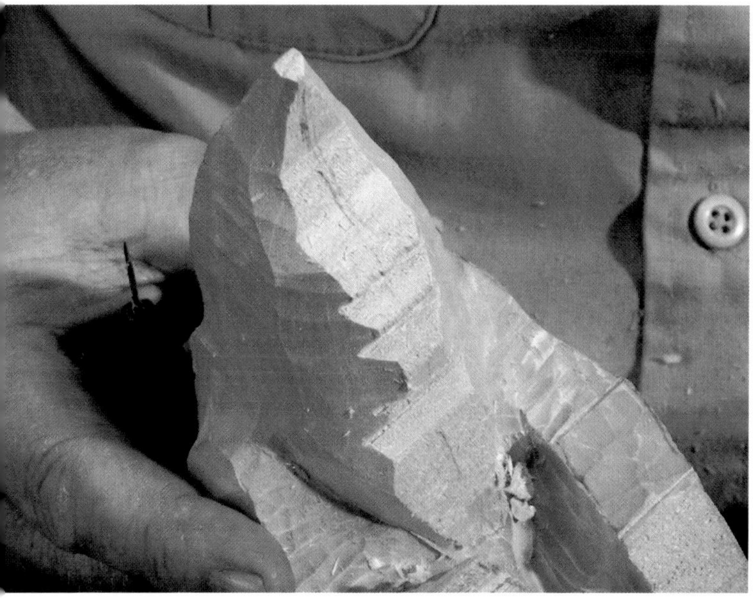

Carry the cuts up to the top of the hat. I always take a carving to an octagonal shape before going to round. This keeps me from creating a figure that is too flat or out of proportion.

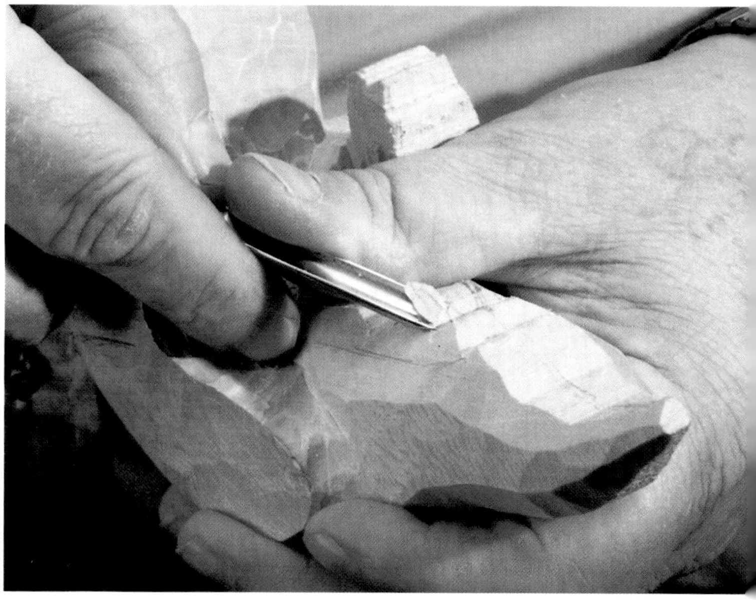

Come up beside the nose with a gouge.

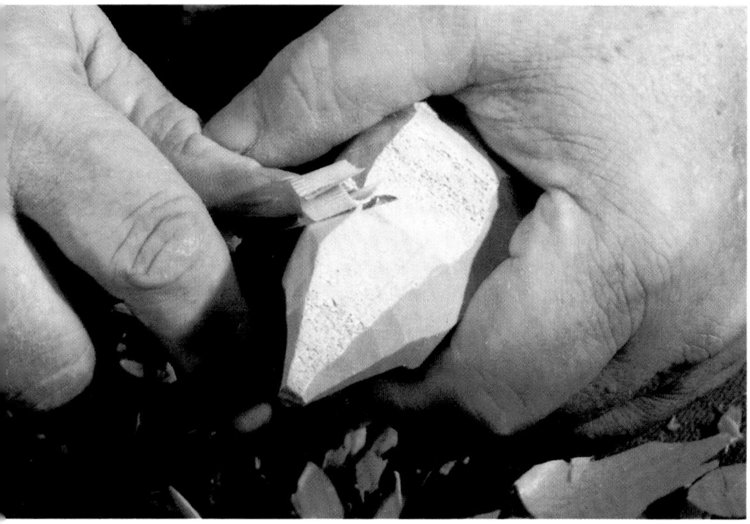

Do the same on the back corners.

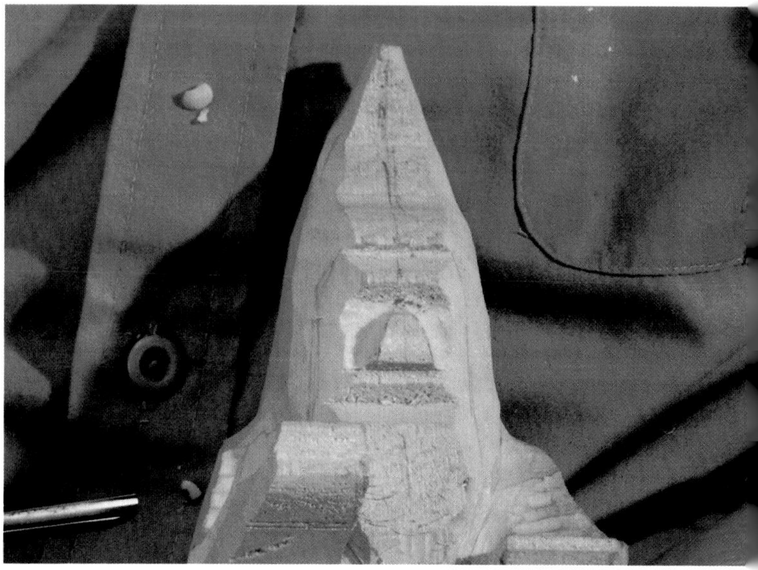

Progress.

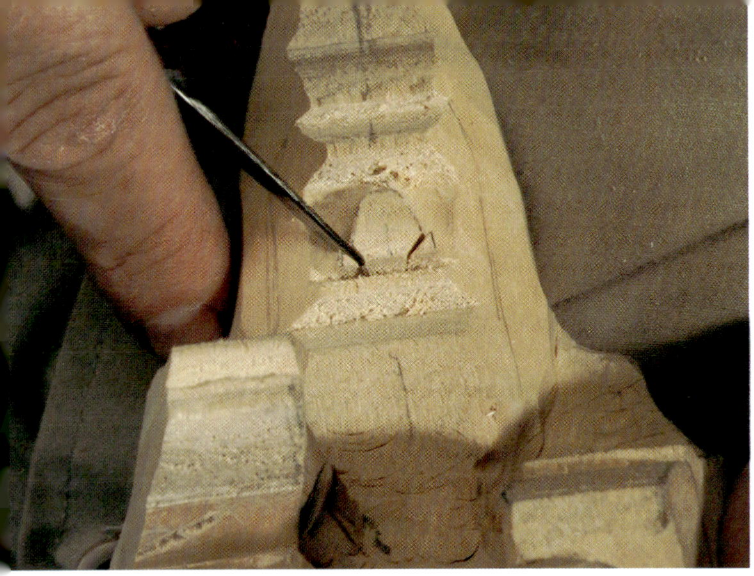

Cut straight in at an angle at the nostrils...

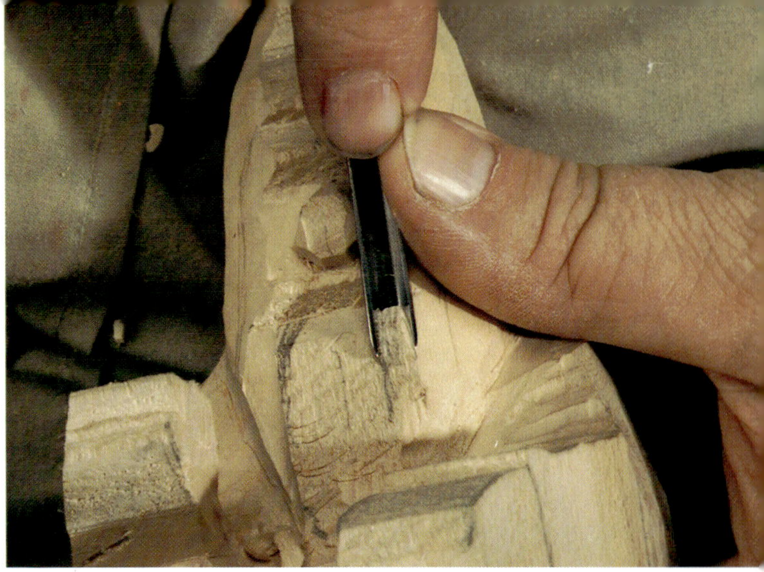

A gouge does this nicely.

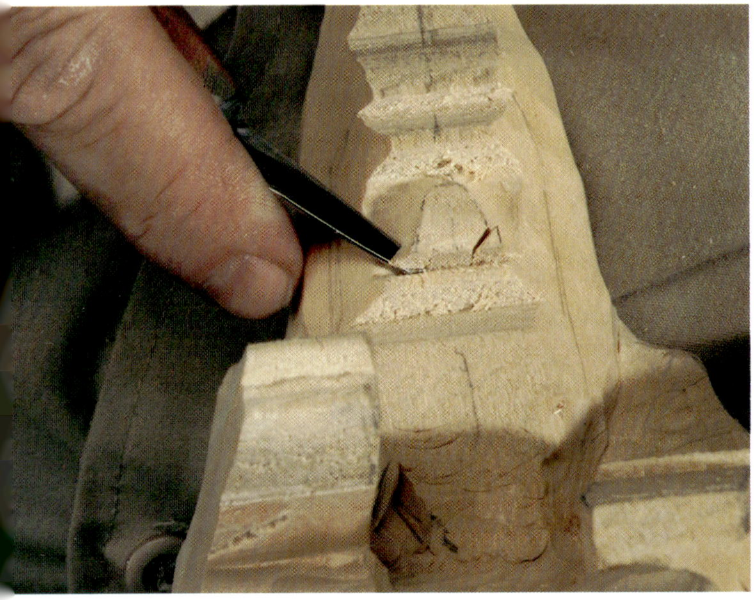

and trim the corners off from the cheeks.

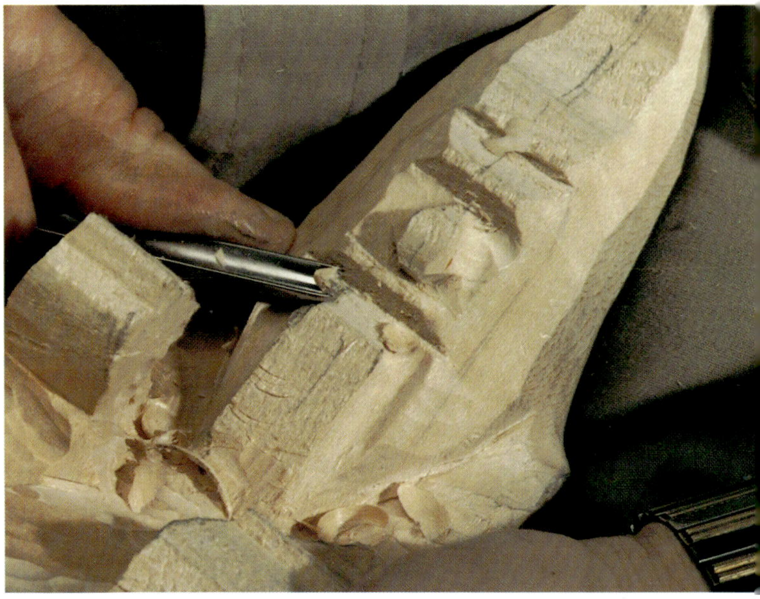

At the top bring the beard in under the mouth.

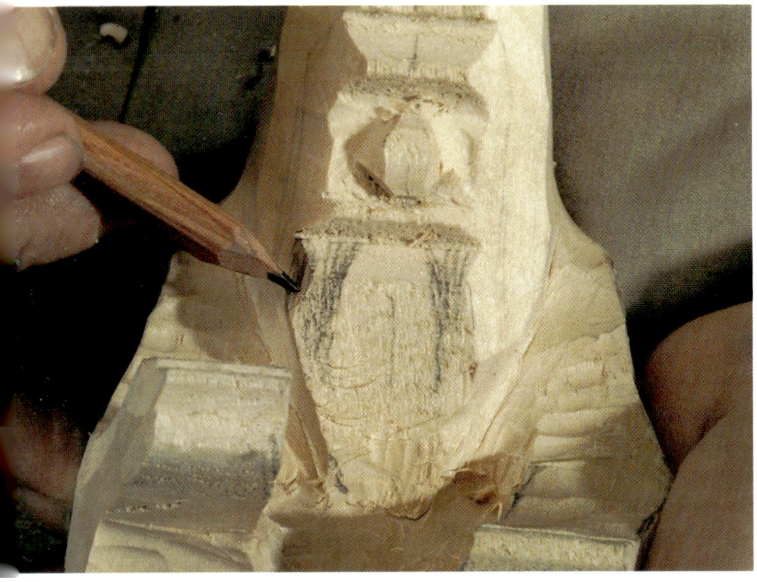

I need to contour the outer edges of the beard.

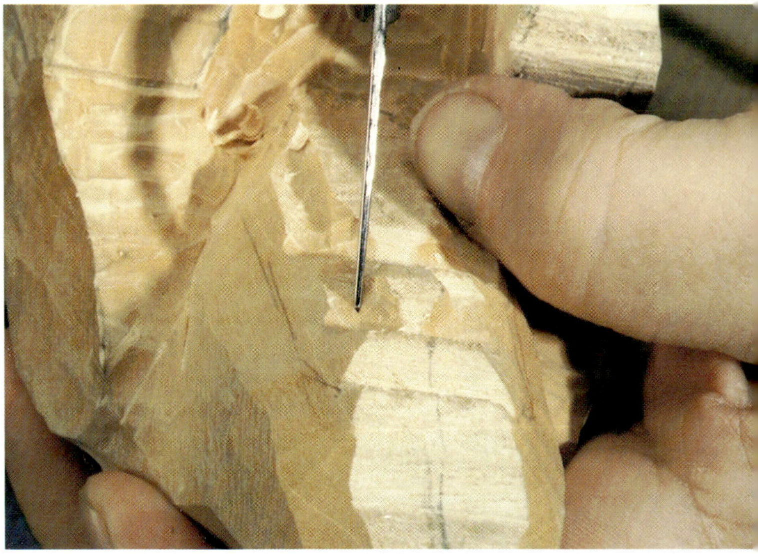

The intersection of the nose and the cheek is made by cutting straight in beside the nose...

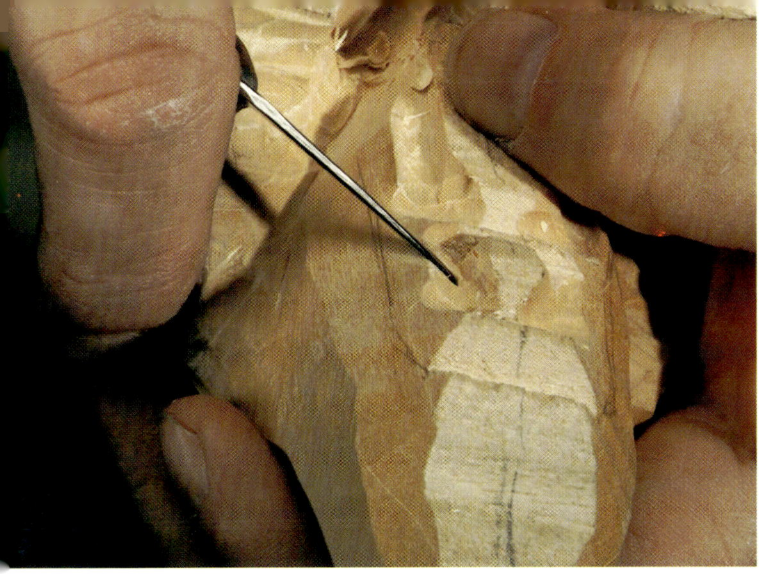

cutting straight in on the cheek line...

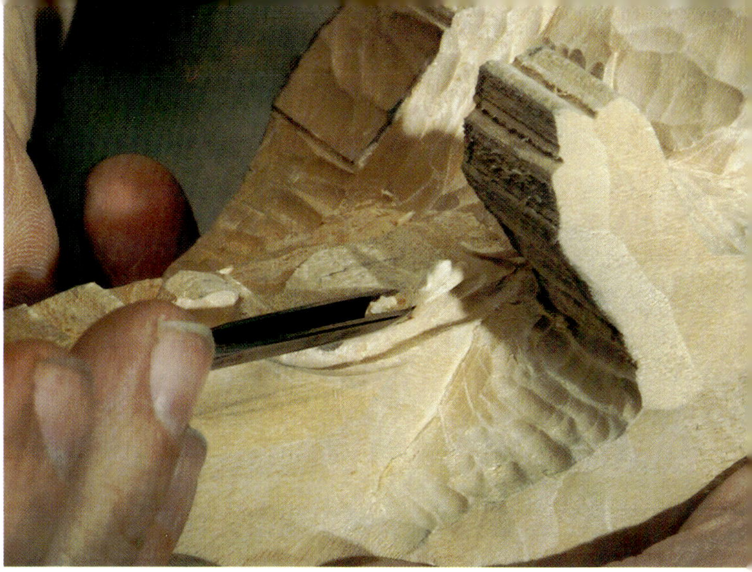

Another, parallel cut on the inside of the moustache raises it.

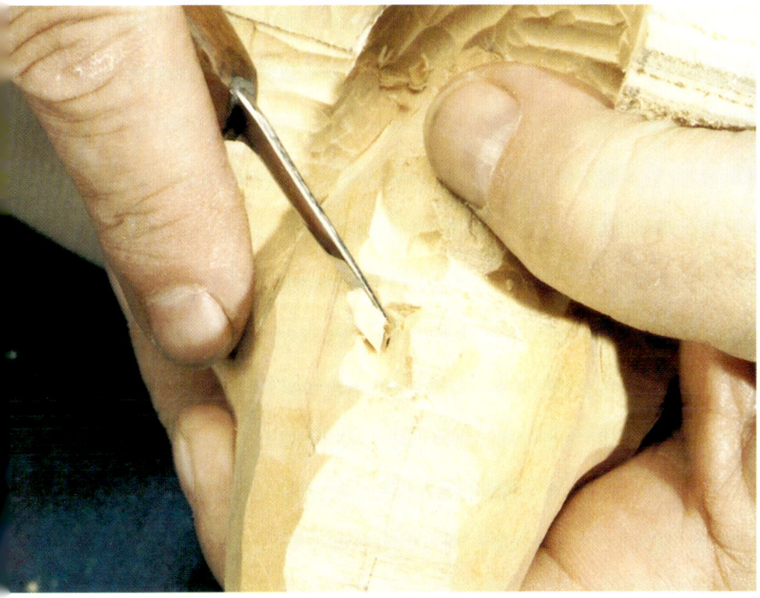

and coming back into the corner of these two cuts with the blade flat against the lip.

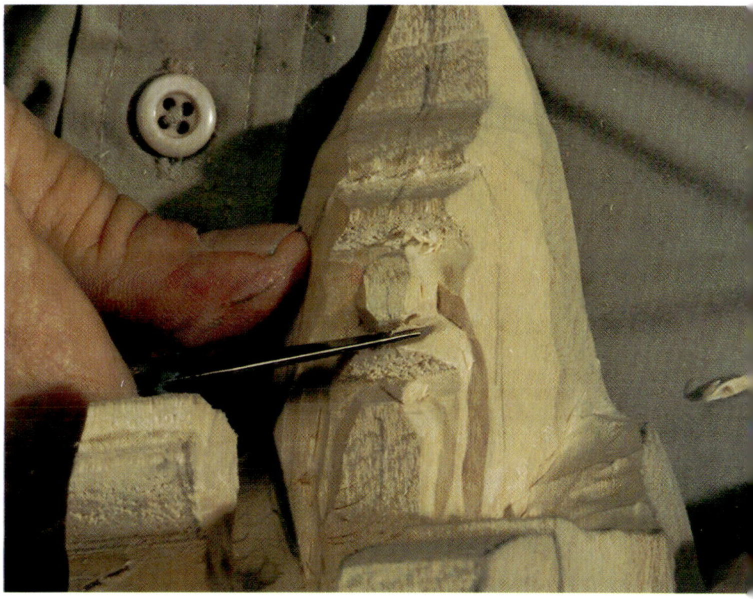

Shape the moustache under the nose.

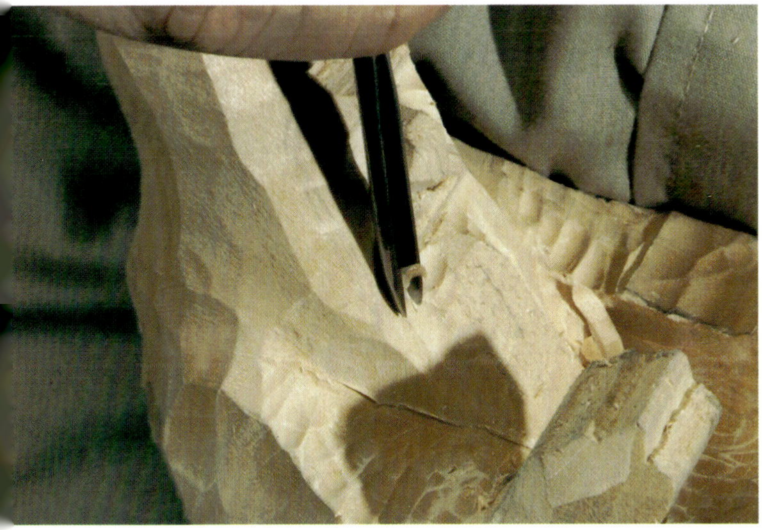

Carry the cheek line down into the beard with a gouge to establish the flow of the long moustache.

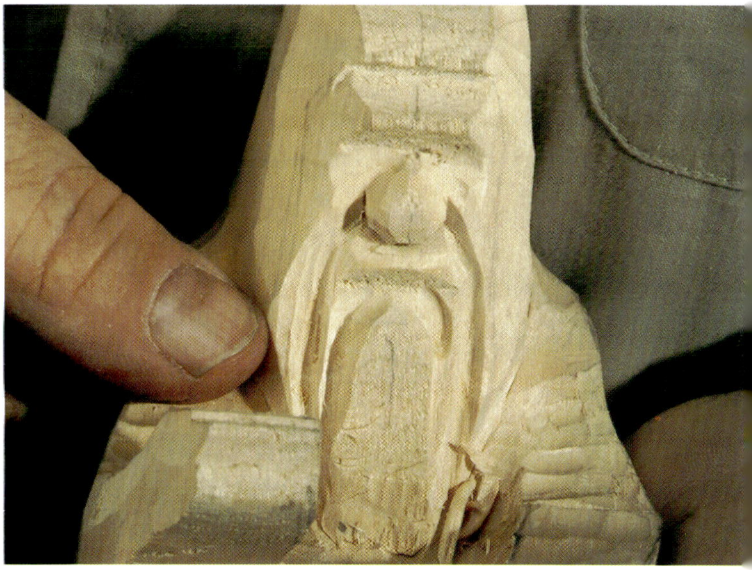

Progress.

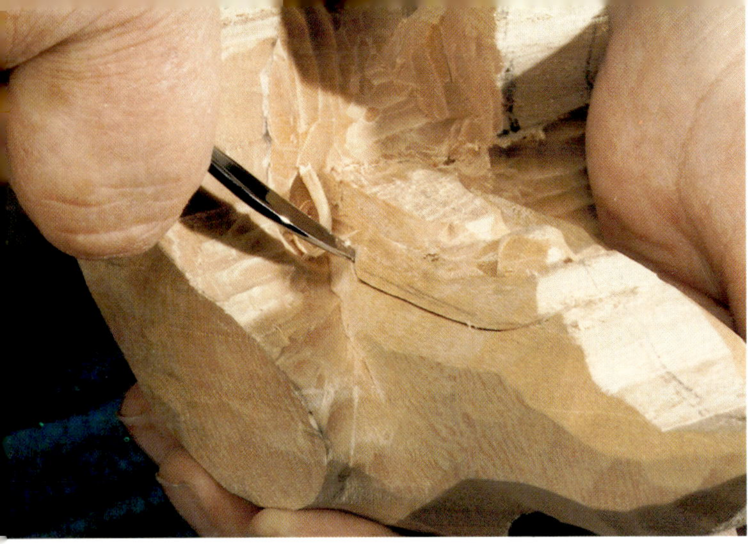

Cut a stop around the opening of the hood, going all around the face and coming back under the jaw until it disappears beneath the beard.

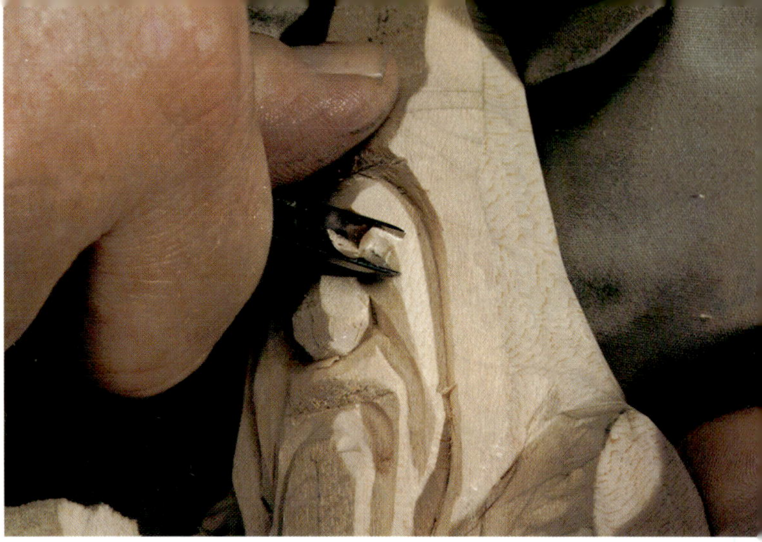

Carry the eye socket around into the temple.

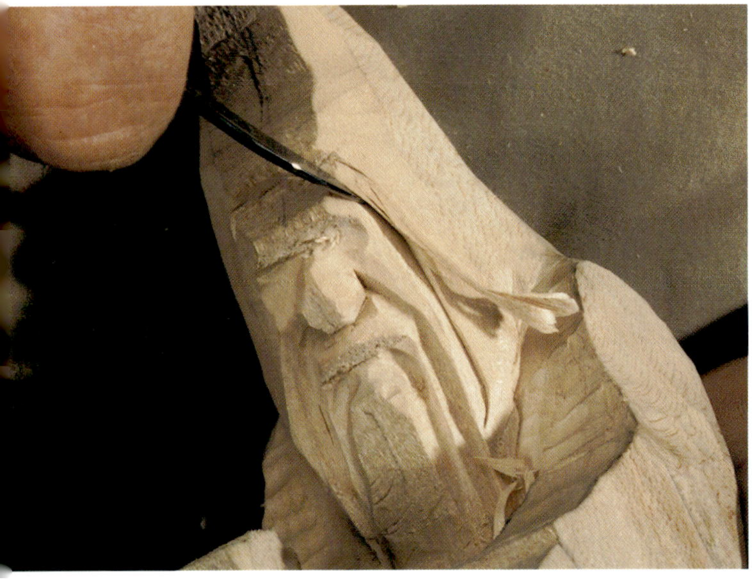

Slice back to the line from the face.

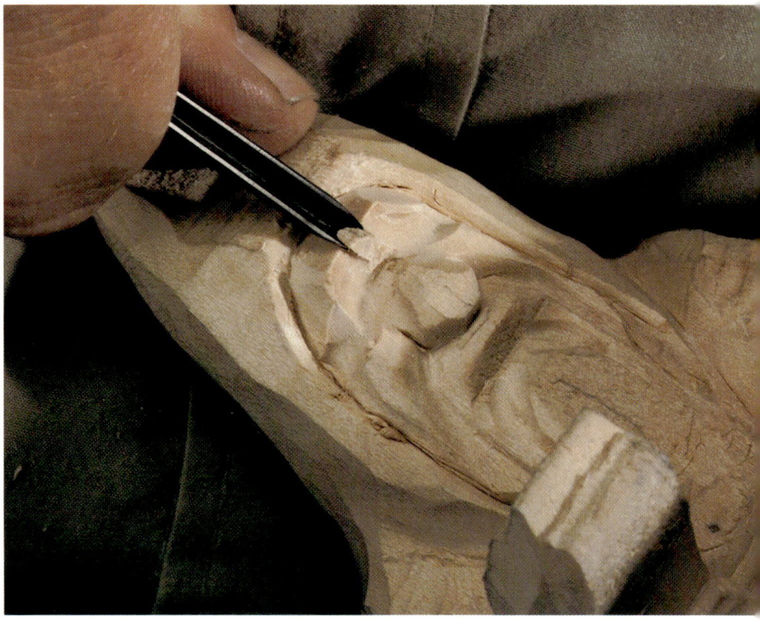

With a smaller gouge create a separation between the eyebrows.

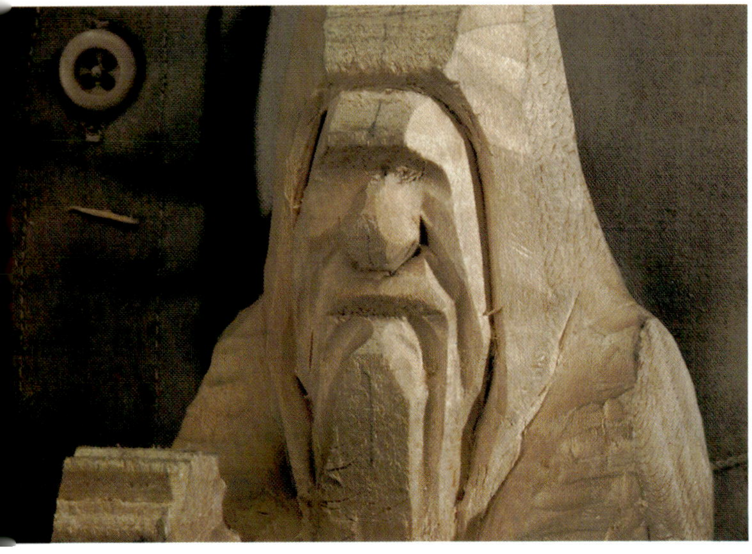

Progress. There is a pretty strong demarcation between the hood and the face.

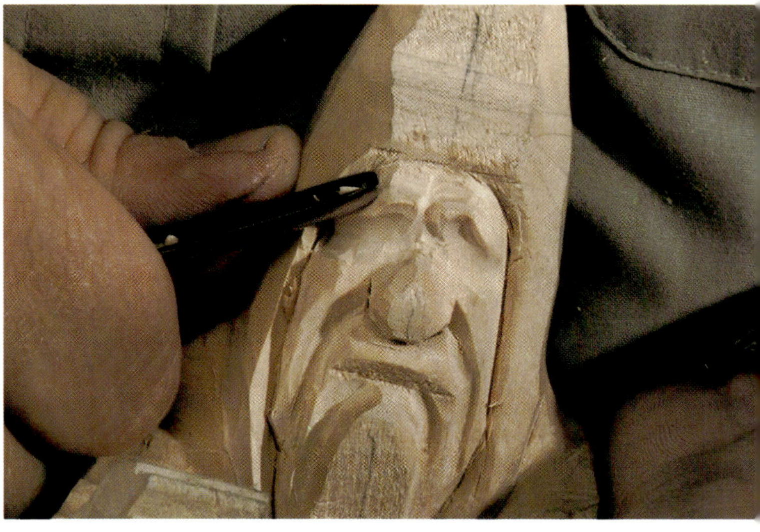

Come over the top of the eyebrow with the gouge, bringing it out.

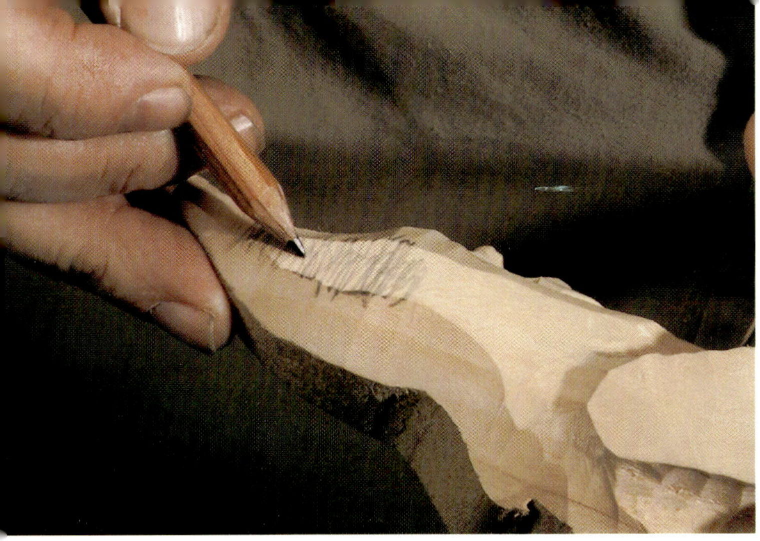

I've noticed that the sides of the hat need to be narrowed. Since I won't do this until later, I mark it now to remind me.

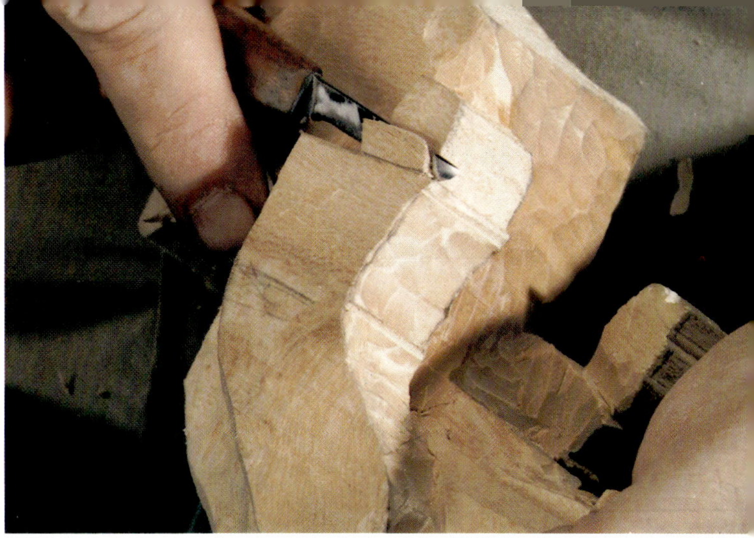

Repeat on the other arm.

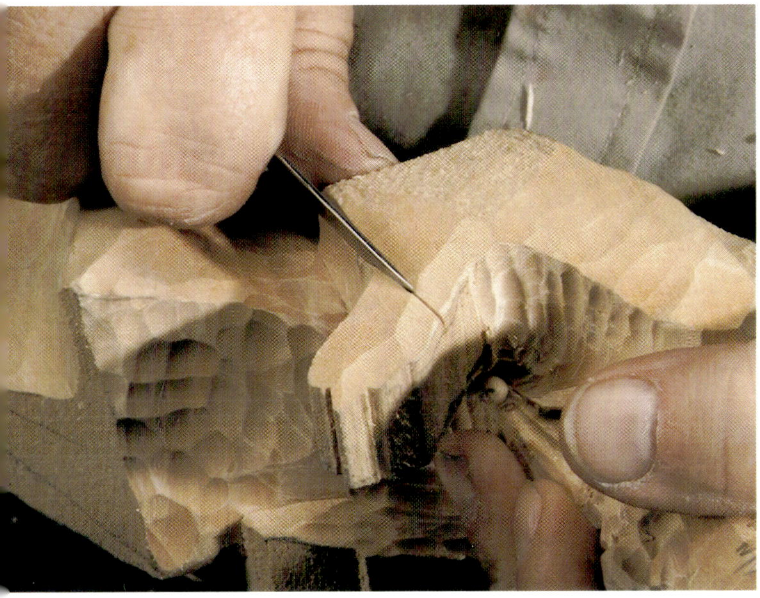

Cut a stop in the line of the sleeve around the raised hand.

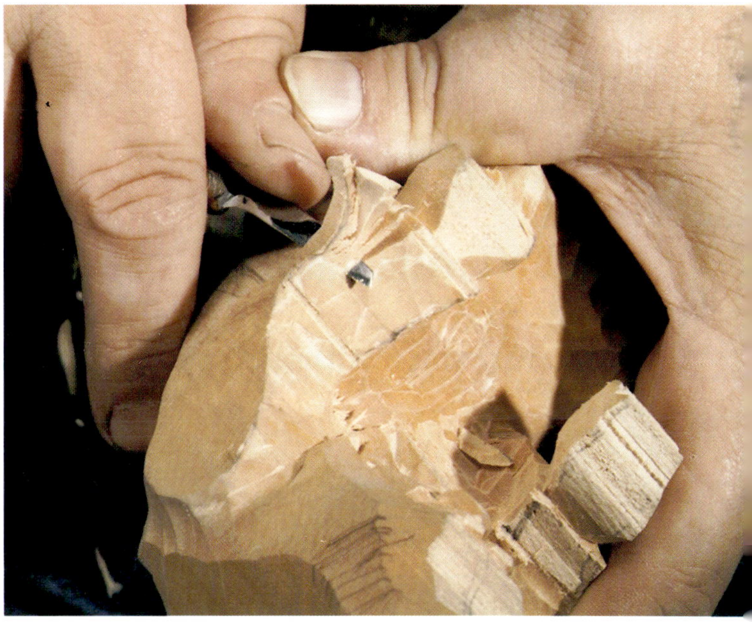

Before detailing I want to go over everything, taking square shapes to octagonal, like here on the arm...

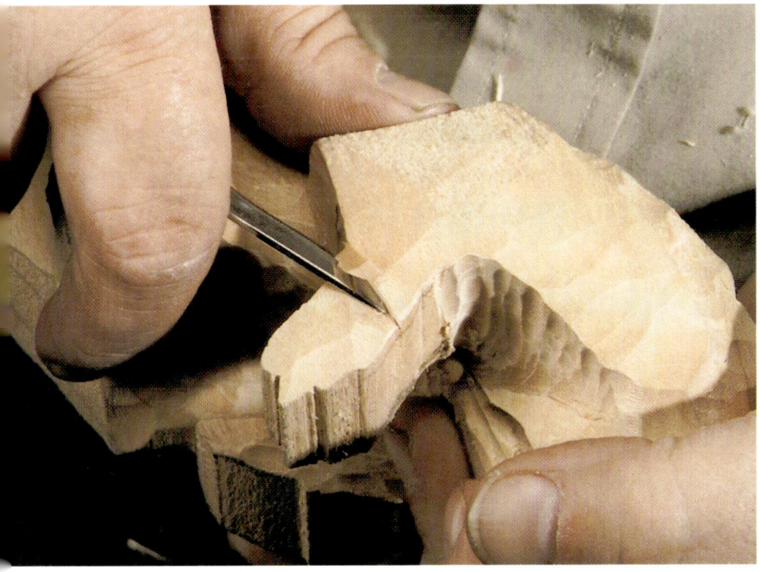

Cut back to it from the hand. Continue all around the wrist.

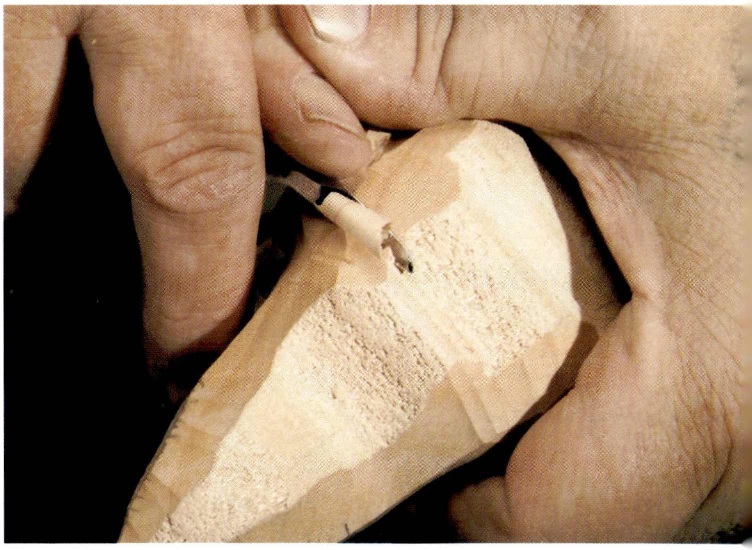

and here on the back.

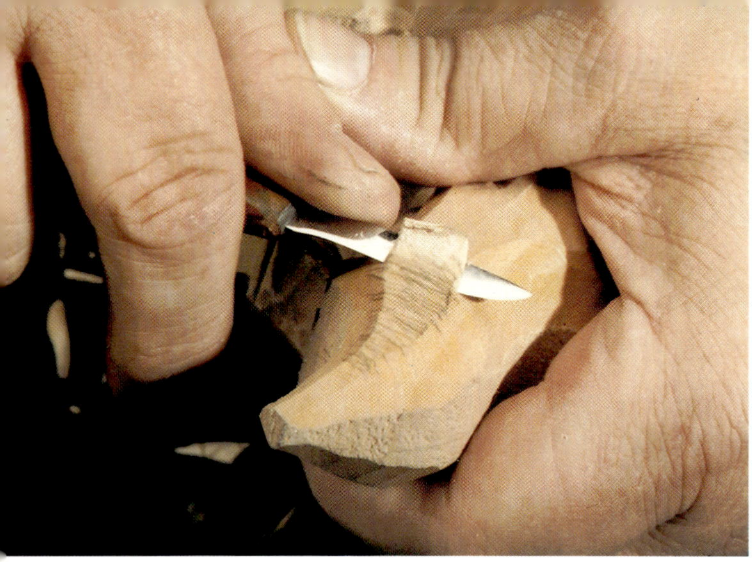

Narrow the head.

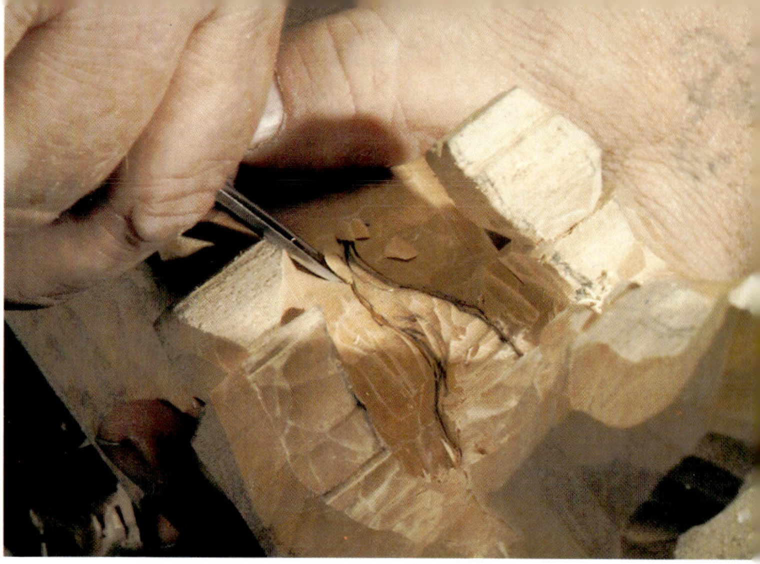

Cut back to the stop from the body with a gouge.

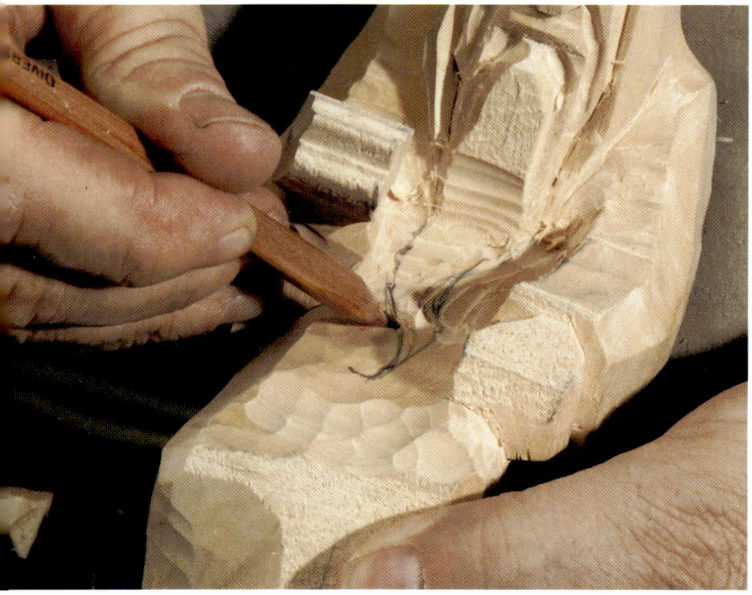

Carry the beard lines down into the Wizard's lap.

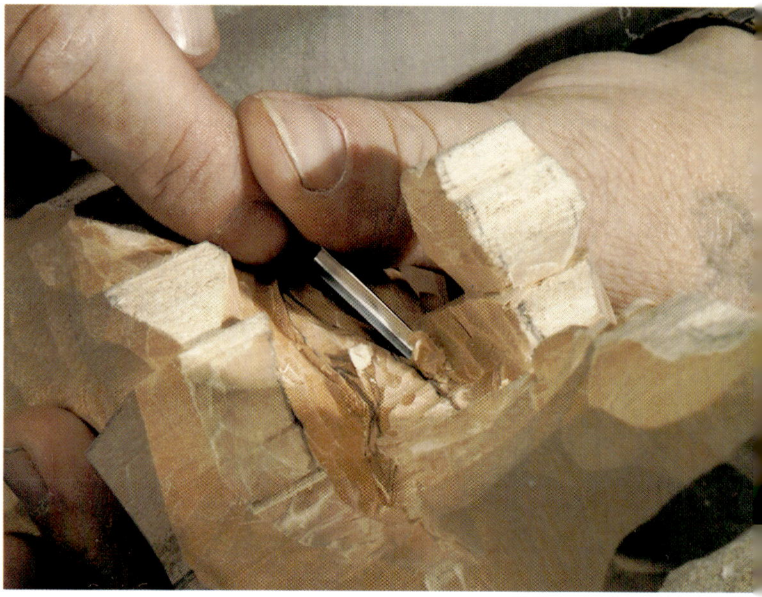

Where I can't cut back to the stop, I cut along it with a gouge.

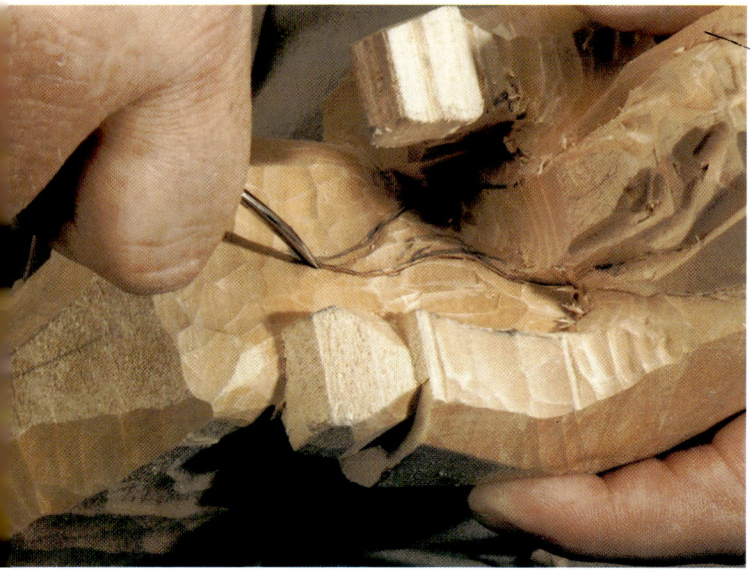

Cut a stop around the beard.

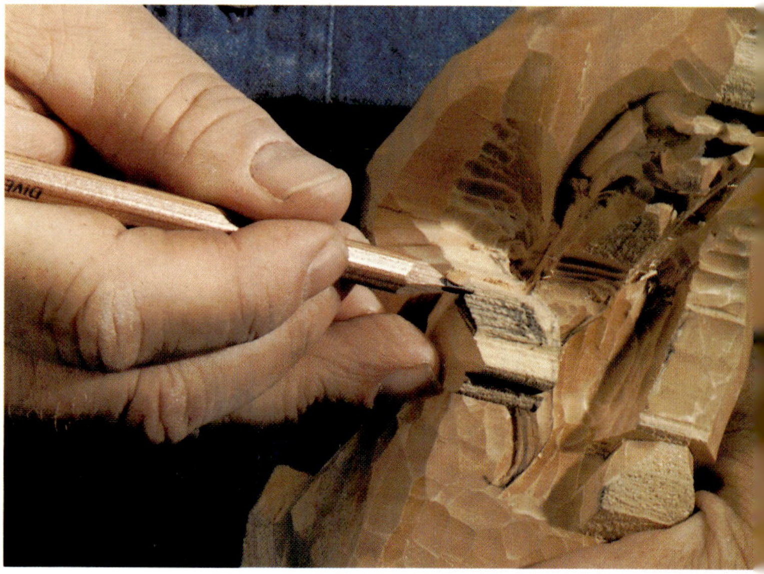

Mark the area beside the thumb to be removed.

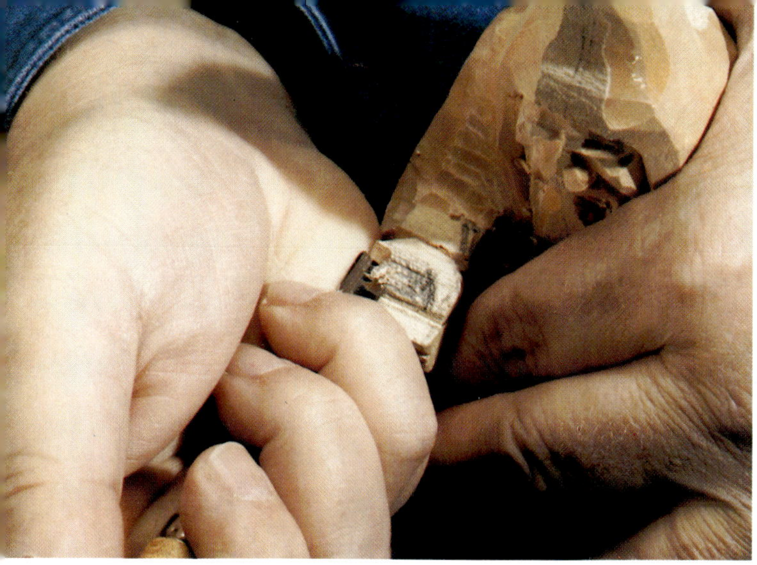

Scoop it out with a gouge.

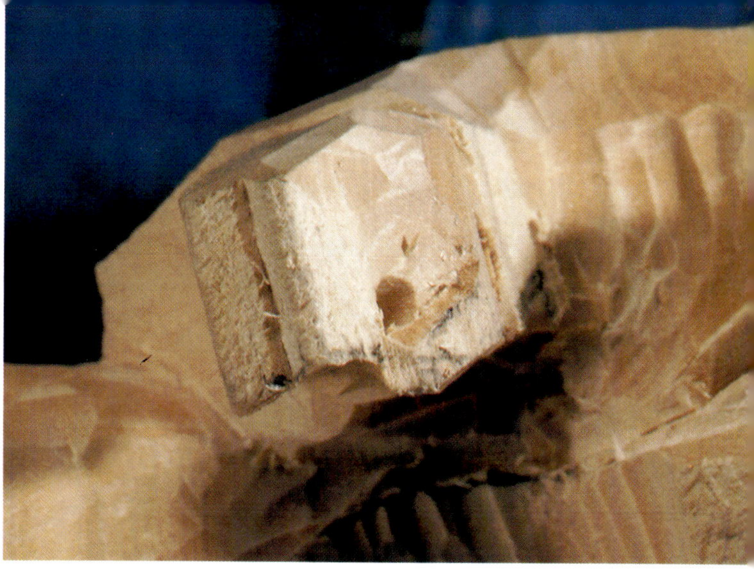

About this time I need to decide what the hand will be doing. Since this is a Wizard, it seems right that he should hold a magic wand. I've drilled a 1/16" hole in the hand on the drill press.

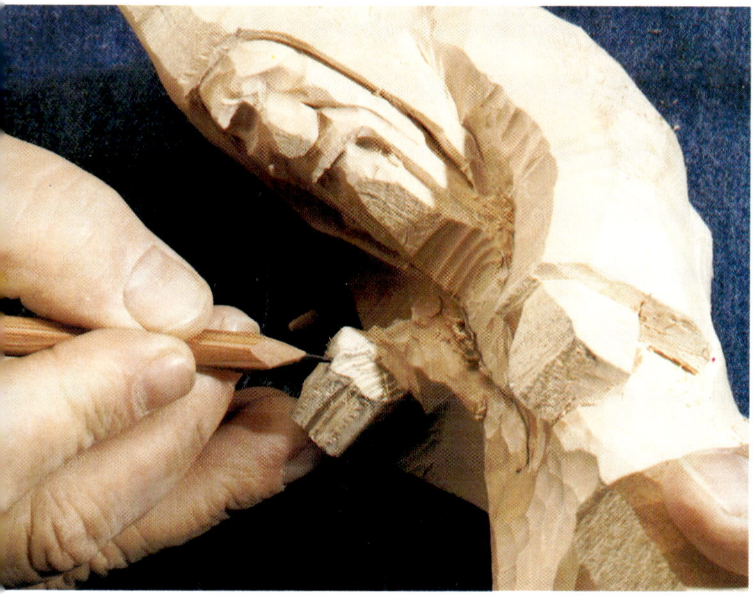

In the same way, mark the area of the palm to be taken away.

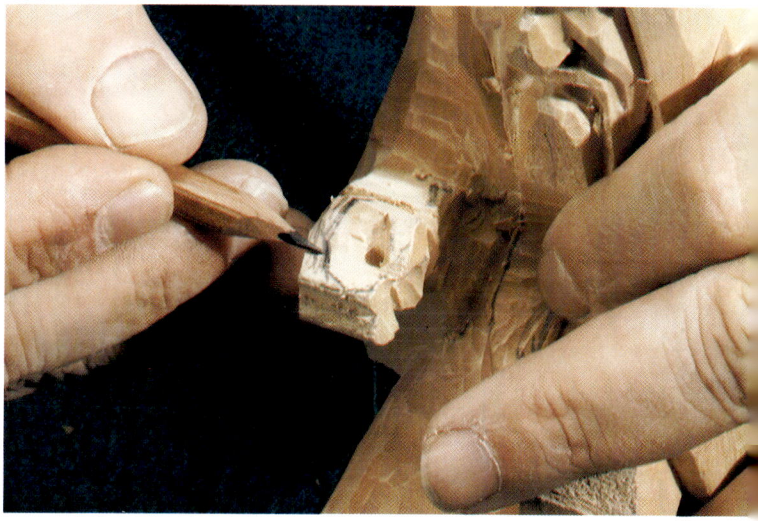

Now I can mark the shape of the outside of the hand.

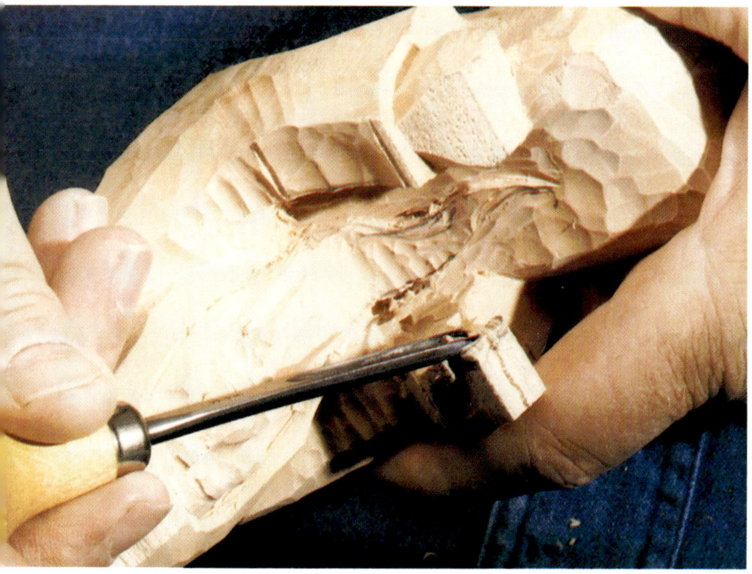

The gouge gets in this spot well.

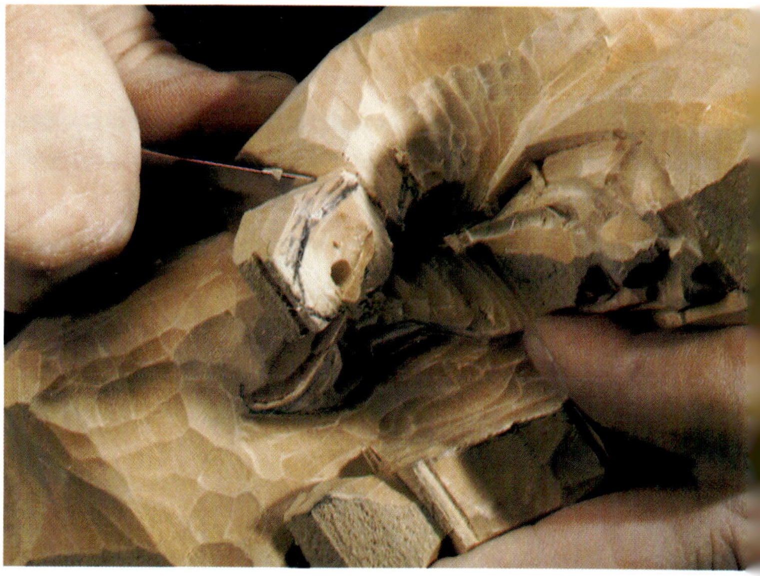

Cut a stop at the cuff...

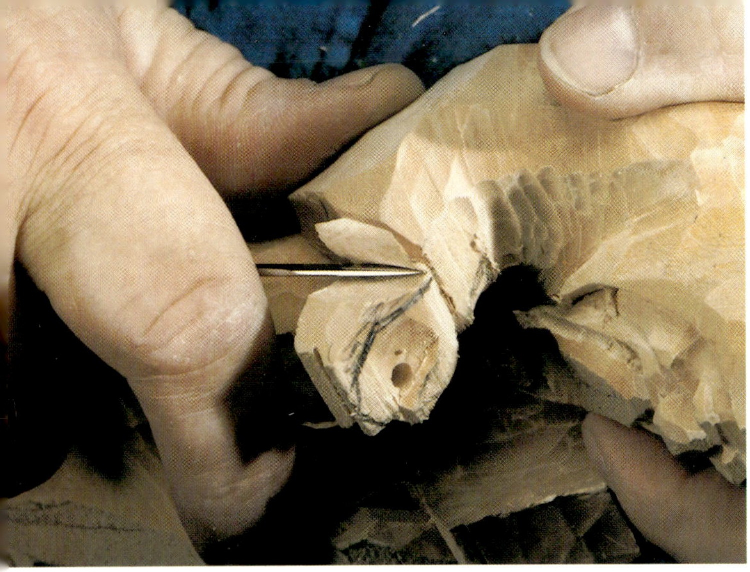

and come back to it.

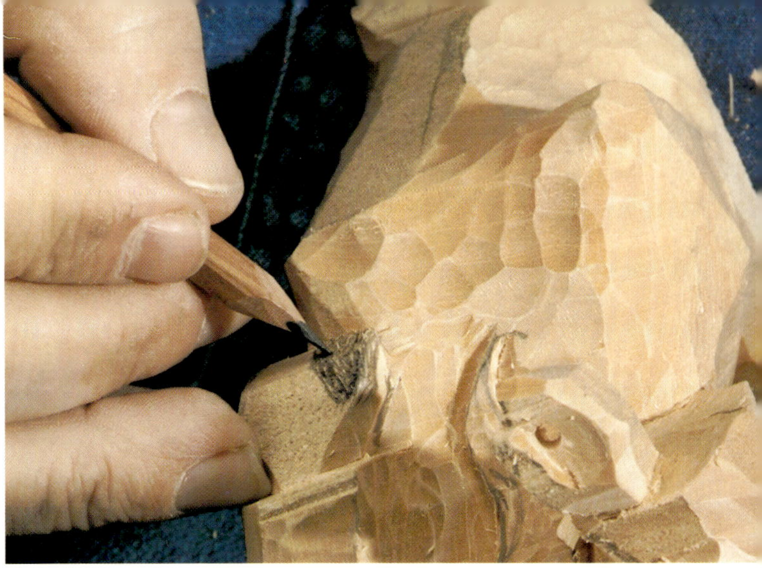

Mark the left thumb.

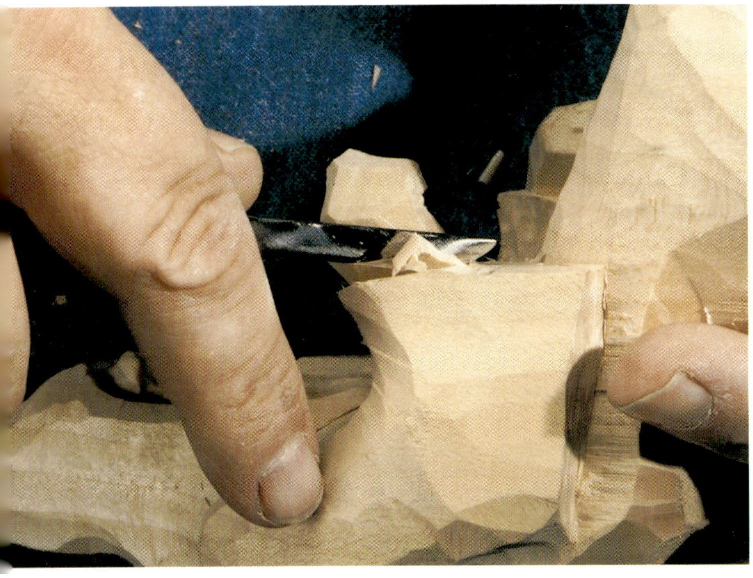

Knock off the corner to establish the overall shape of the hand.

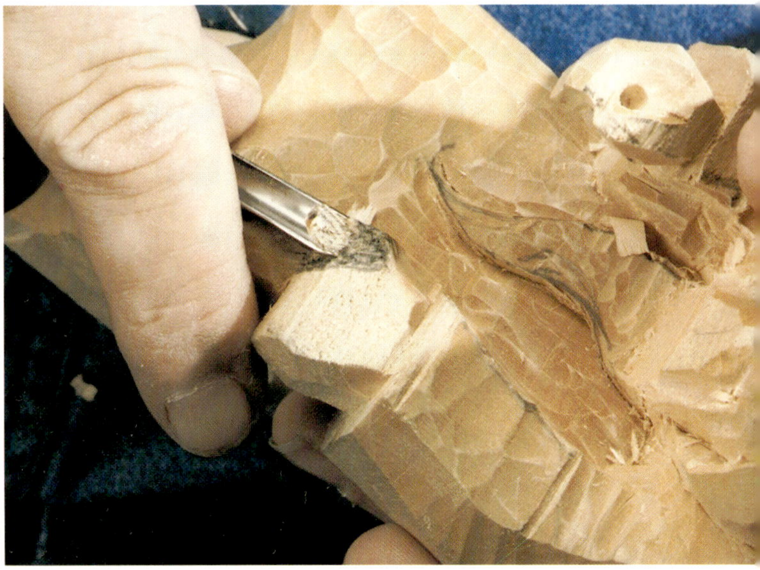

Remove the area between the thumb and fingers with a gouge.

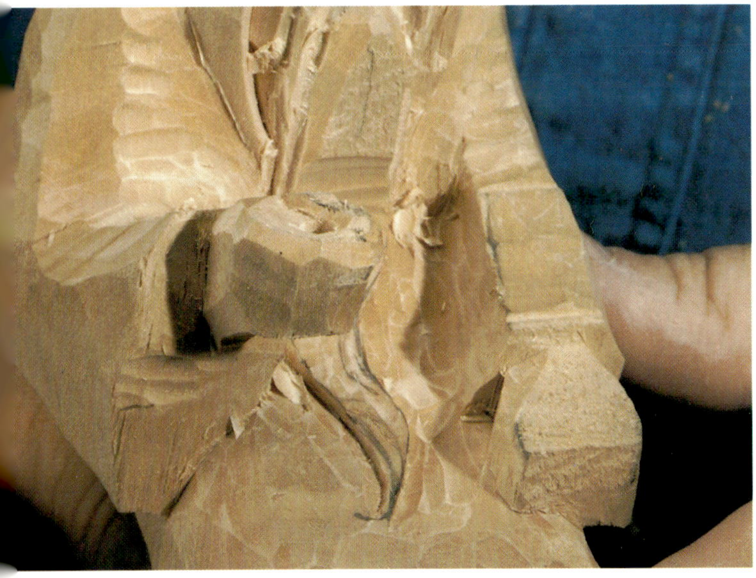

The result.

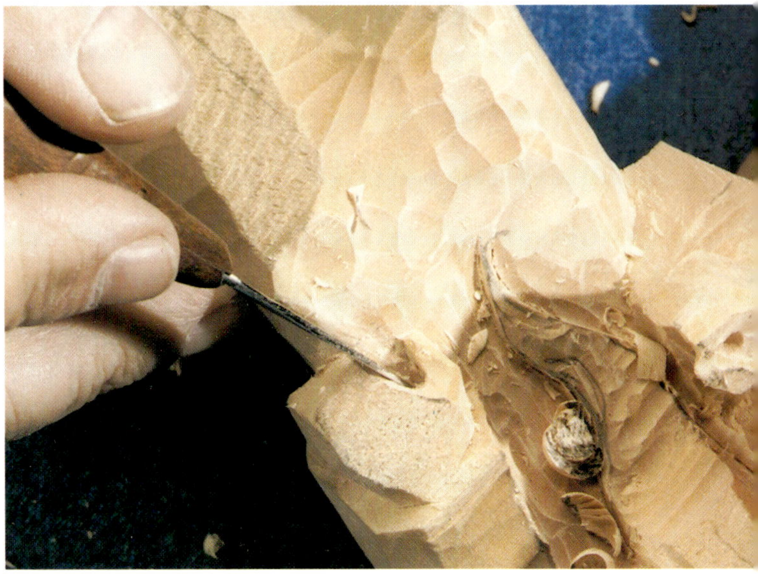

A long-bladed knife gets into the deepest spots.

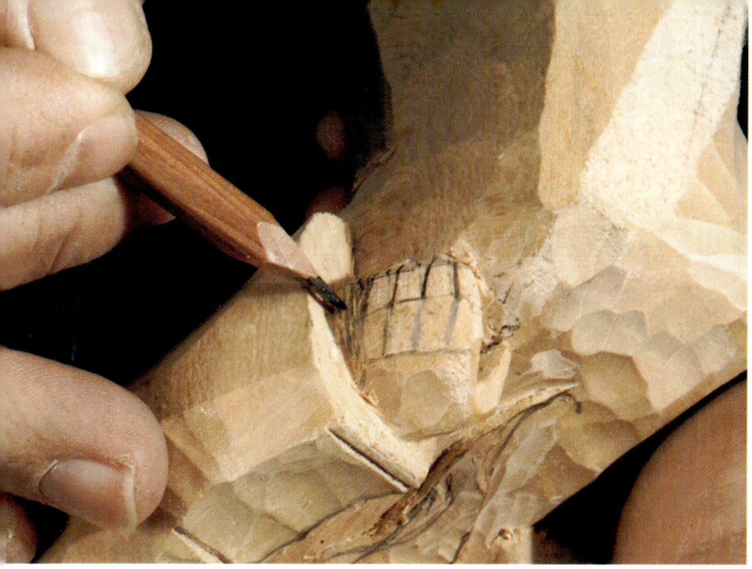

Draw in the fingers. Start by establishing the line of the knuckles, and the lines of the two joints. Then draw in the lines between the fingers. The body of the hand has four planes: the back of the hand, the surface between the knuckle and the first joint, the surface between the first and second joint, and the end of the fingers.

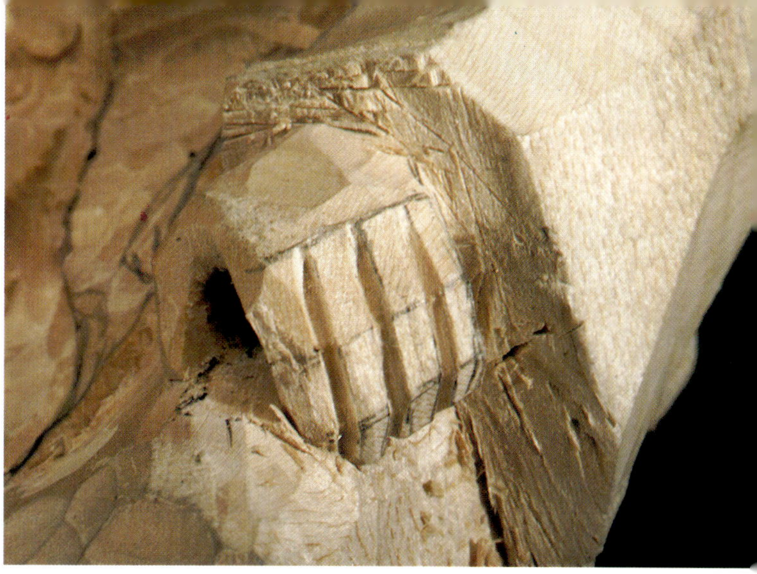

The left hand done.

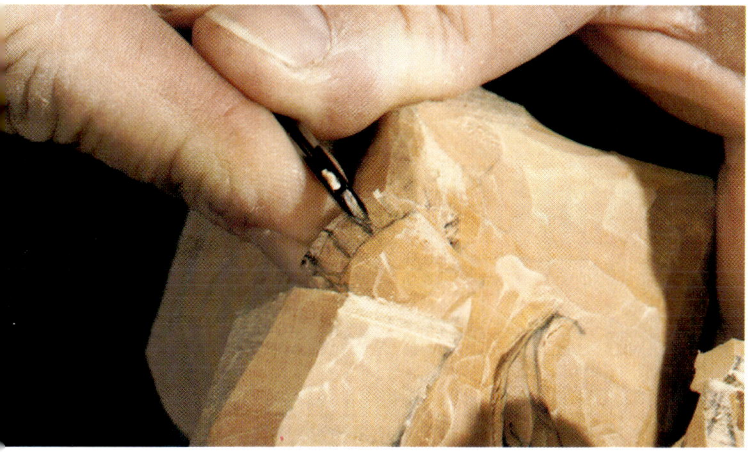

Gouge between the fingers with a veiner.

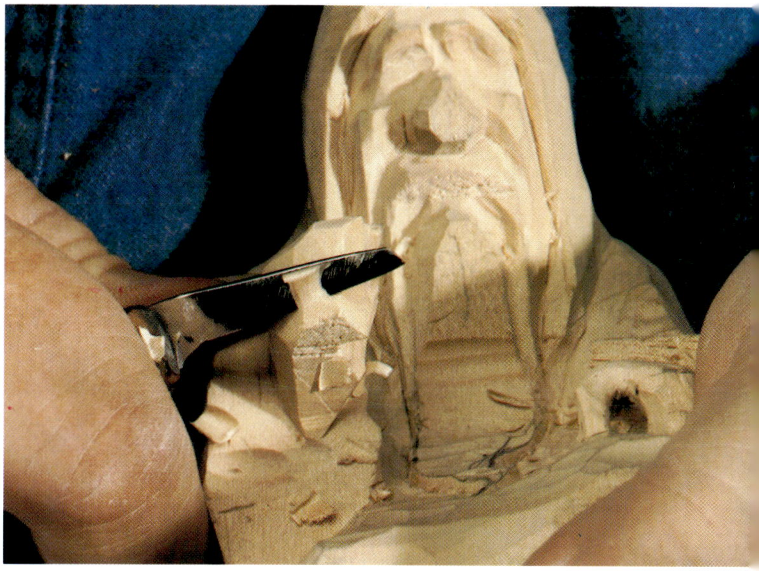

With one hand done I can set the size of the other and establish the planes.

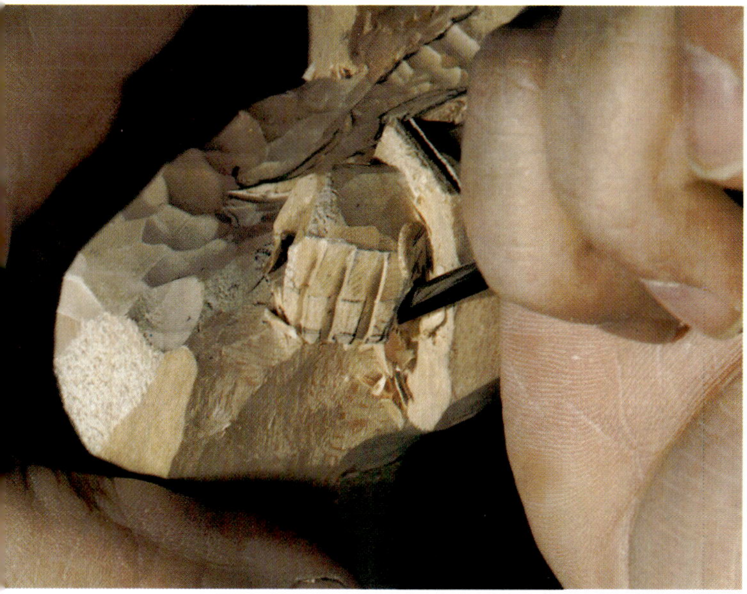

Remove the extra matter at the back edge of the hand.

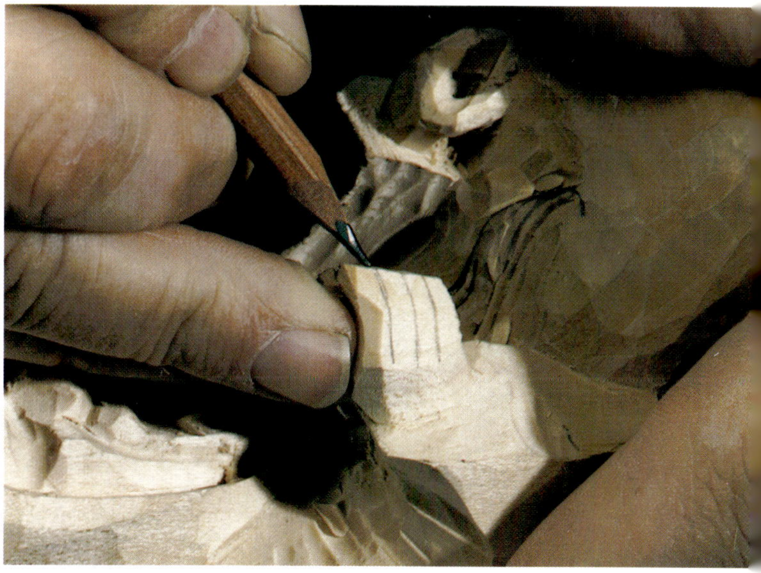

Draw in the finger lines.

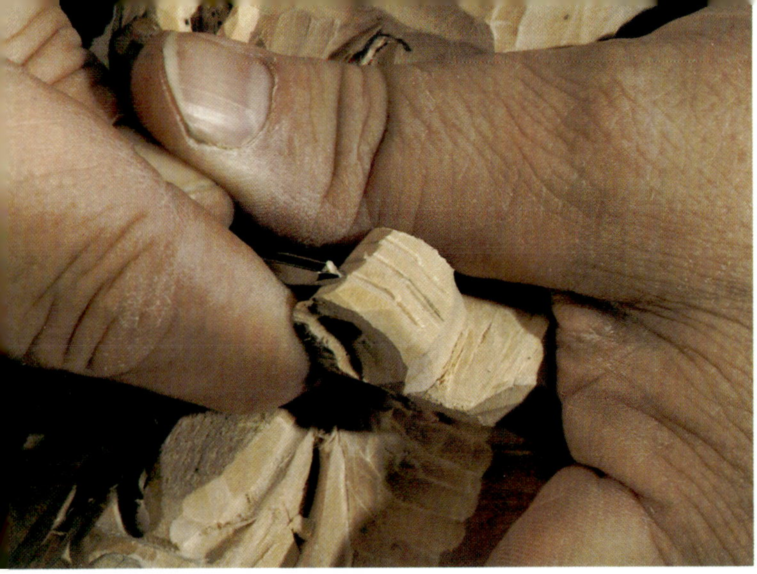

Run between the fingers with a veiner.

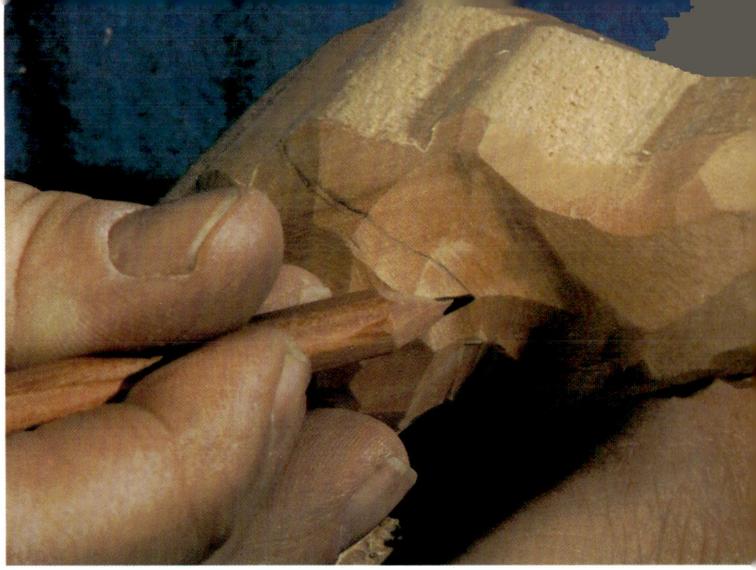

Draw in the folds, as the hood goes over the shoulder.

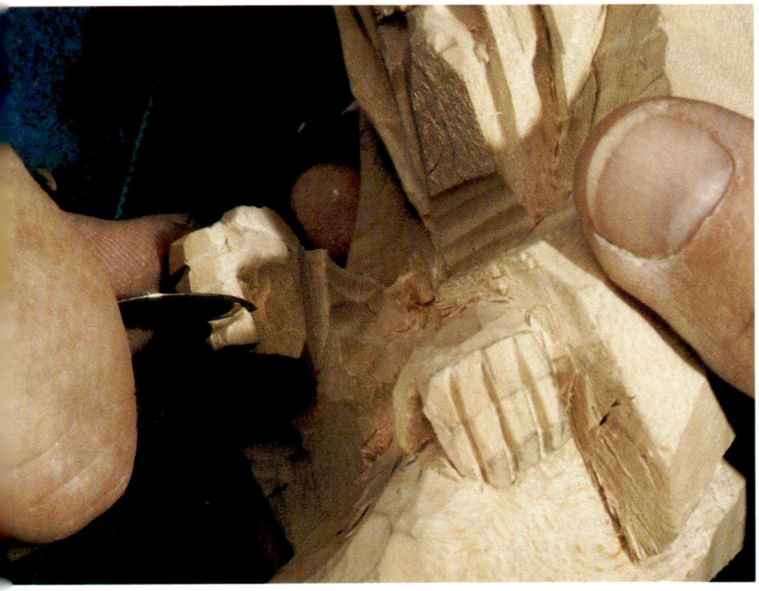

Shape the ends of the fingers and they are done.

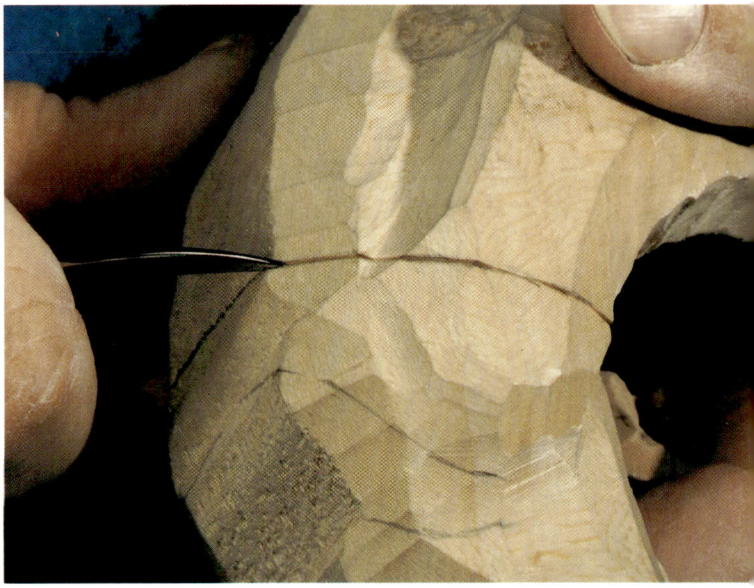

Cut a stop in the line of the hood.

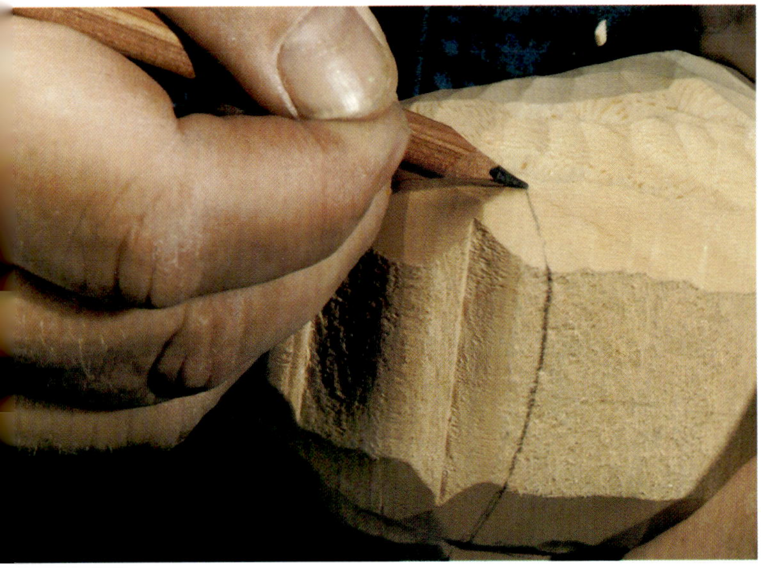

Mark the line of the hood in the back.

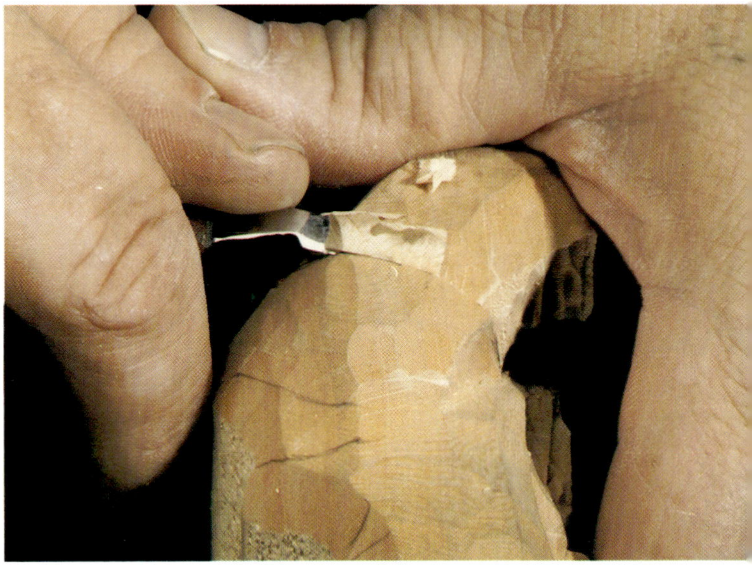

Cut back to the stop from the line.

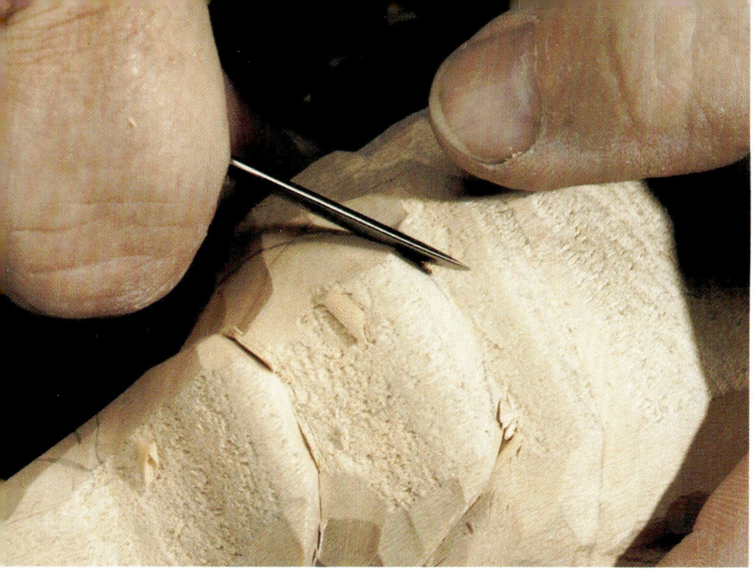

Cut a stop straight in on the fold lines then trim back to it from the surface below. You want the effect of the material being folded over the lower surface.

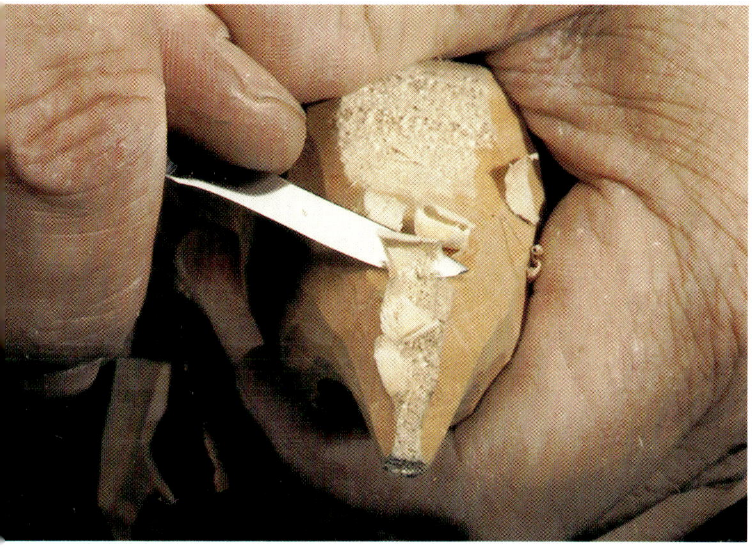

Clean up the saw marks on the hood.

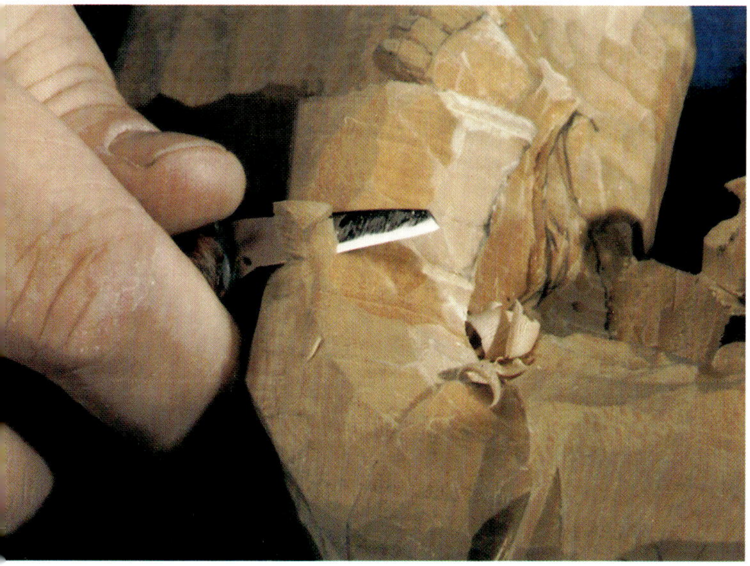

Continue down the arm, dressing it up.

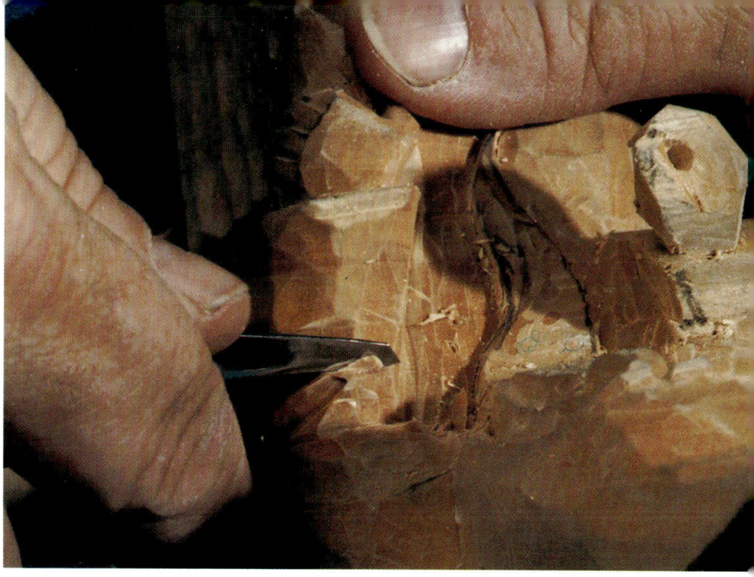

Carry folds across the arms at the elbows.

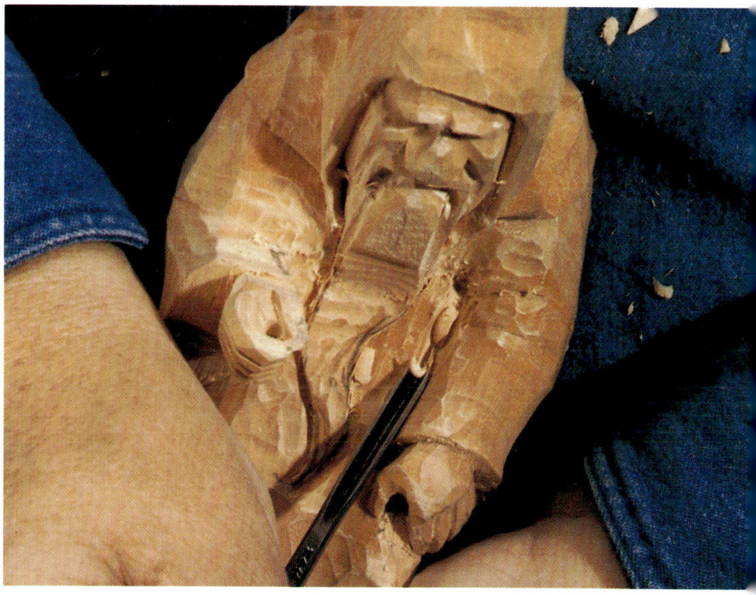

Begin to distinguish the arm from the body by running between them with a pretty good sized veiner.

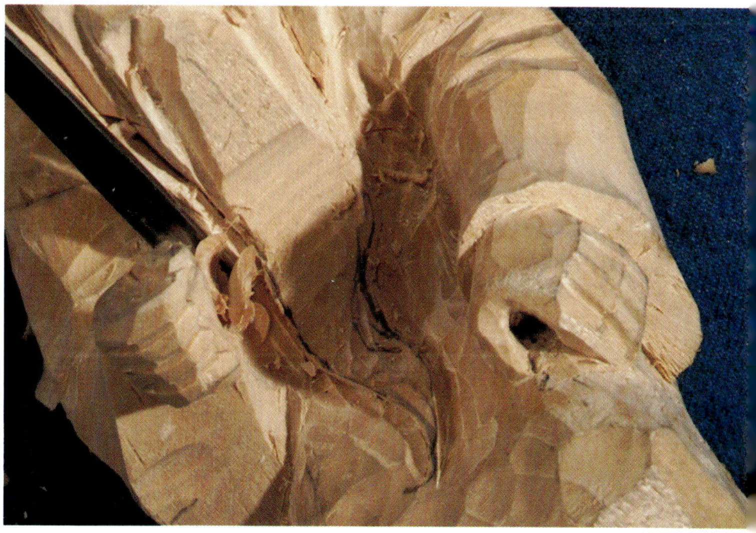

The right arm needs to be moved over a little, away from the body. To do this we widen the chest on that side.

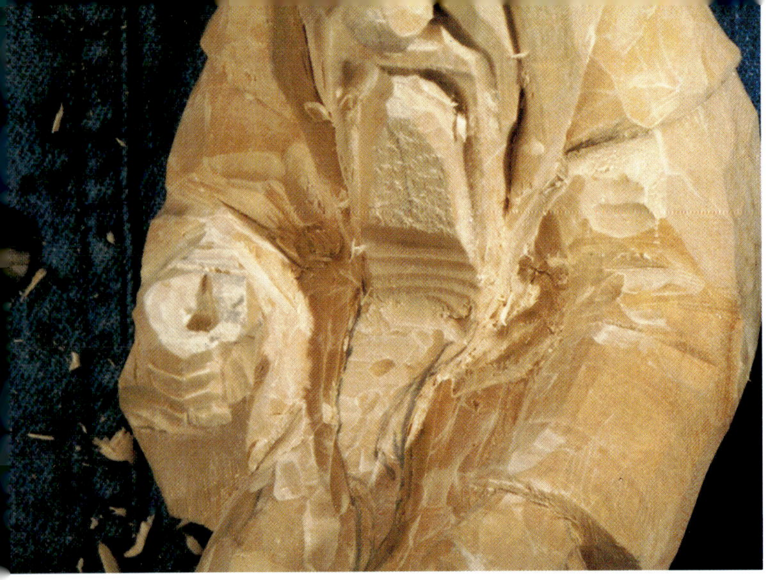

You can see how this brings depth to the carving.

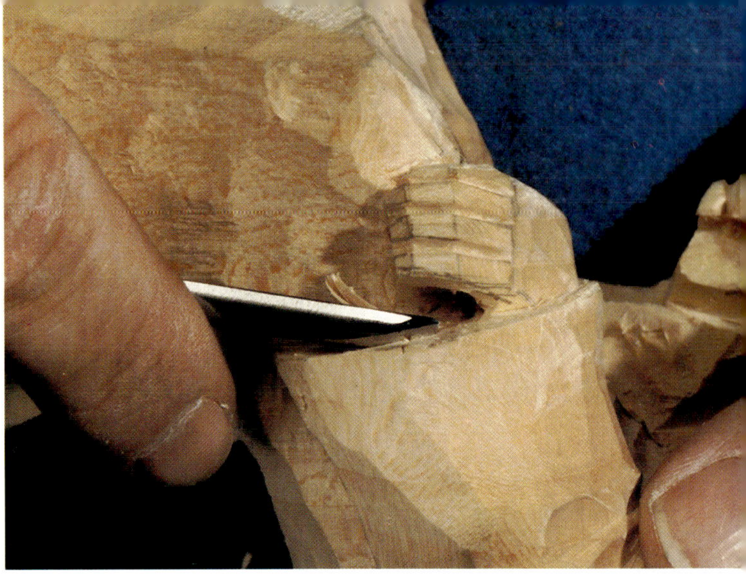

Do the same on the left sleeve. Remember there is no stop, so stay alert.

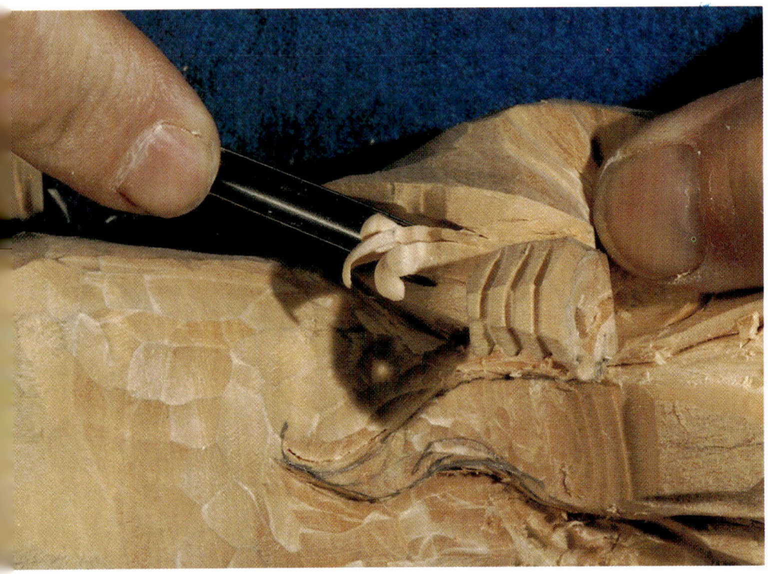

To get the appearance of the sleeve being open, clean it out with a gouge. Be sure you don't go into the arm.

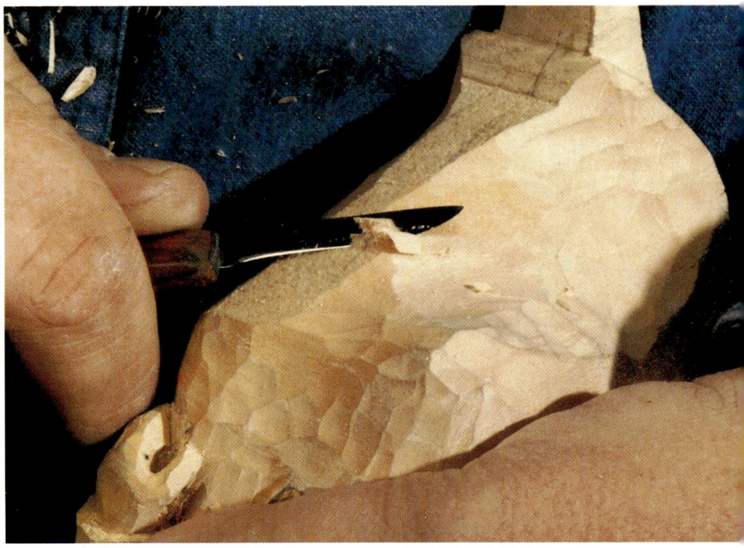

Continue the clean-up process on the skirt of the robe.

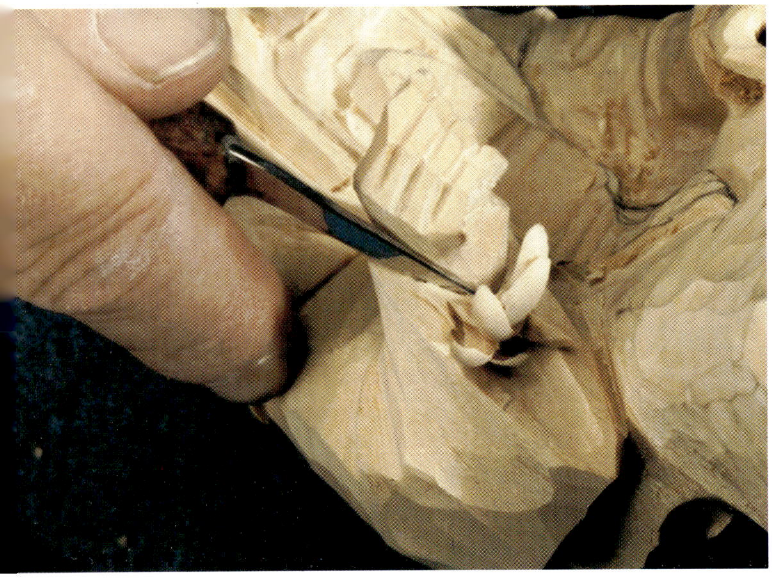

Cut the shavings at the arm with a knife.

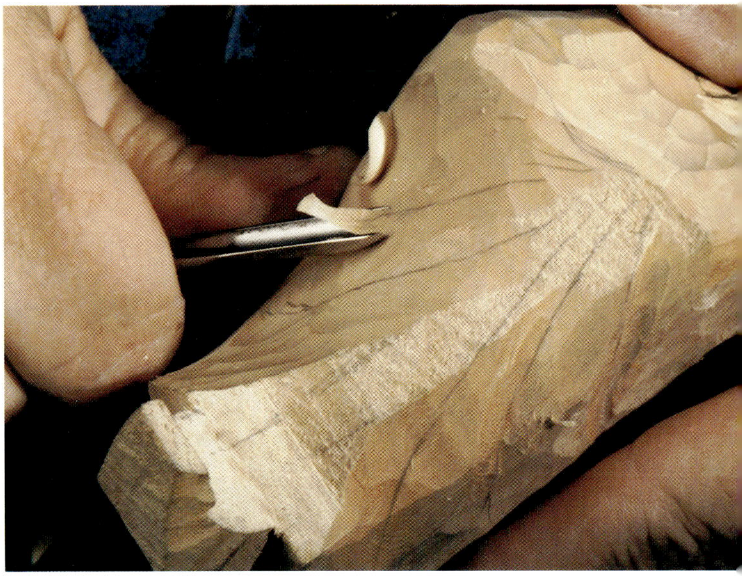

Draw a pattern of stress folds from the knees and start to carve them with gouge.

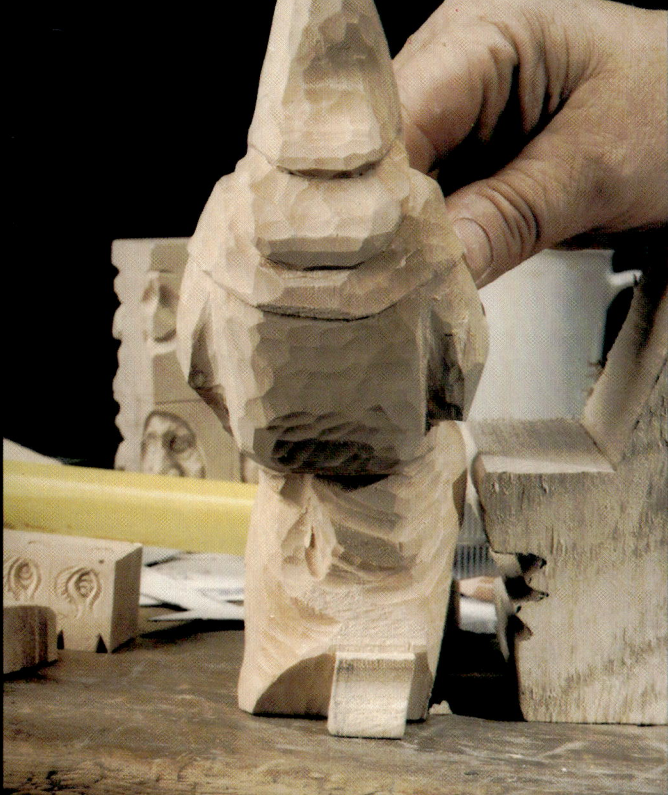

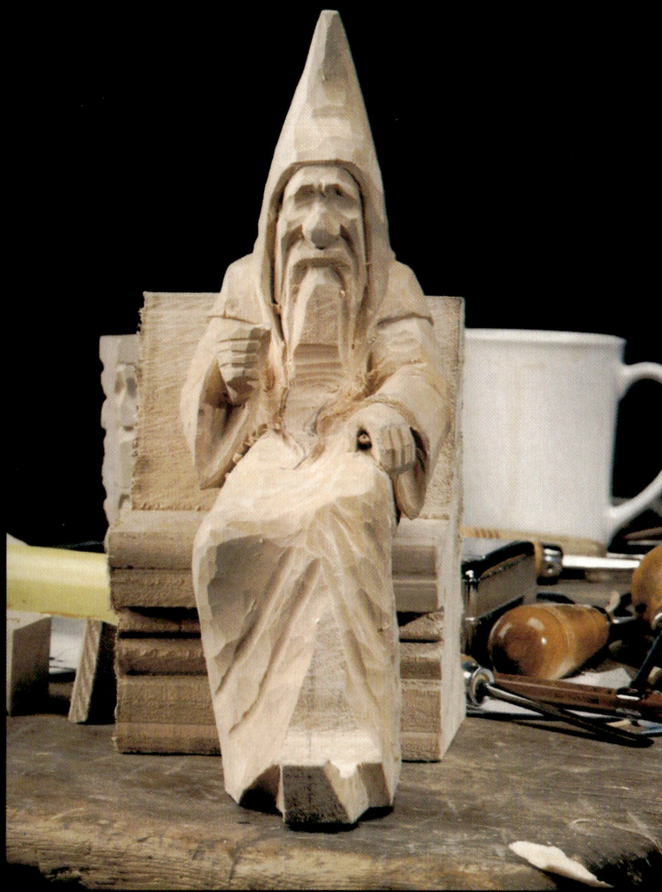

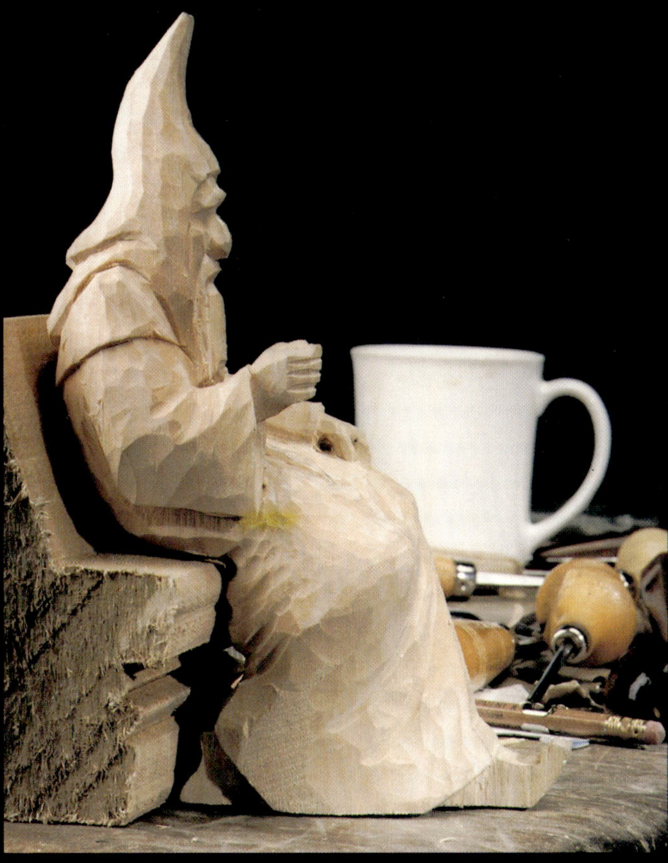

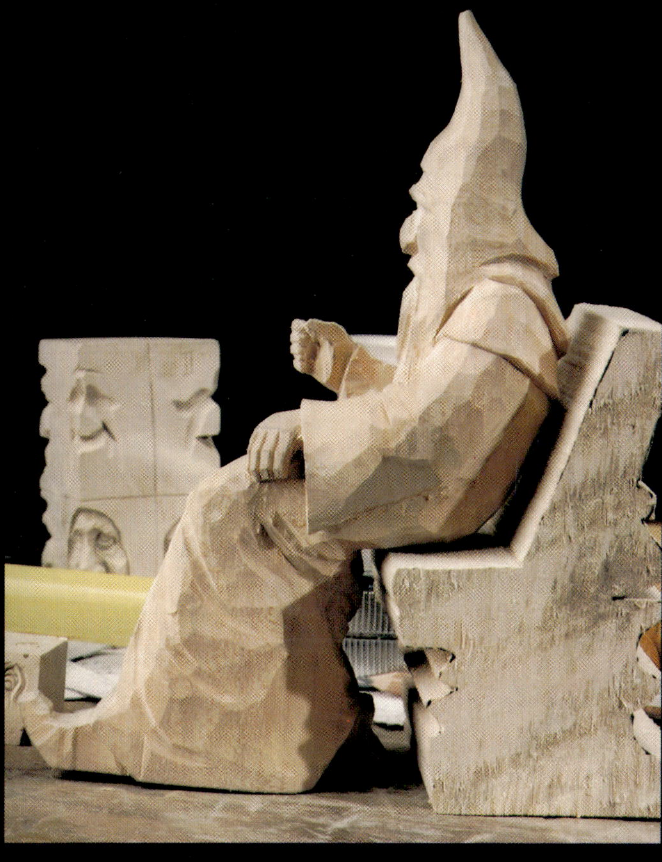

Progress.

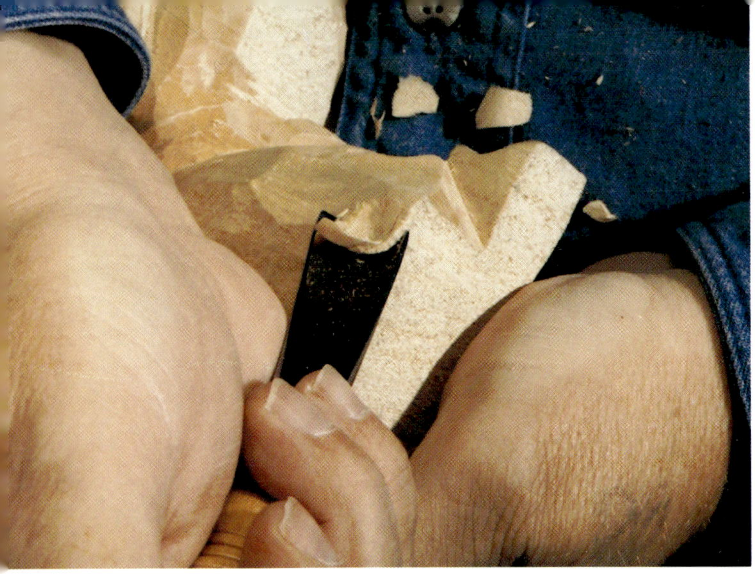

The hem of the robe seems a bit square, so I'm going to round it around the heel.

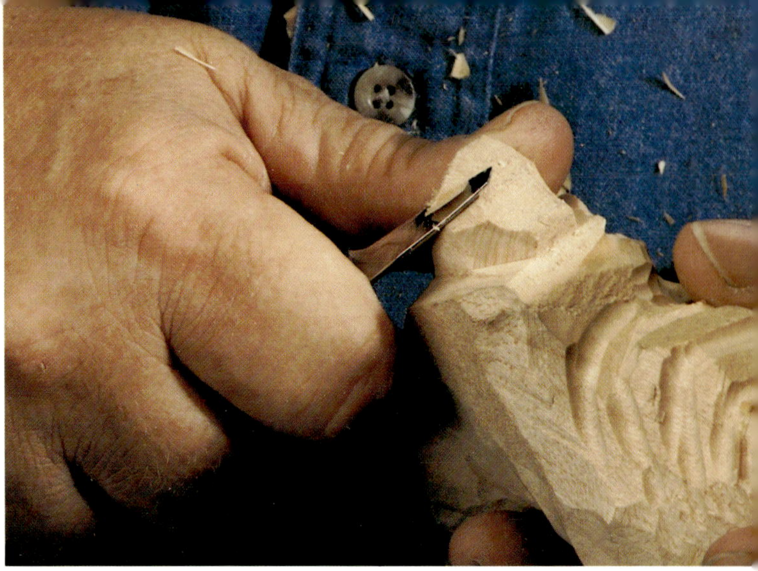

and knocking off the corners of the heels.

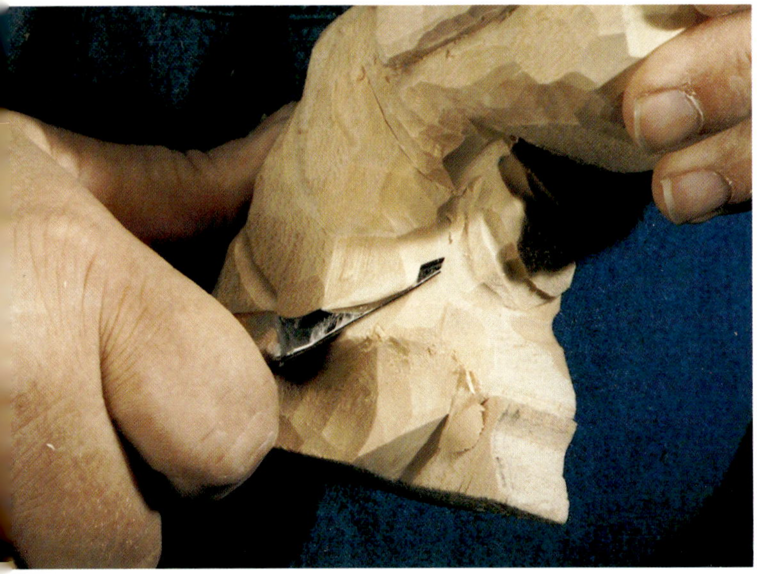

Make adjustments to the skirt. You want the baggy look, but you want it to conform to the position of the leg.

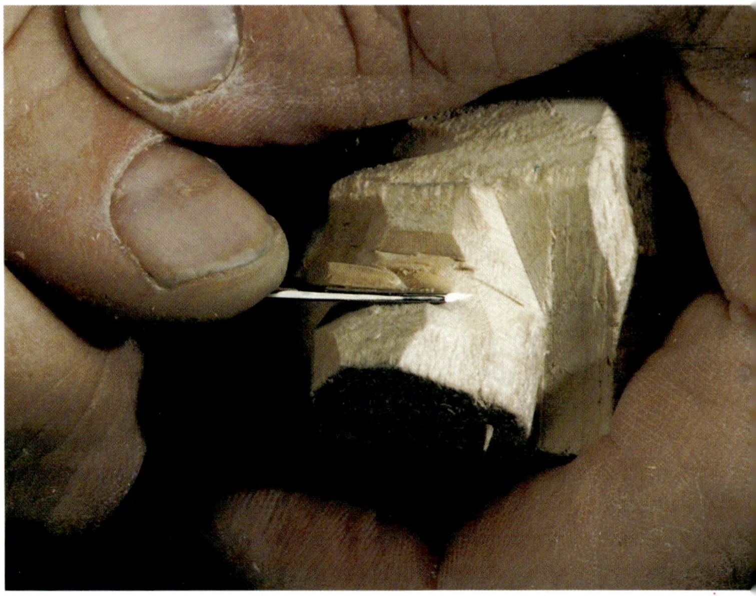

Cut two notches across the back of the shoe for the folds.

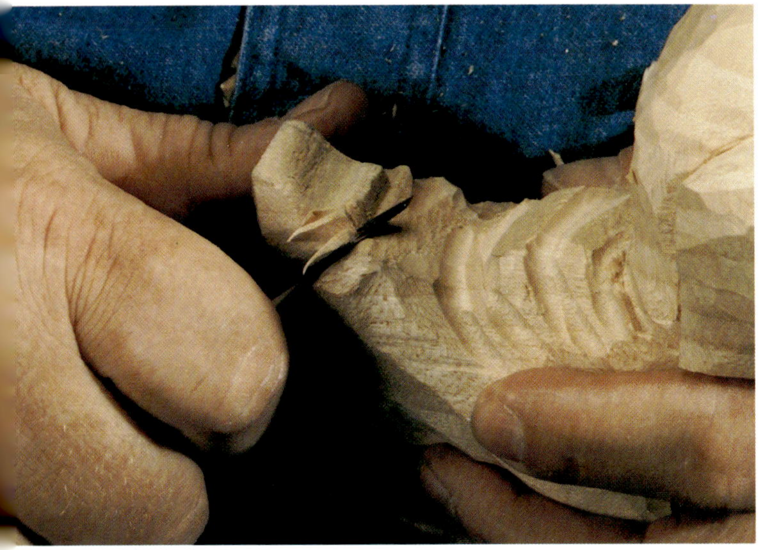

Begin to shape the back shoe by narrowing it...

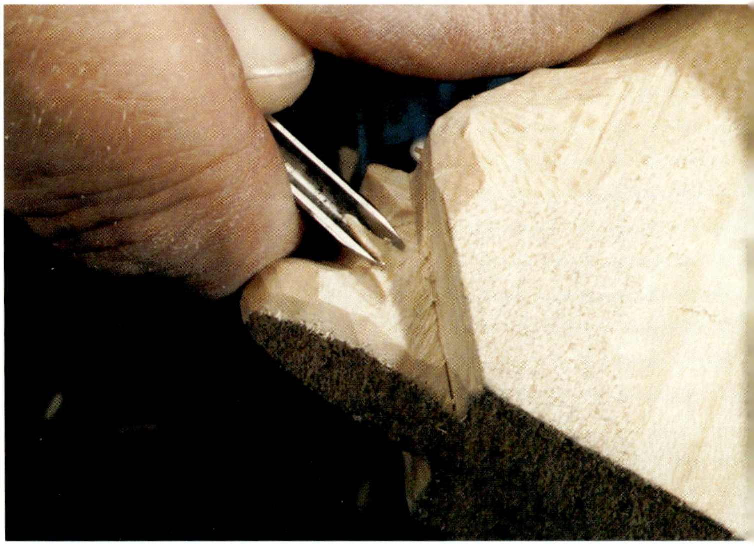

On the side, one fold heads down and the other up, with a nitch in between them cut with a gouge.

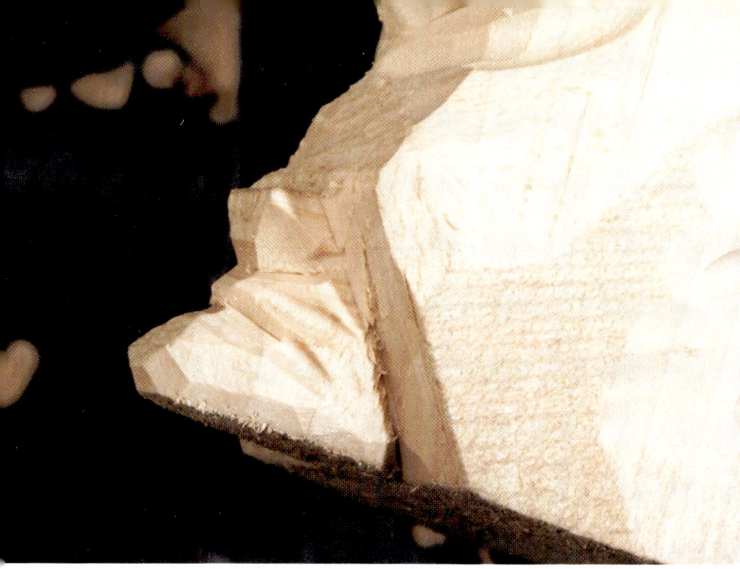

The result.

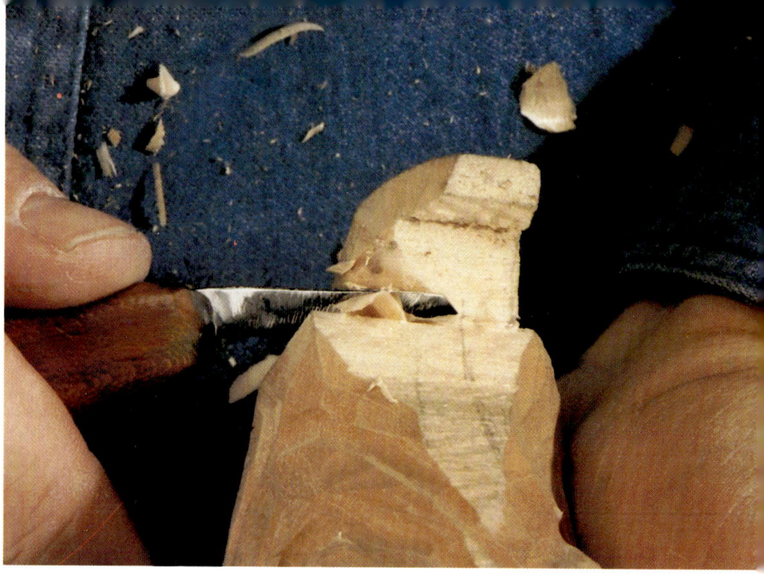

Shape the forward foot in the same way.

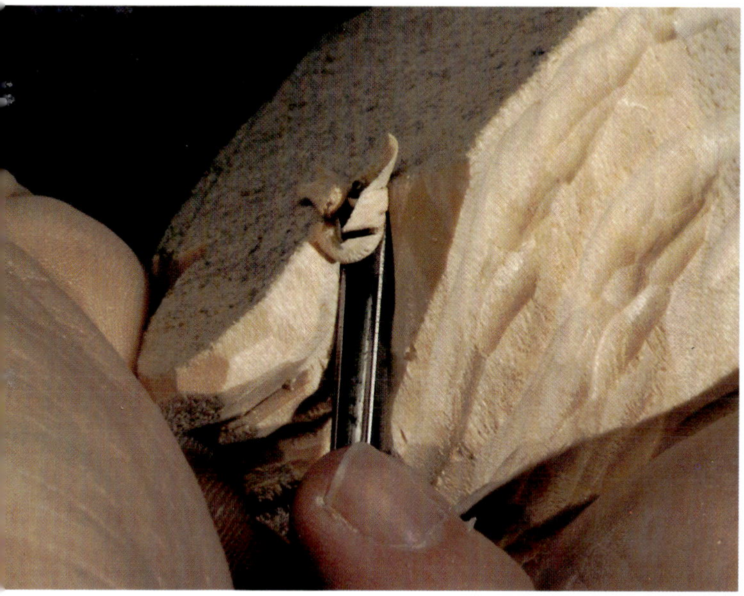

Clean away the robe beside the foot with a gouge so it appears to open up underneath.

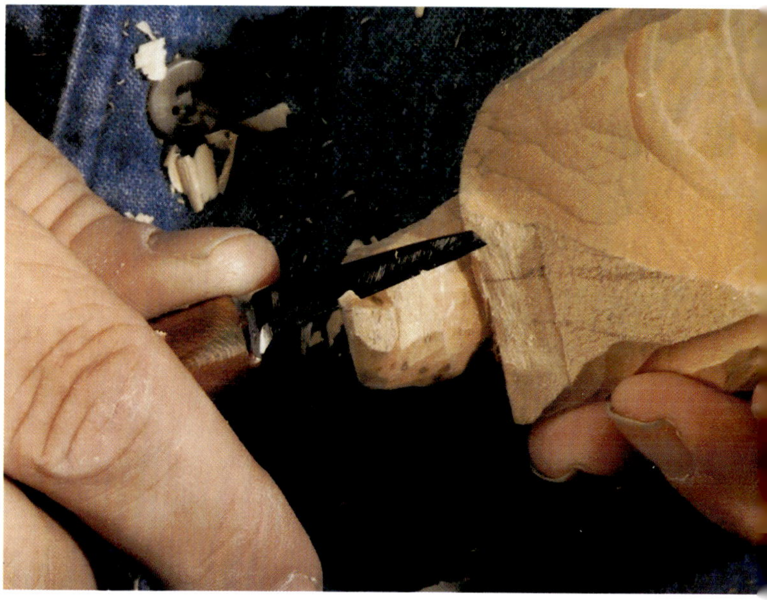

Bring the toe to more of a point, giving it little bit of an elfin look.

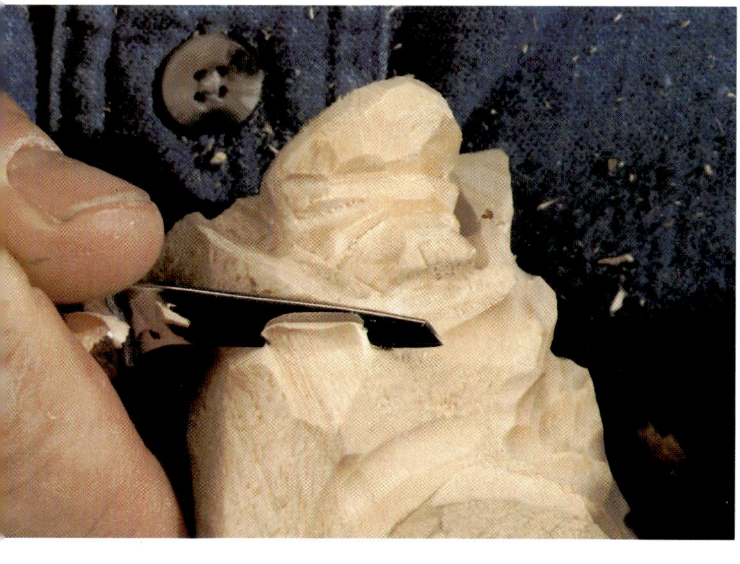

Adjust the fold of the robe to the new lines around the foot.

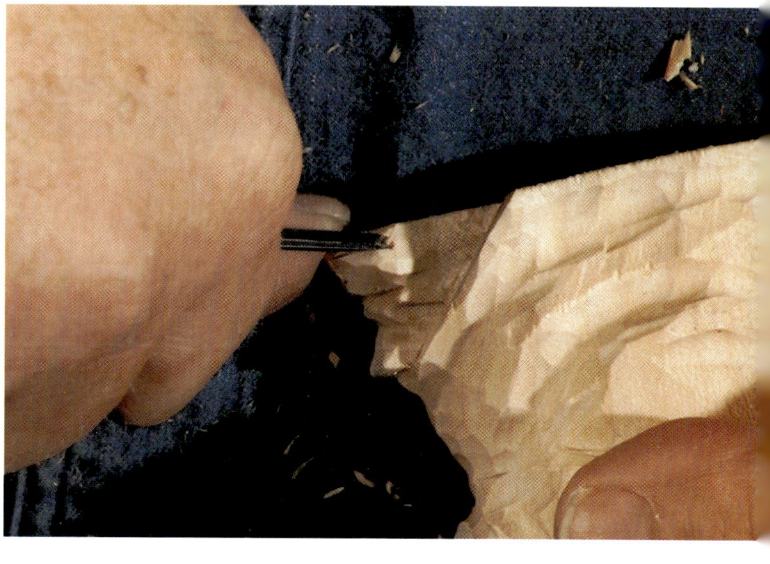

Cut the line of a seam around the sole with a small veiner.

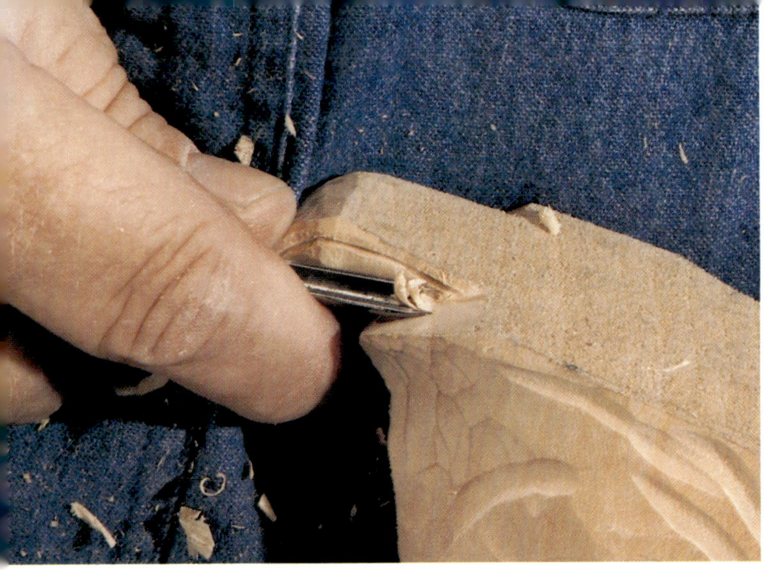

Undercut the skirt with a gouge.

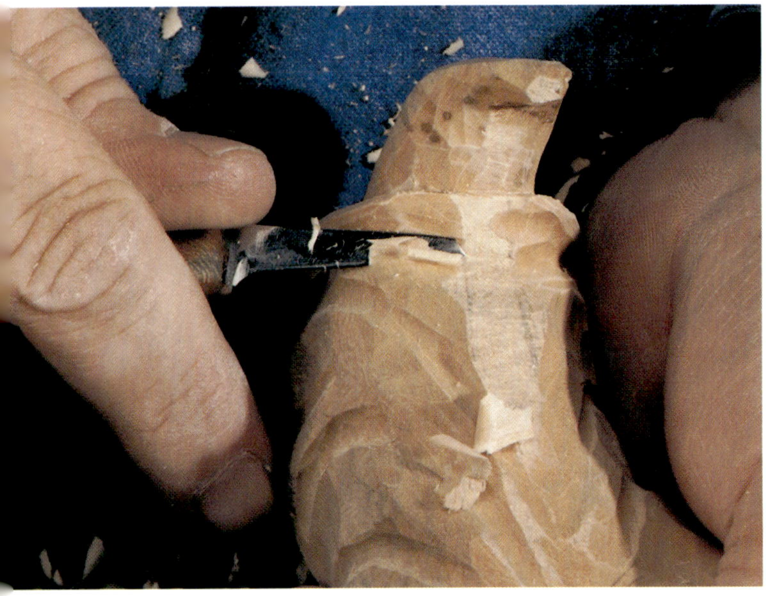

Shape the skirt.

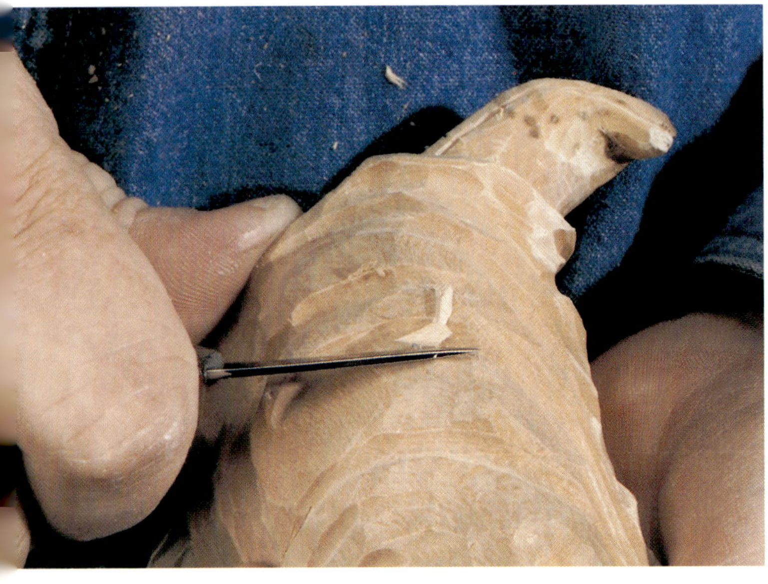

Go back and soften the folds in the skirt.

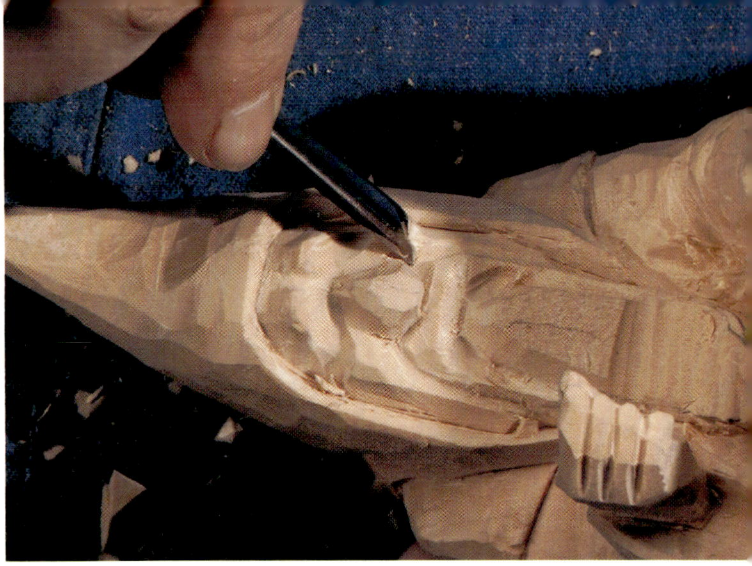

Returning to the face, come over the cheek with the gouge, keeping the cup side against the cheek.

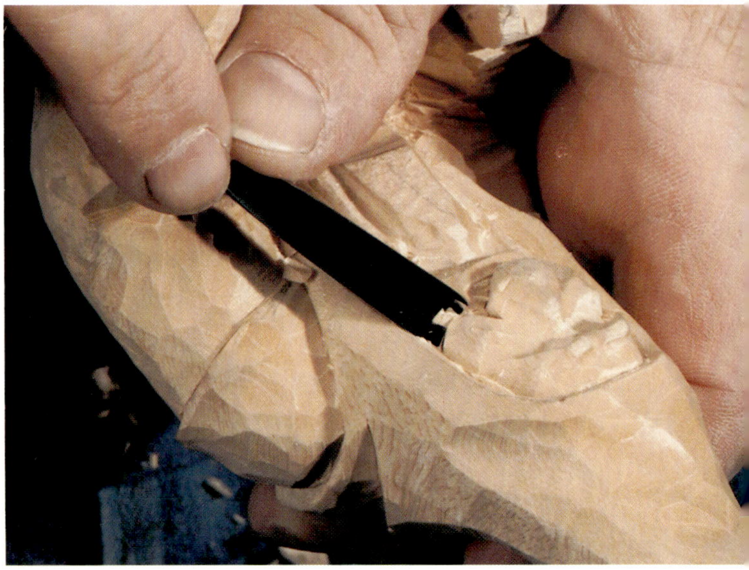

Come back to the cheek from below, with the cup of the gouge away from it. This will establish the roundness of the cheek.

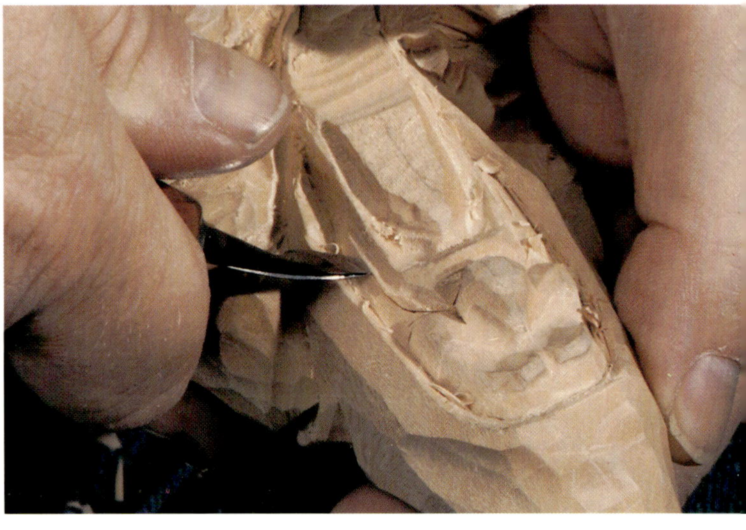

Cut a stop in the upper moustache line...

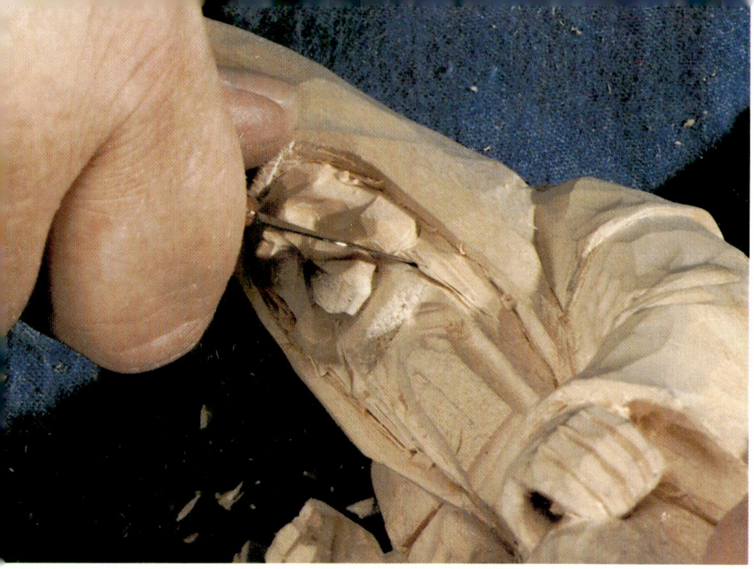

and slice back to it from moustache.

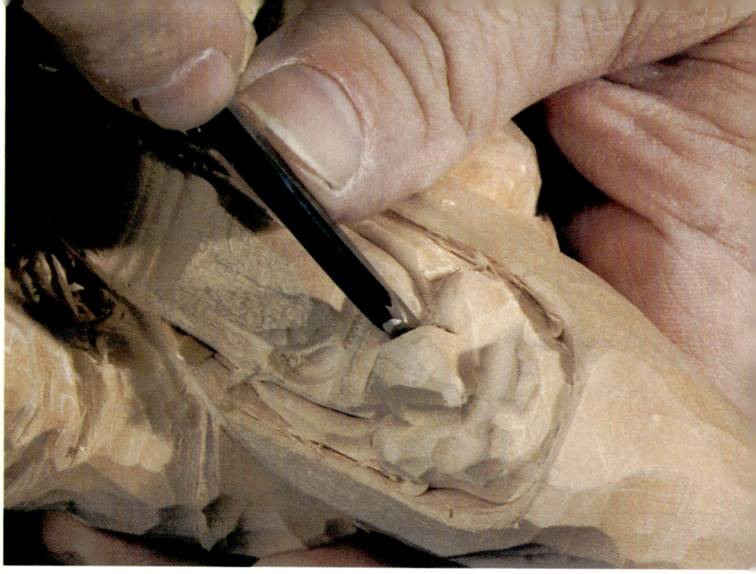

Come straight into the nostril with a small round gouge to create the hole.

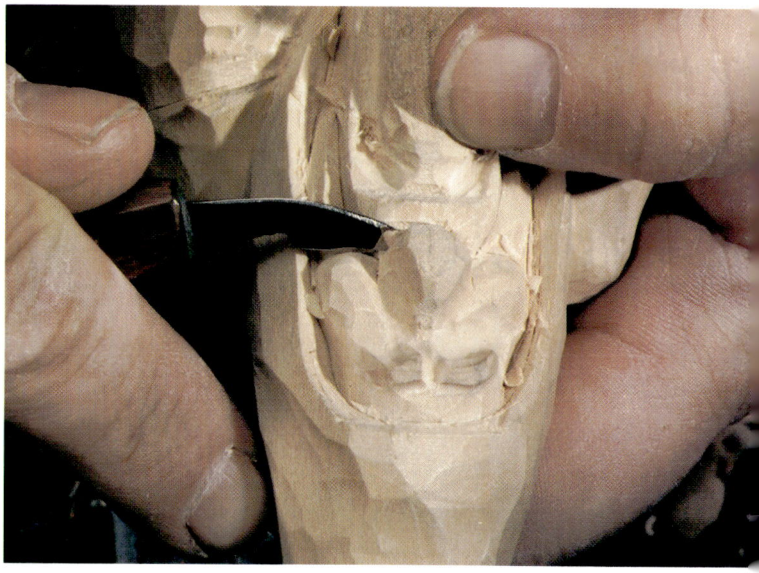

Clean it out with a knife.

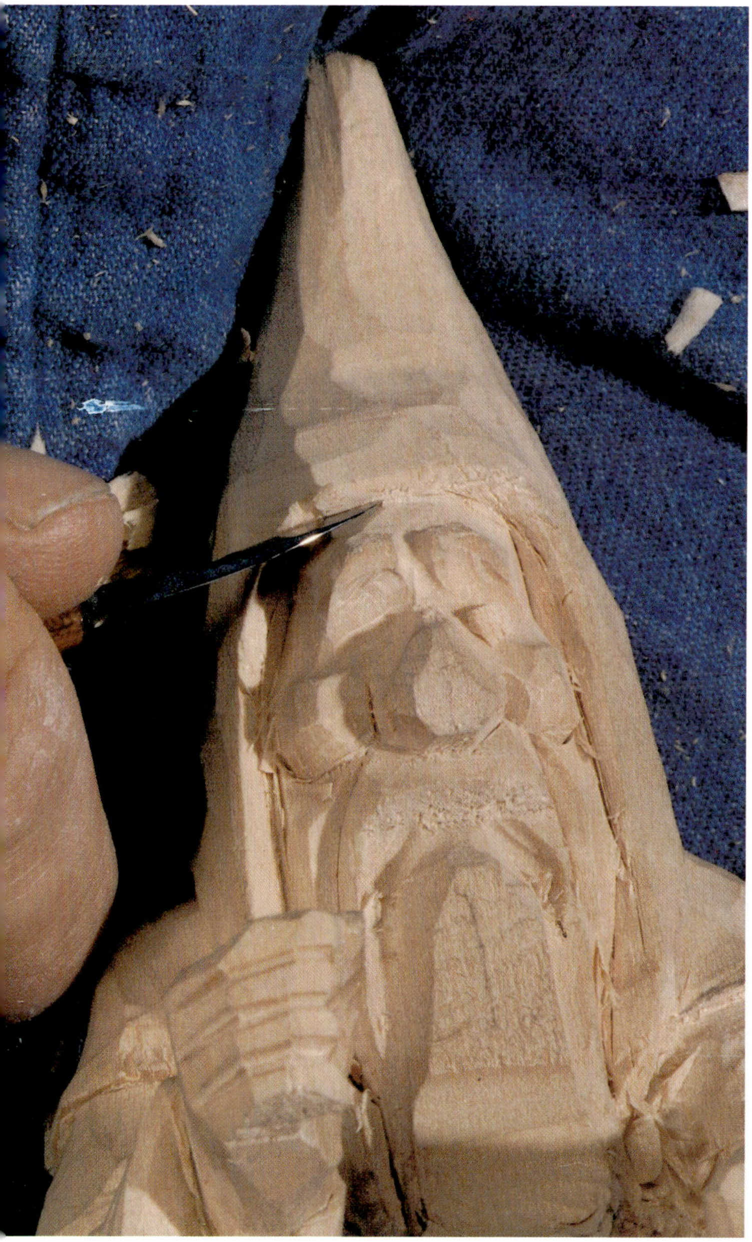

The face is a little too jovial, so I need to thin it down.

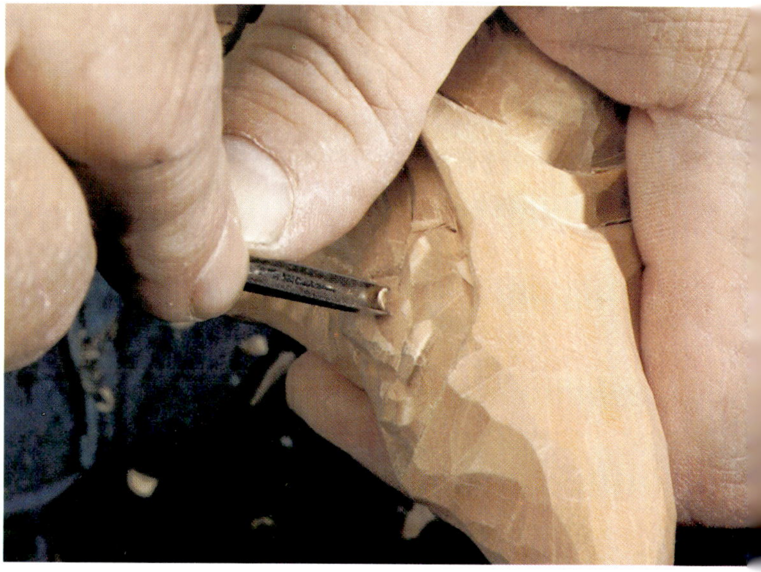

Come over the nostril flange with a small half round gouge.

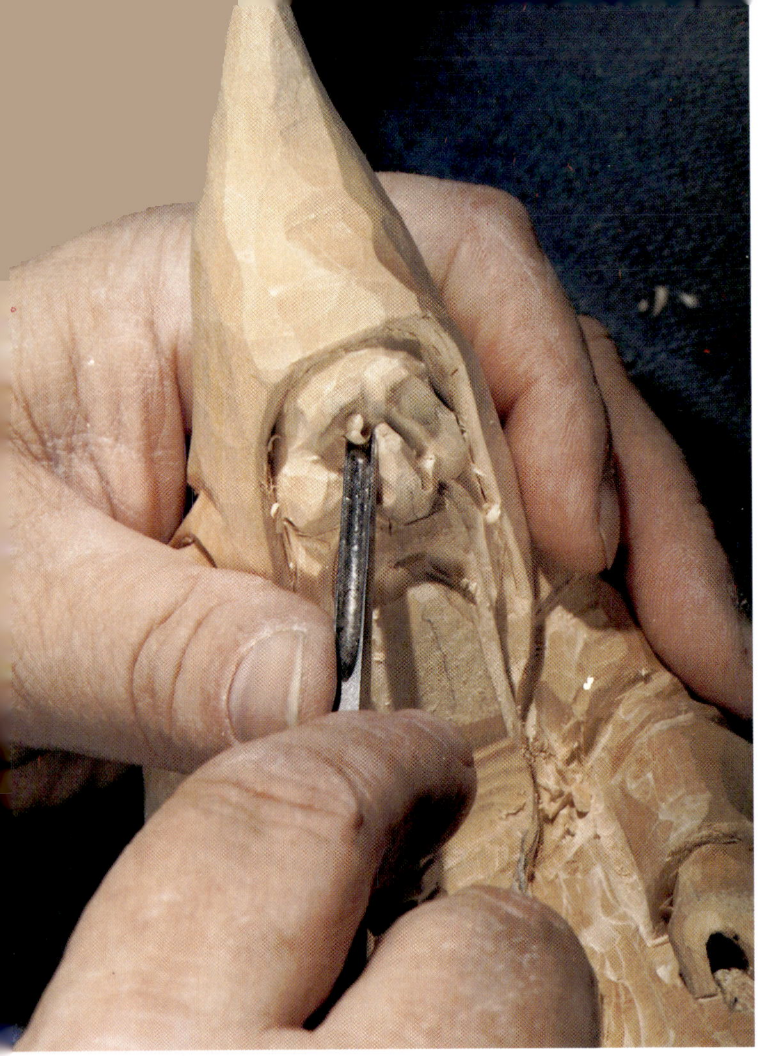

With the same tool come up beside the nose....

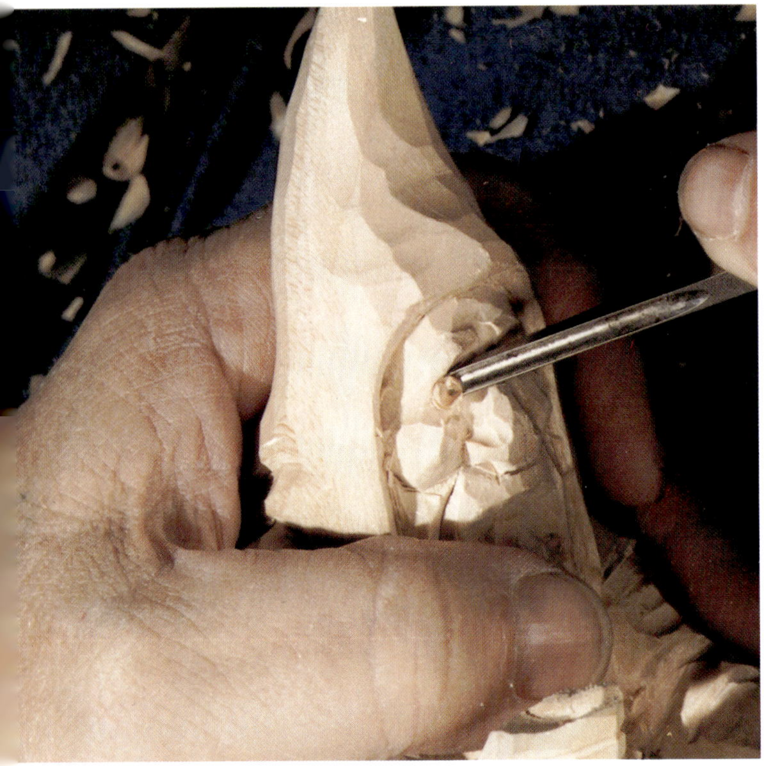

and continue the movement out through the eye socket.

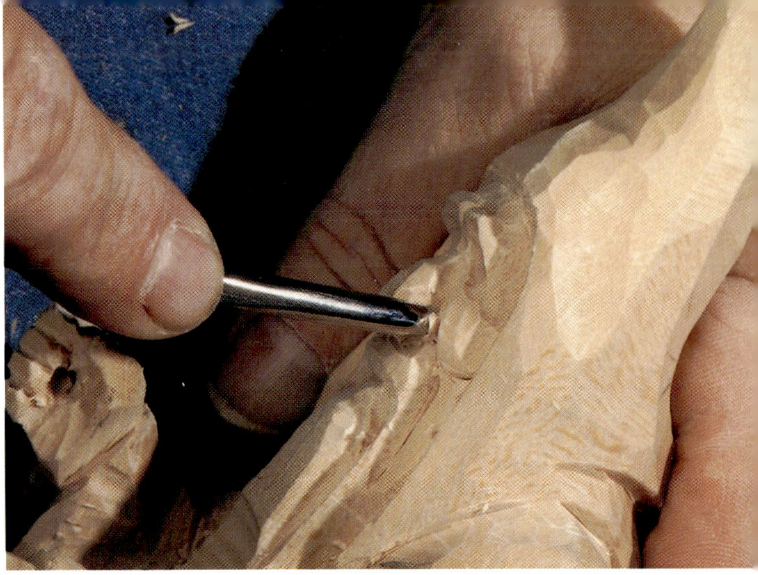

With the cup of the tool against the nose, push it over the nostril flange to round it. This also makes both nostril flanges the same size.

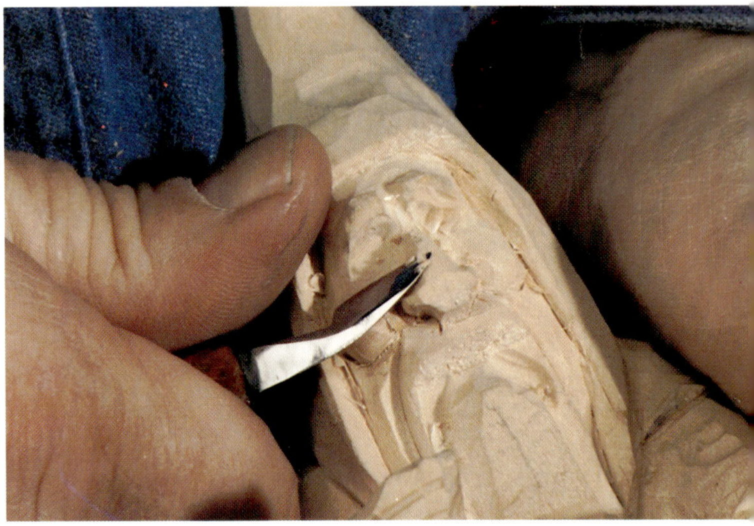

Smooth everything out with a knife.

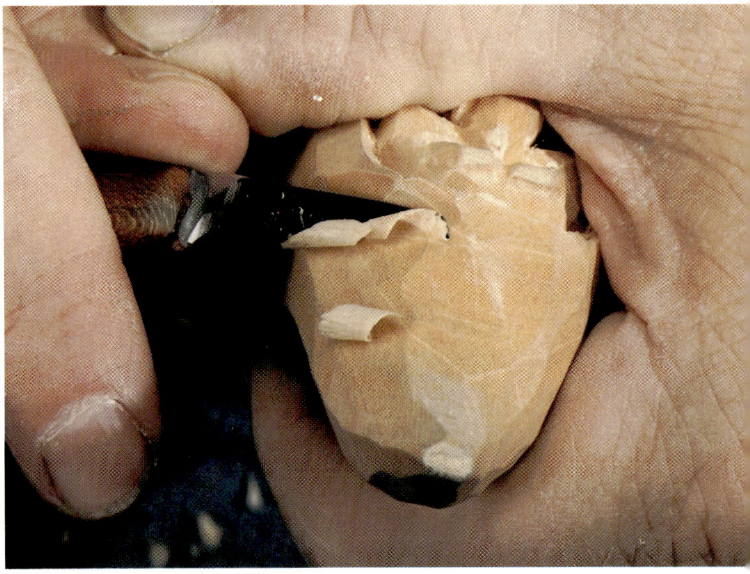

The hat needs some shaping to make it look like cloth. Begin with a curved knife cut at the brim...

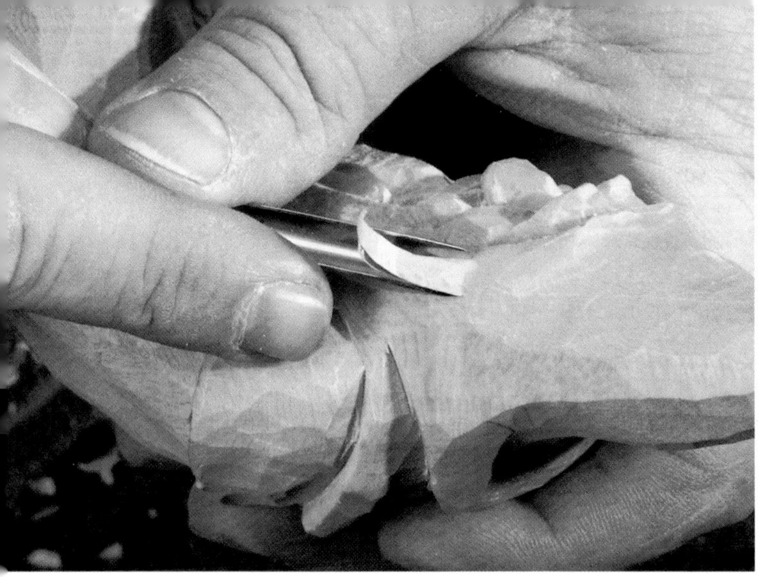

then, with a gouge, bring a curve up the side to meet it.

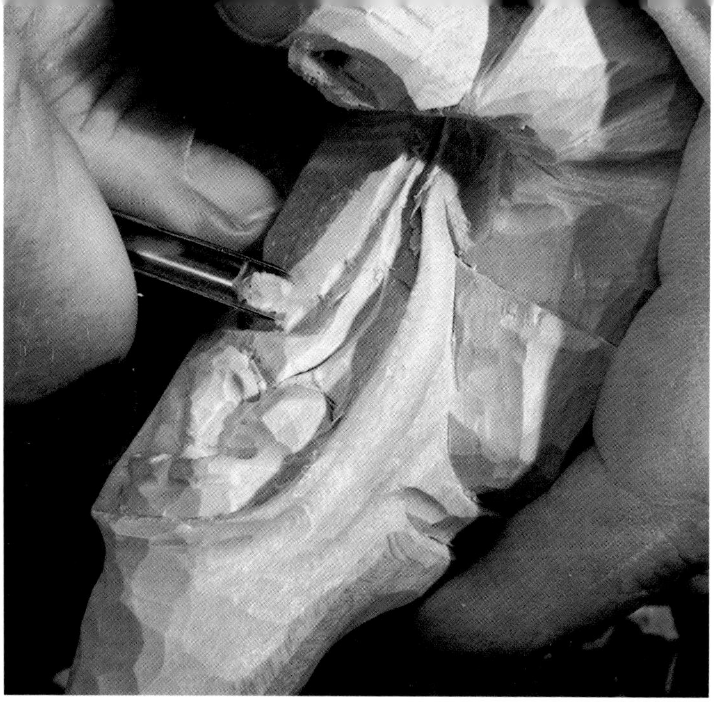

Run a gouge across the jaw to establish the bottom lip.

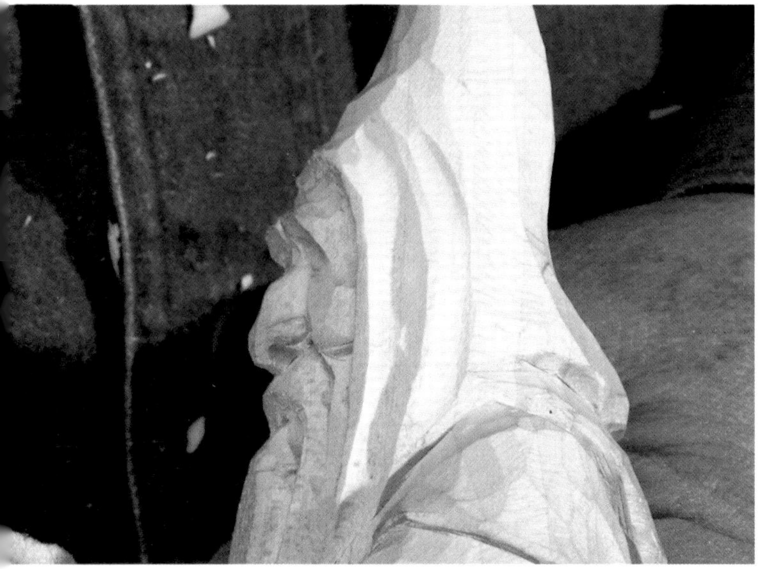

Continue with a couple more folds to give the hat some contours.

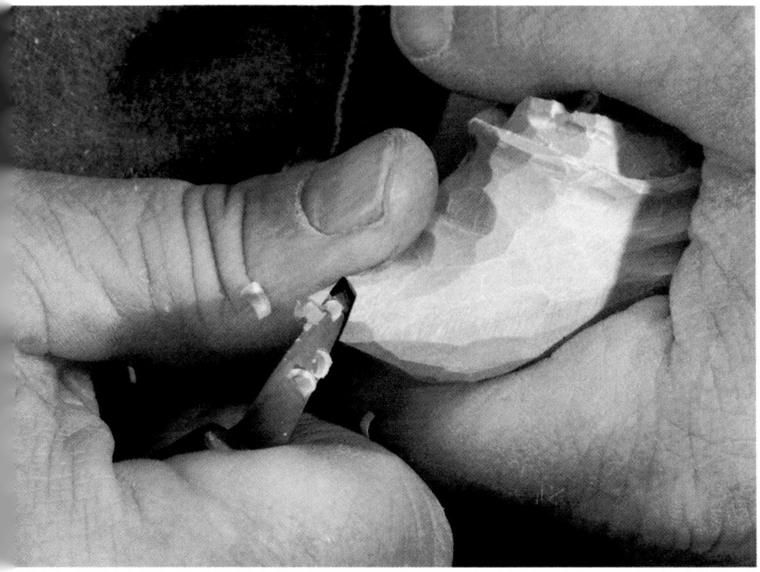

Sharpen the point of the hat.

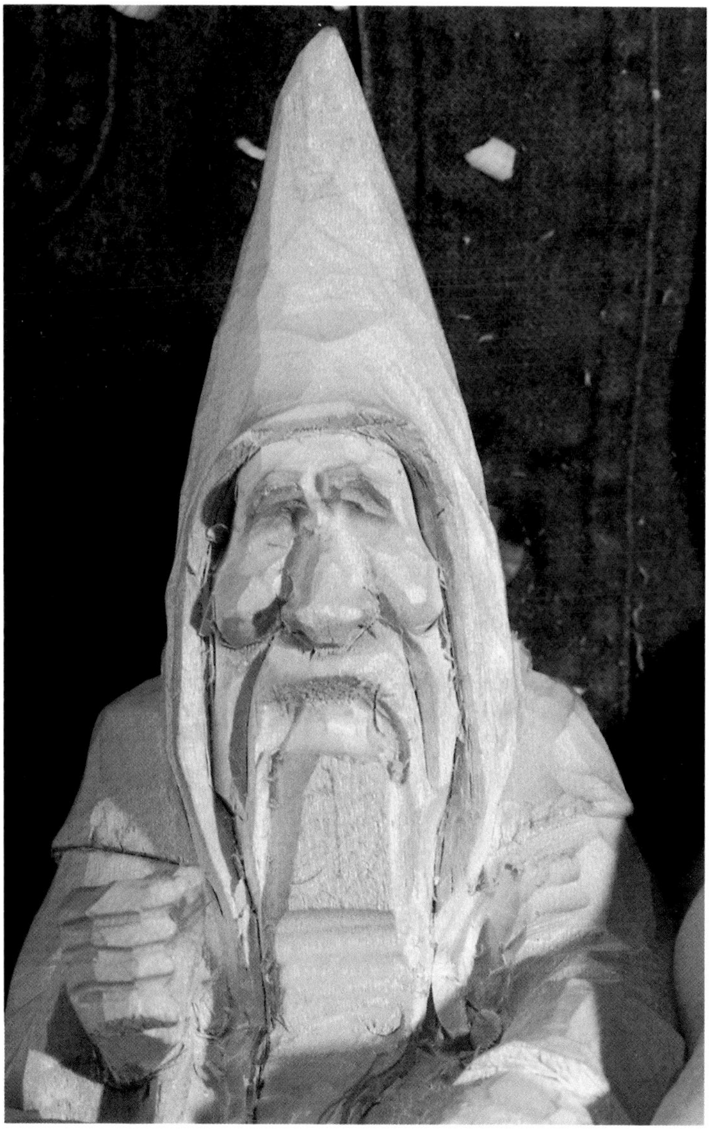

Progress.

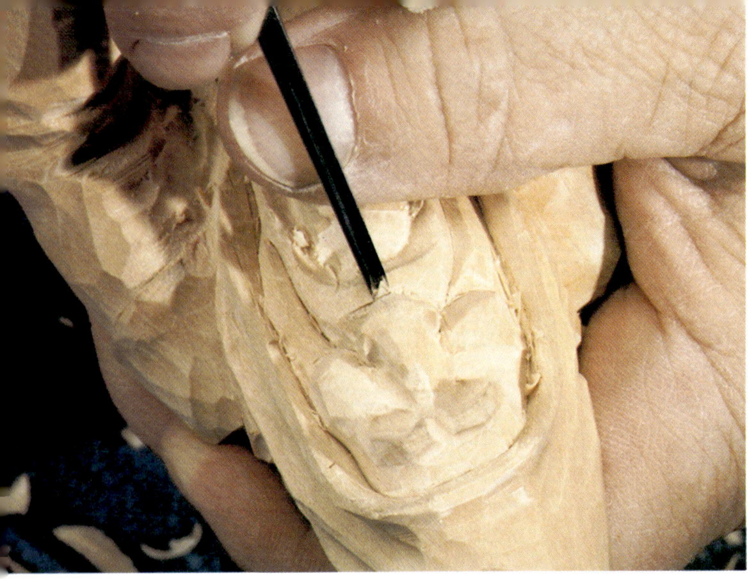

Separate the moustache with a v-tool.

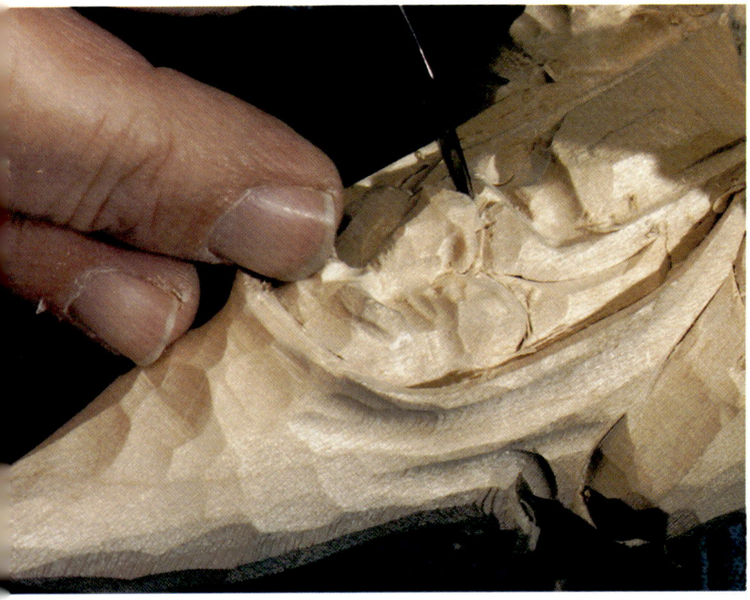

Cut the shaving off with a knife.

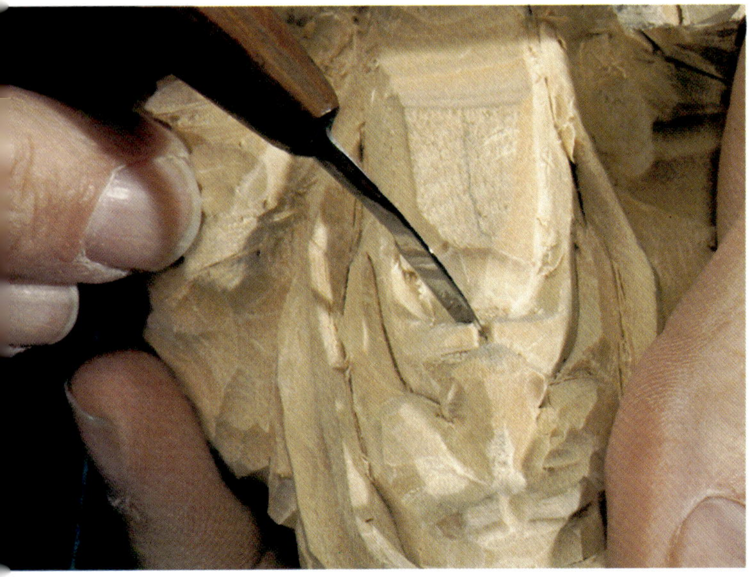

At the bottom of this separation cut at an angle, one way...

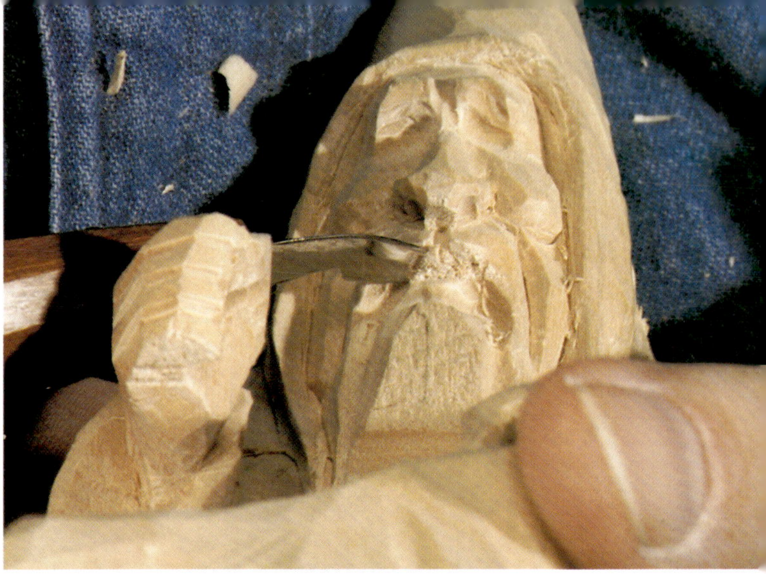

then the other...

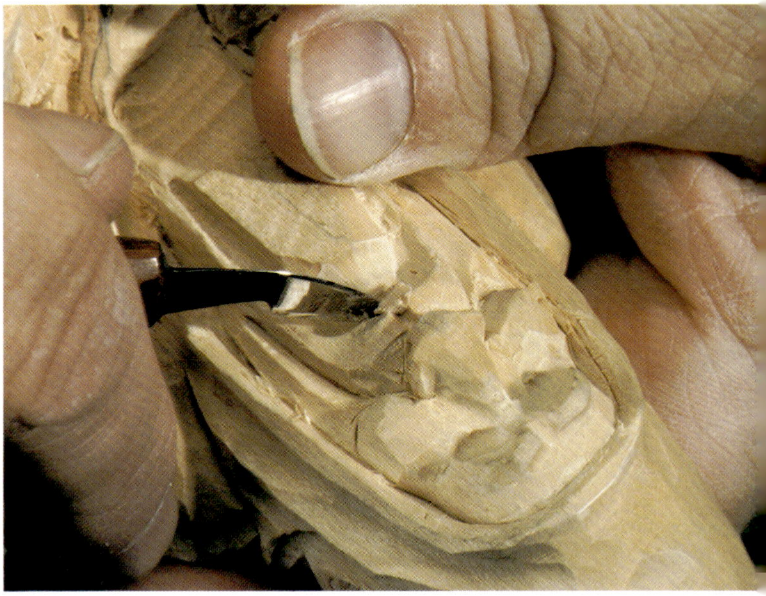

and back into the triangle from below. This should pop out the nitch where the halves of the moustache come together. It also gives the mouth the appearance of going under the moustache.

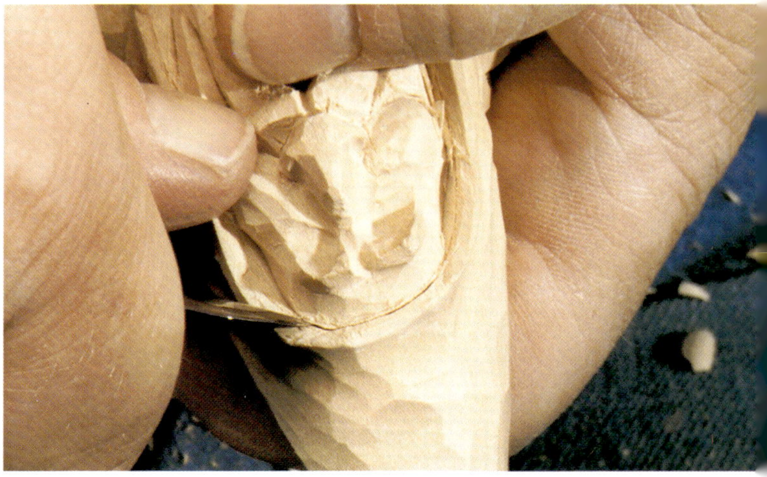

Undercut the front edge of the hat so the head appears to go underneath it.

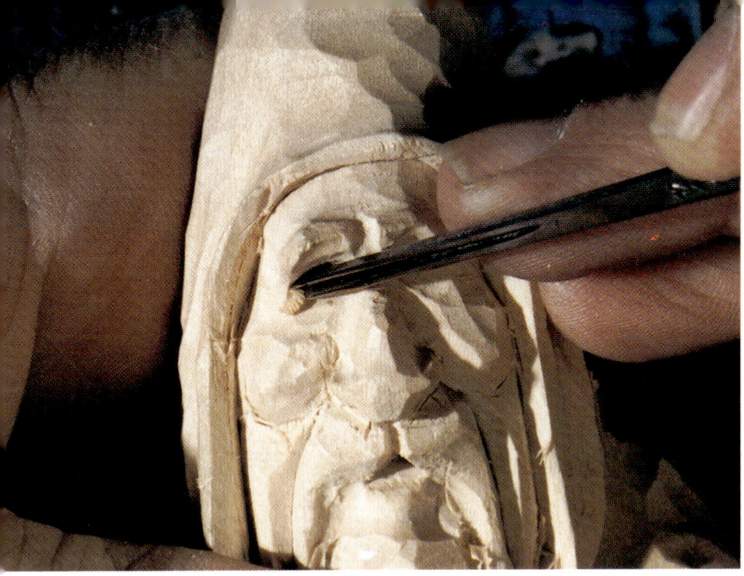

Cut the top eyelids with a v-tool...left...

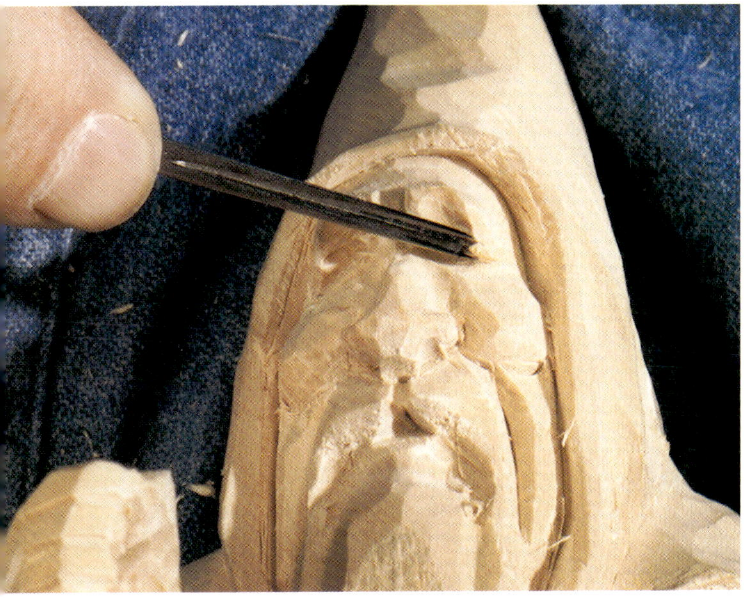

and right.

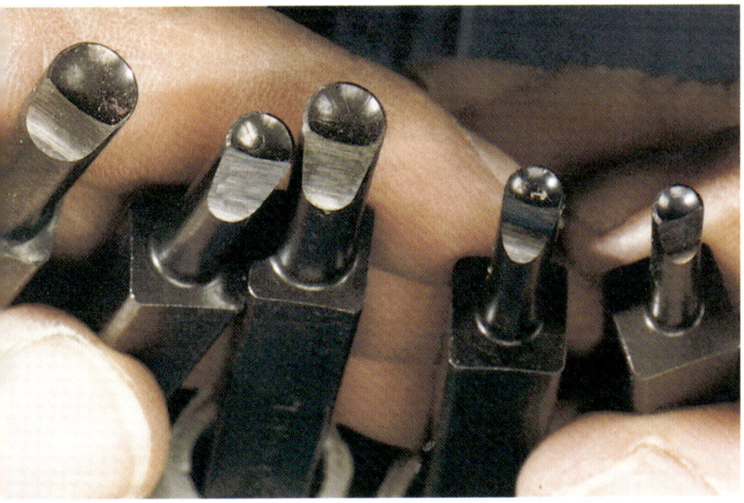

This is new way of doing eyes for me, a variation of the eyepunch method I introduced years ago. I've taken a regular set of eyepunches and ground one side down, not quite halfway.

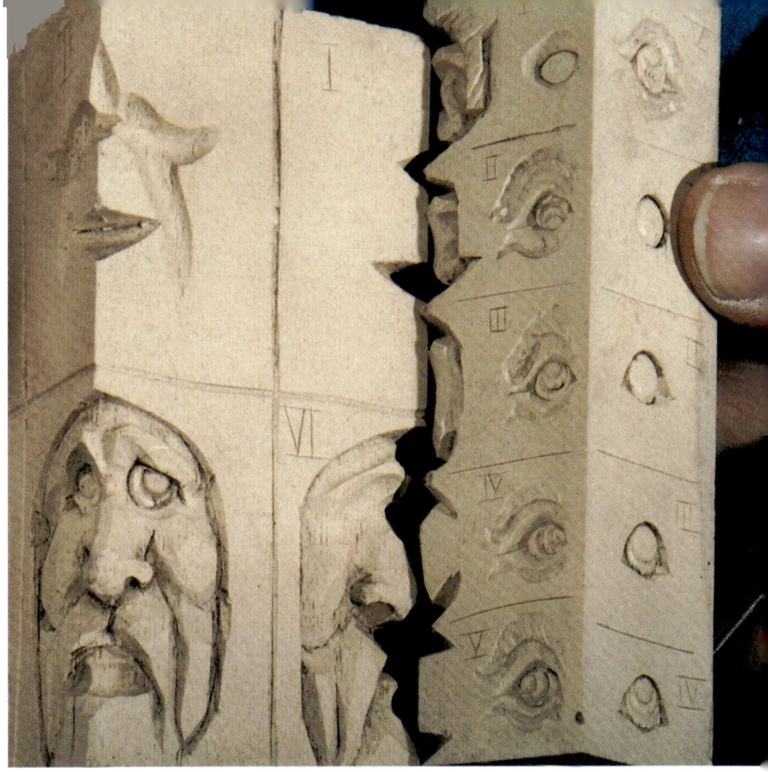

These study casts give you some idea of the process.

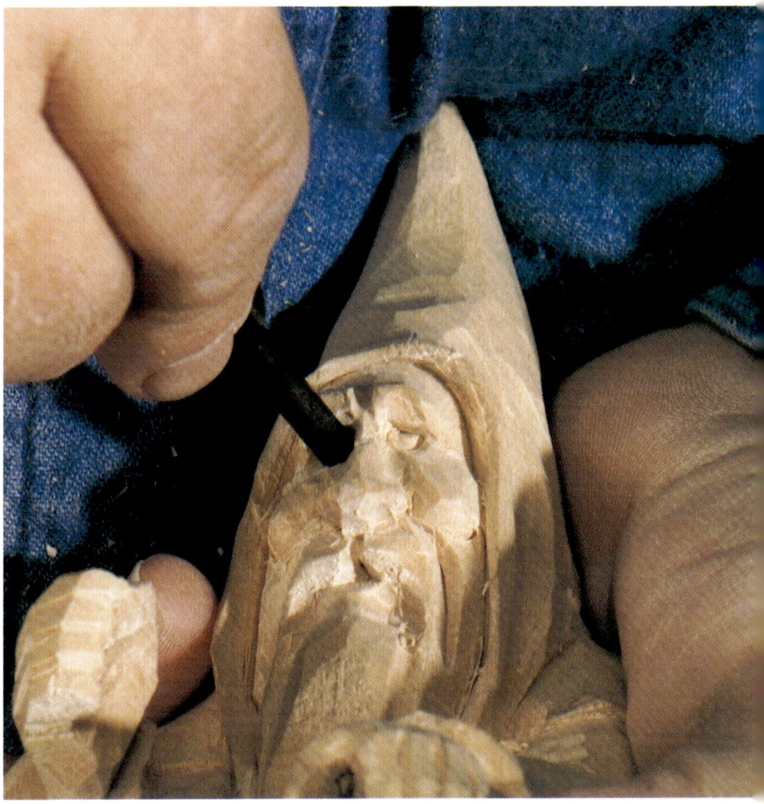

In this particular eye, I use two half-round eyepunches. The larger is 3/16" and the smaller is 4/32". This skips one size eyepunch. If I don't skip one size, the lines of the eye are too close together. Line the flat edge of the larger punch against the top lid and rock it side to side and up and down. This creates the general shape of the eyeball.

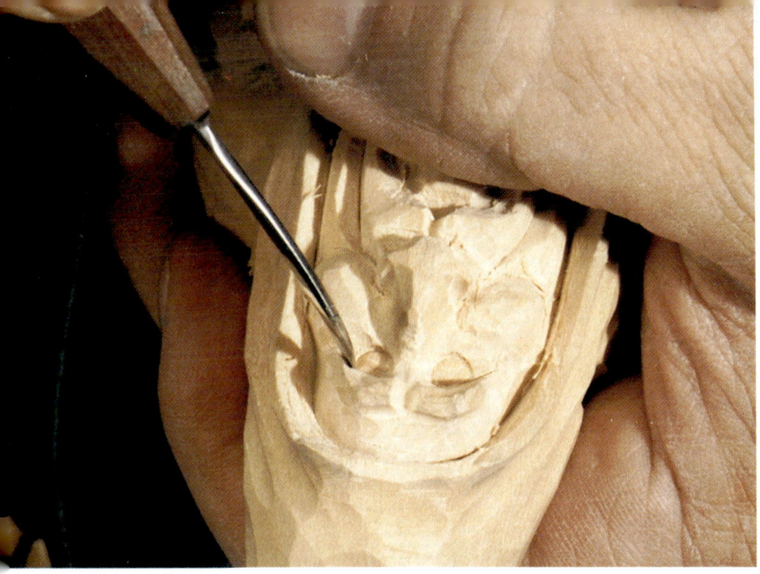

Cut into the corner with a knife along the top lid...

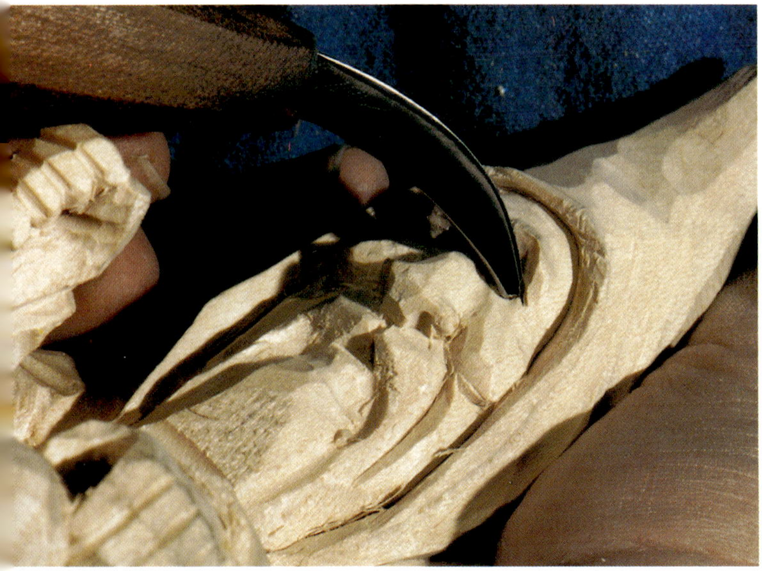

over the surface of the eye...

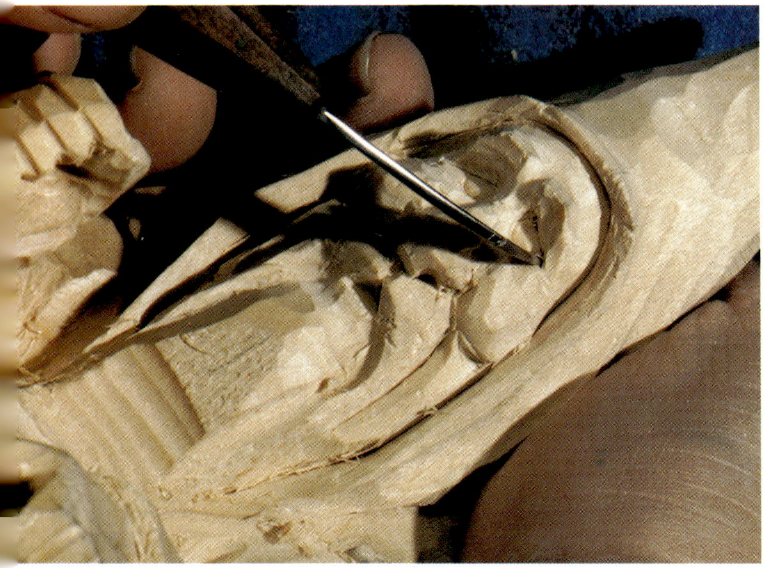

and along the bottom lid. The sequence is not as important as it is that the cuts be clean.

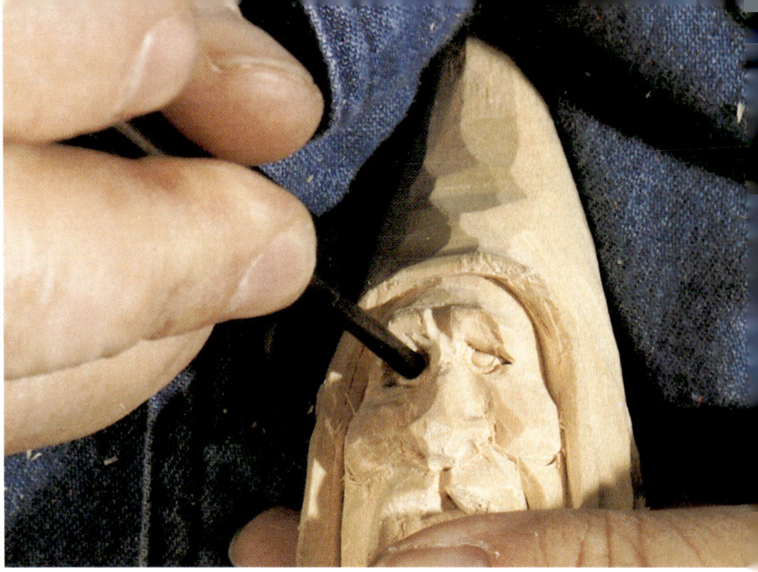

With the smaller half-eyepunch make the iris, rocking it in the same way.

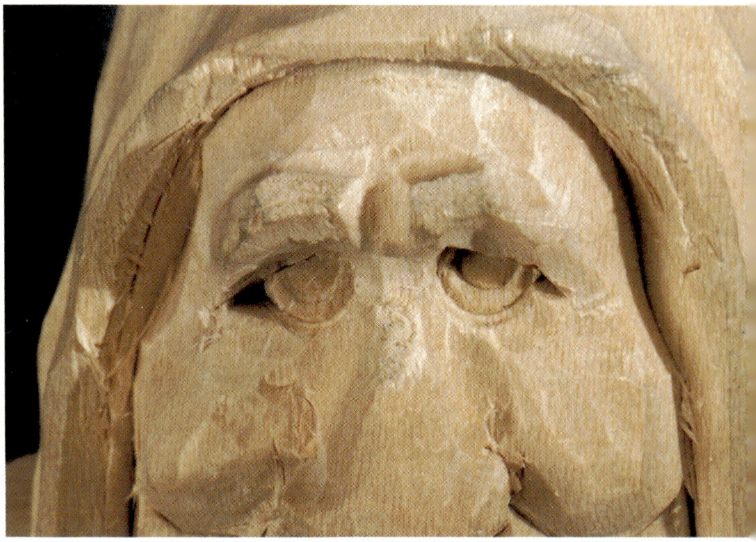

The result.

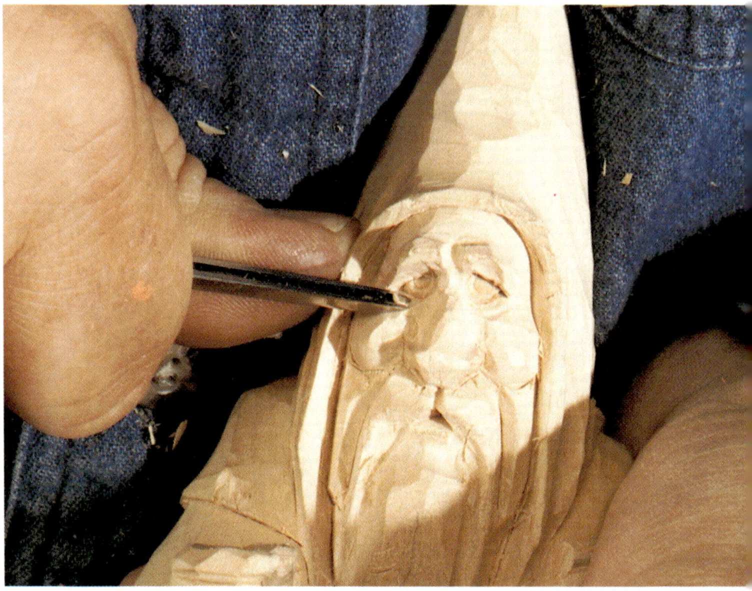

Use a veiner to create bags under the eyes.

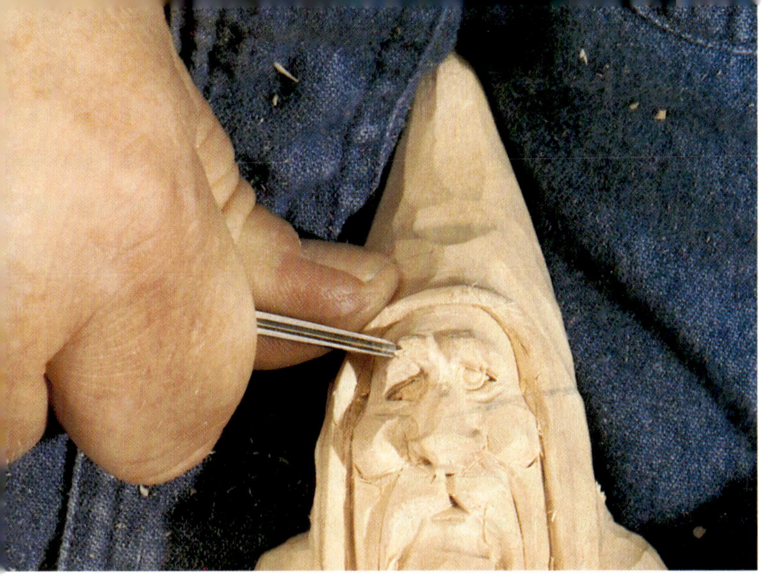

While you have the veiner, make some hair lines in the eyebrows.

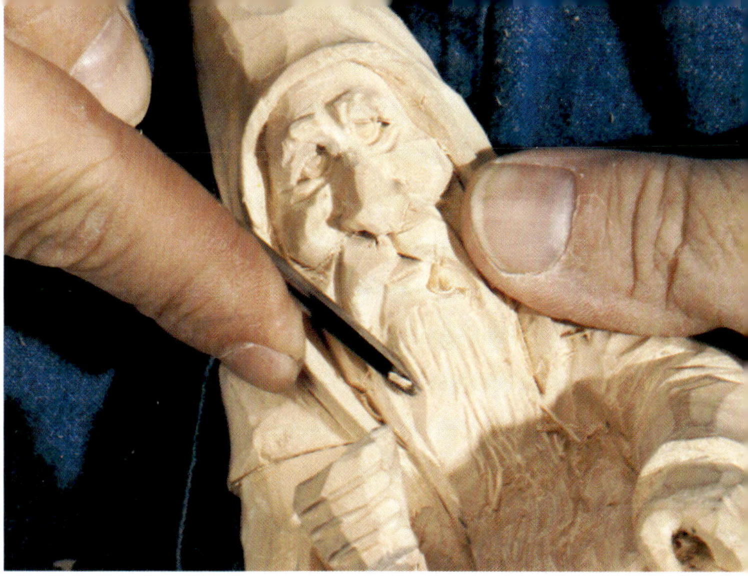

Continue up to the lower lip.

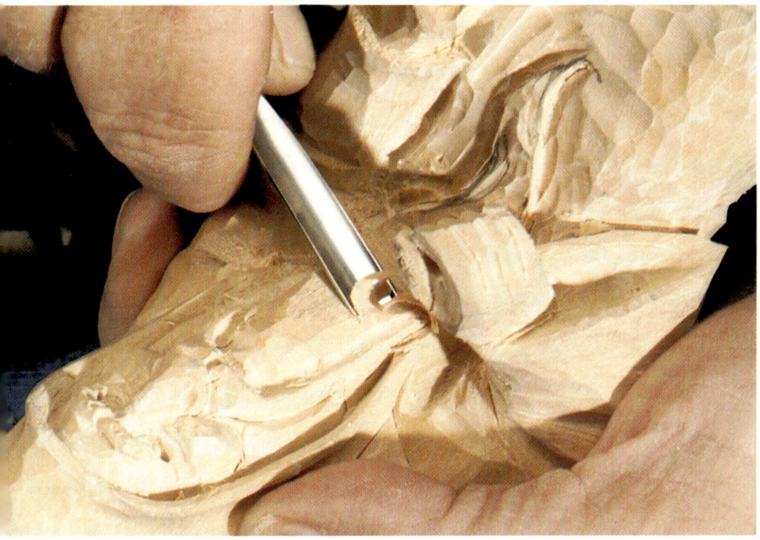

Straighten and shape the lines of the beard.

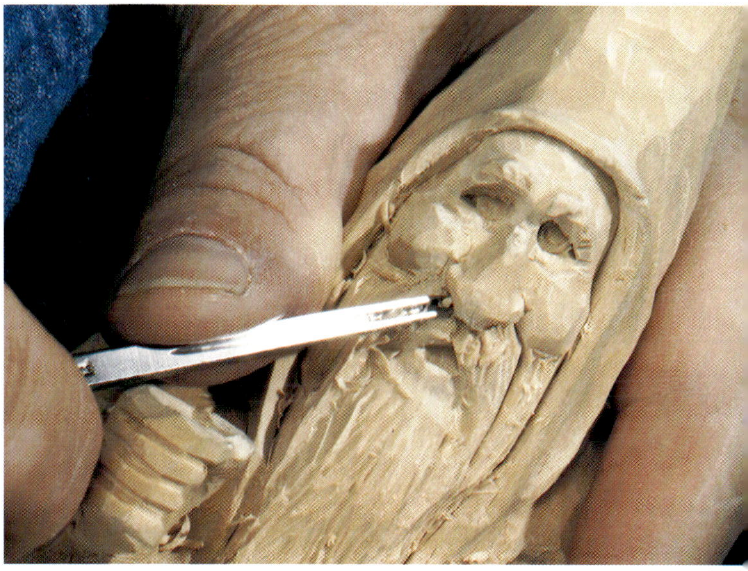

Finish the beard beside the face and the hair of the moustache.

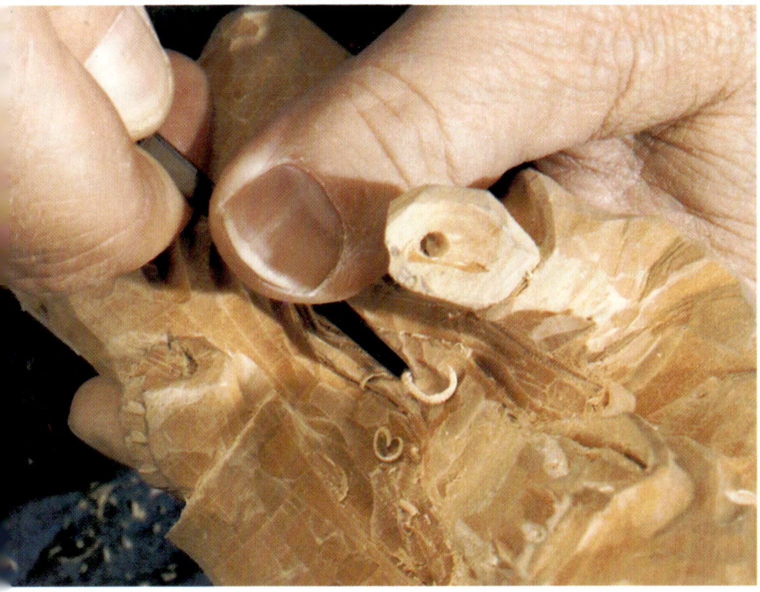

Add some hairlines to the beard.

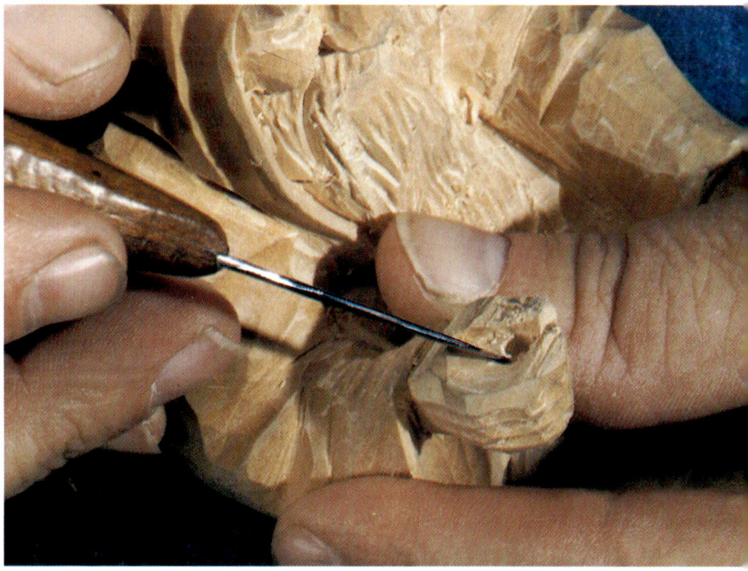

Ream the drilled hole a little bit so it looks more natural.

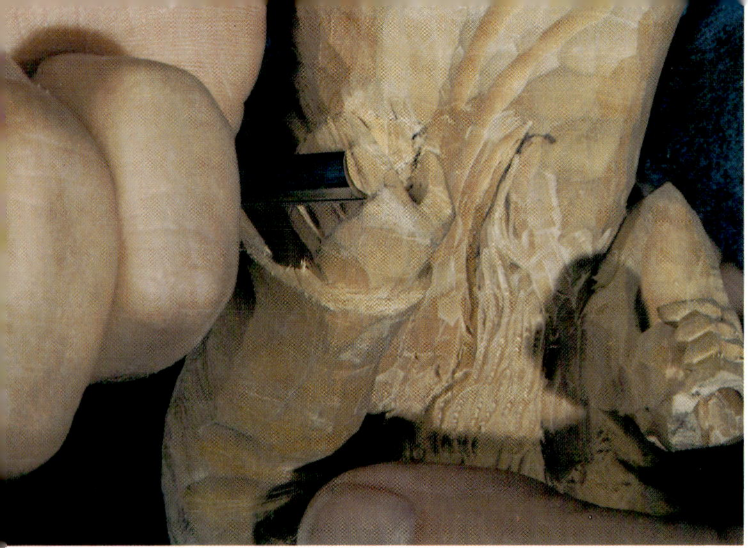

Bring contour to the planes of the hand using a gouge that fits the particular plane. Come across to the line between the fingers from one side...

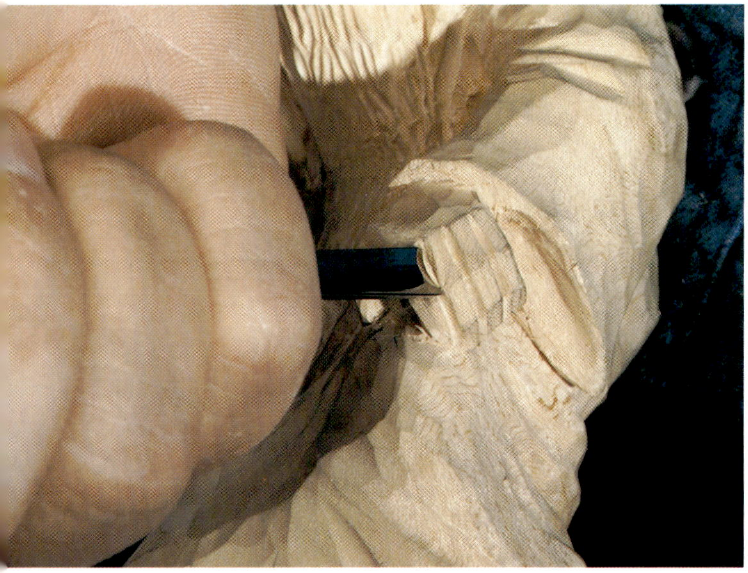

and the other.

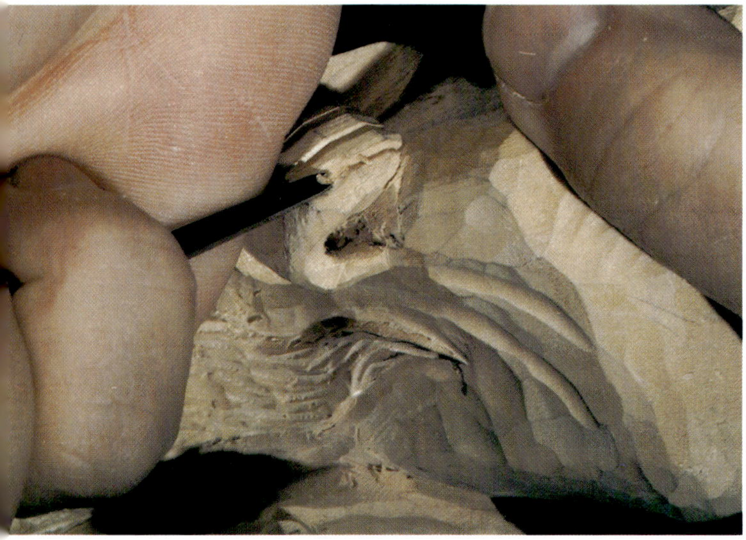

Clean up the cut with a little veiner. Continue between all the fingers.

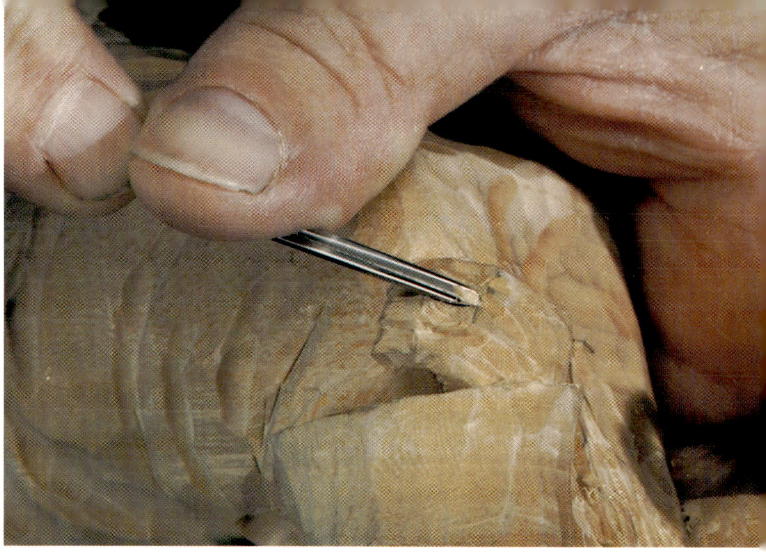

A v-tool will give me a definite line between the fingers. It makes the figure look a little arthritic, but that is in character with the Wizard.

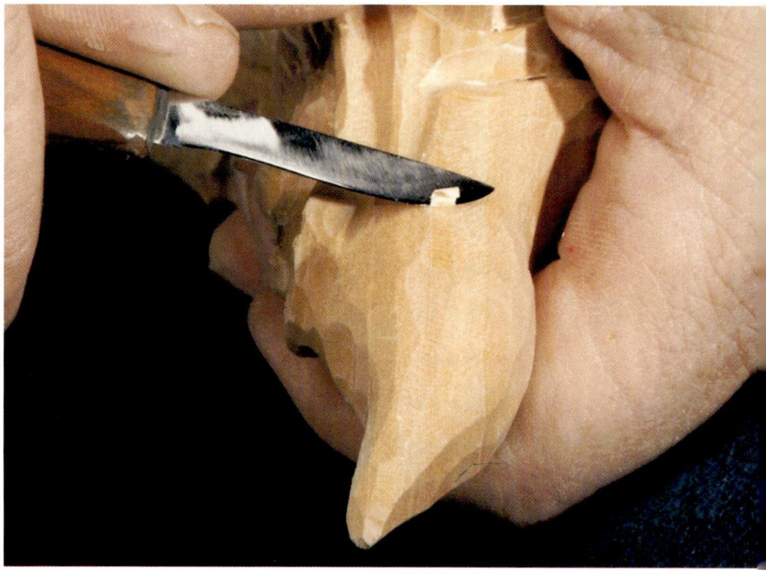

Go back and smooth the piece, breaking up any long lines, like this one.

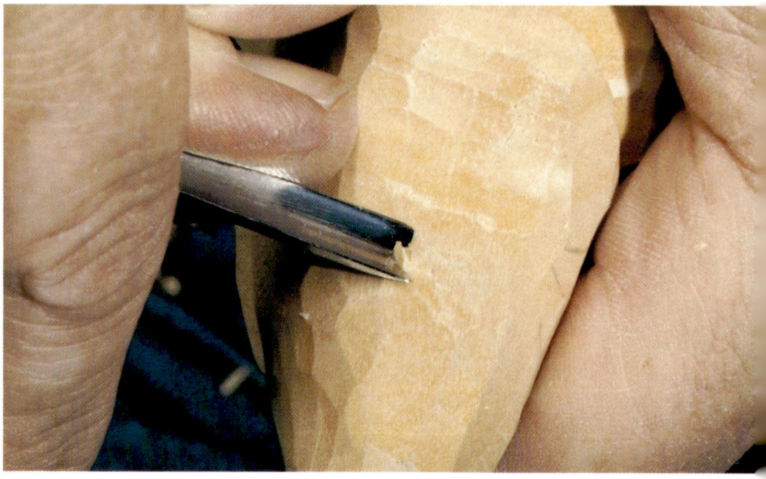

There are some spots, like here, where the grain runs both ways making it impossible to smooth with a knife. In these cases find a gouge that fits the contour and come across the grain with it.

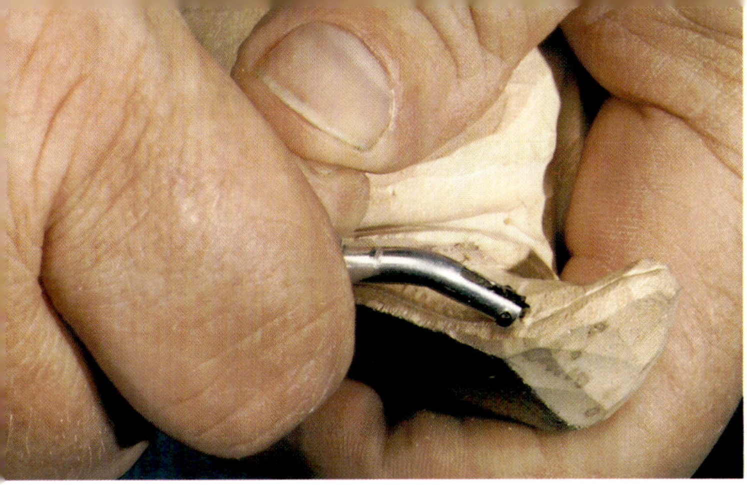

Add seams to the clothing with a tracing wheel. Start with one set of stitches above the sole lines of the shoes.

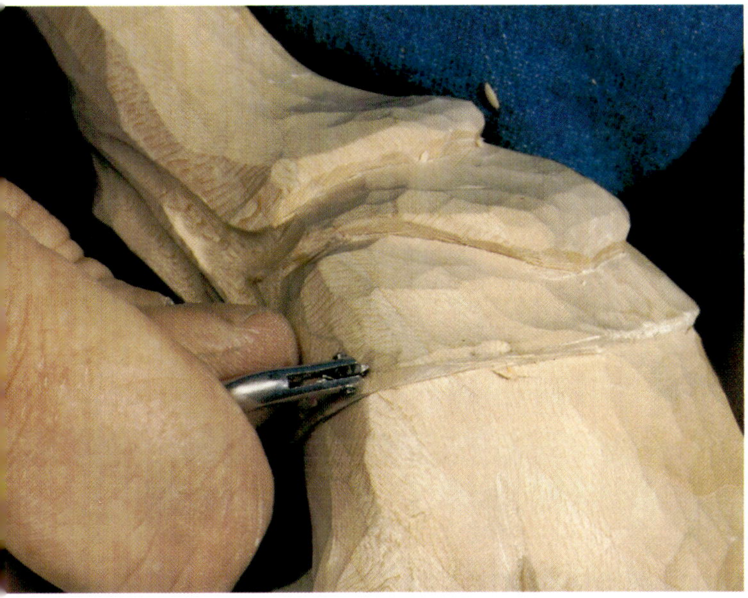

Continue around the hem of the hood and any other place that seems appropriate.

The throne is constructed of rocks piled around. Draw them in as a guide before carving.

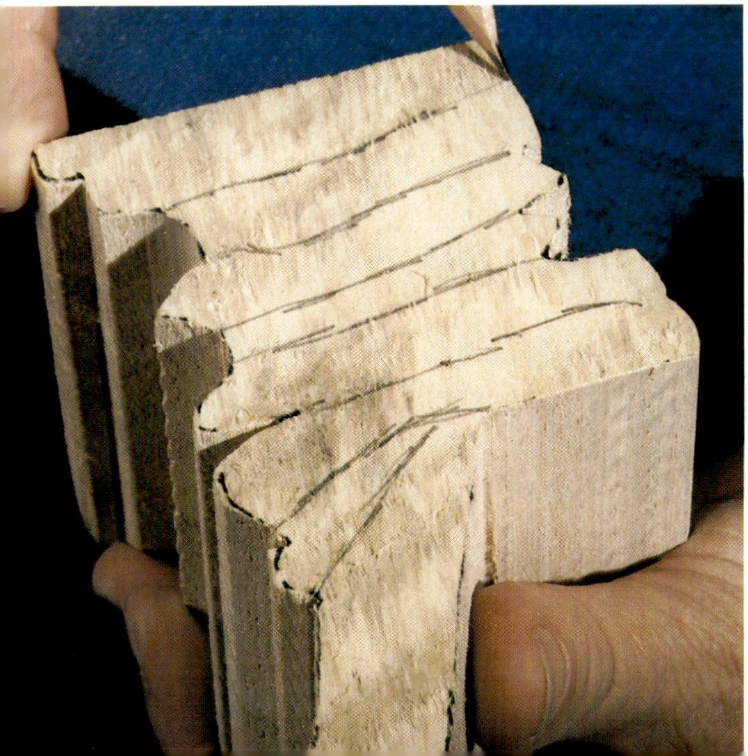

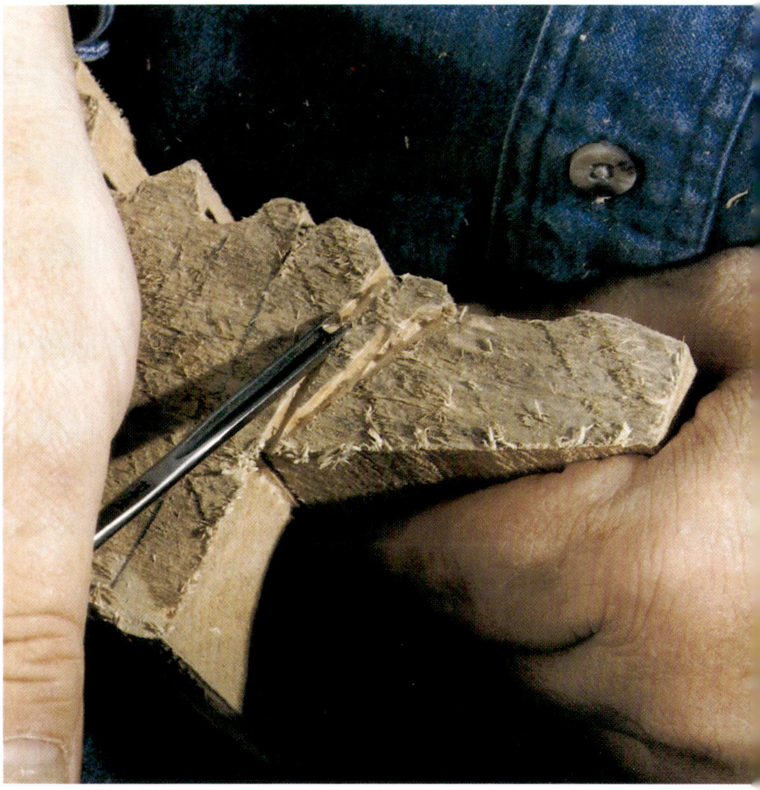

Cut the major lines with a gouge. This will give the power tool something to follow.

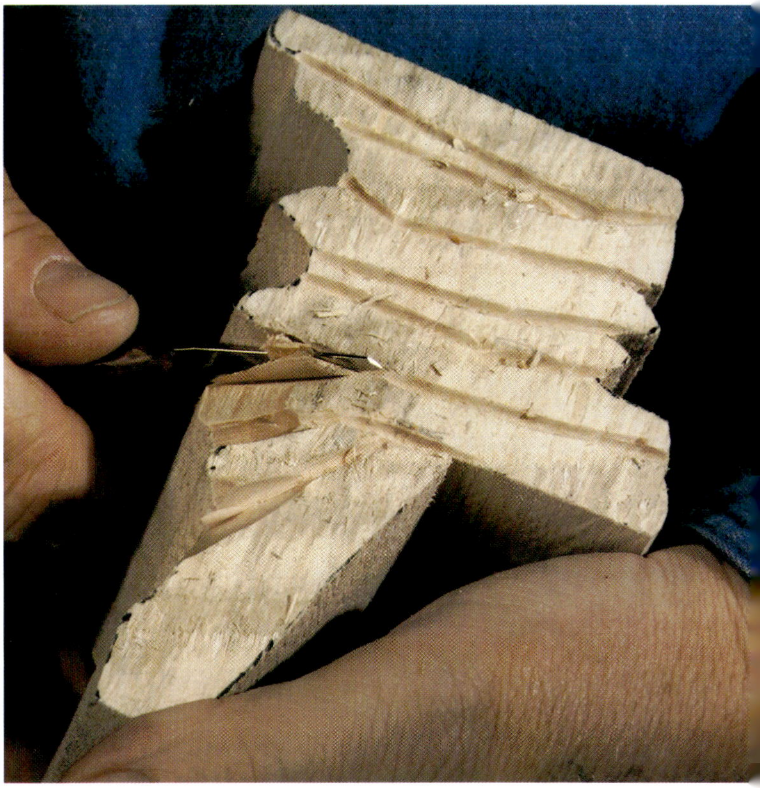

Cut in at the corners of the rocks with wedge cuts to get some dramatic movement. You don't want a regular pattern in this throne. It should appear natural.

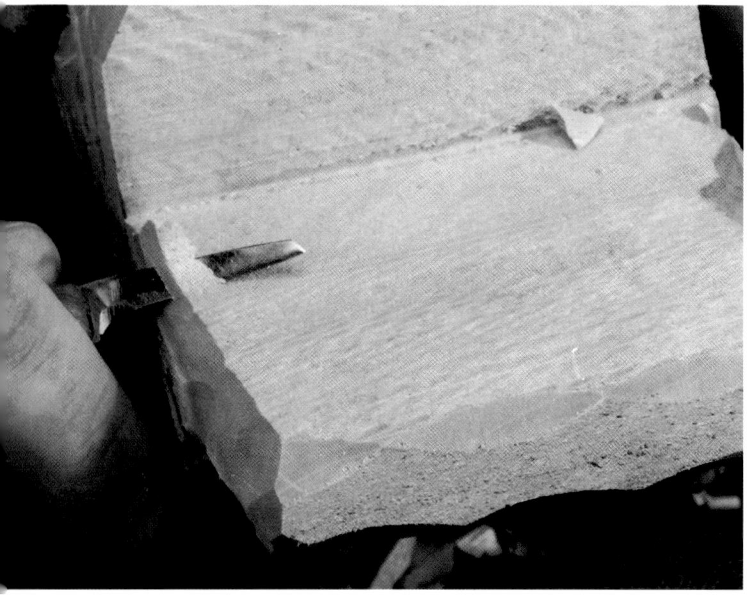

Knock the corners off the back of the chair.

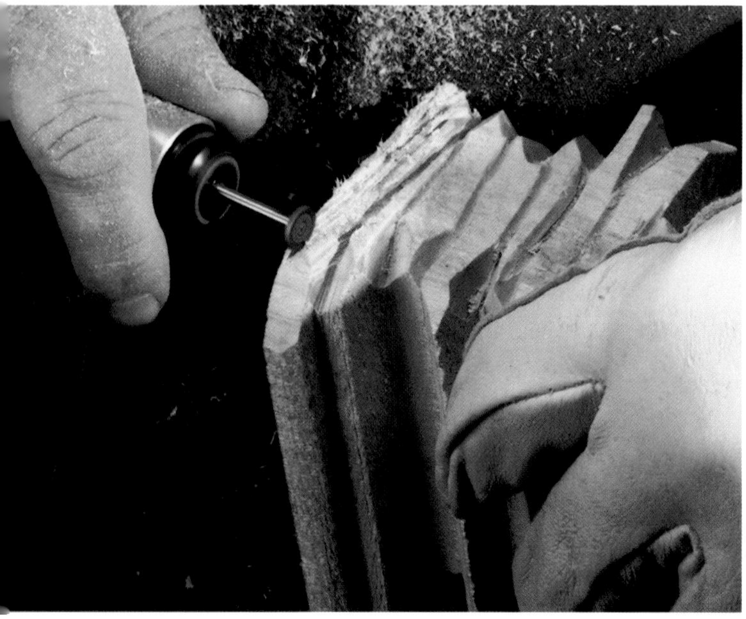

With a round saw blade on a flexible shaft rotary tool, create the shale-like layers of the rock. This job is best done with a glove on the holding hand, and while wearing something other than a sweater. I've had more than one sweater wound around the blade.

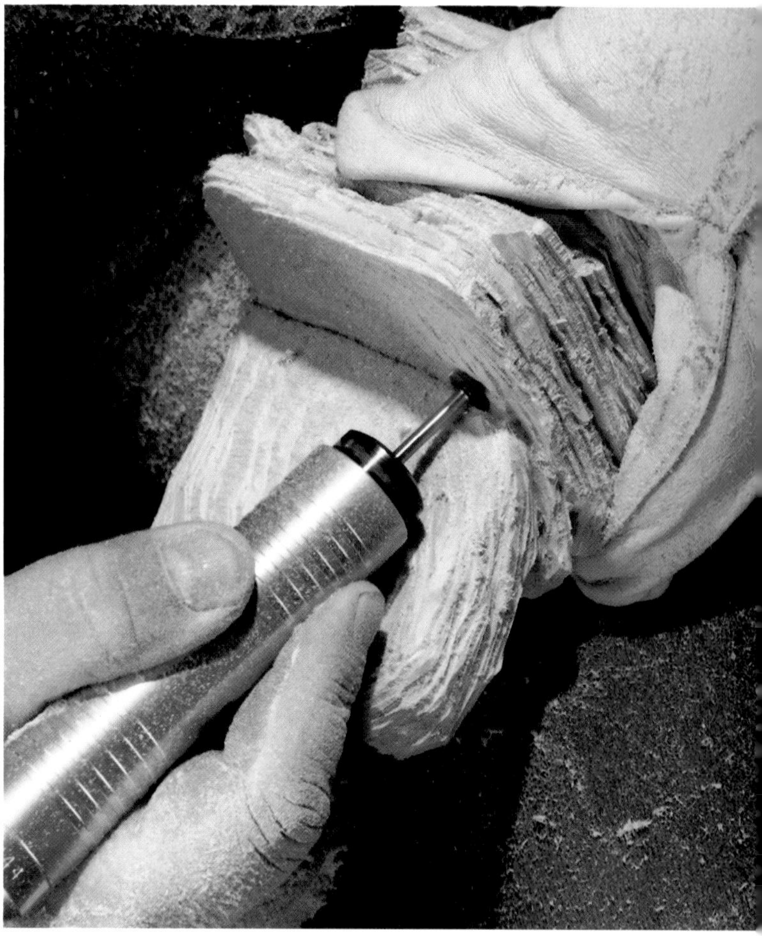

Create the separation between the bottom and the back of the chair.

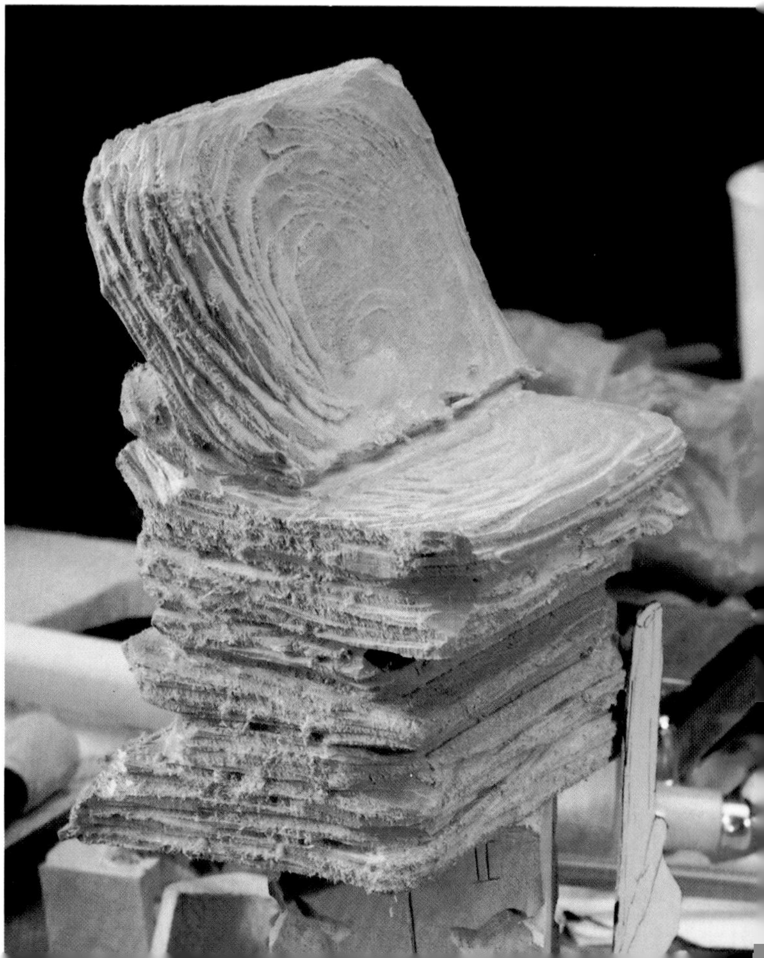

Progress.

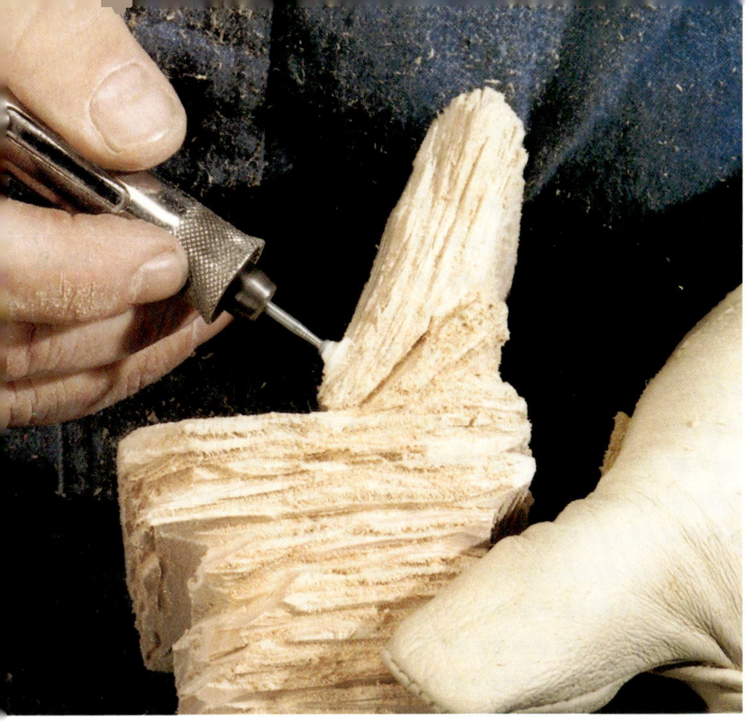

Go over the piece with a stone bit, smoothing out the roughness and fuzz of the saw. This will also add a few new "in between" lines.

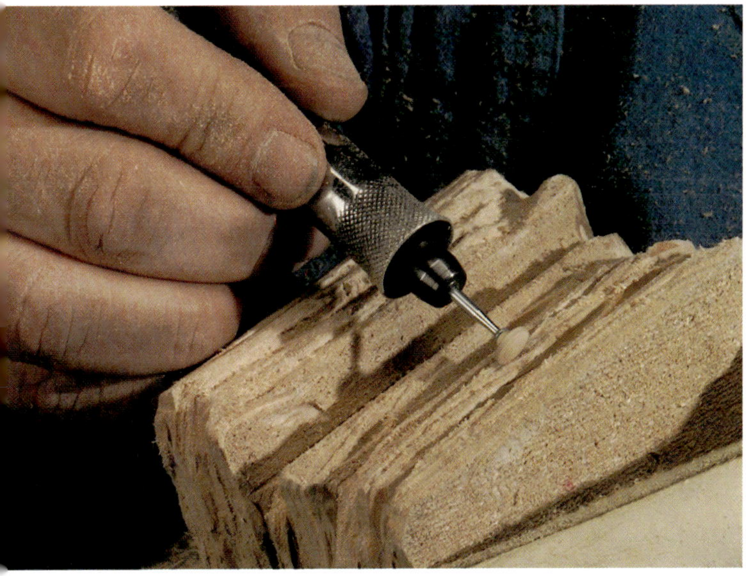

This is a reversible tool, and going over it again in reverse takes off most of the rest of the burrs.

On the flat surface of the rock the grain shows. It is nicely done with the stone bit.

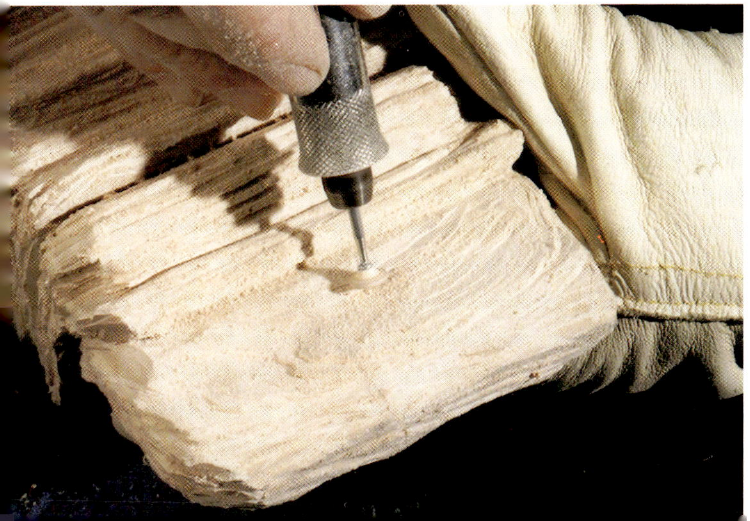

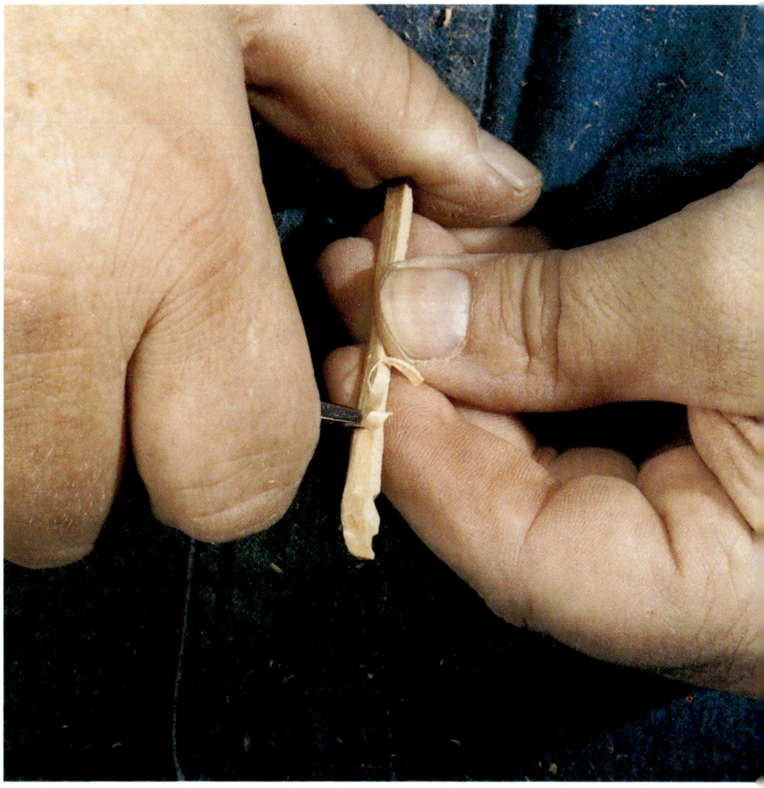

The wand can be carved from a piece of scrap. This is a place to let your imagine go. I saw a magical dragon toe at the end so I carved it, then rounded the shaft to fit in the hole of the hand.

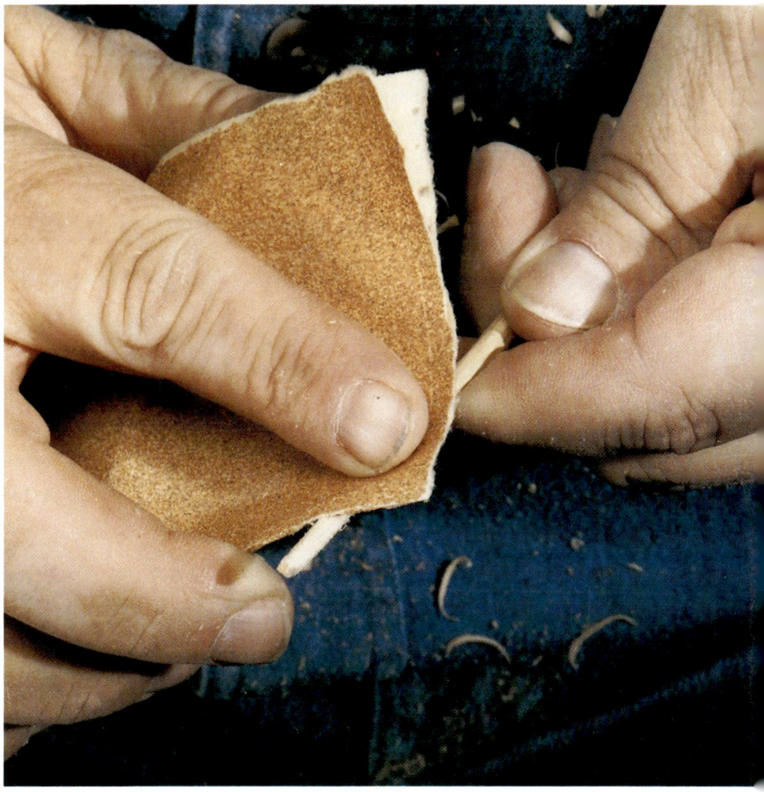

Sand it smooth.

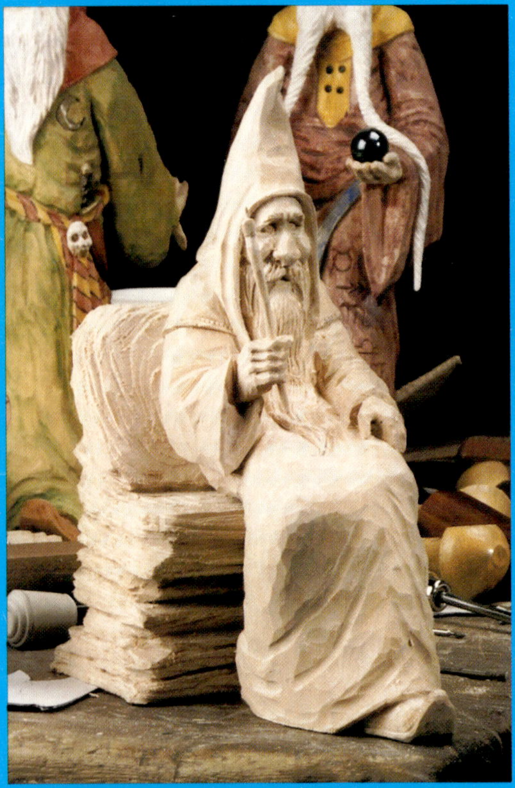

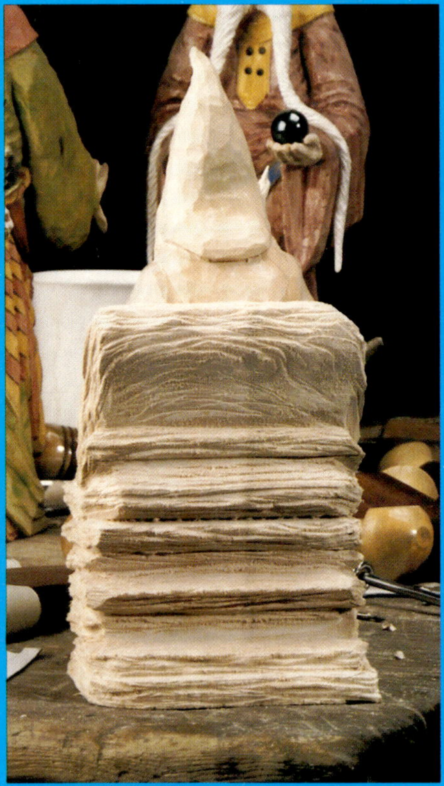

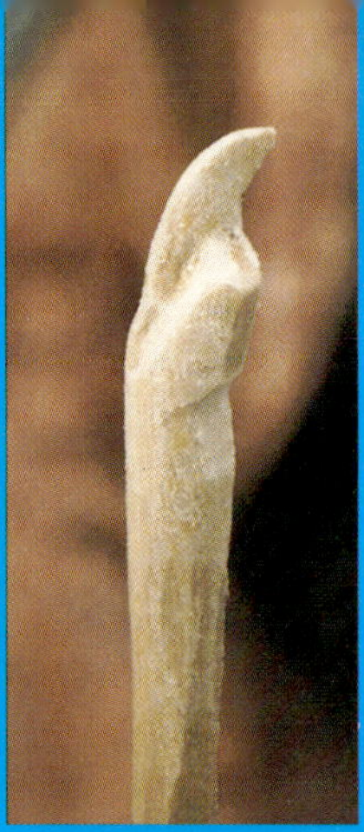

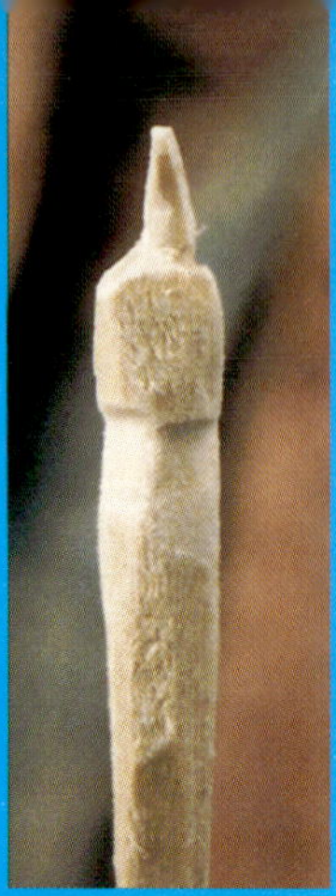

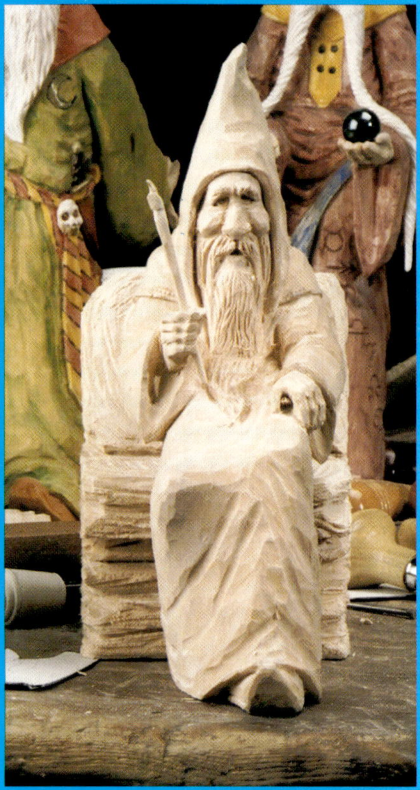

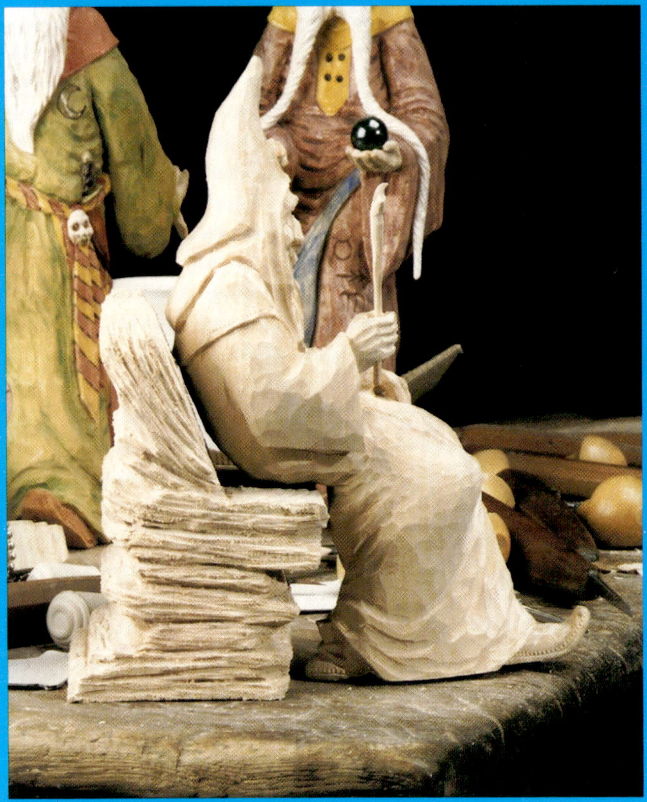

Ready to paint.

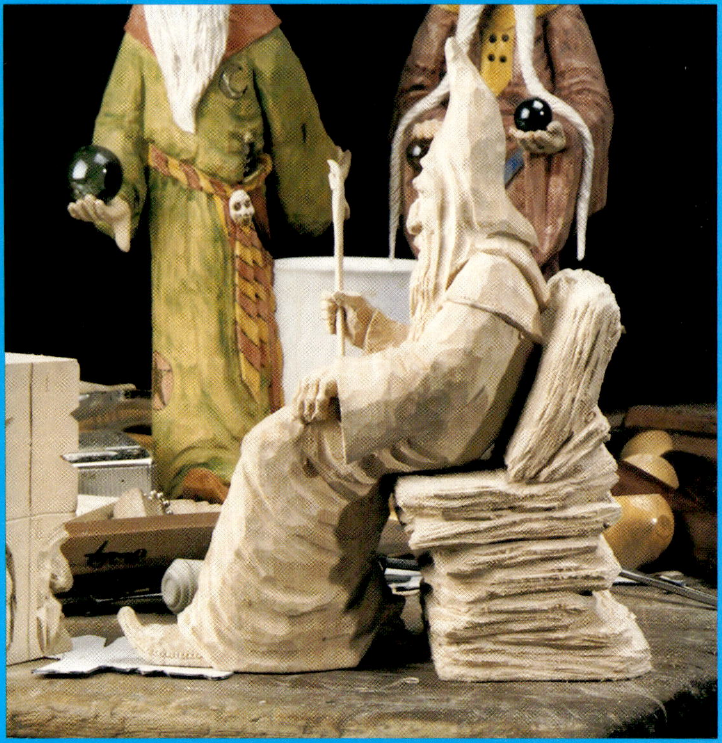

Painting the Wizard

For wood carving I use Winsor and Newton Alkyd tube paints. Most coats are thinned with pure turpentine to a consistency that is soaked into the carving, giving subtle colors. What I look for is a watery mixture, almost like a wash. In this way the turpentine will carry the pigment into the wood, giving the stained look I like. It has always been my theory that if you are going to cover the wood, why use wood in the first place. It should be noted that with white, the concentration of the pigment should be a little stronger.

I mix my paints in juice bottles, putting in a bit of paint and adding turpentine. I don't use exact measurements. Instead I use trial and error, adding a bit of paint or a bit of turpentine until I get the thickness I want.

The juice bottles are handy for holding your paints. They are reclosable, easy to shake, and have the added advantage of leaving a concentrated amount of color on the inside of the lid and the sides of the bottle which can be used when more intense color is needed.

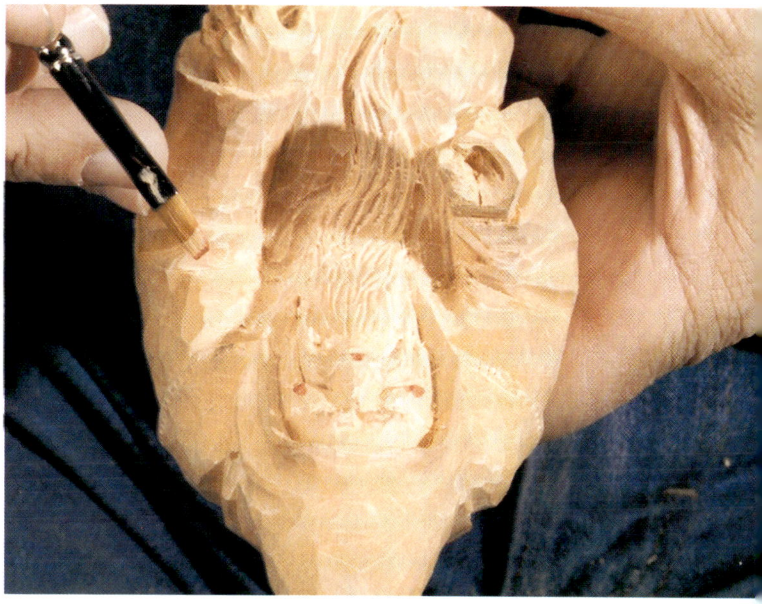

Add dots of red to the cheeks, nose, lips, and the back of the hands.

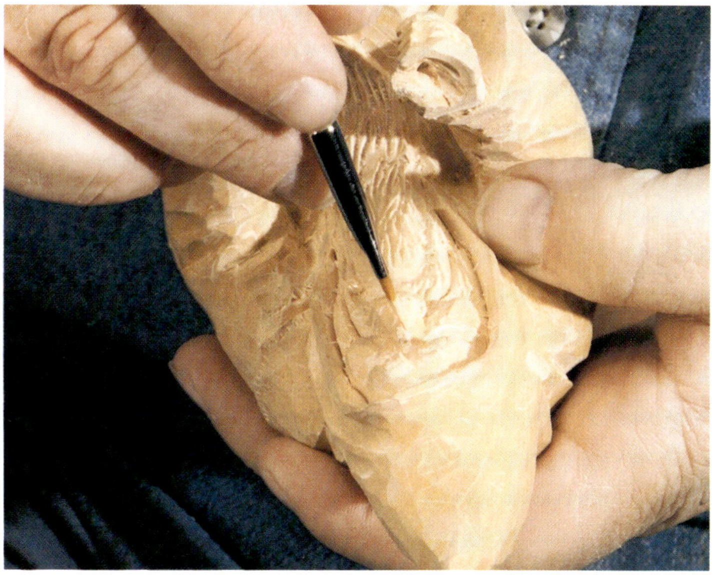

The flesh tone is a mixture of raw sienna and white with a touch of red. Apply to the face and hands.

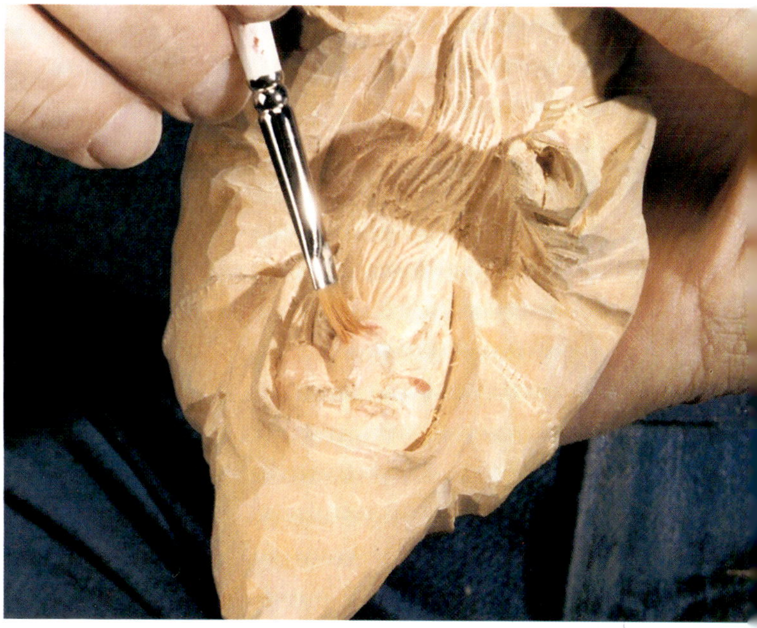

Blend it into the flesh.

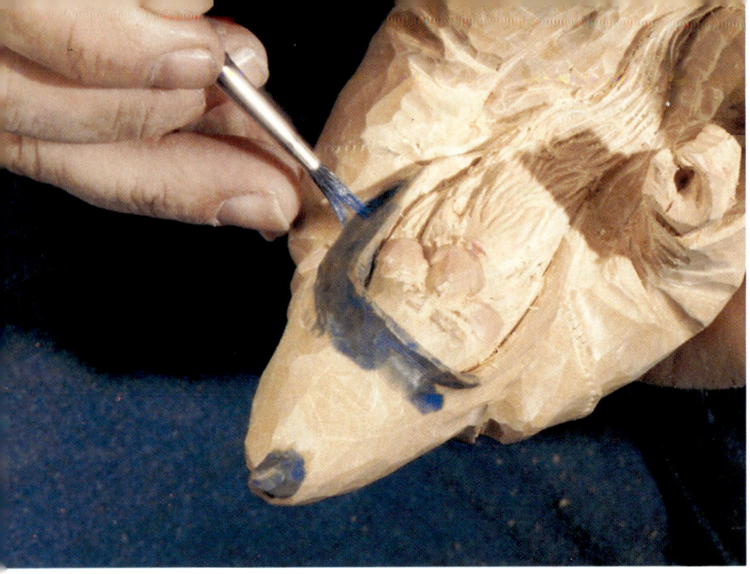

The color of the outfit of the Wizard is totally up to your imagination. A fantasy figure can stand most any color. I'm going to start with a sky blue for the hat, though I may come over it with a darker color later.

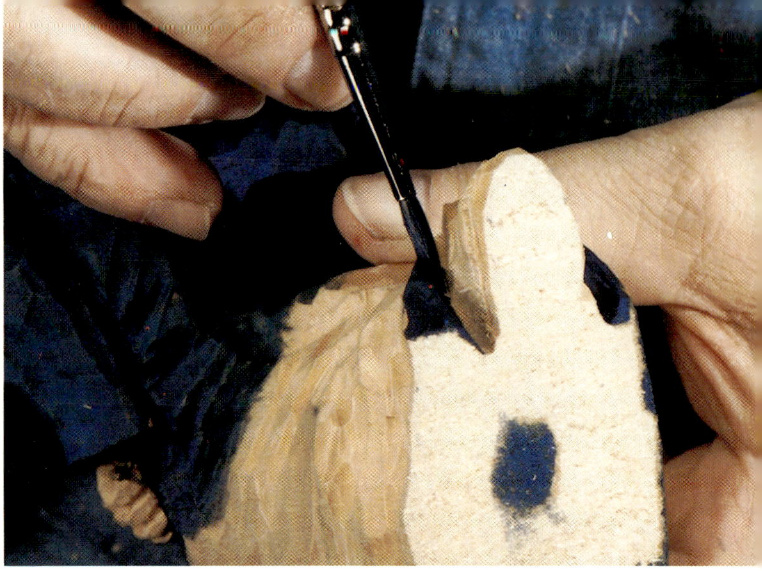

A smaller brush works around the feet...

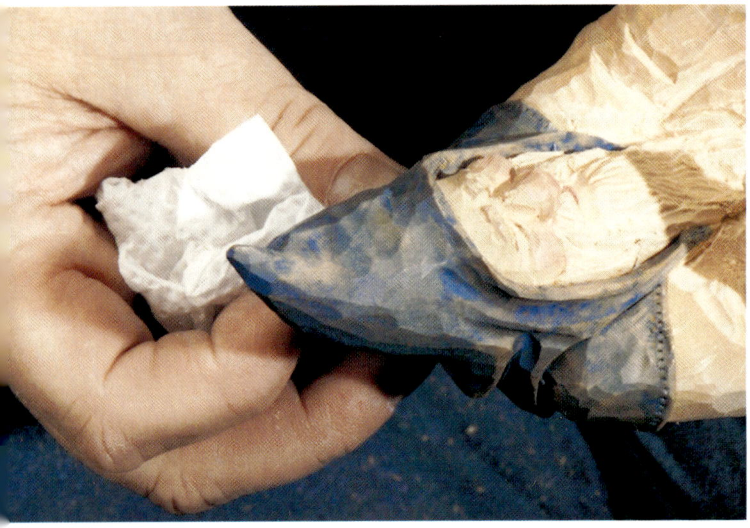

Rubbing it down with paper towel helps take away the excess and keep the color light.

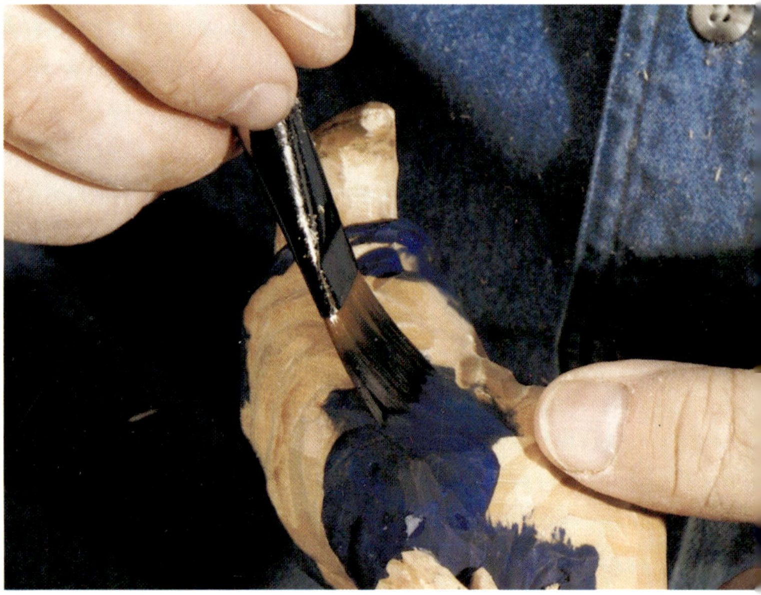

and a larger brush fills in the wide open spaces.

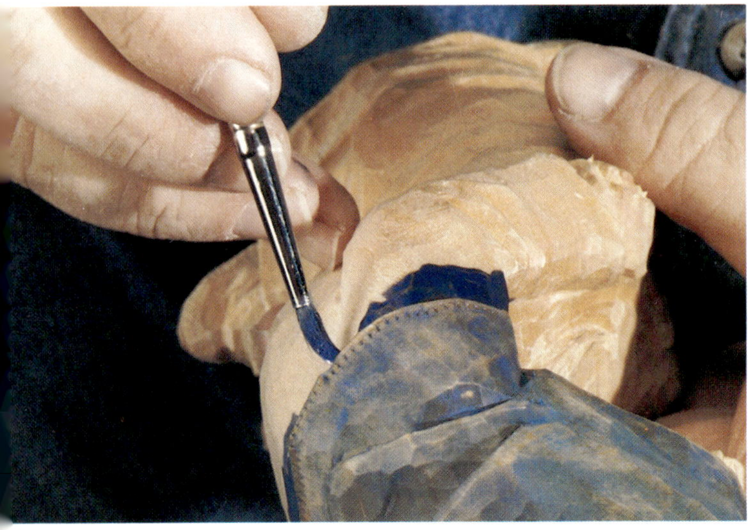

Apply the robe color, beginning at the borders with other colors. I am using an ultramarine blue.

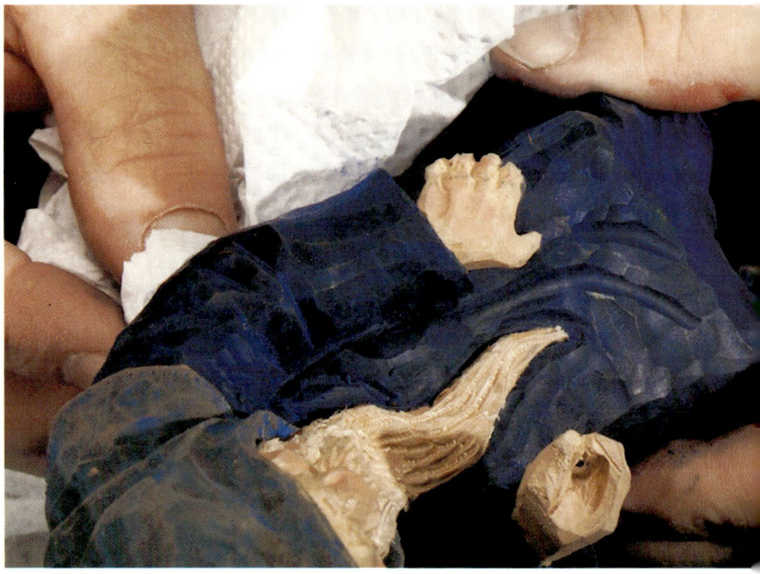

Wipe the surface down with paper towel.

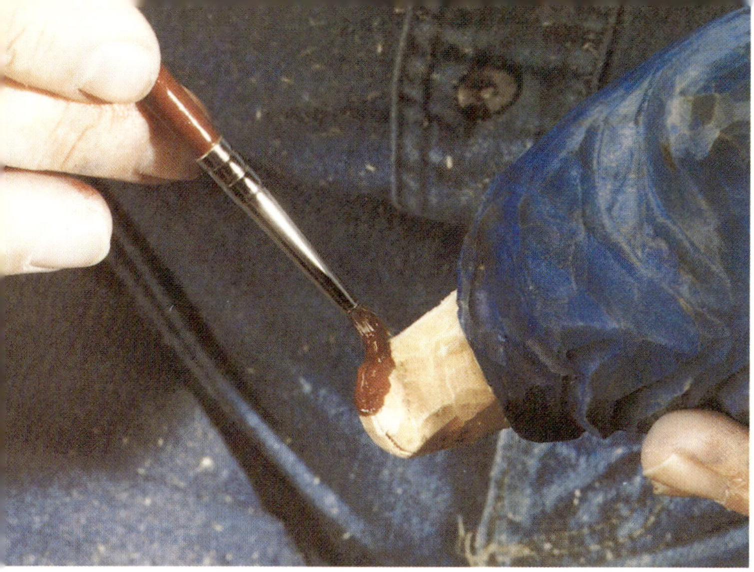

Apply burnt sienna to the shoes.

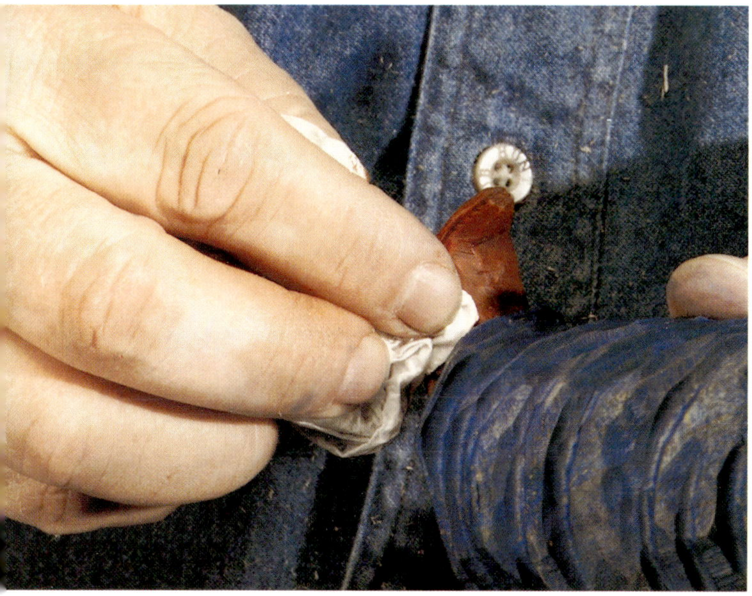

Wipe it down.

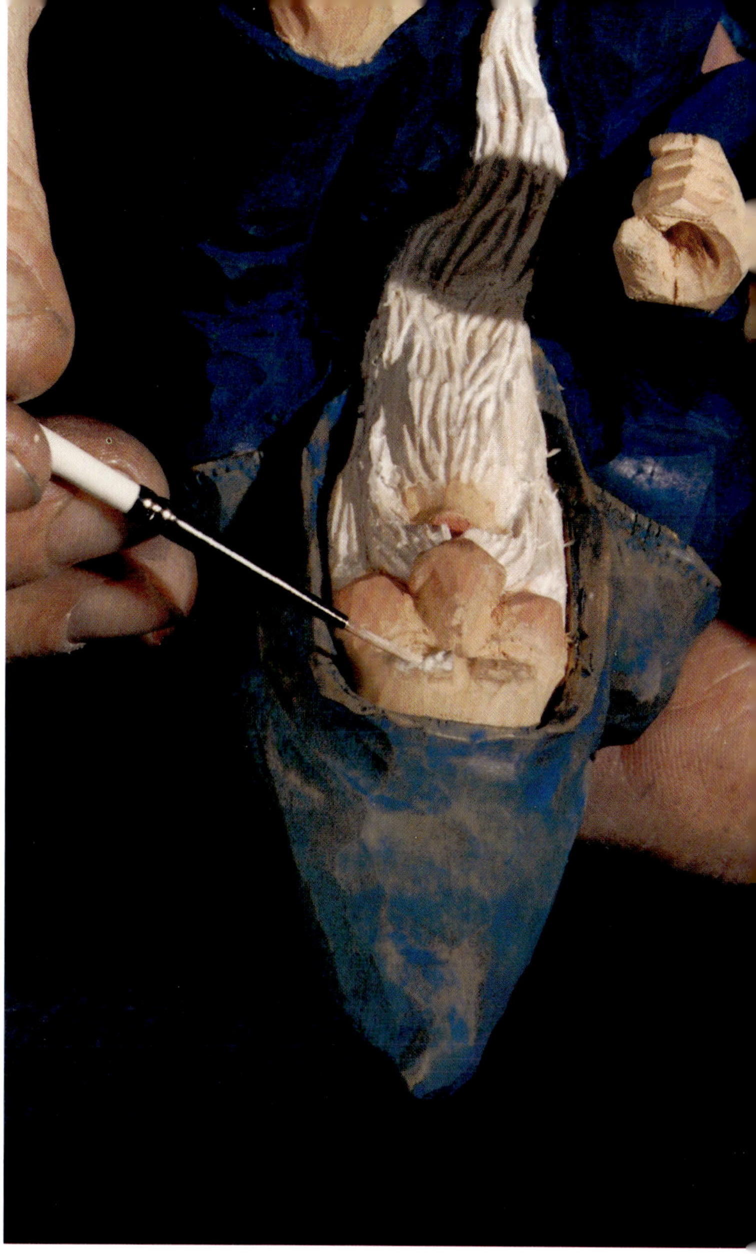

and the eyebrows white.

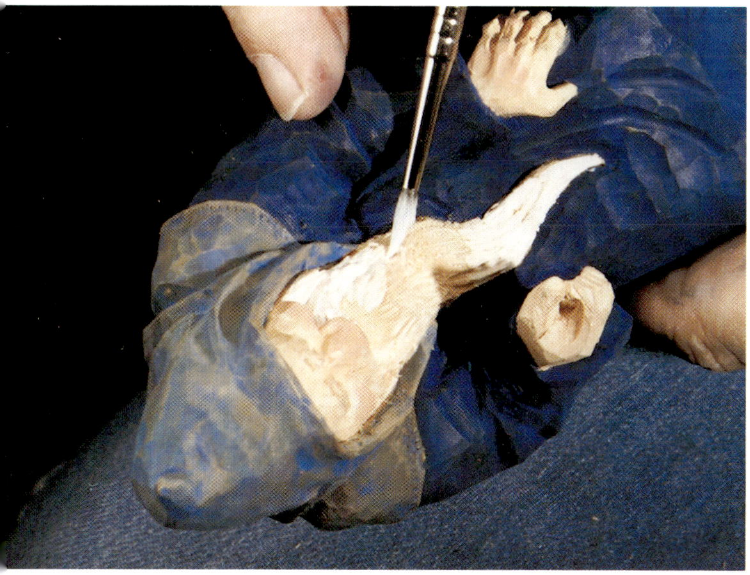

Paint the beard...

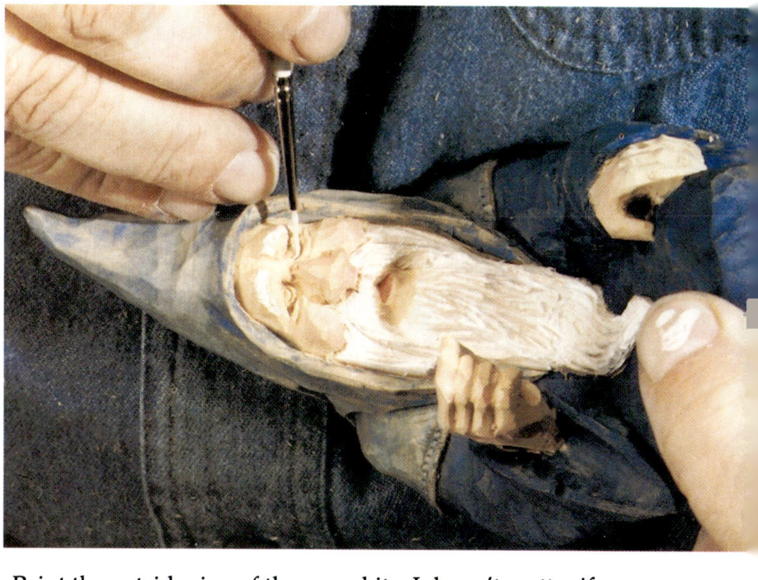

Paint the outside ring of the eye white. I doesn't matter if you get a little white on the iris.

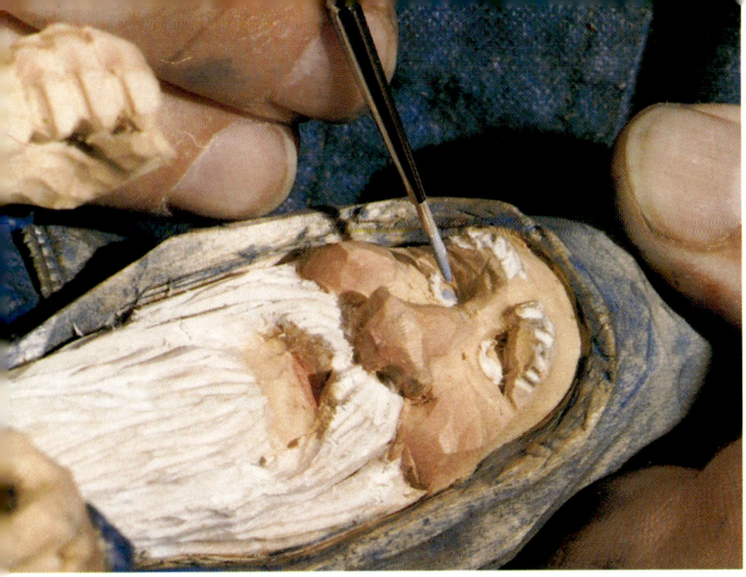

Add some light blue to the iris.

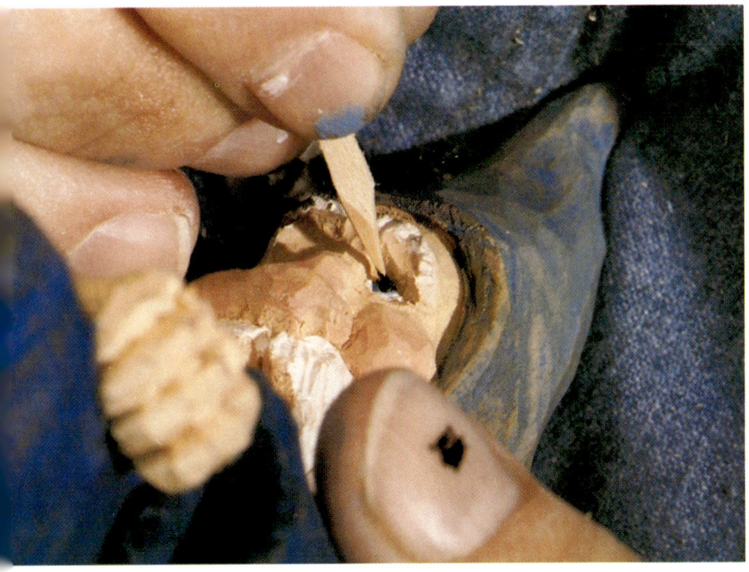

A sharpened stick applies the black to the pupil.

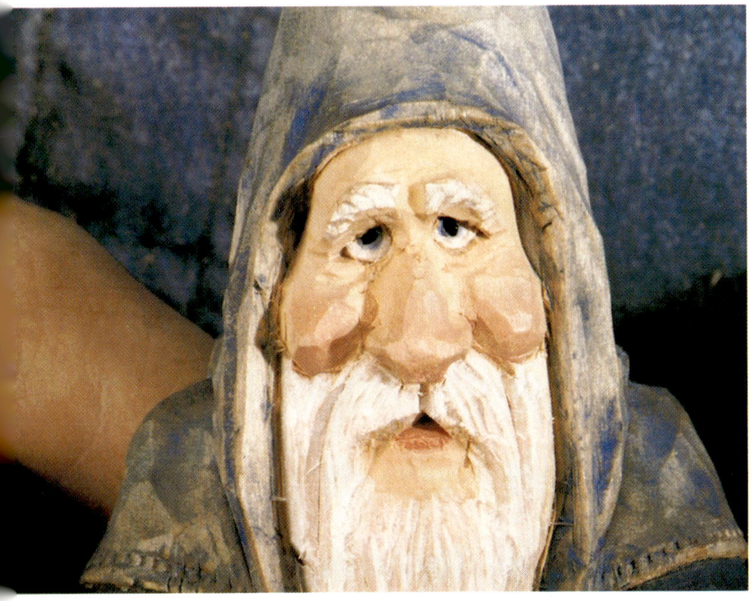

The eyes complete.

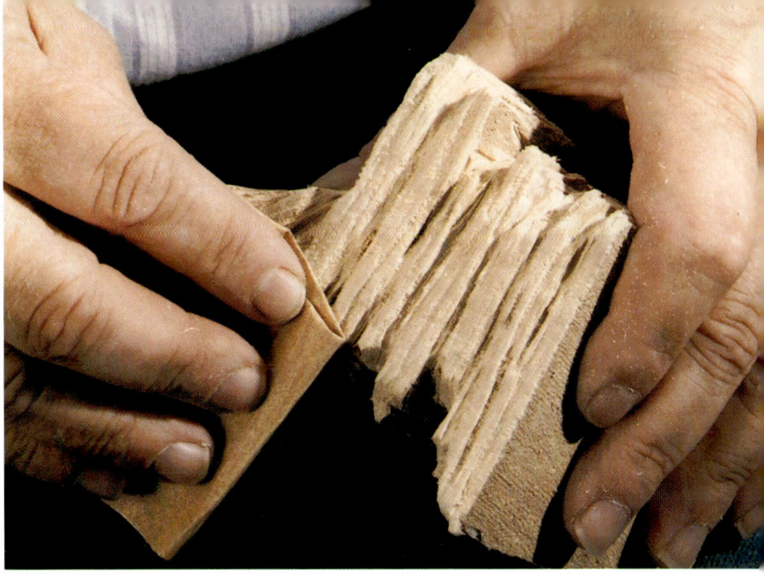

Before painting the throne, I want to knock off some of the fuzzies with sand paper.

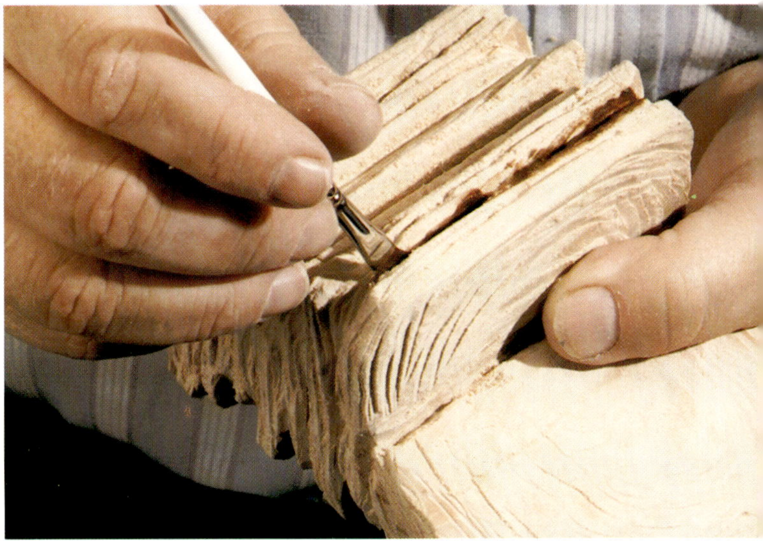

The colors for the rock are all earth tones. I begin with a dark brown applied to the deeper crevices. I'll probably come over this with black, but if I did black first it would be too dark.

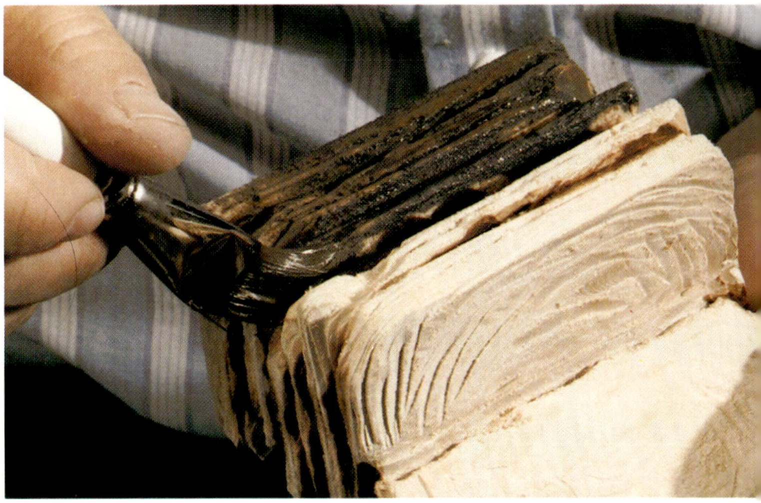

Wash over the throne with a gray. This particular color is from the jar where I store the rinse turpentine from cleaning my brushes. Waste not, want not!

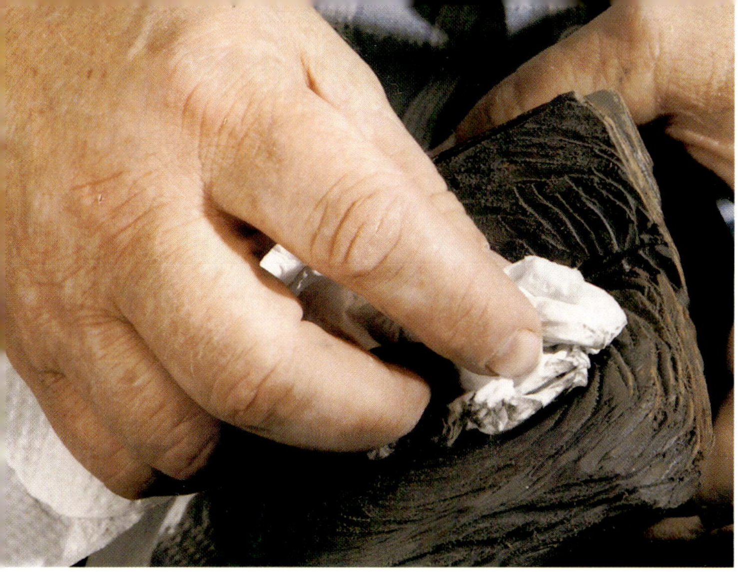

Wipe the excess with paper towel.

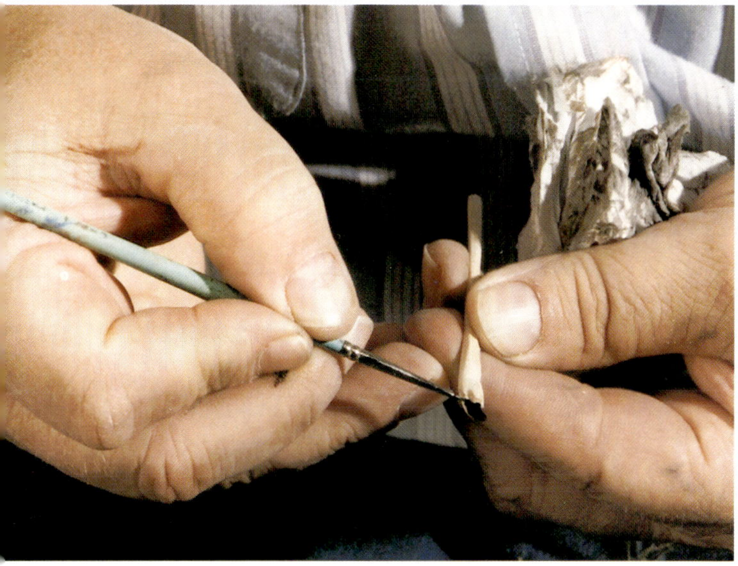

Apply black to the toenail of dragon's claw of the wand.

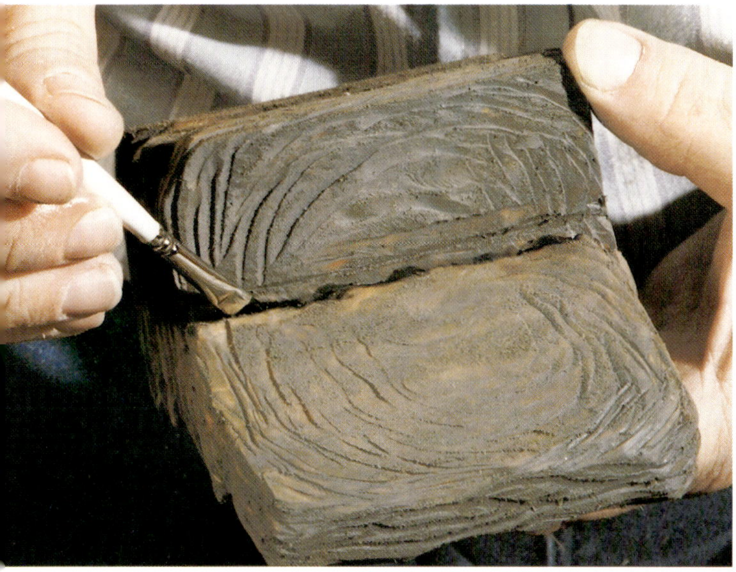

Apply black to the deepest shadows of the throne, and blend it into the gray.

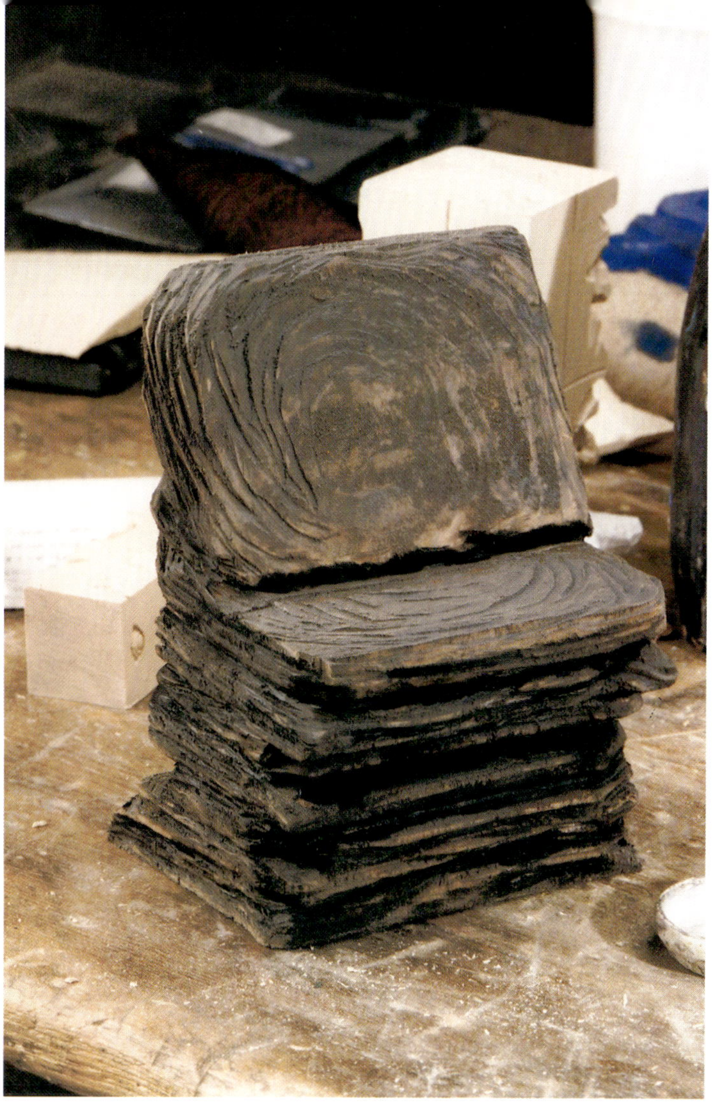

Ready for dry brushing.

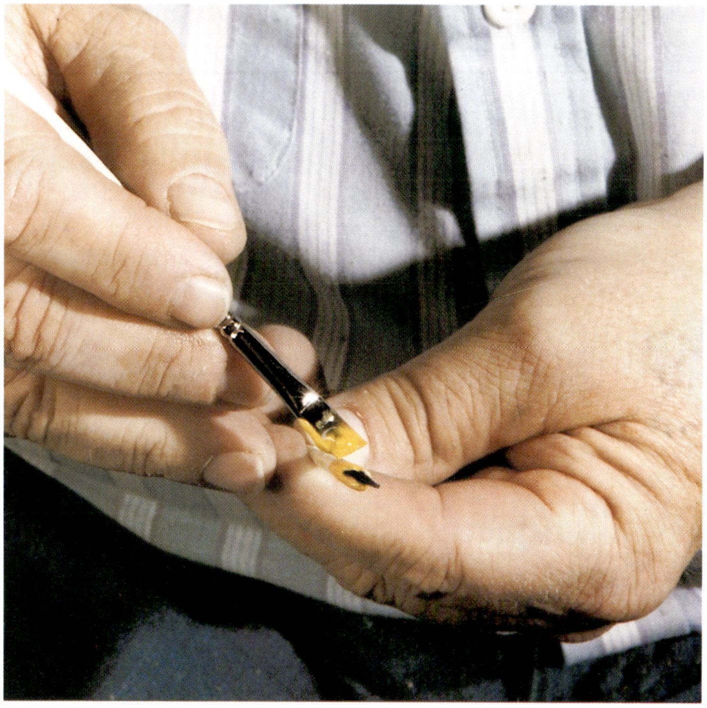

To the wand I think I'll add a little yellow around the claw...

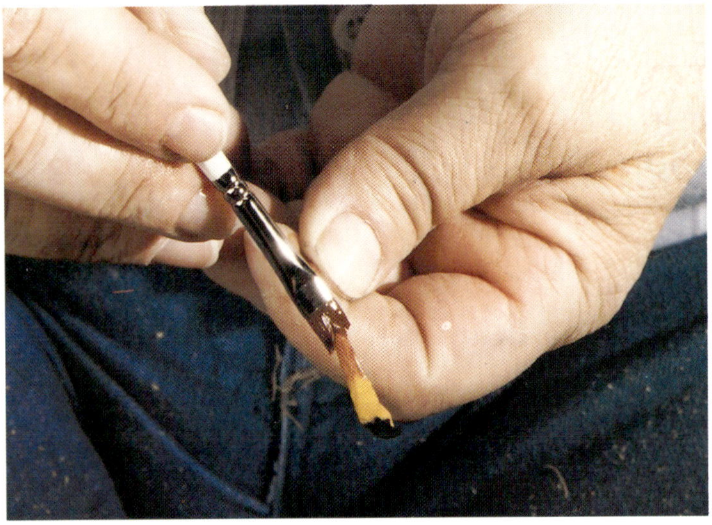

and burnt sienna to the shaft.

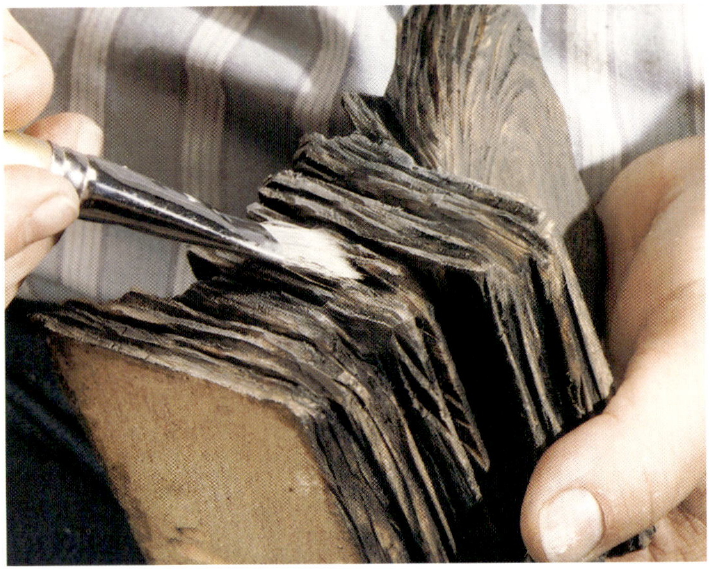

Spray the throne with a sealer like Deft™ semi-gloss clear finish. Dry brush the throne with white. The paint hits the raised surfaces, giving the throne lively highlights.

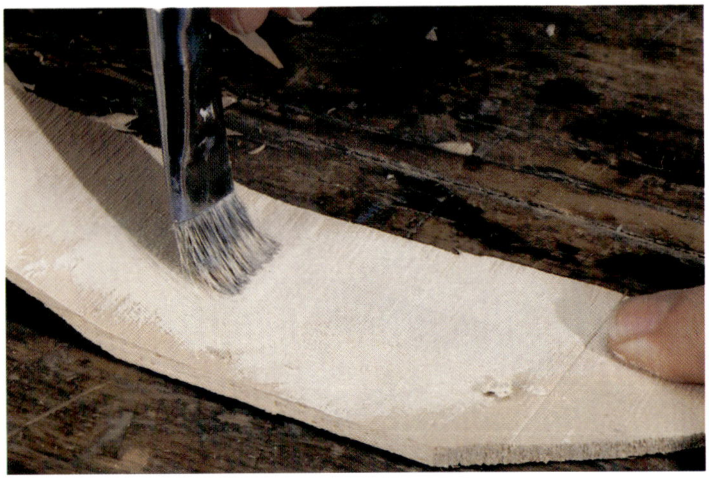

To dry brush I apply the paint to a piece of scrap wood. The wood absorbs the turpentine from the paint leaving the pigment dry on the surface and ready to be picked up by the brush.

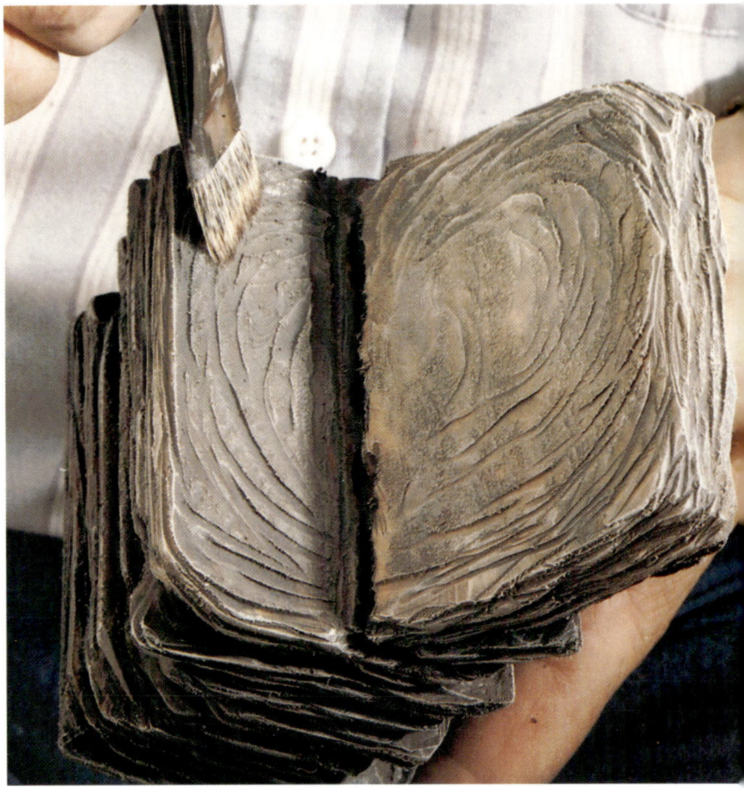

The first pass with the dry brush will not leave much pigment, but going over it again and again will cause a gradual build-up of pigment.

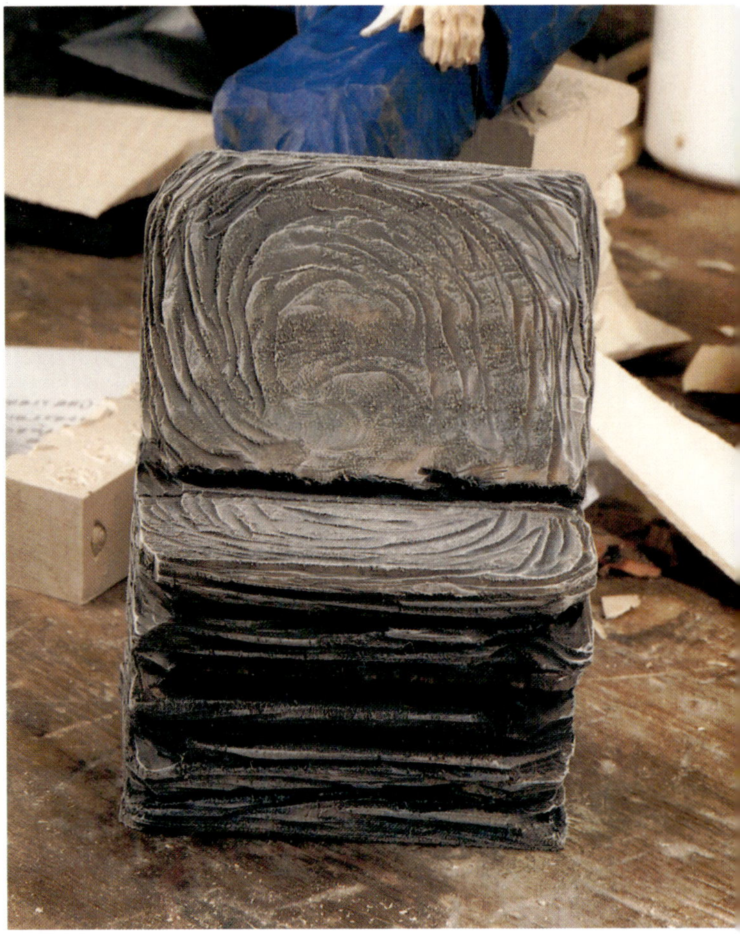

The result is a very rock-like throne.

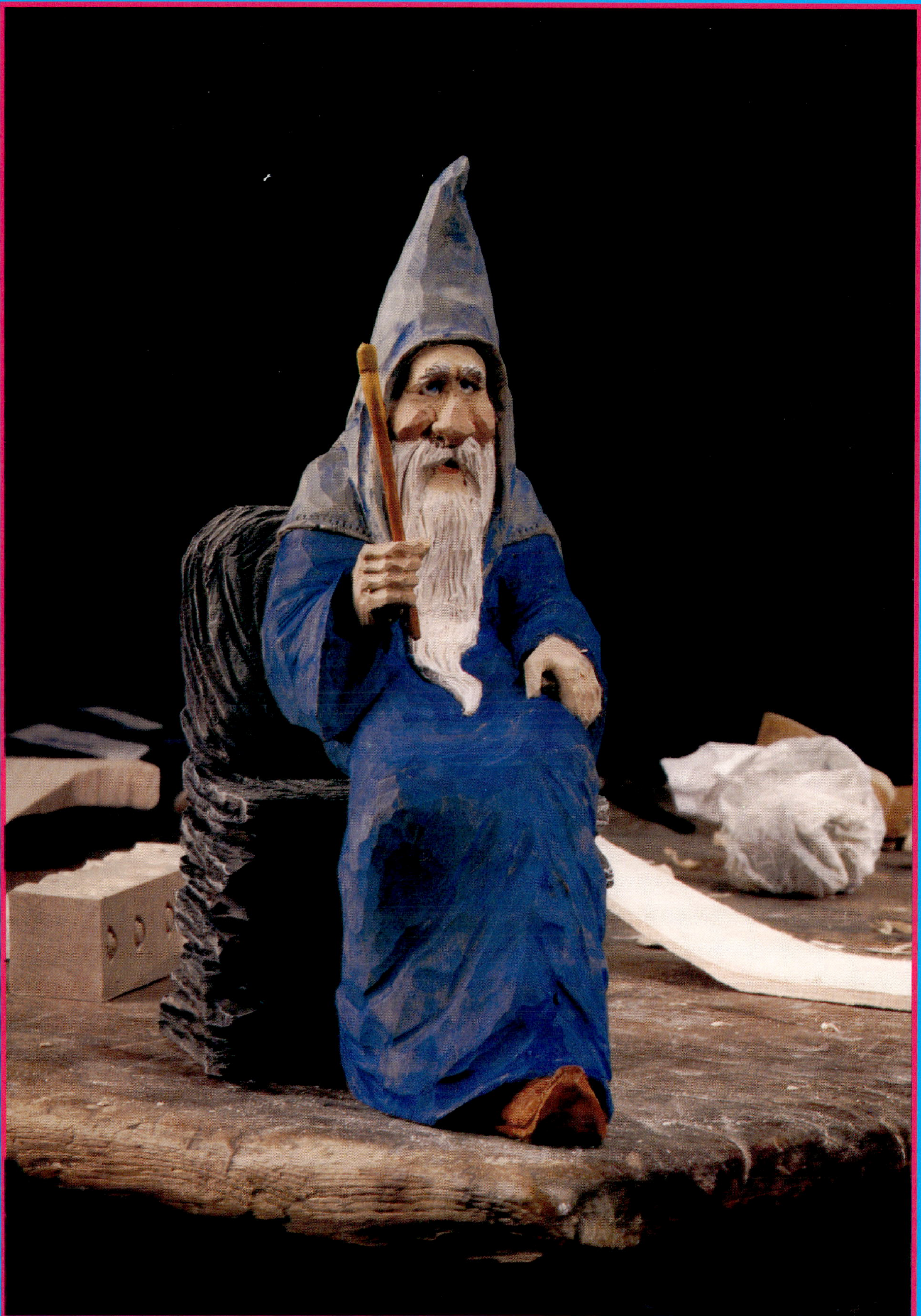

Finished.

Gallery

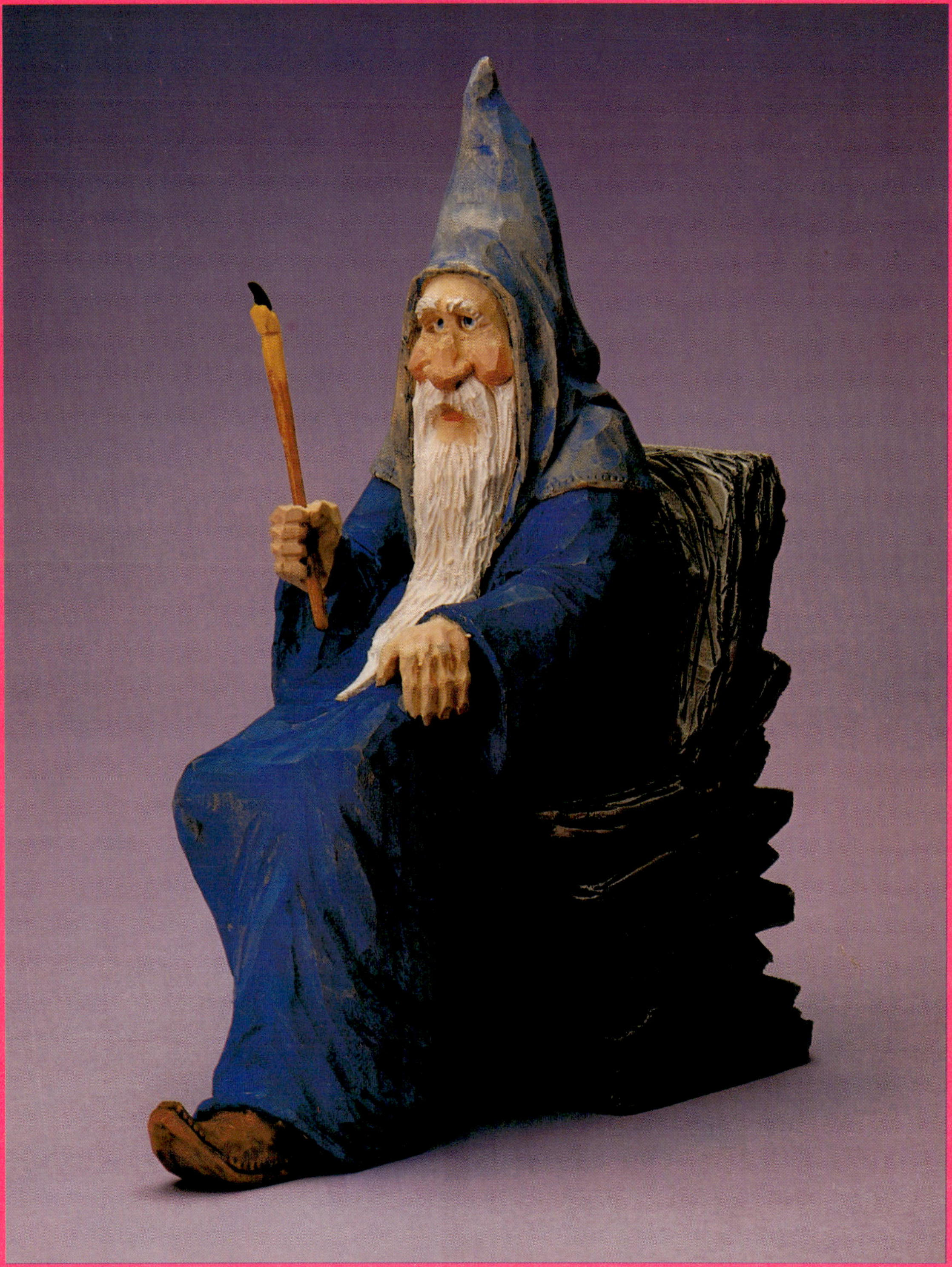

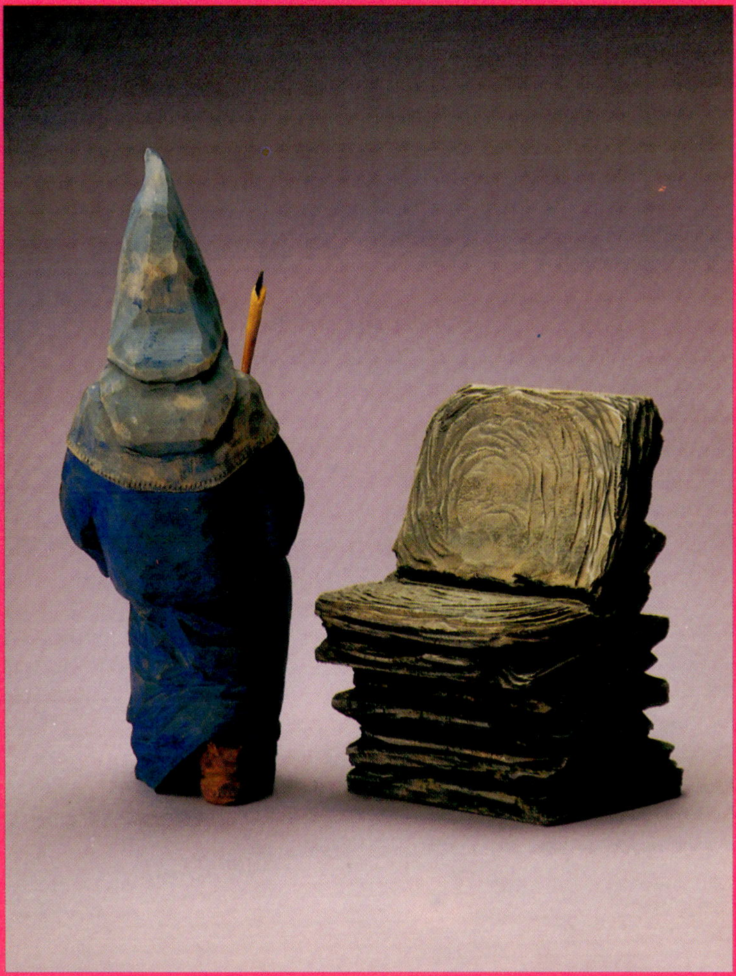

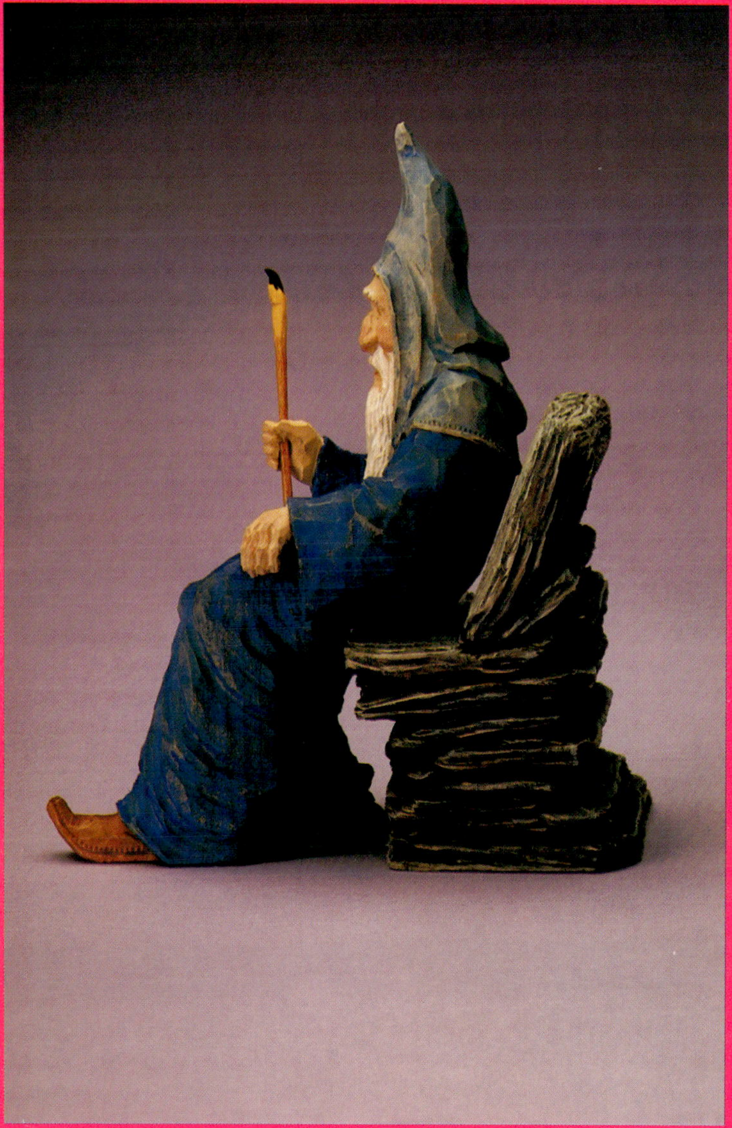

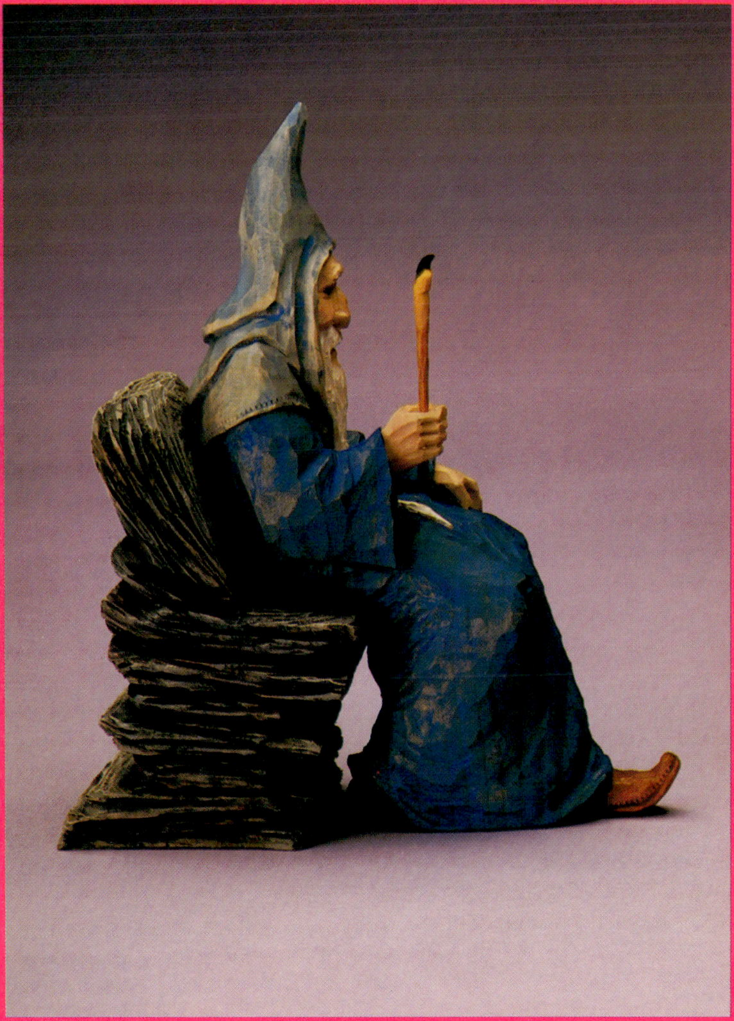

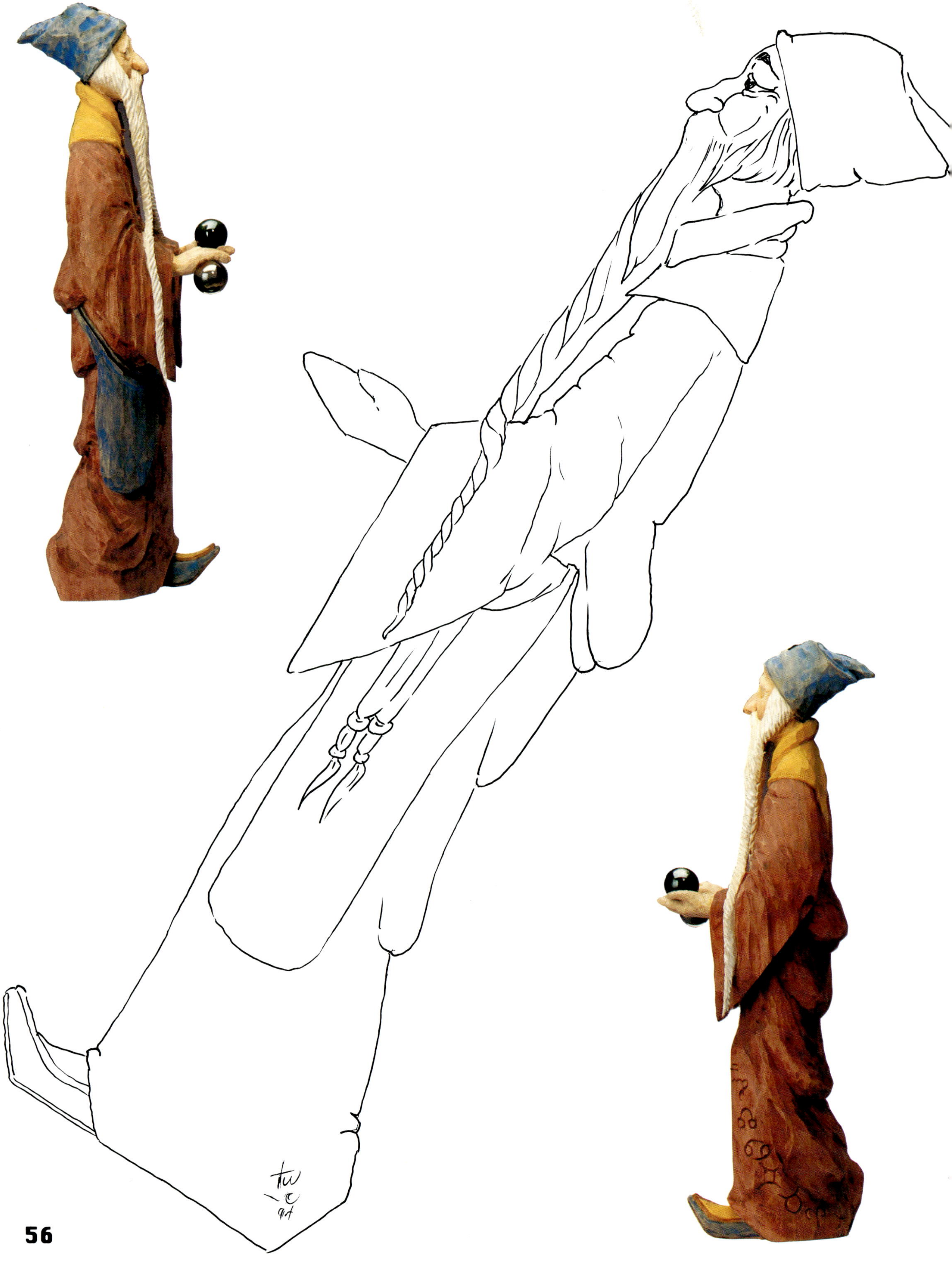

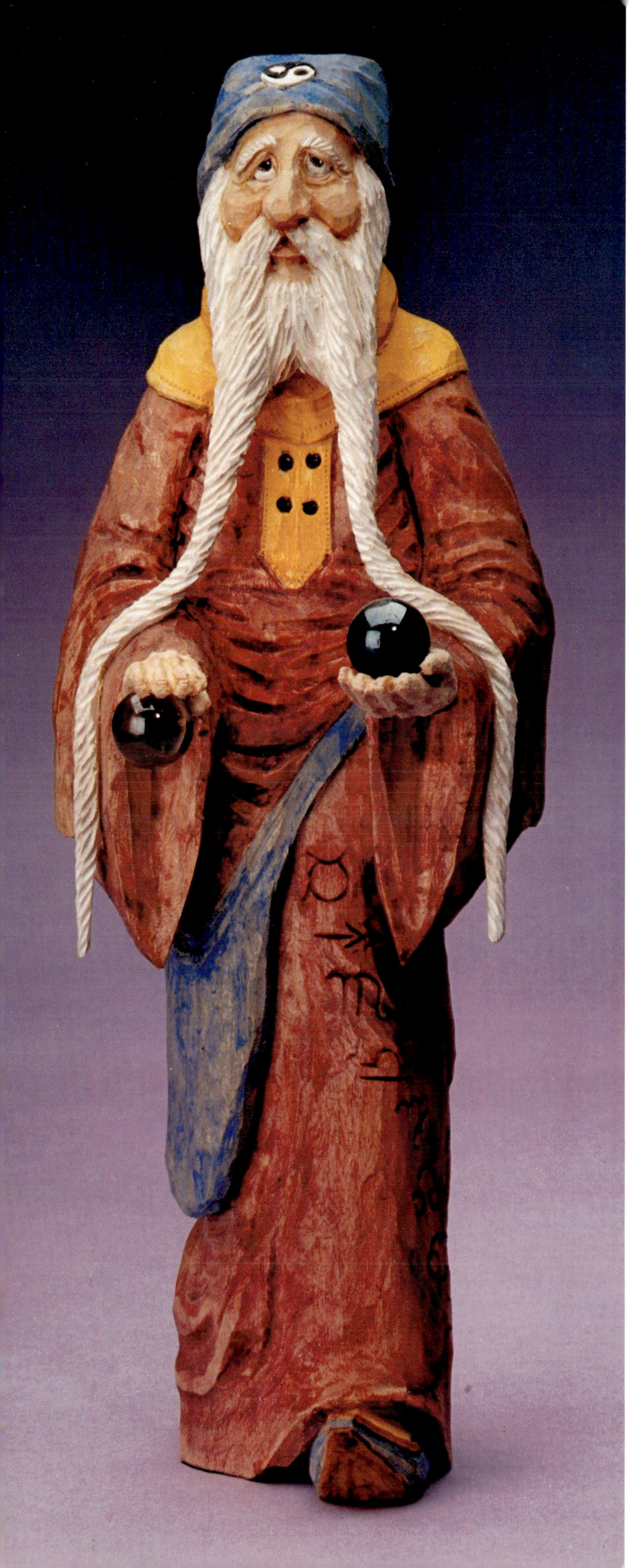

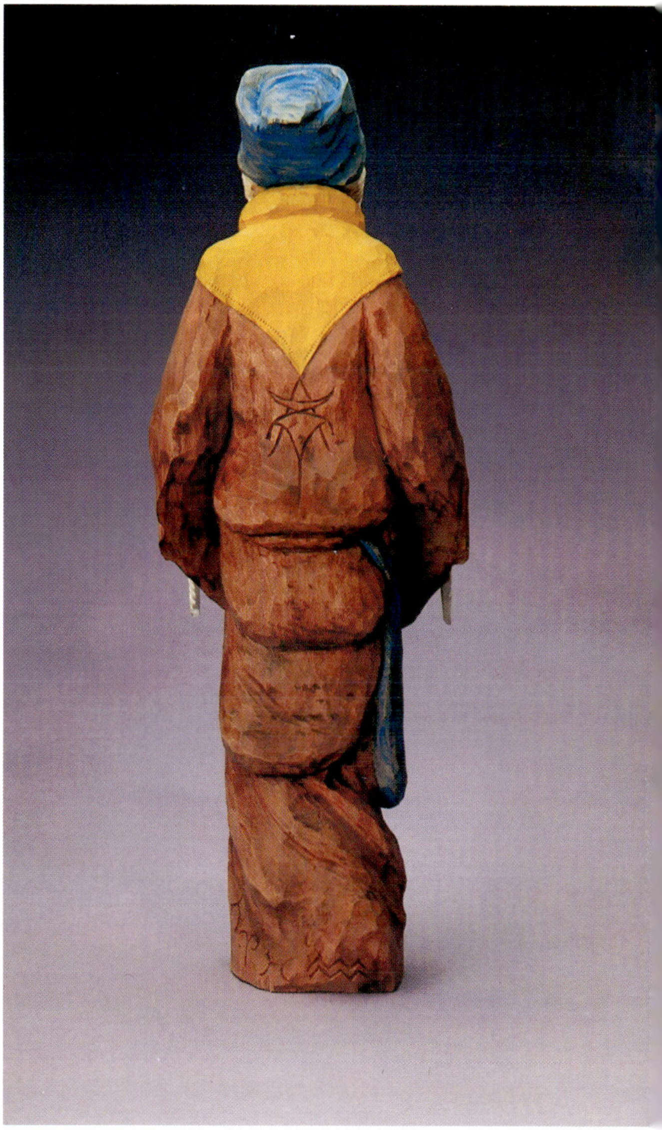

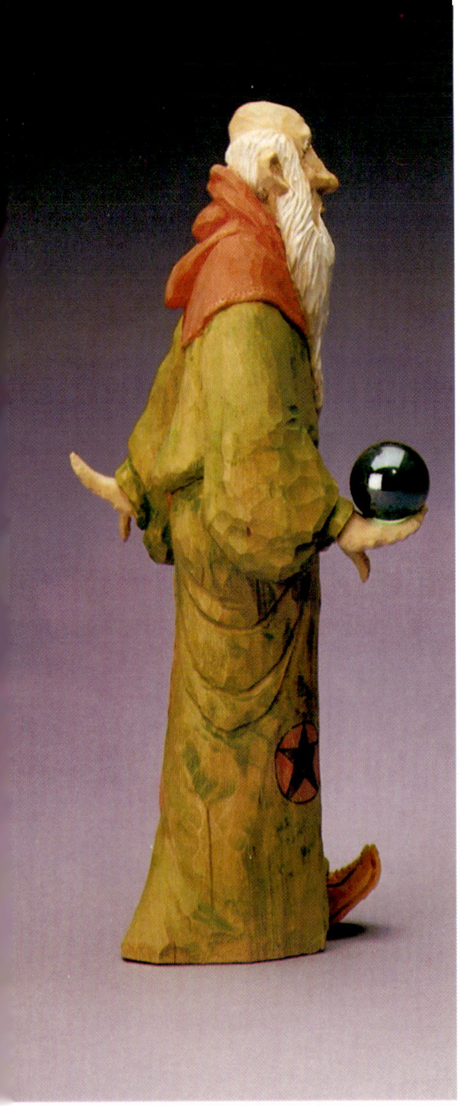

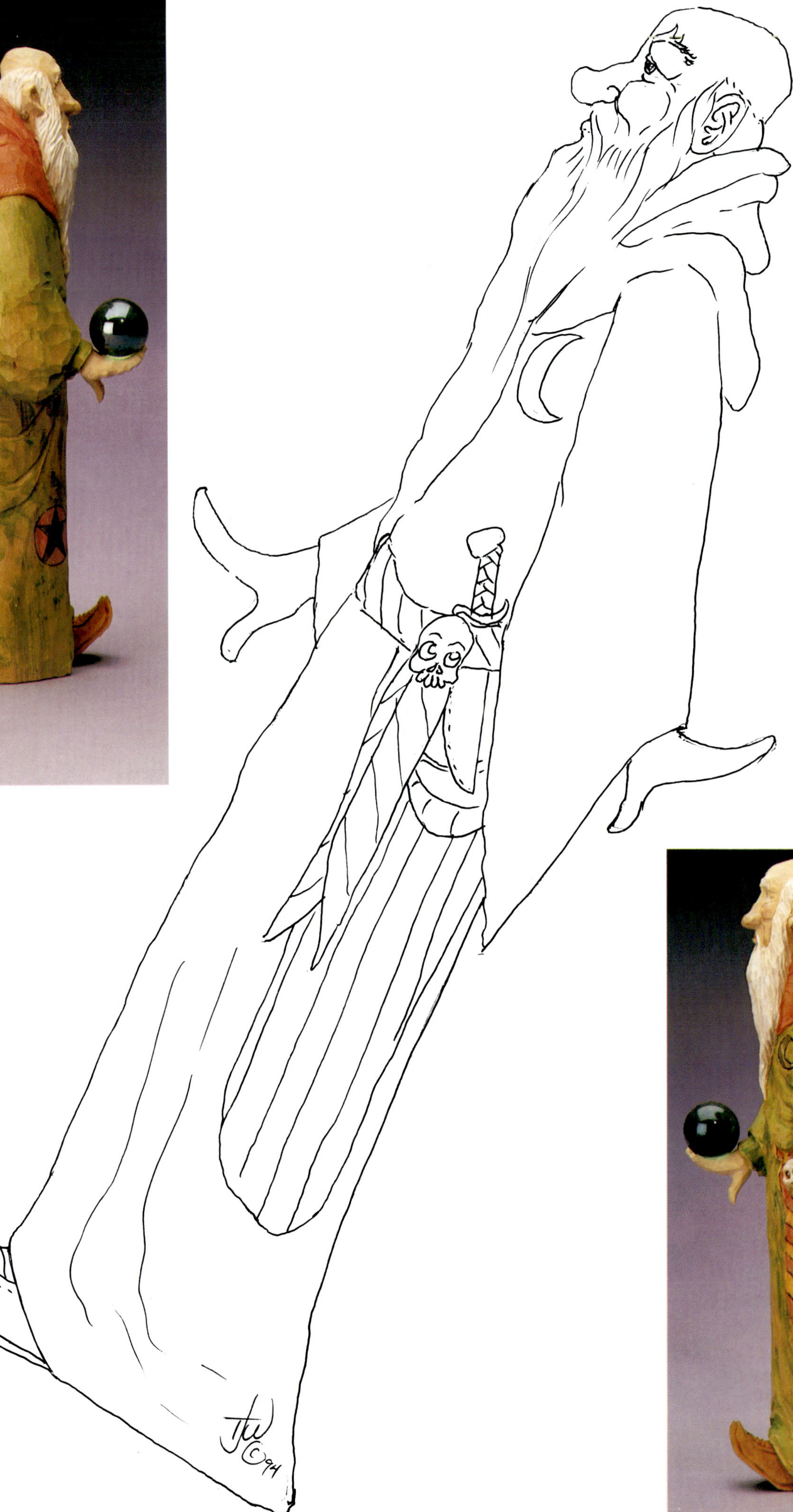

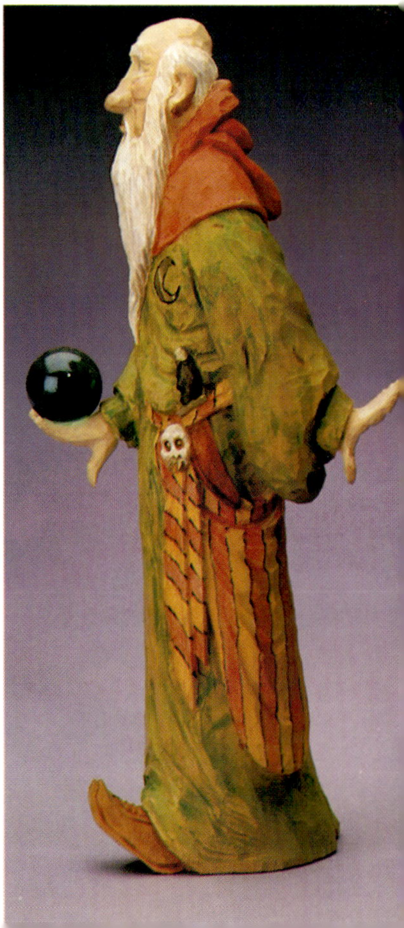

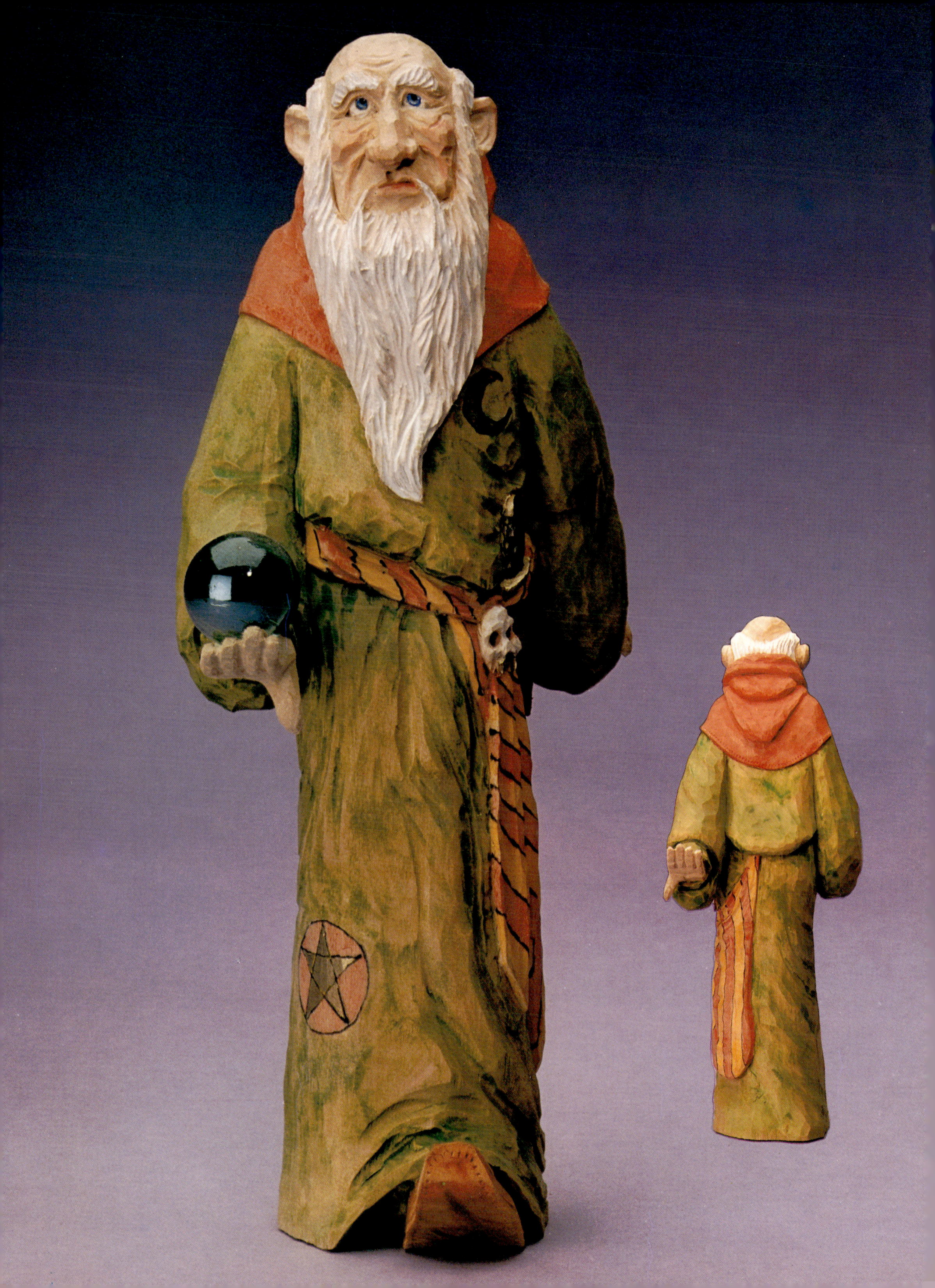

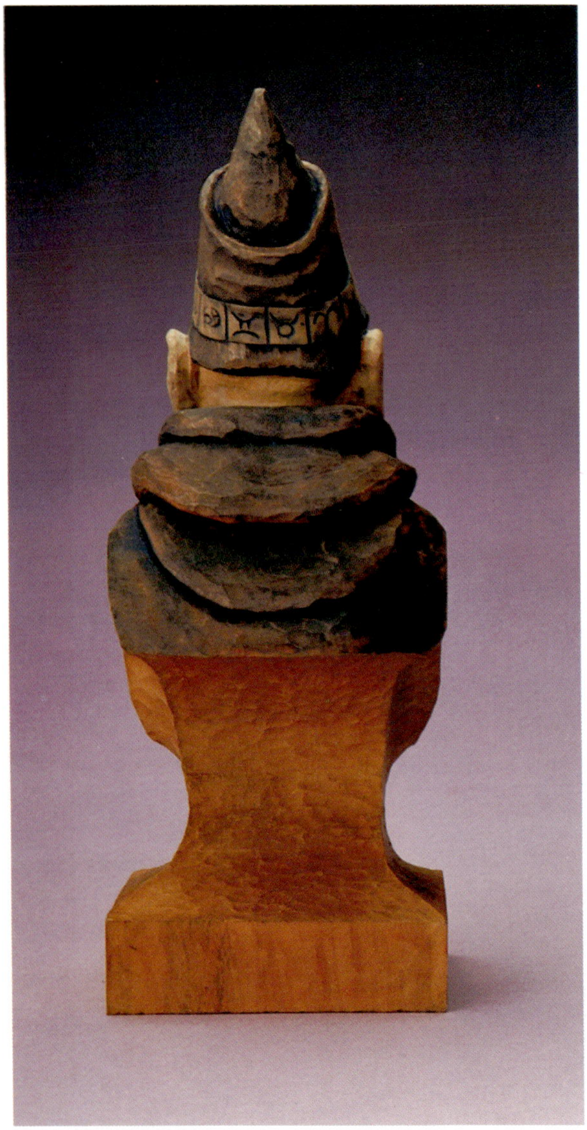

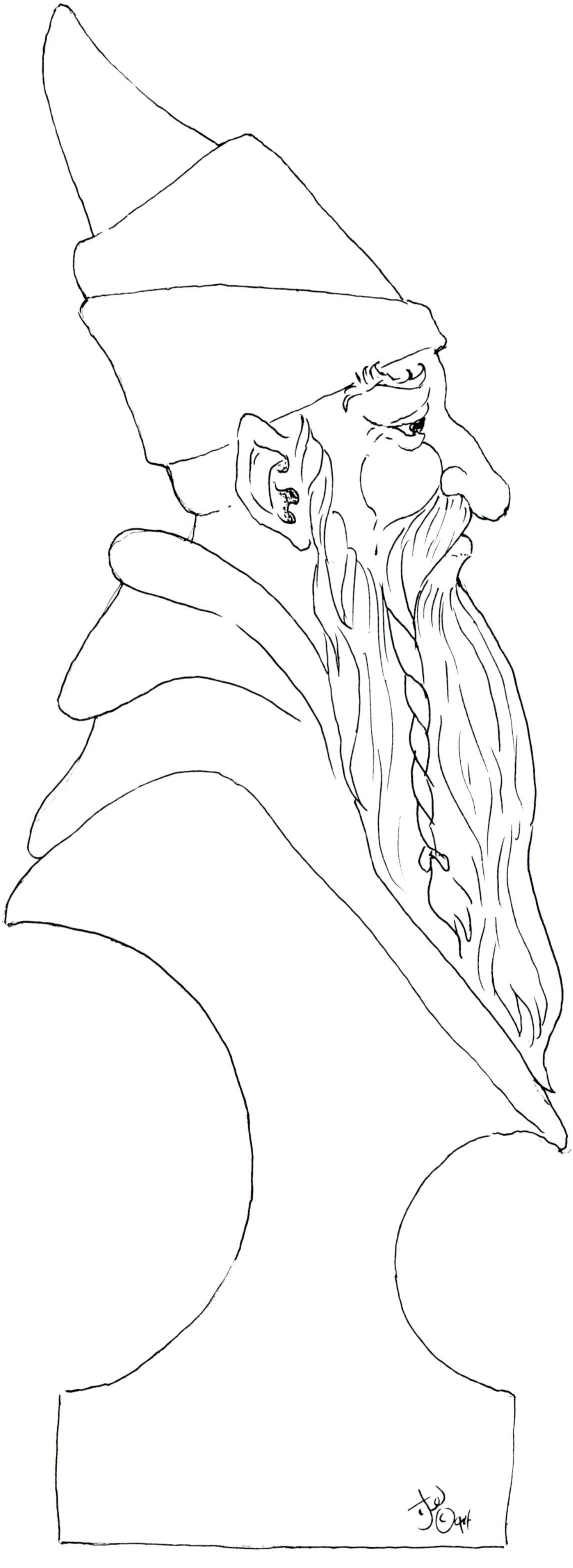

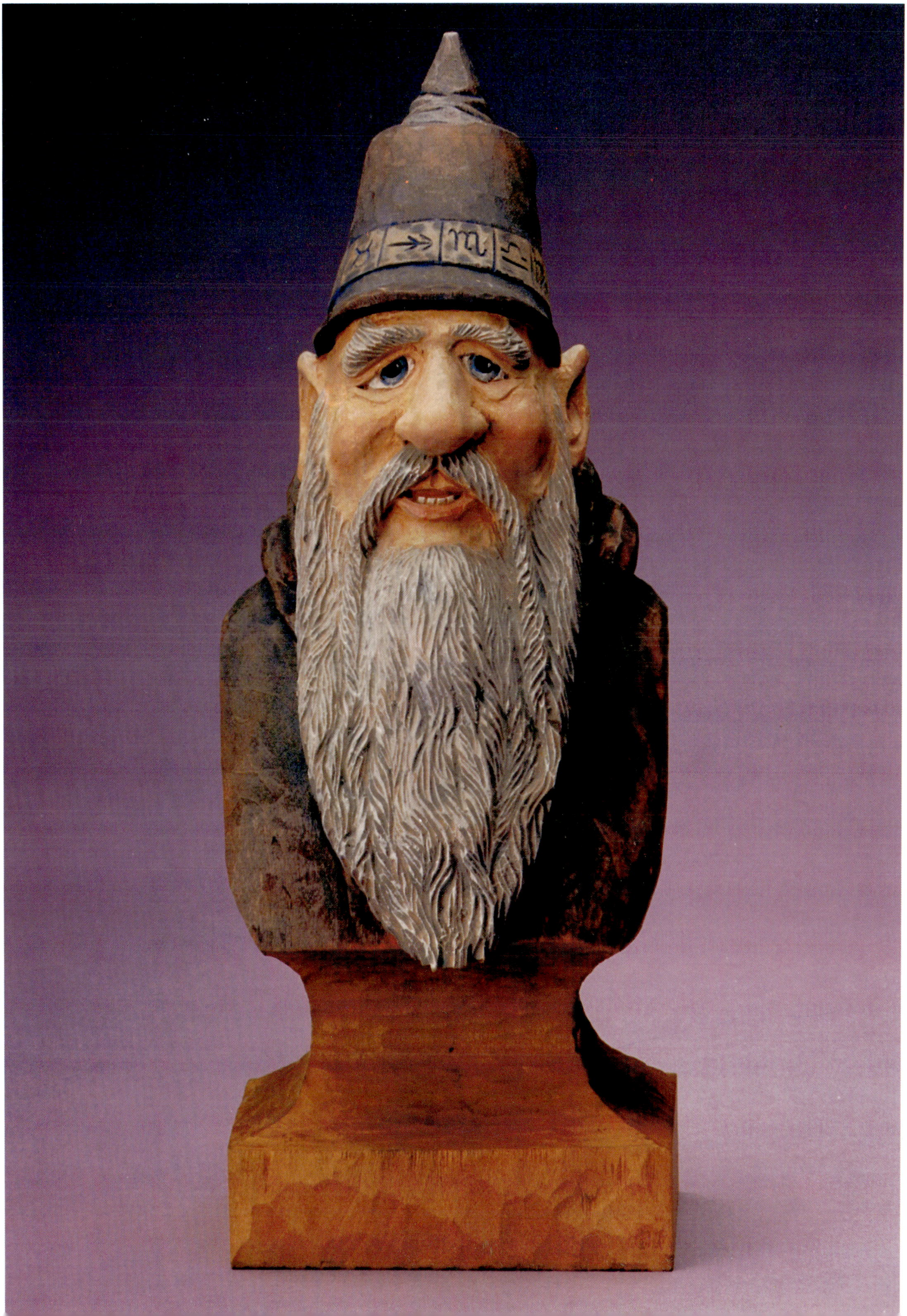

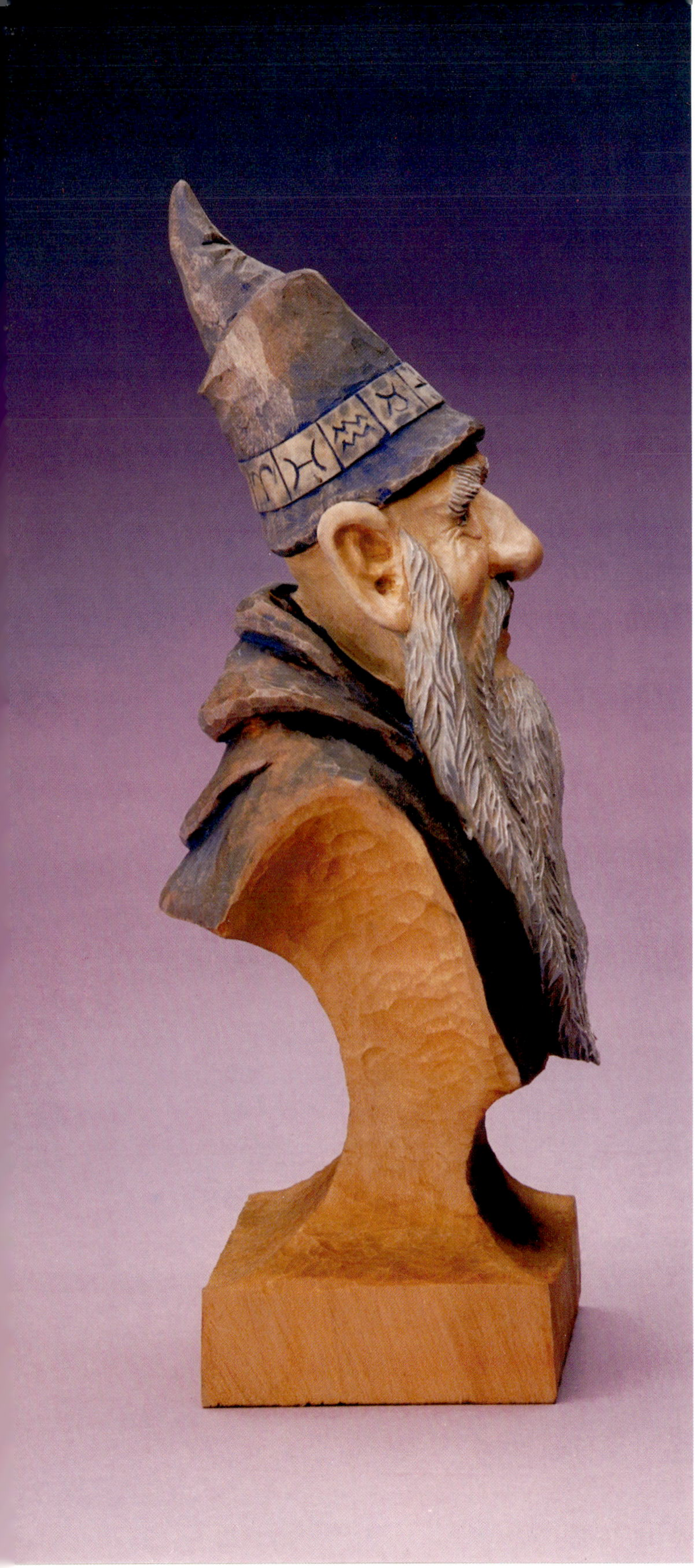

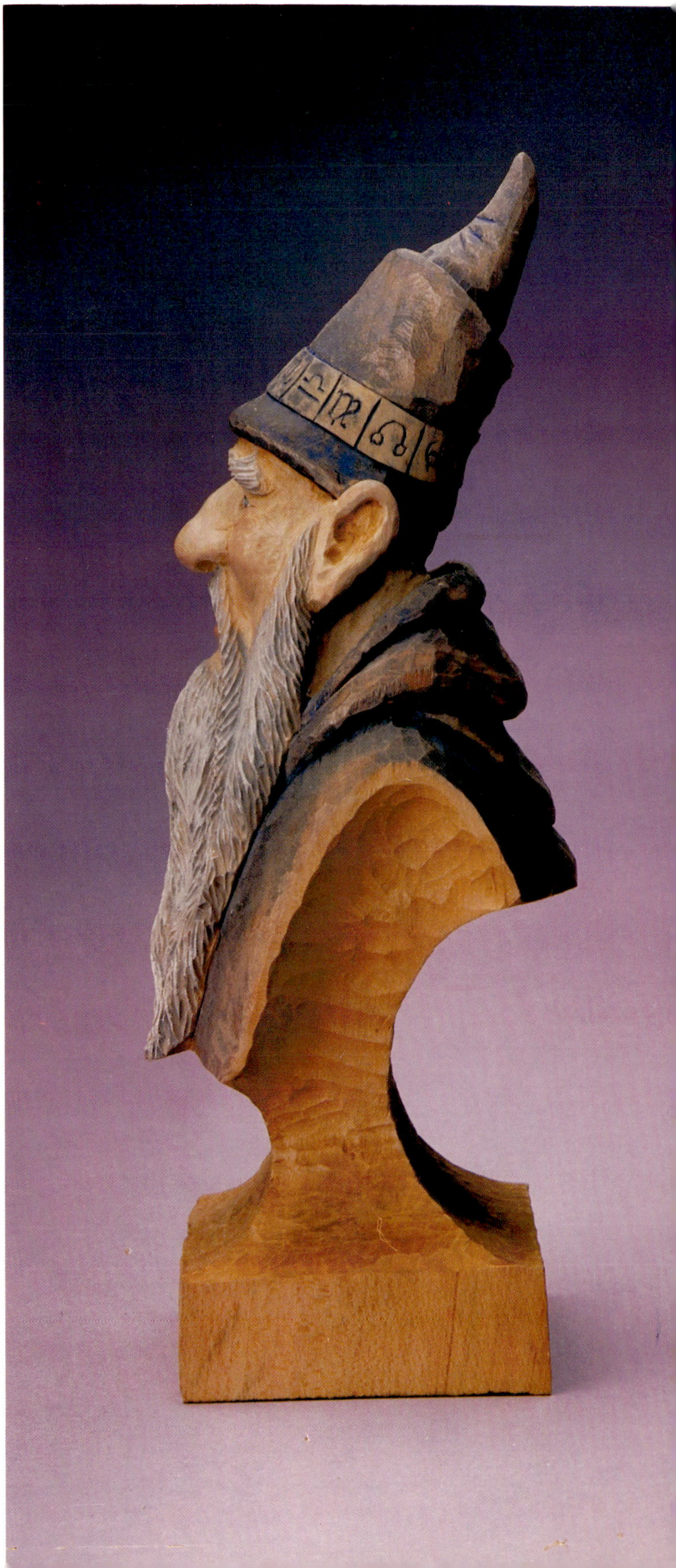

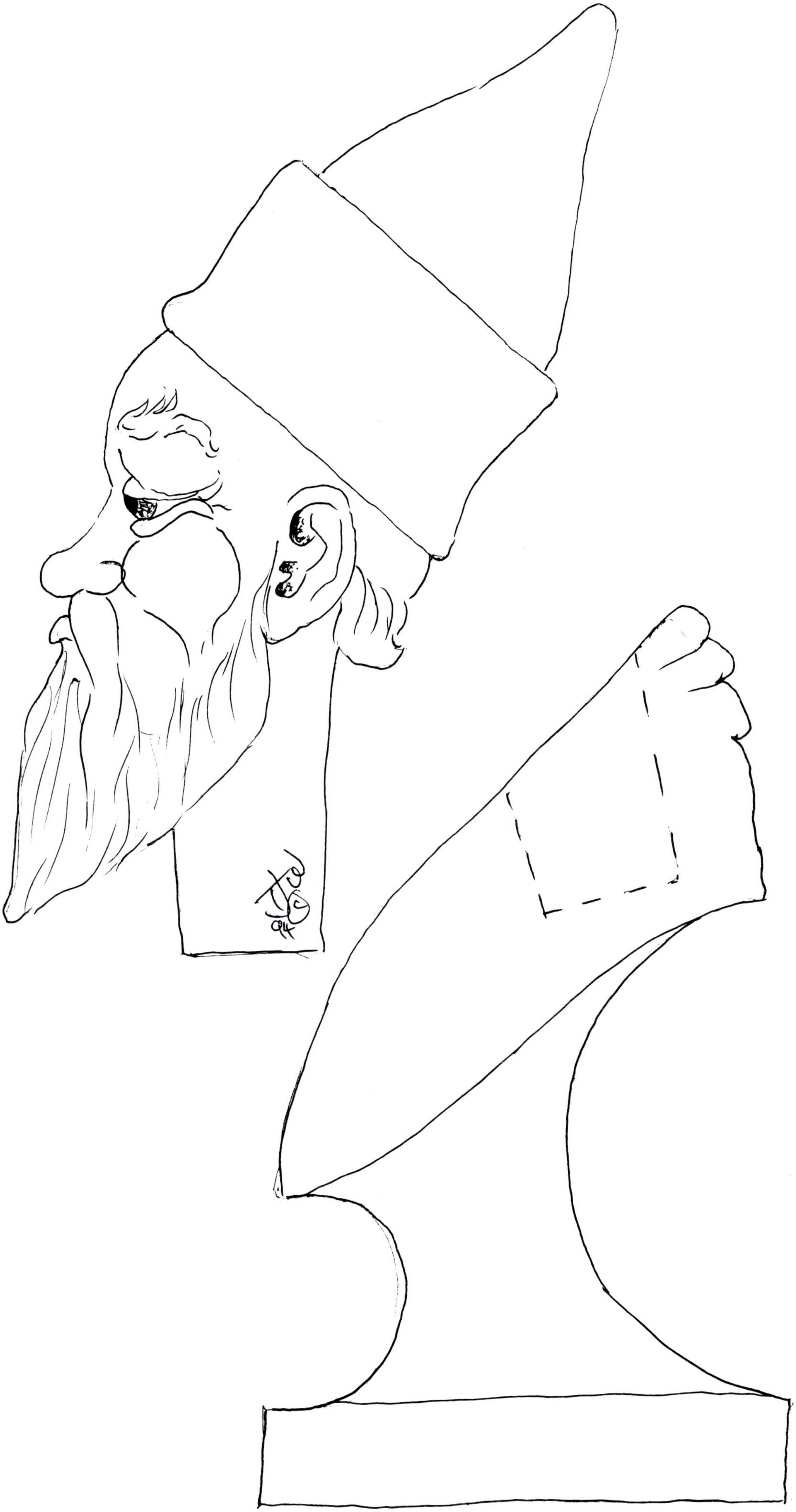

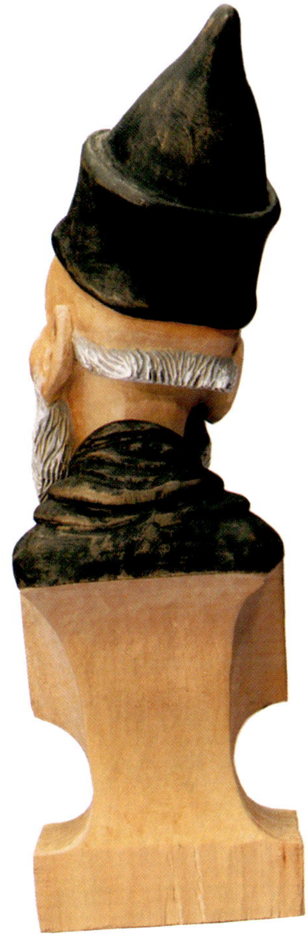

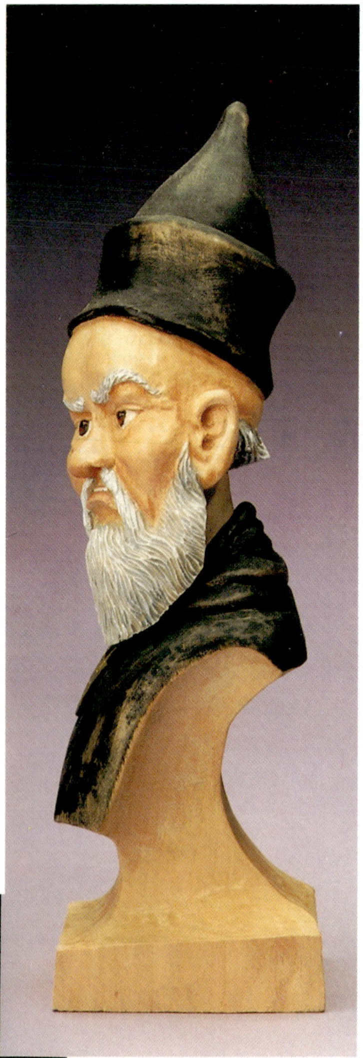
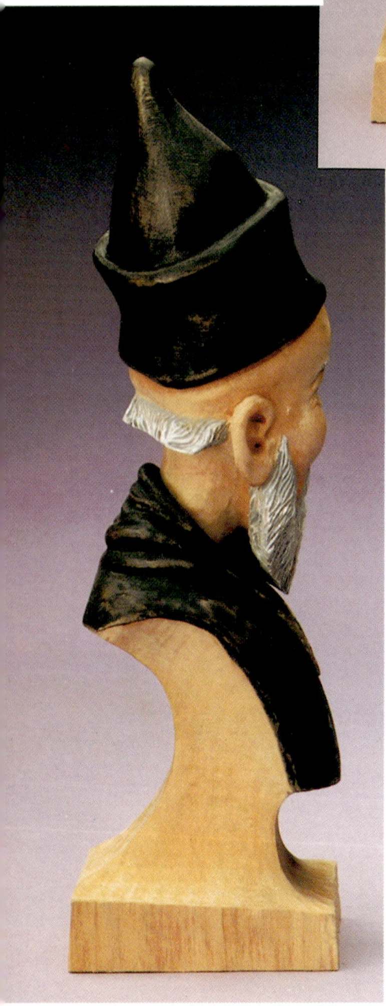
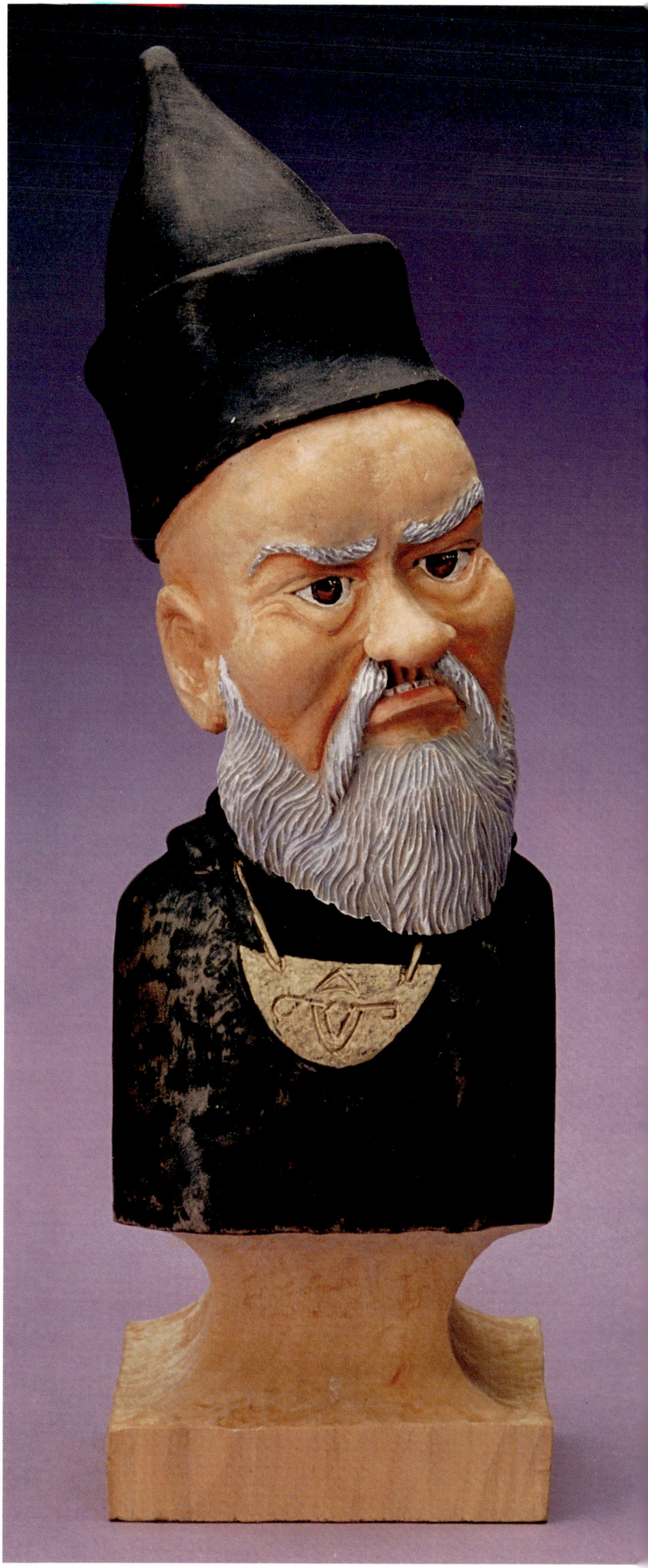

Foreword

The current fascination with angels probably reveals an undercurrent need for the sacred in a highly secular society. God seems remote, even absent, but maybe an angel is hovering close by. We live in a society of big government, big business, and big church. Few of us would walk up to a CEO, shake his hand and ask a favor, so how could we dare approach God? But maybe an angel — an agent — would hear.

In our need for a Greater Power, we run the risk of inventing beings to suit our pleasure. Some of our attention to angels may become a pursuit of our own fantasies instead of a genuine seeking of God.

Ron Ransom's angels-to-be-carved provide a healthy balance. At the same time, they offer a means of pursuing an interest widespread enough for a *Time* cover story, an opportunity to carve out an angel which exactly (or approximately) represents the fantasy you desire most, and a set of ideas and techniques that will keep you from taking the whole thing too seriously. In other words, with this book you can devotedly remind yourself and your friends, with pieces they can see and touch, of a God who cares and sends agents of his caring. With these angels, God can be seen to care about every part of life — even golf. But at the same time, the whimsical patterns preach the truth that our representation of God's agents are just that: the best our hands can do to express the fancies in our heads.

So, I commend Ron's angels to your heart as well as to your carving. They tell us gentle things about God's presence and love, but refuse to let us pretend we can make something holy with our hands.

Happy carving to you!
Proud to be Ron's Pastor.
James O. Speed
Pastor
First Presbyterian Church of Marietta, Georgia

Introduction

If you have used my other carving books, you know I like to keep my designs simple enough for the beginner but challenging enough for the more advanced carver to take the design and add to it with his or her own creativity.

I have carved these designs using basswood measuring one inch thick or less. They may be cut out with a reciprocating (sabre) saw, a scroll saw, or — for the more adventurous — a coping saw.

If I may be of additional help, send your questions or comments to Ron Ransom, Box 4101, Marietta, GA 30068. If you want an answer, send a self-addressed, stamped envelope.

Good carving!
Ron Ransom

Carving The Angels

Angel One

I know we all feel sometimes as if our guardian angel is having a little trouble getting off the ground. A few years ago, my wife and I were going through some nagging health problems and our faith seemed to sag at times. This design was the result of that tough period in our lives. We are both doing great now ... and maybe this angel will too.

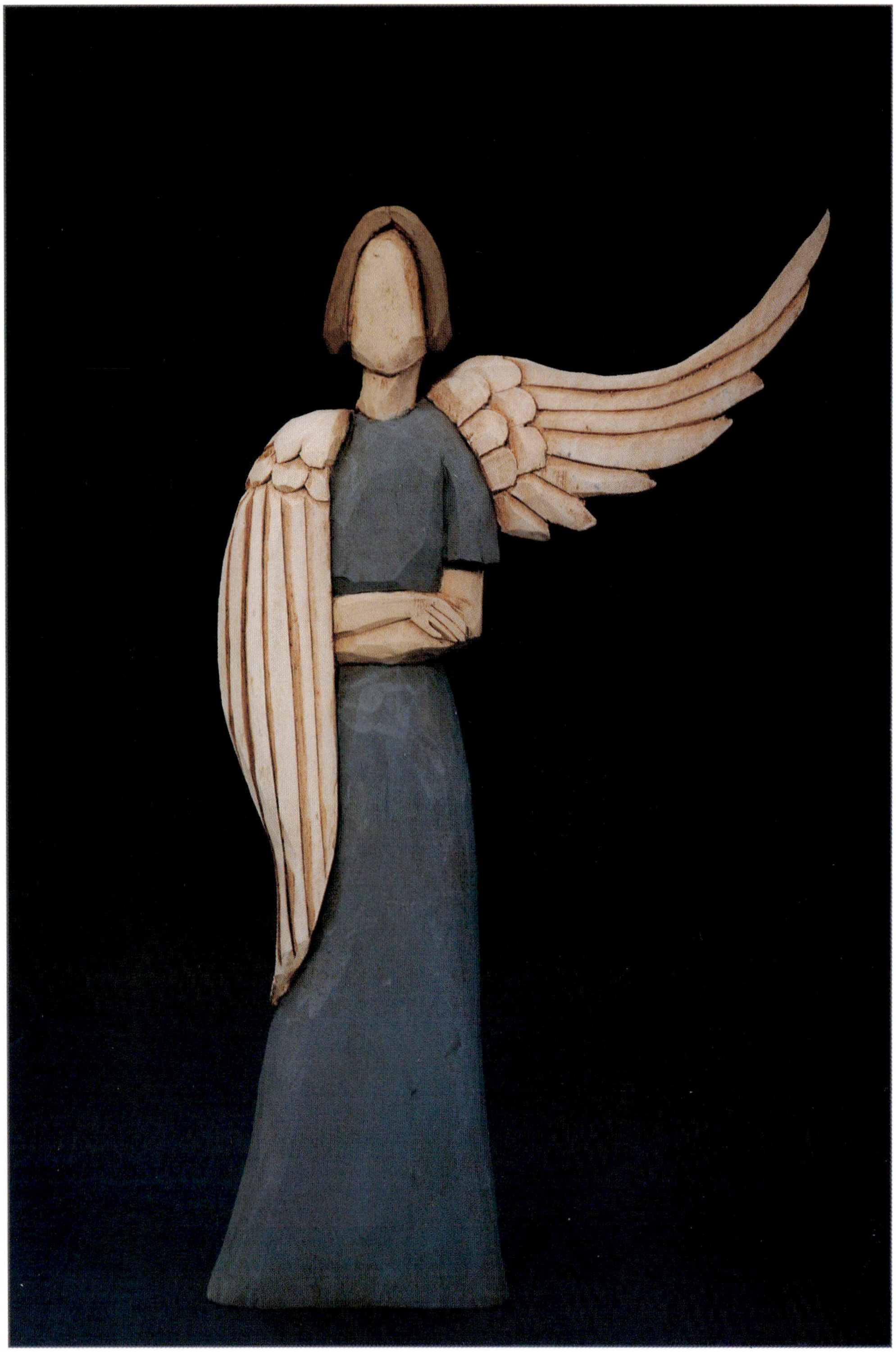

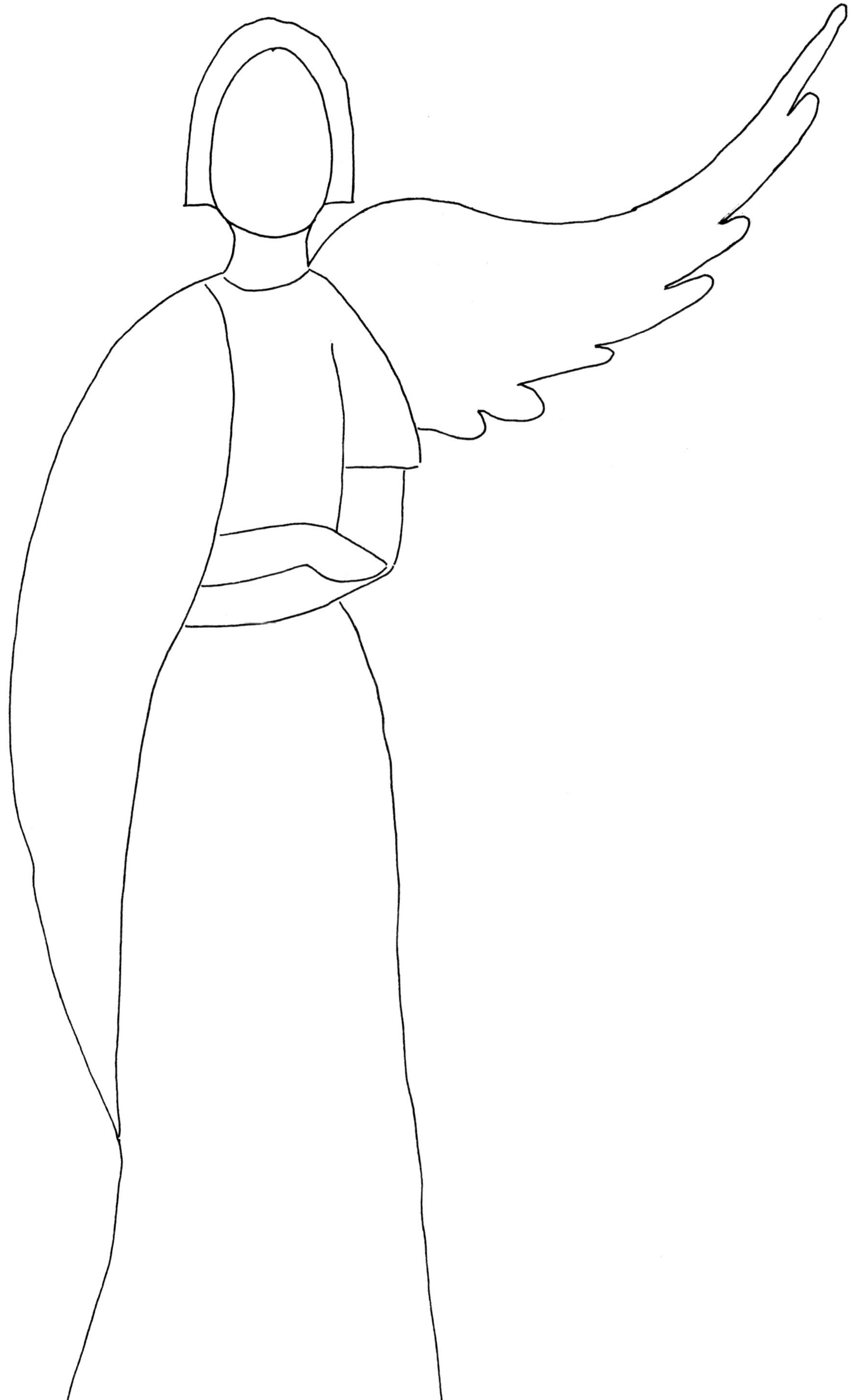

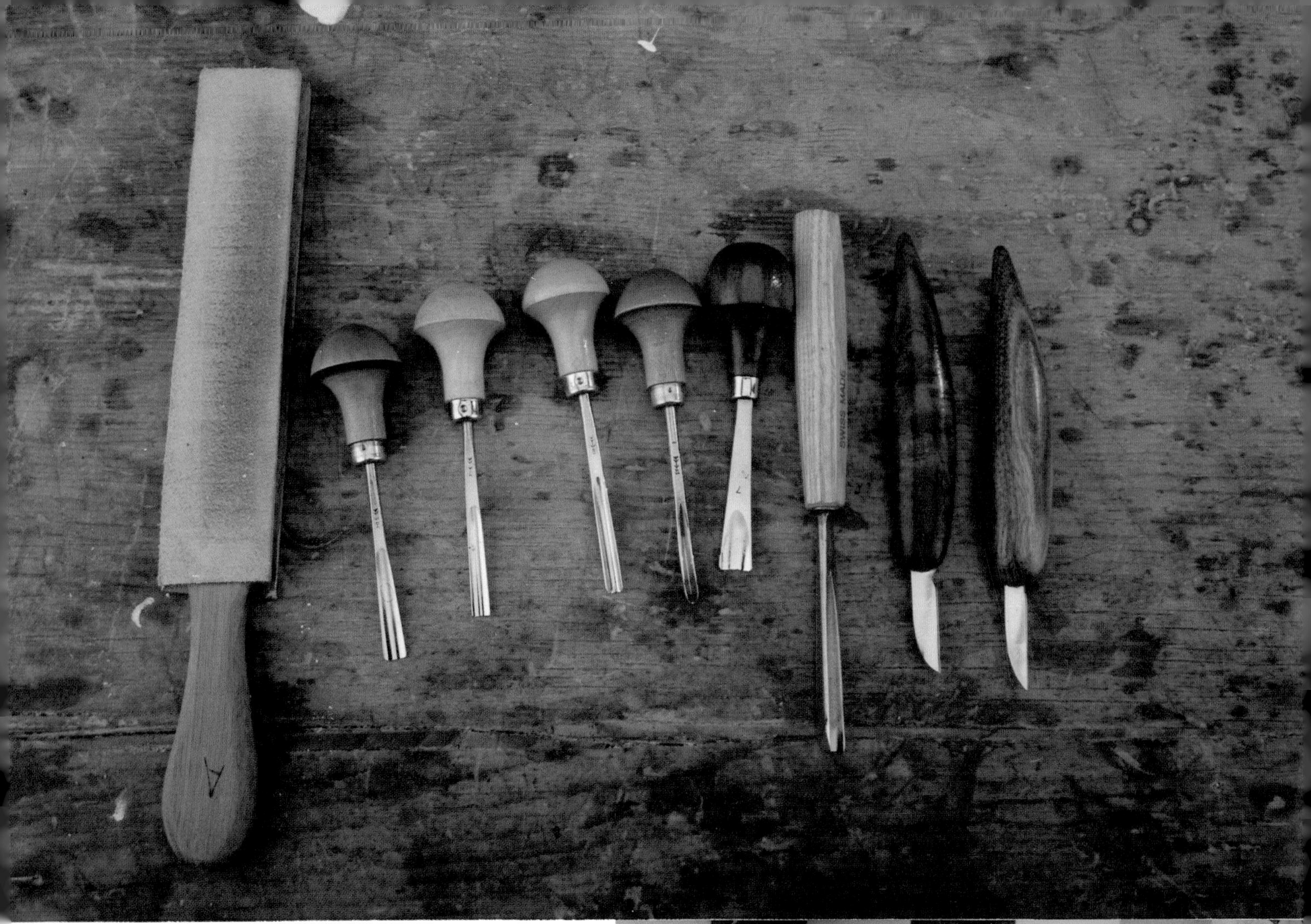

These are the tools you will need for the angel carving projects.

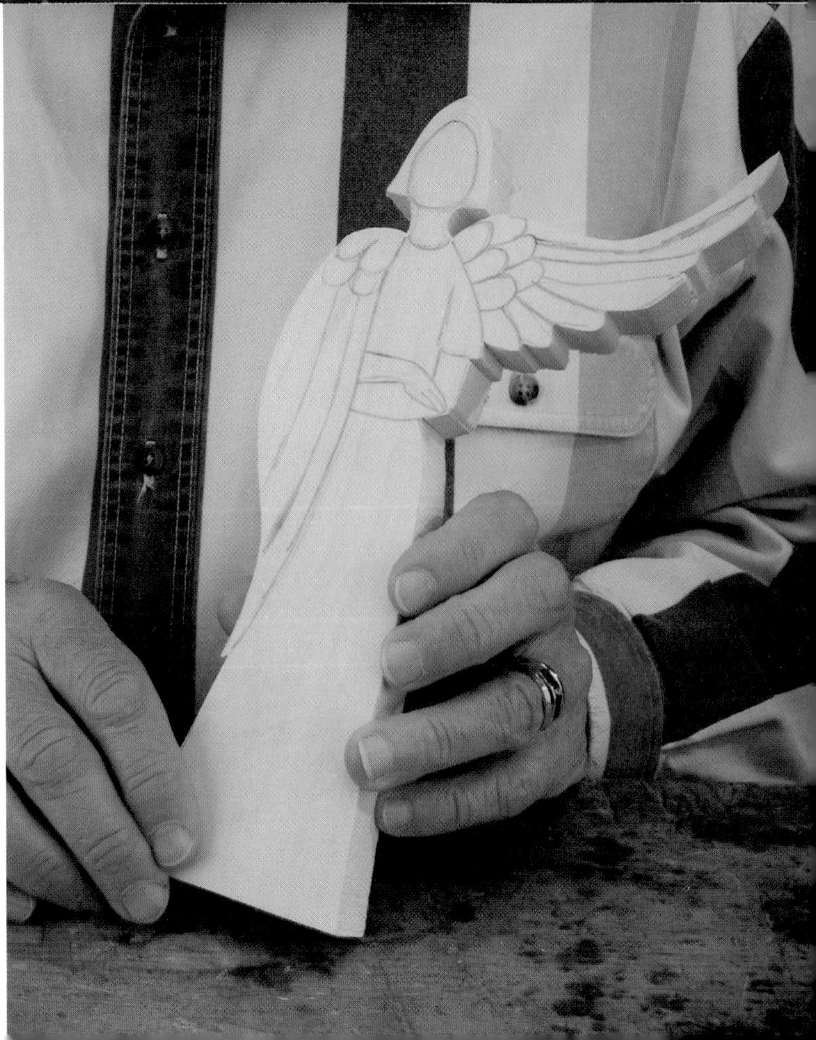

In this book I'm using the 1" or less wide basswood.

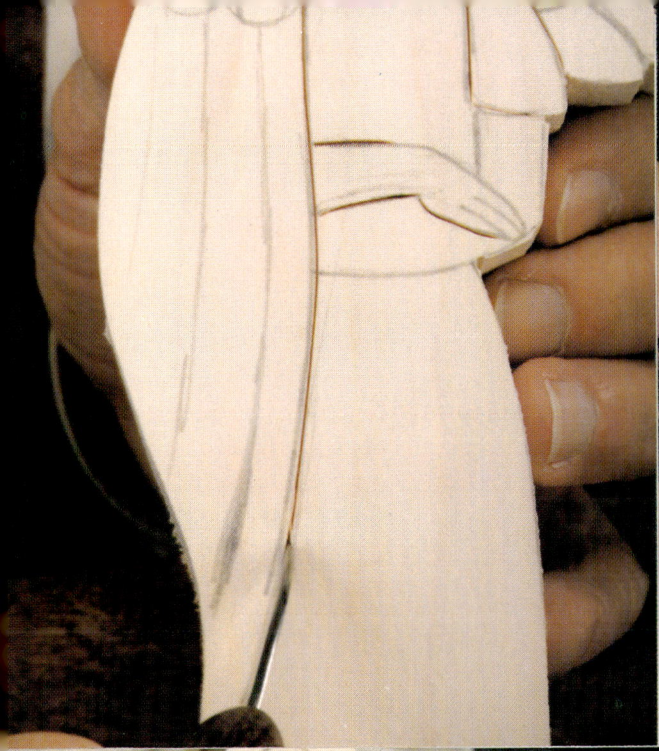
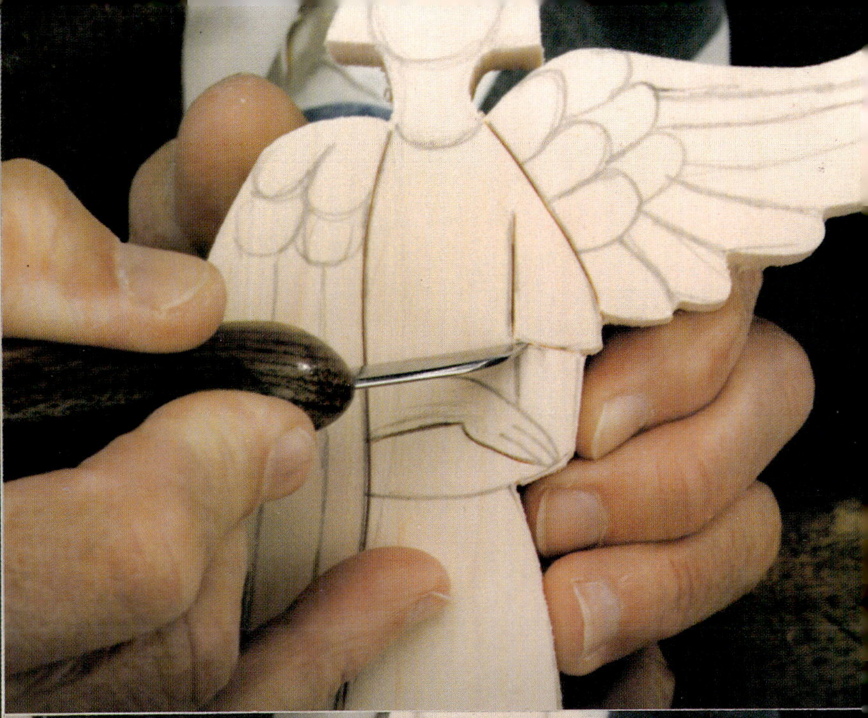
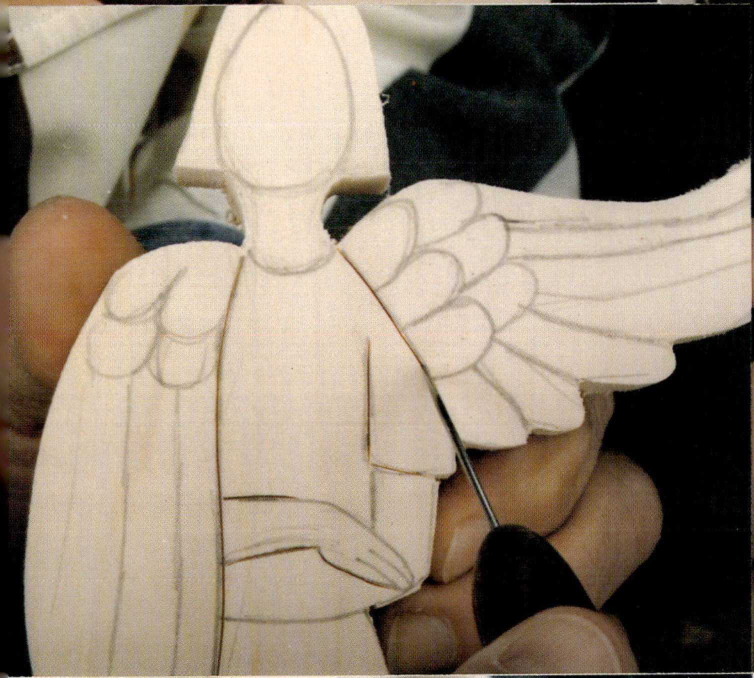
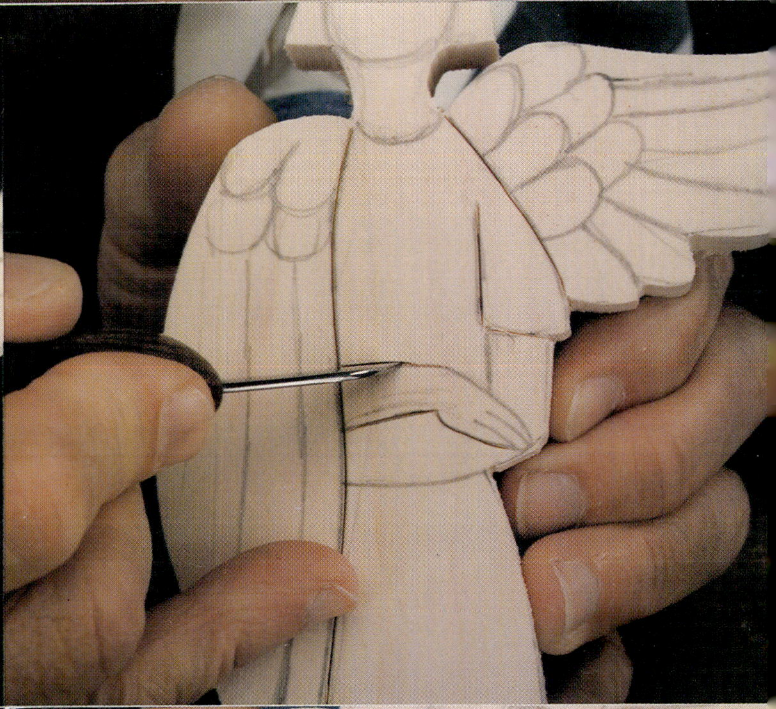
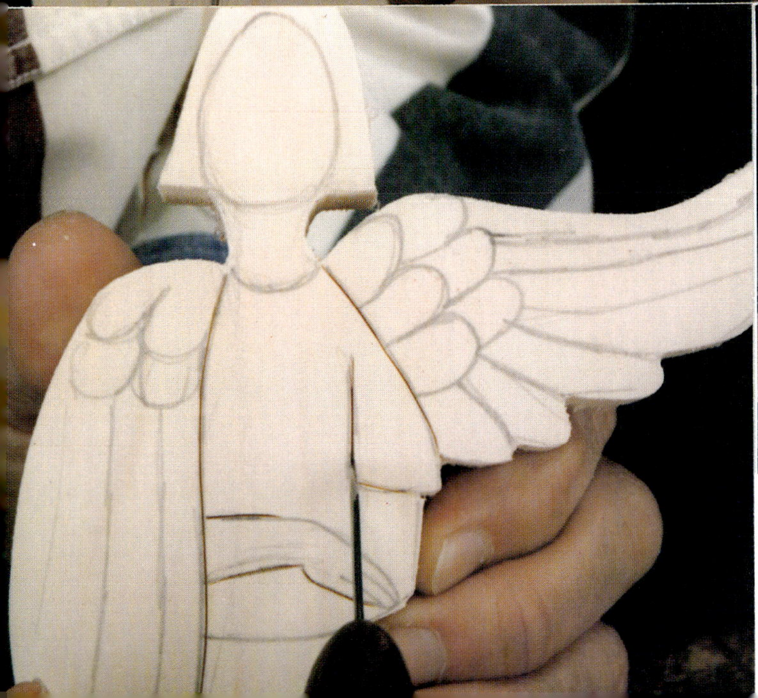
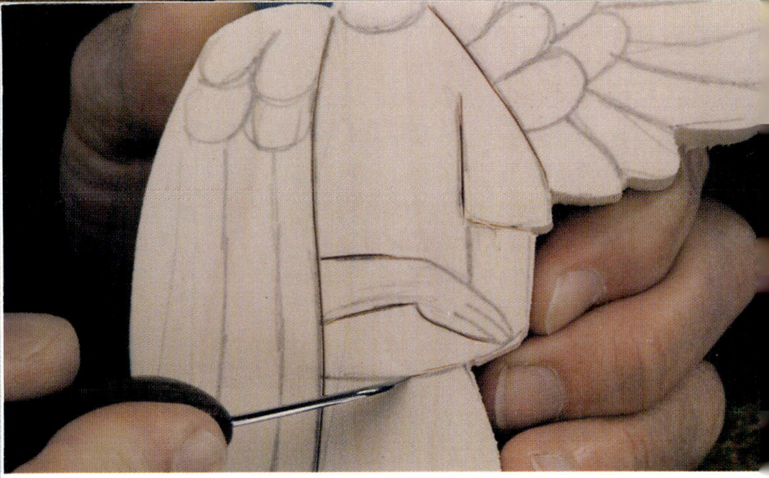

With my bench knife I am scoring the lines on the front of the angel that I want to start with. This is simply to give me something to carve to.

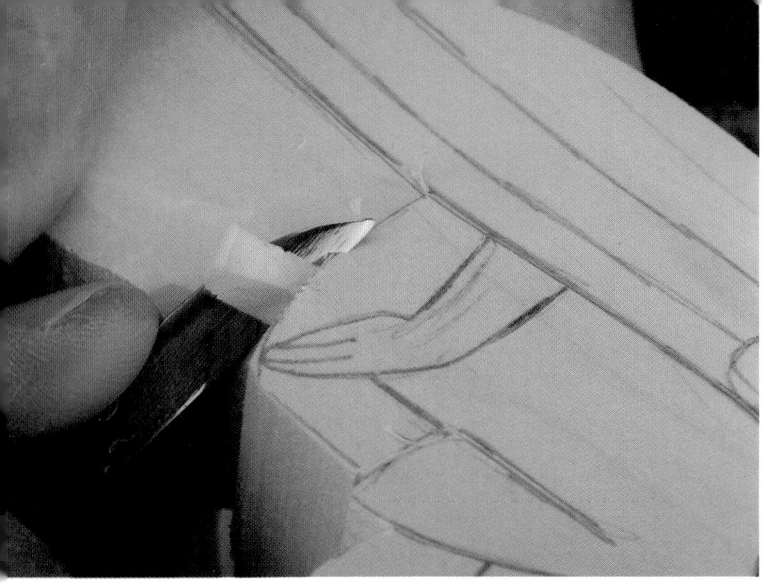

With a piece this narrow, you need to be careful how you hold it for safety's sake. Wear a carver's glove if you have one. Round the robe.

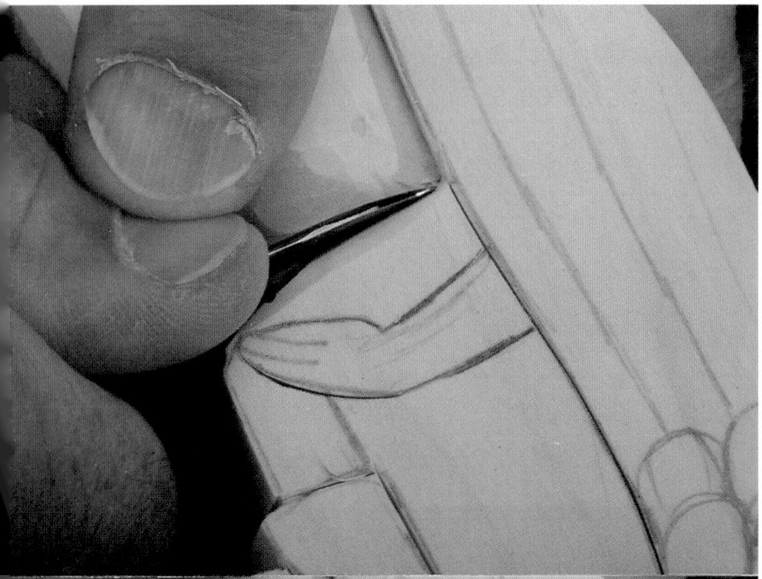

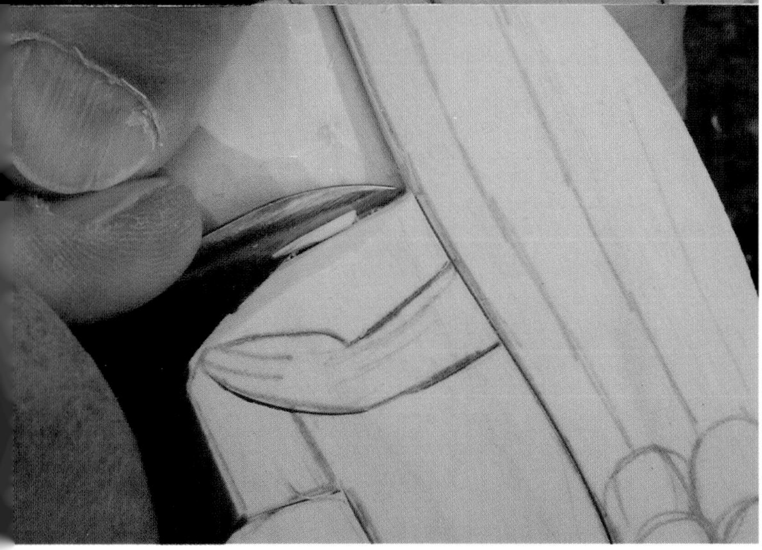

I am going to assume this is the first of my books you have read, so I want to emphasize that you should use your thumb to push your knife blade for control and leverage. Rounding the arm using a series of stop cuts that cut straight down and then angle up to give the arm its shape.

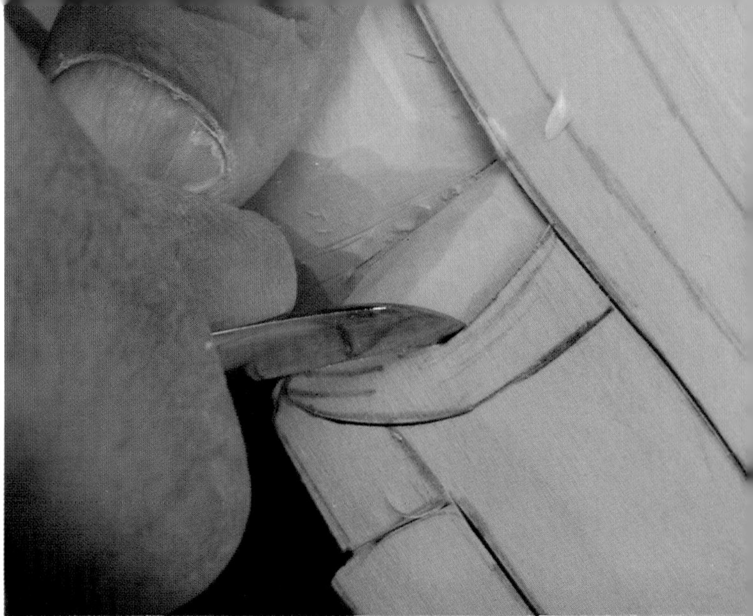

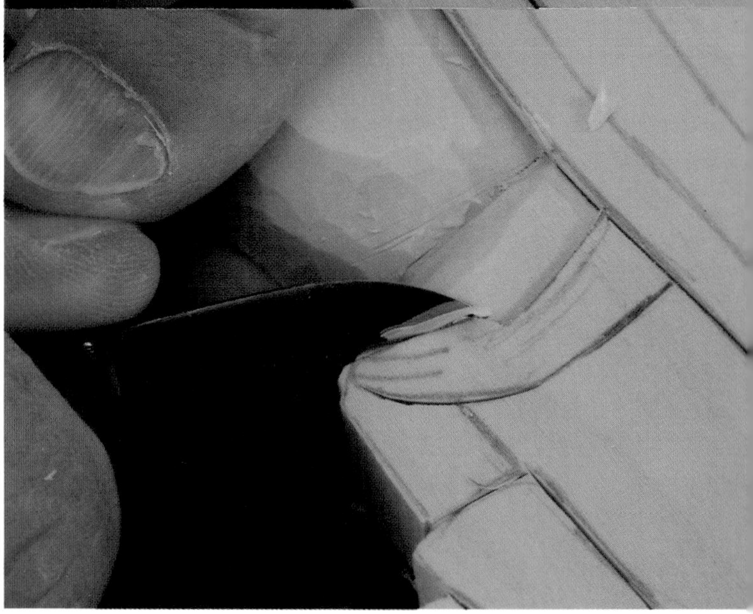

Do the same thing to define the right (upper) arm, using a series of stop cuts along the bottom of the arm and hand.

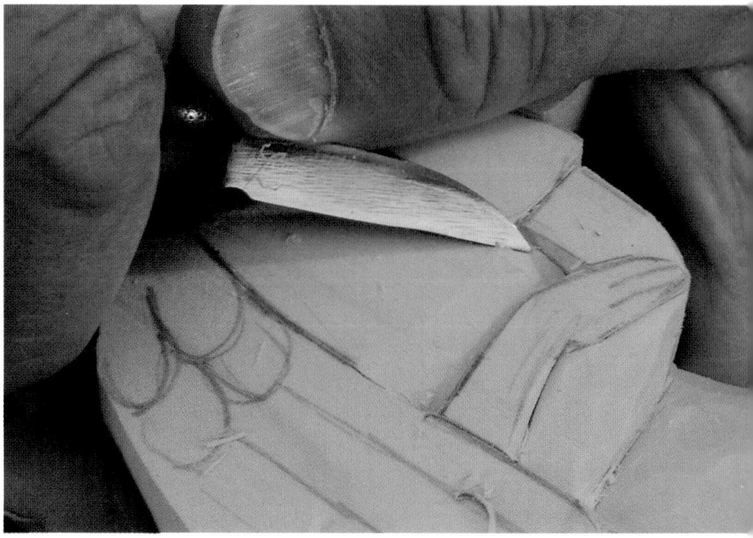

Use a series of stop cuts along the top of the right arm to give it some shape as well.

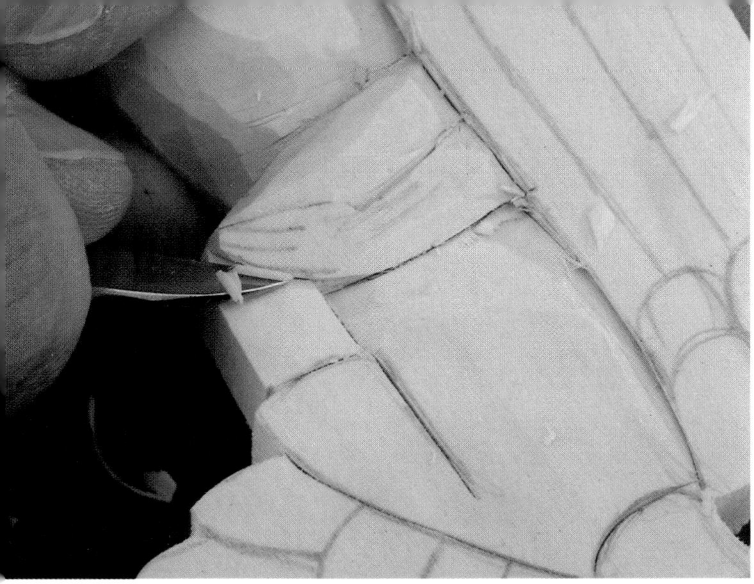

Round down the arm to the hand. Be careful not to cut off the fingers.

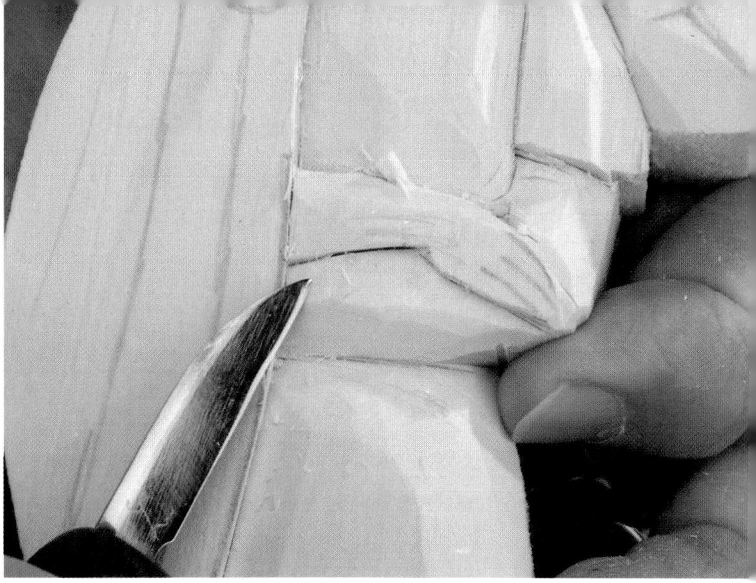

The left arm goes under the right arm so we have to cut it back, recess it. Continue to carve down the forearm, you don't want this angel to have forearms like Popeye.

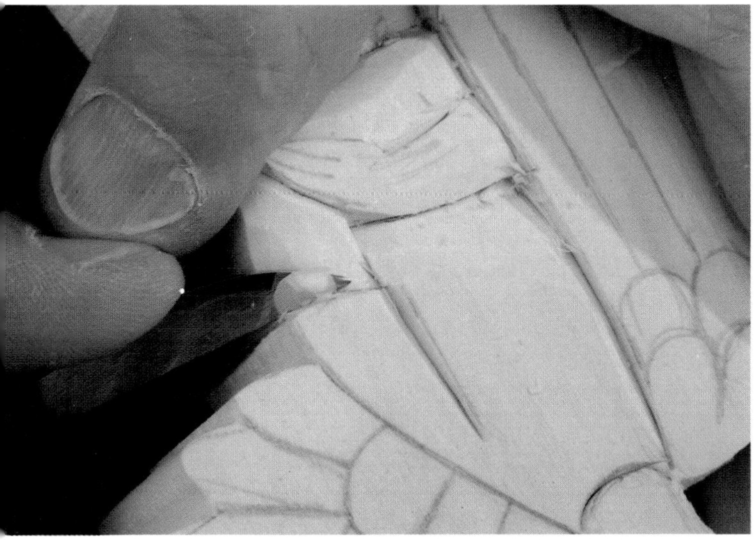

Round the upper part of the left arm where it goes into the sleeve.

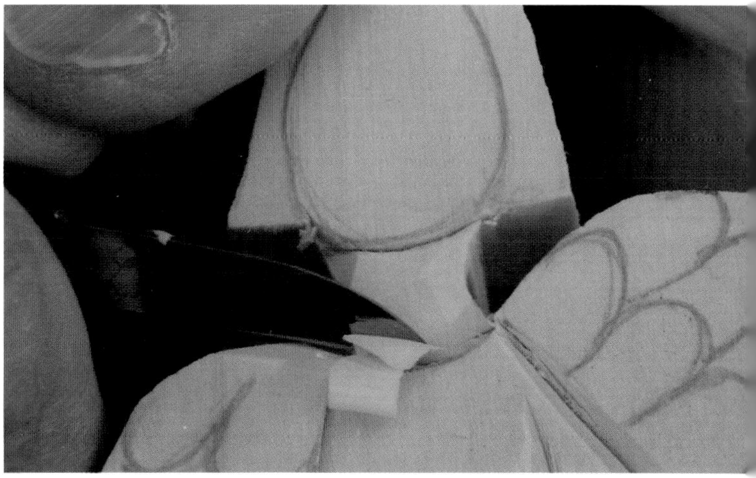

Shape the neck into the jawline.

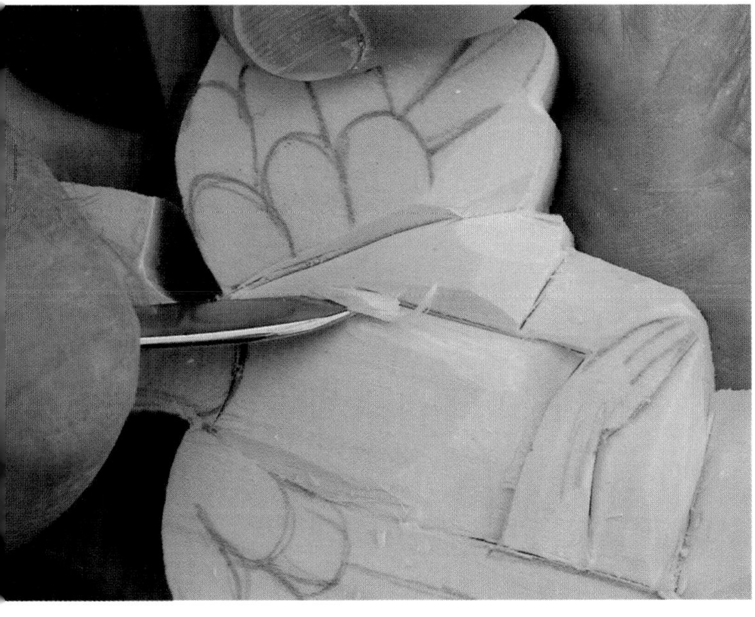

Round the upper part of the body where it meets the arm.

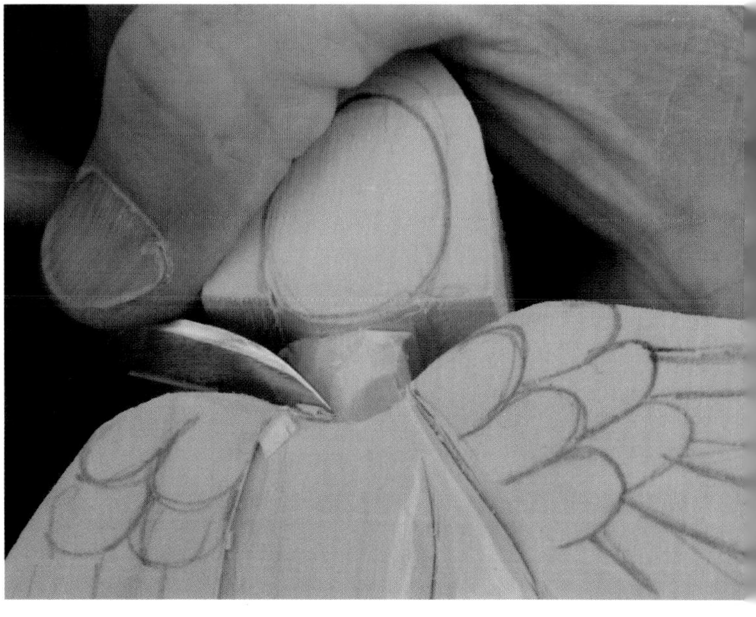

Continue rounding the neck to give it some shape.

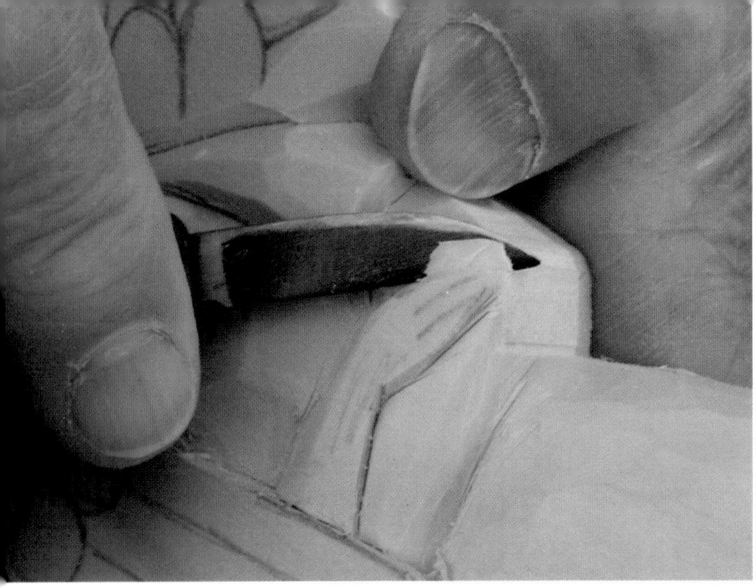

I want the hand to be more prominent so I'm cutting the arm down more. Don't worry about cutting off your pencil line guides, they can be redrawn.

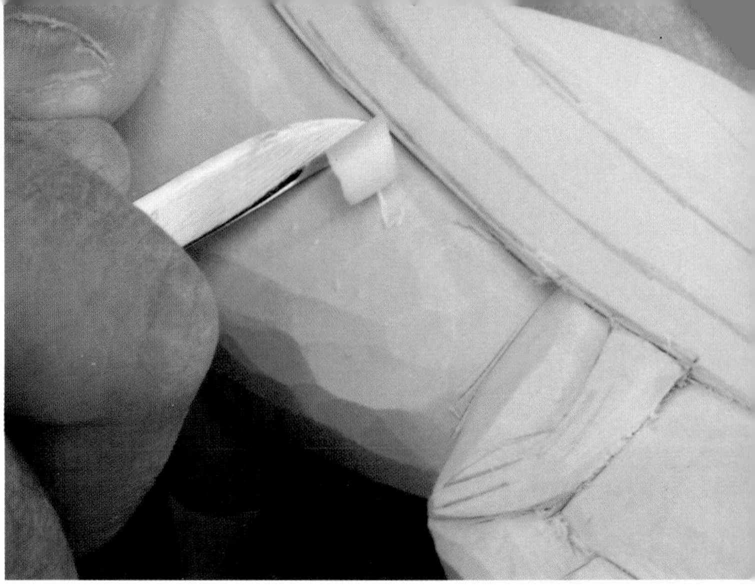

Rounding the robe under the wing. We are going to make the wing a little more prominent.

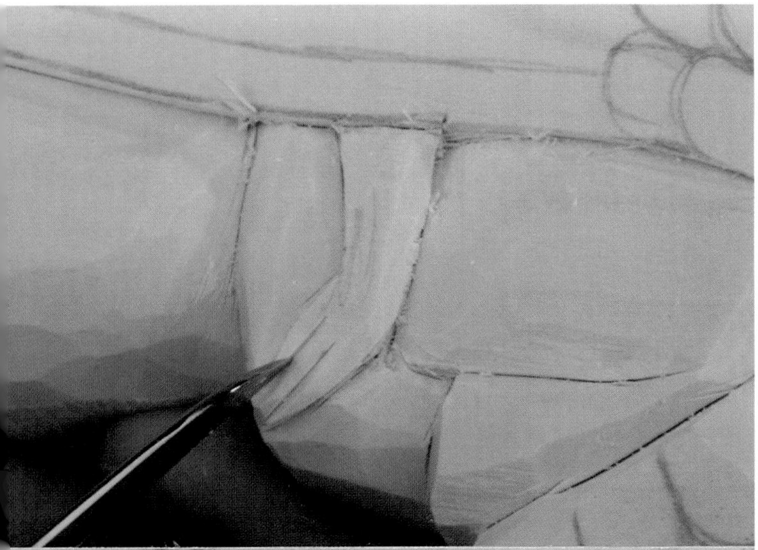

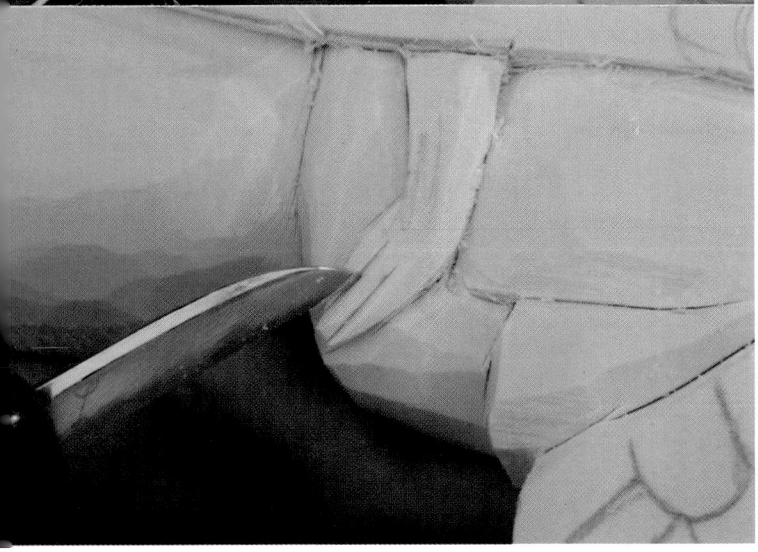

To define the fingers, just take your knife and rock it along the line where you want each finger to be and then cut at an angle on either side of that line. The piece of wood in the center will pop right out, defining the fingers.

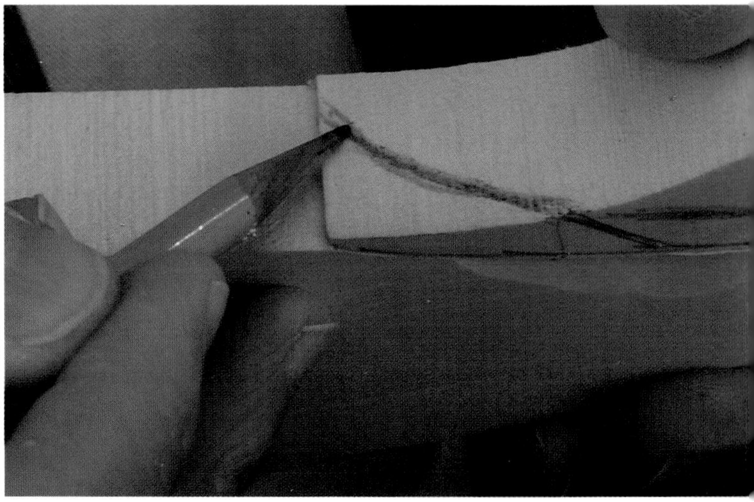

This would be a good time to draw the line on the side of the bass wood block where you want to cut your wing off.

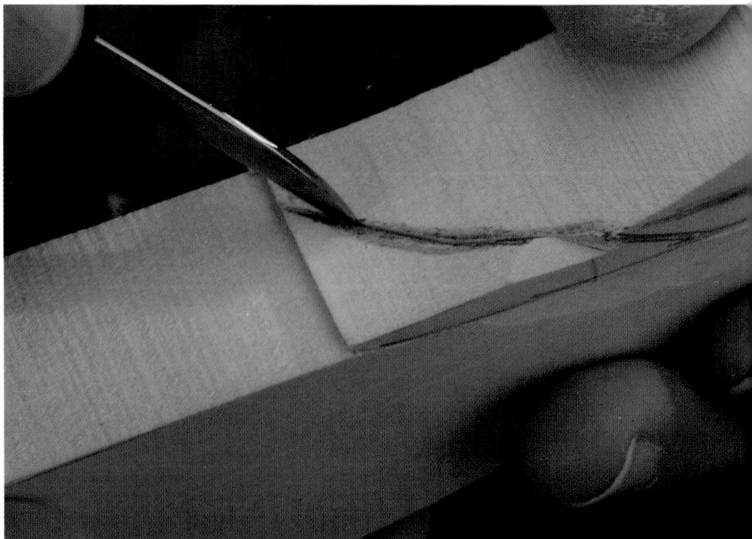

Lightly score this pencil line with your knife.

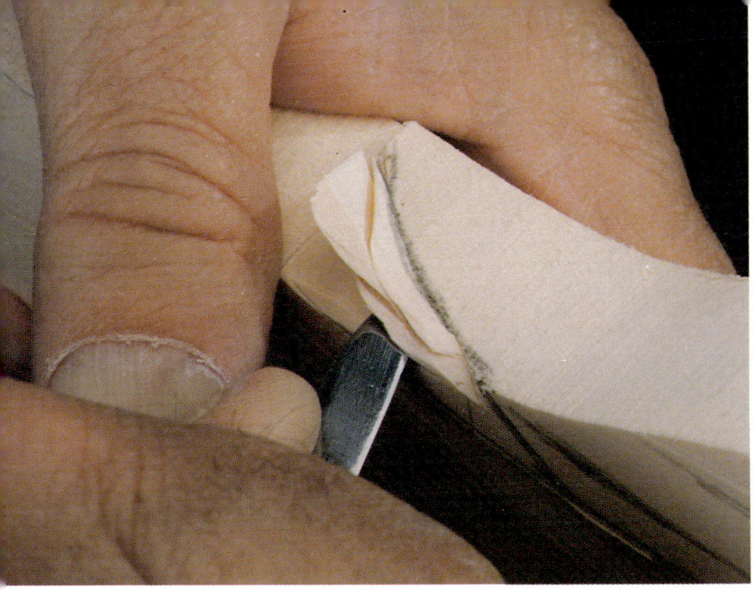

Cut back with your knife to the line you have scored.

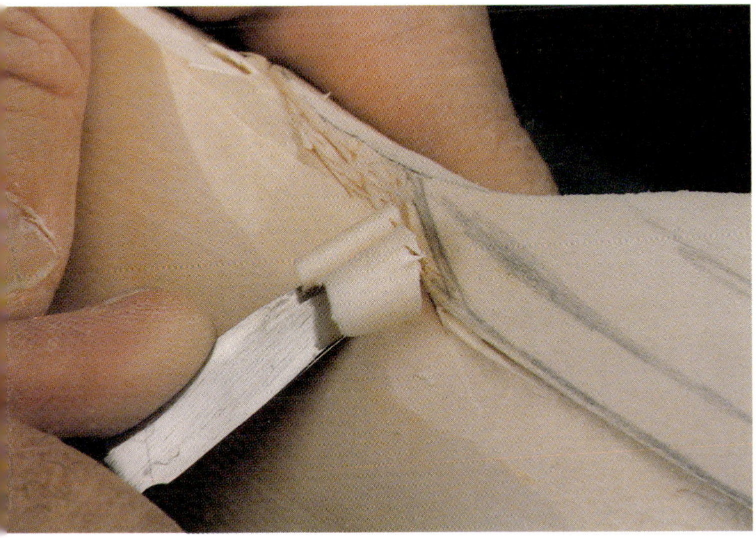

Round the robe in the area we just cut out of the wing.

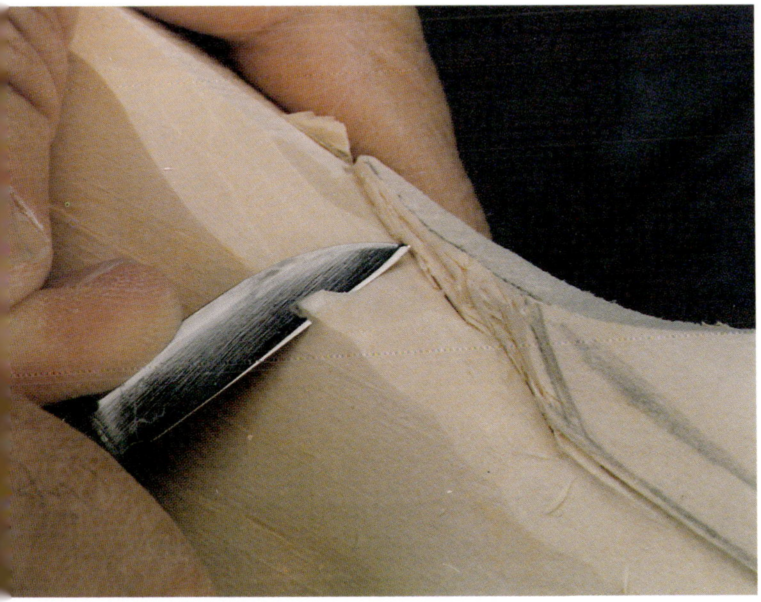

Further rounding the robe into the area of the wing.

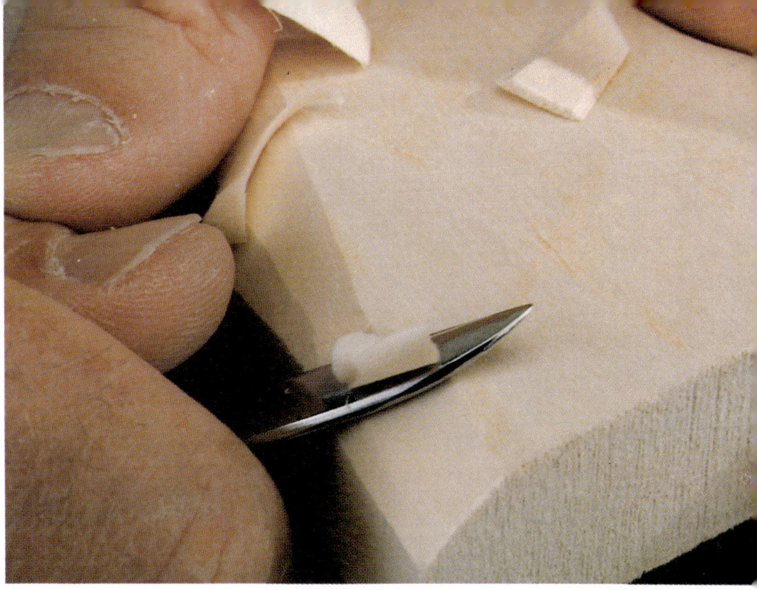

I didn't get a Boy Scout merit badge for carving because I regularly carve toward myself. You'll notice I'm not only carving toward myself, but I'm also using my trusty left thumb to limit the arc of the blade.

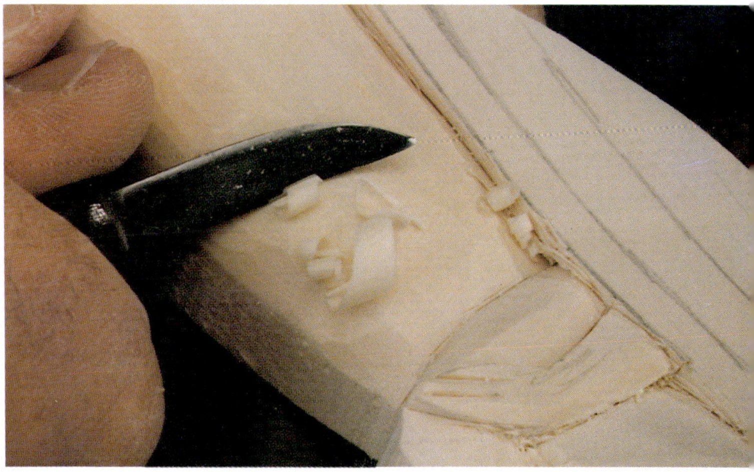

I'm just rounding the robe, moving the blade from side to side to give the robe a symmetrical shape.

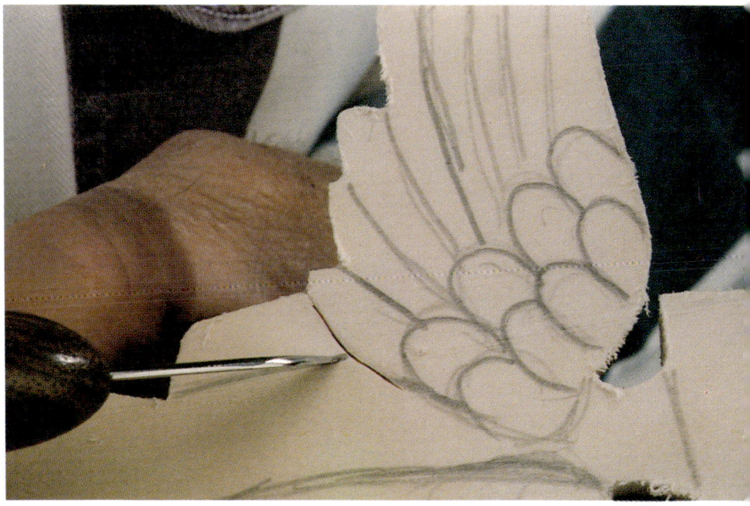

I have darkened these pencil lines in the back to show you where I'm going to incise. Don't worry about cutting these lines off, they can be put back in later. I'm incising the edge of the wings and the left arm.

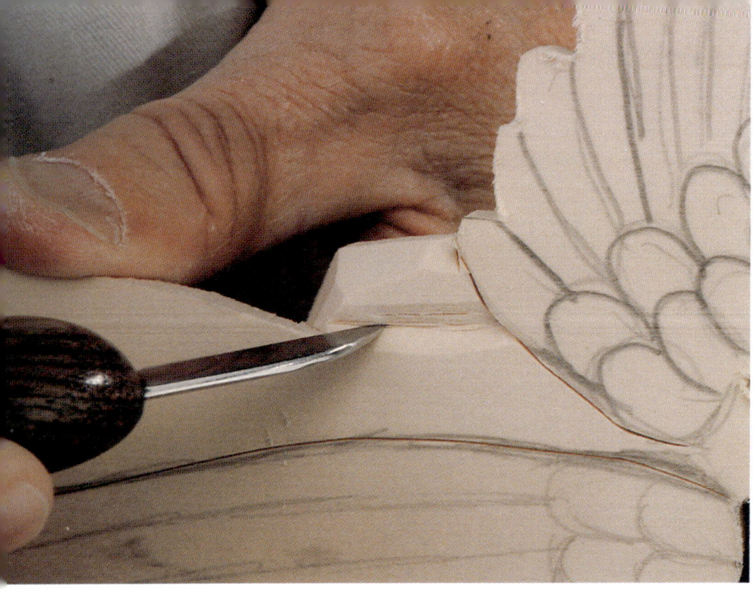

I have made a V cut to show the back of the arm.

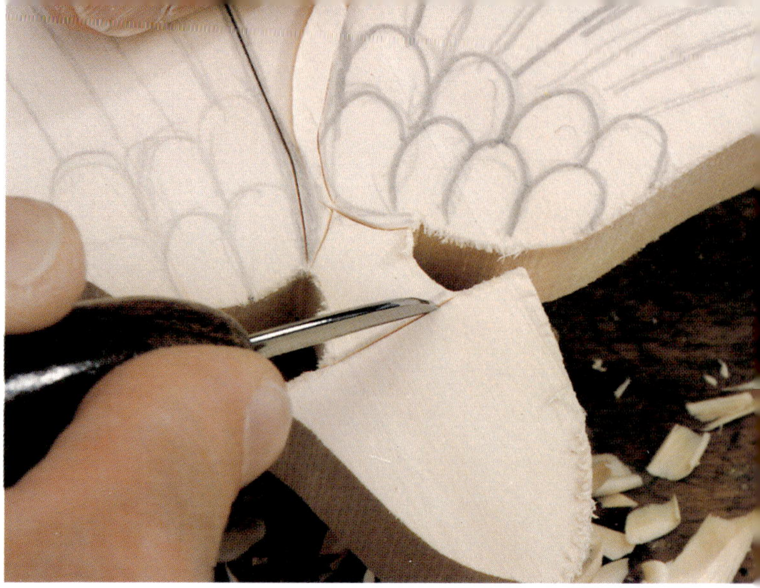

... and incise the hairline.

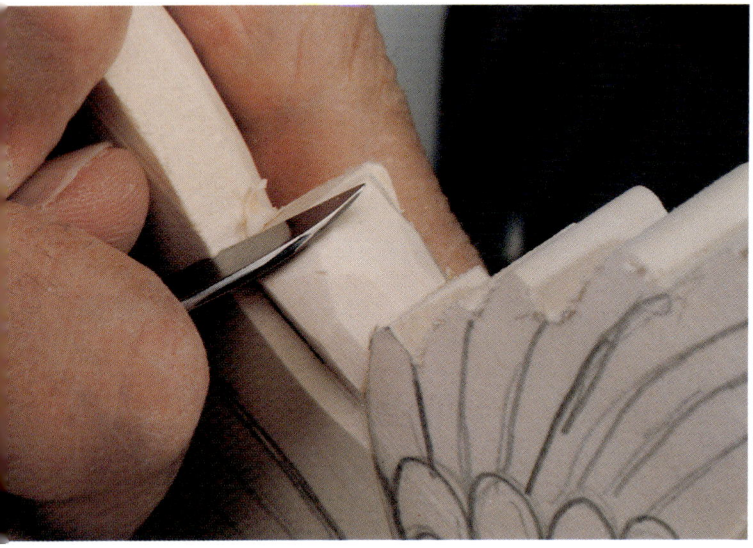

Continue to shape the back of the left arm.

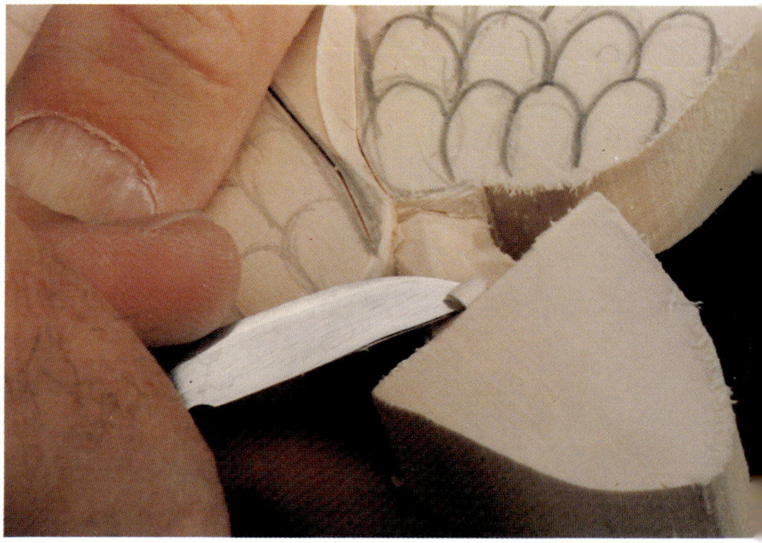

Rounding the neck up into the hairline.

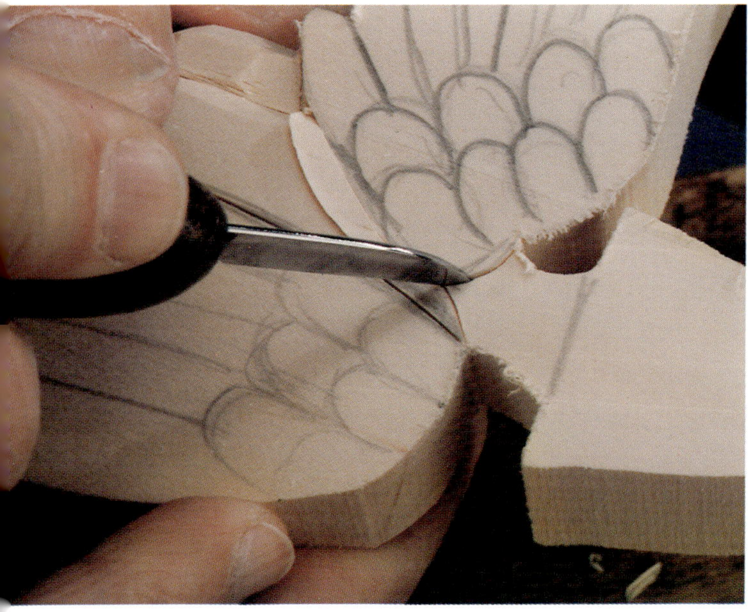

Incise the tops of the wings in the back ...

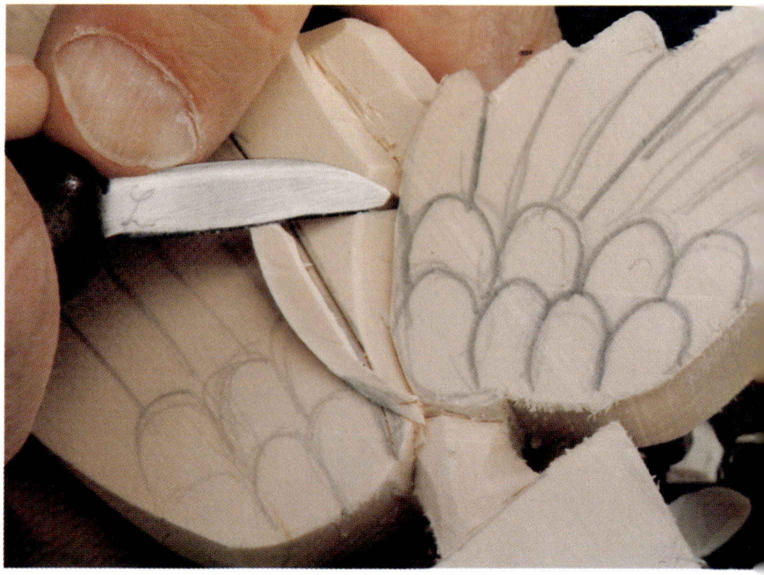

Where you have incised the wing, go back at an angle and the wood should pop right out.

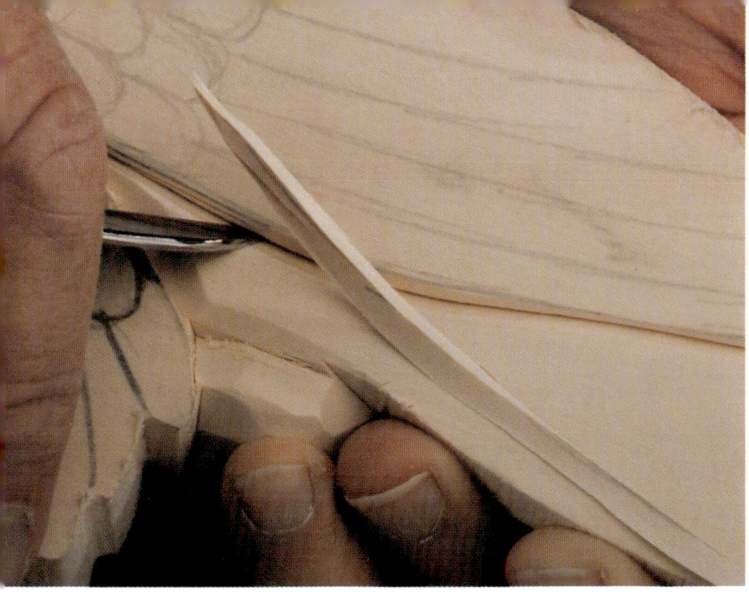

You have incised along the folded wing as well. Go back in at an angle and pop out the longer strip of wood as well. You don't have to take it out all in one piece.

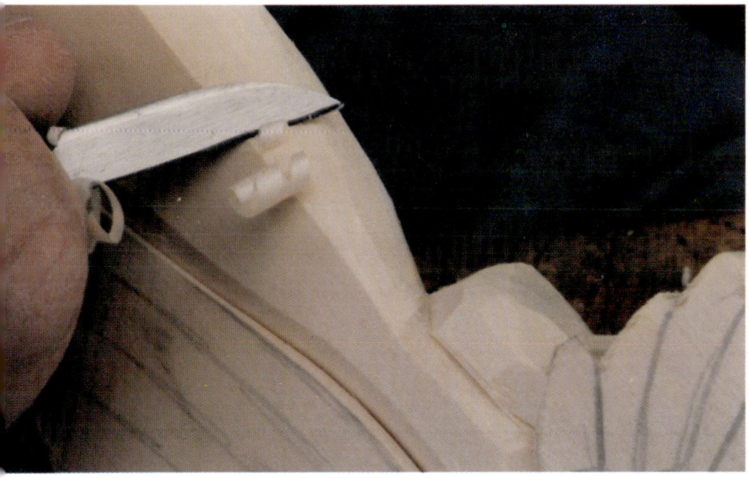

Start rounding the back side of the robe.

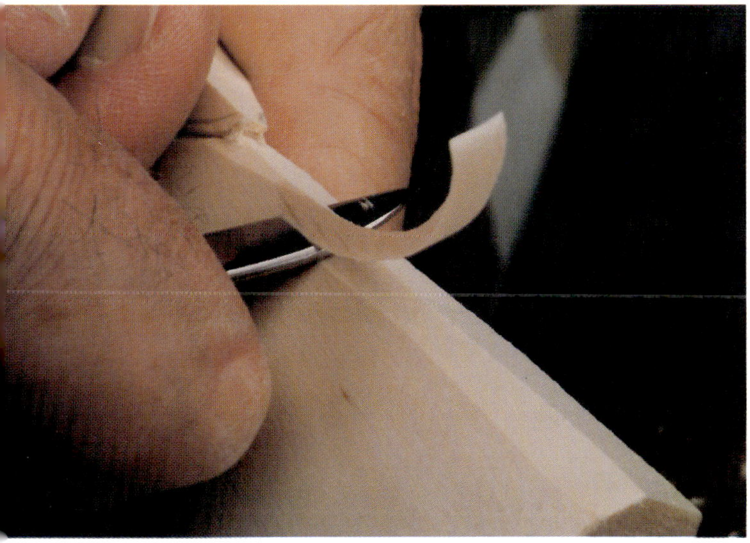

Round the other side of the back of the robe. Notice again how I am holding my thumbs, limiting the length of my cut to avoid cutting myself.

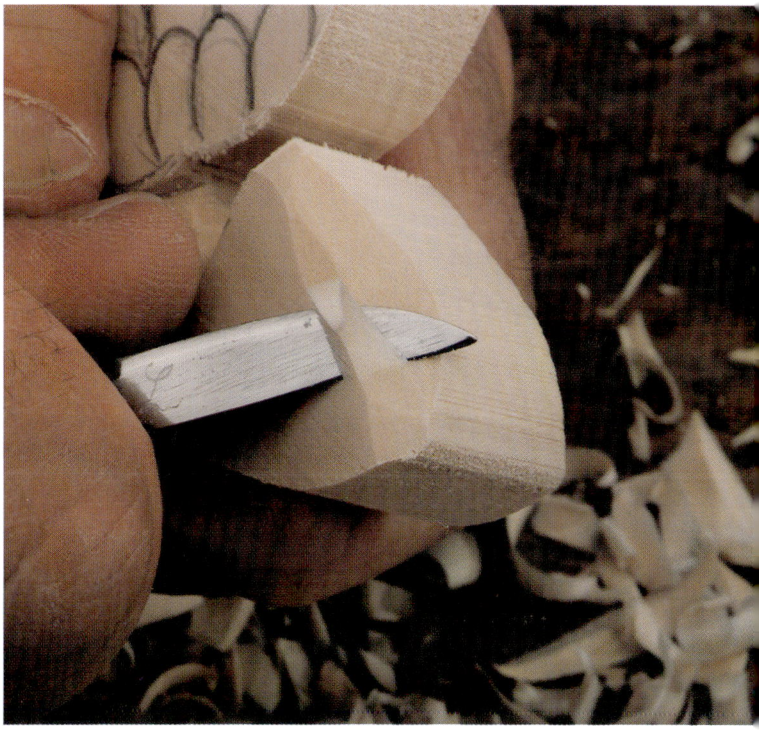

Begin to shape the hair on the back of the head.

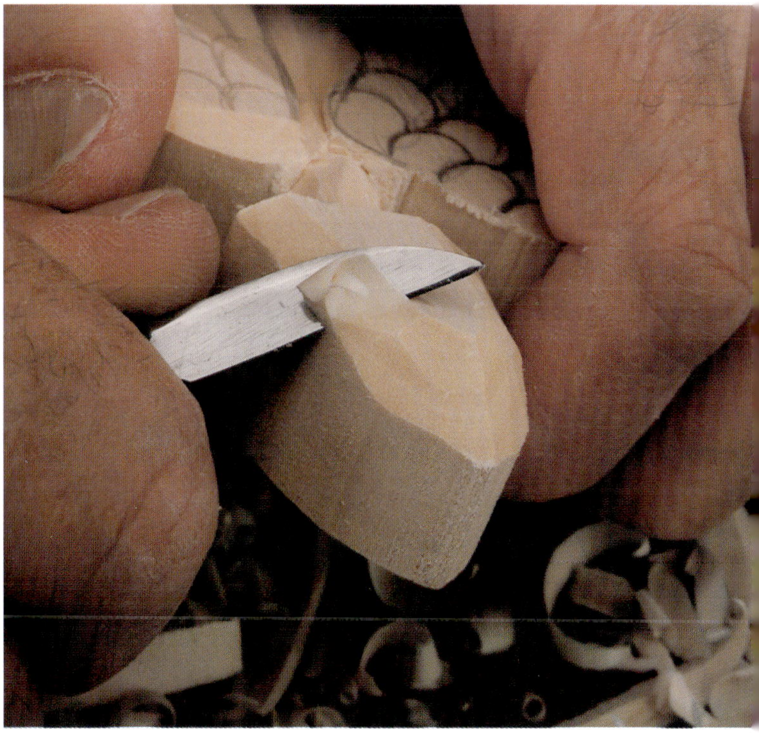

Rounding the other side of the hair.

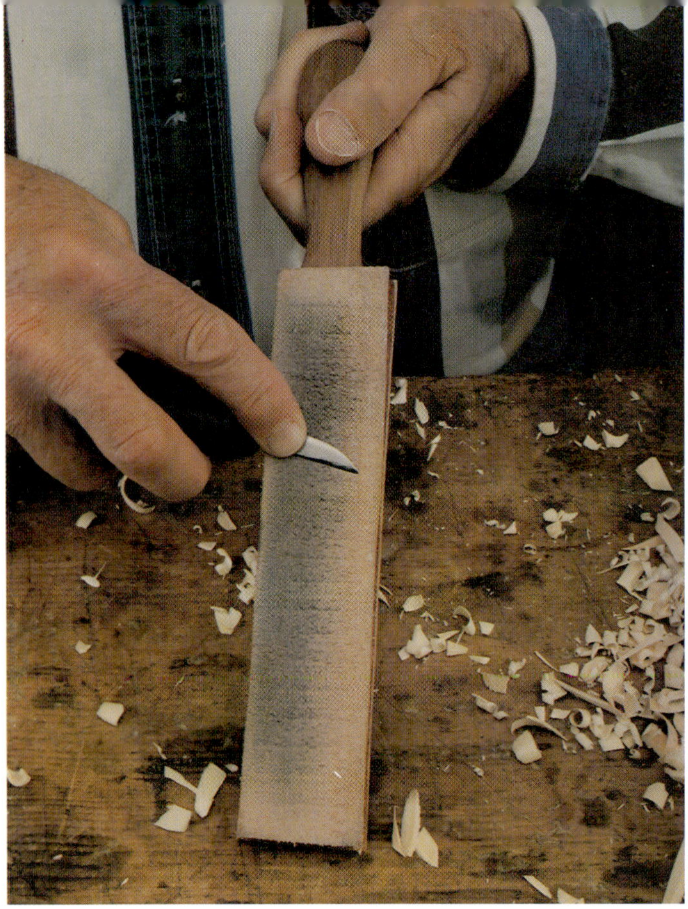

It is a good idea to stop periodically and hone your knife a bit on a leather strop. I suggest doing this about every 20 minutes. A couple of times on the rough side where you have sprinkled some aluminum oxide powder.

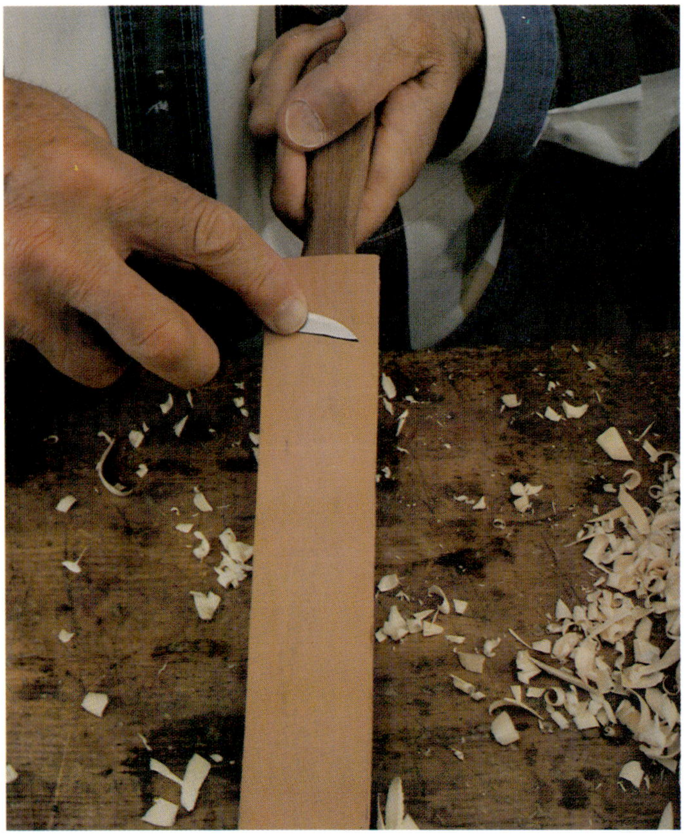

Then a couple times on the smooth side.

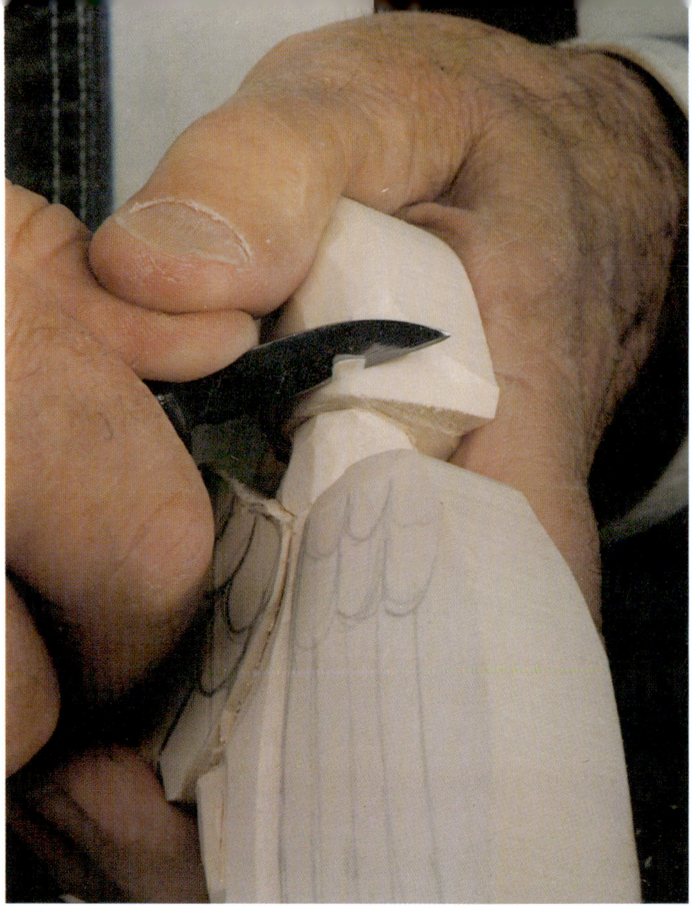

Continue to shape the hair.

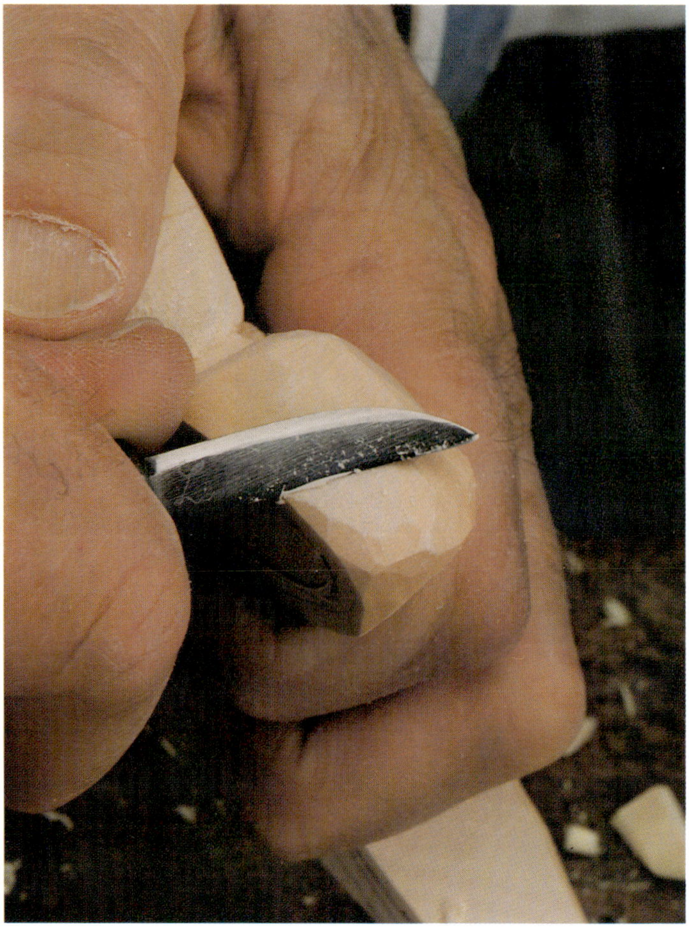

Smoothing, rounding, and removing the saw marks.

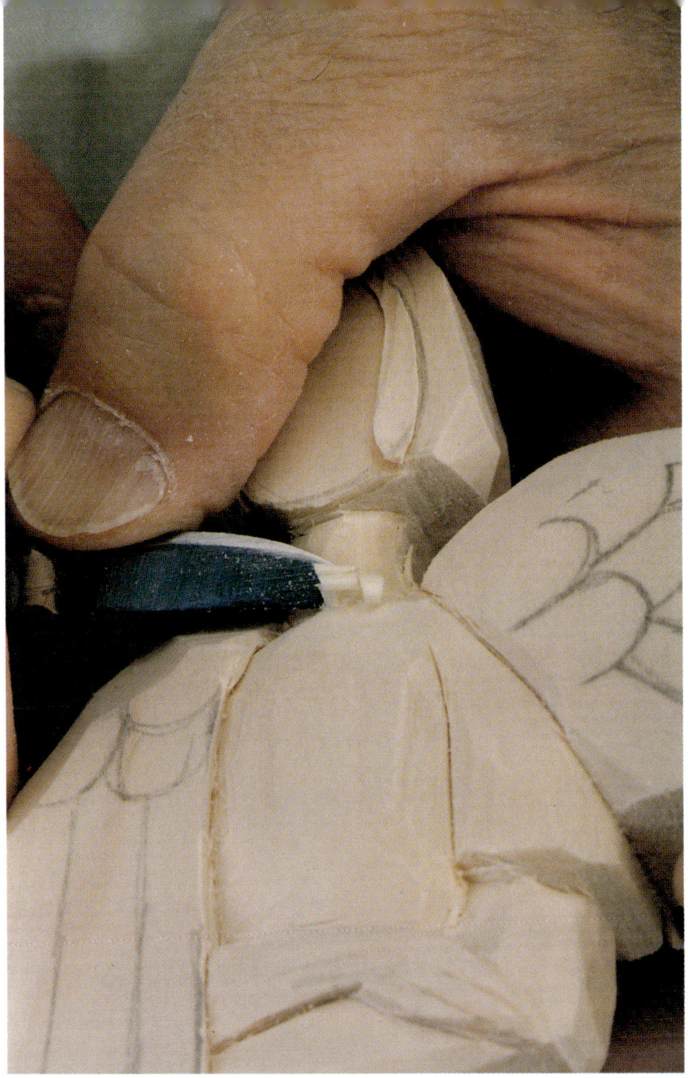

Shaping the neck.

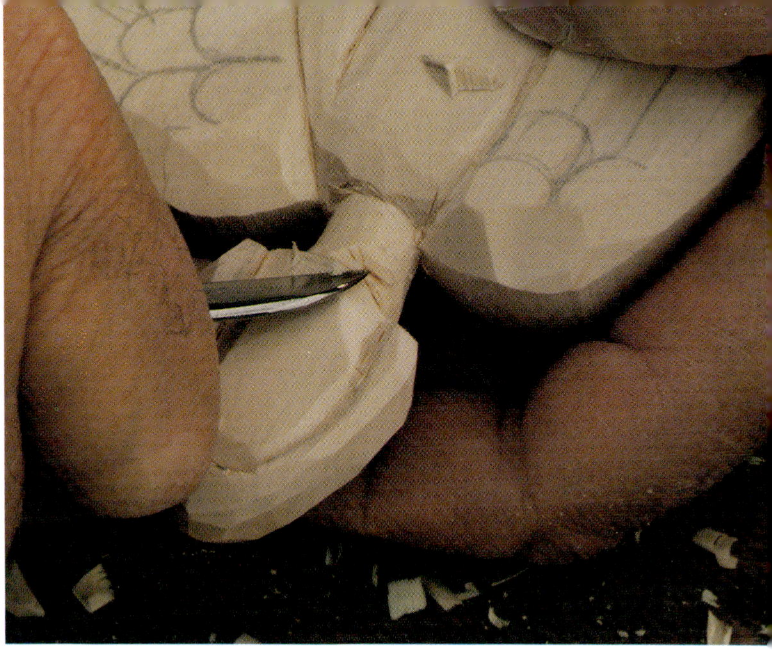

Beginning to shape the face.

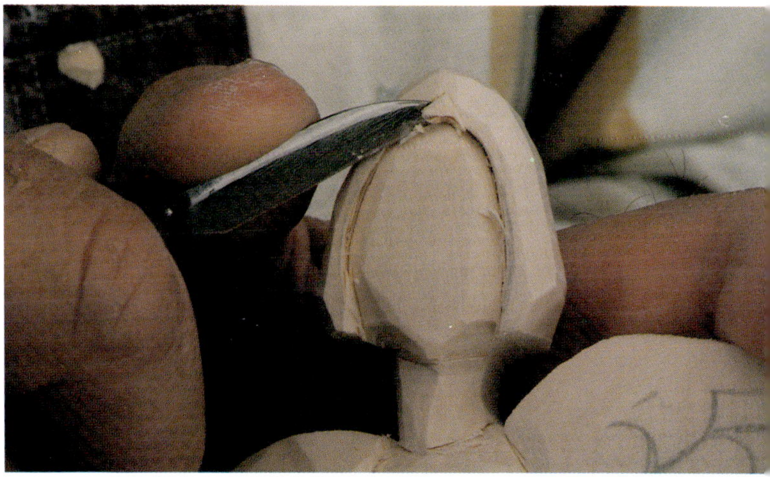

Make a little V at the top of the hair line.

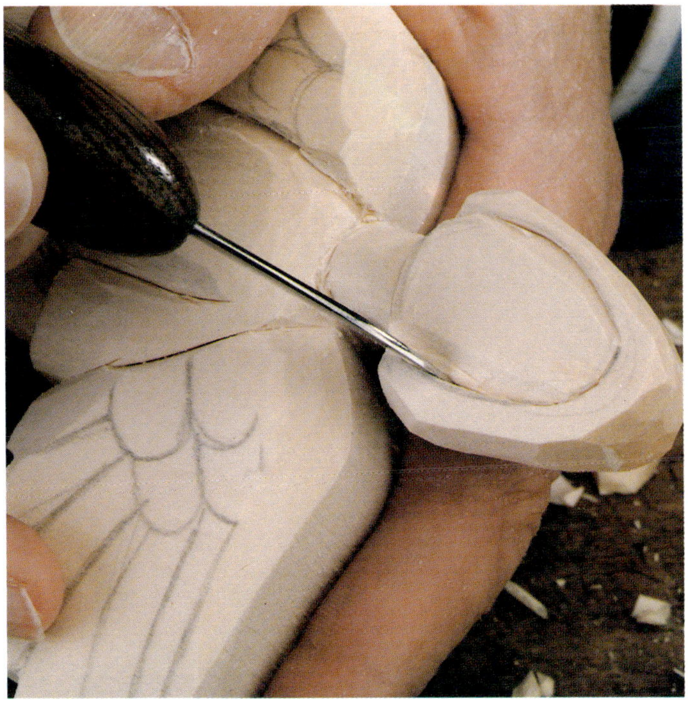

I have scored a line between the face and the hair and I am beginning to round the face.

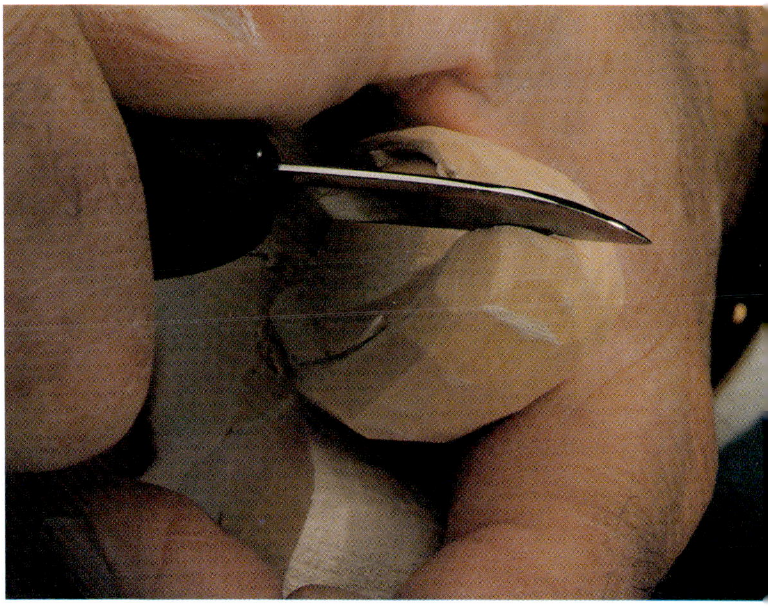

Lay the knife in and make a part at the top of the hair.

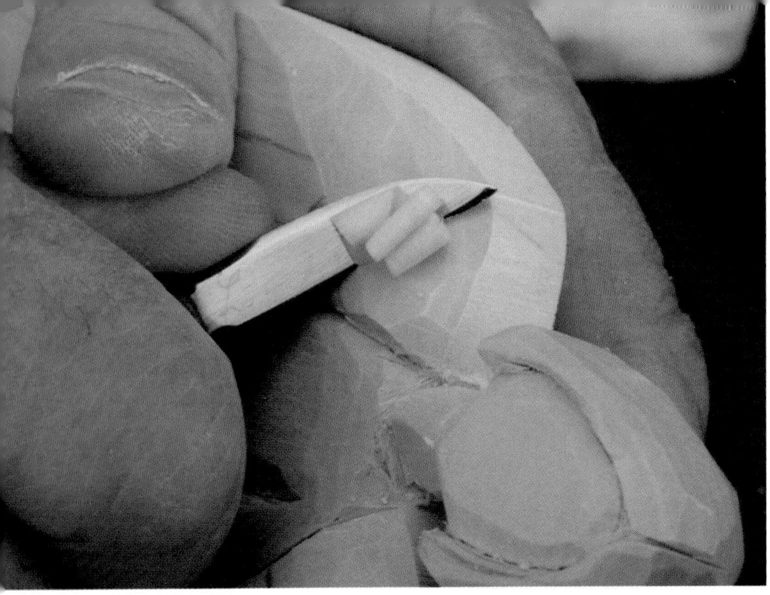

With a piece this small, you have to go back and forth to different areas to keep the proportions proper. So I am going to leave the face now for the wings which are large and important areas. I am going to start by rounding the shoulder of the wing draped next to the body. Again, don't be concerned about cutting the lines off. We will put them back later.

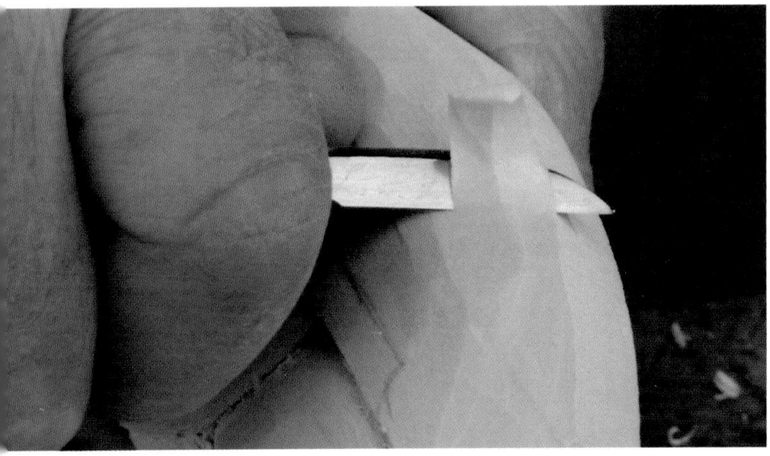

Rounding the wing.

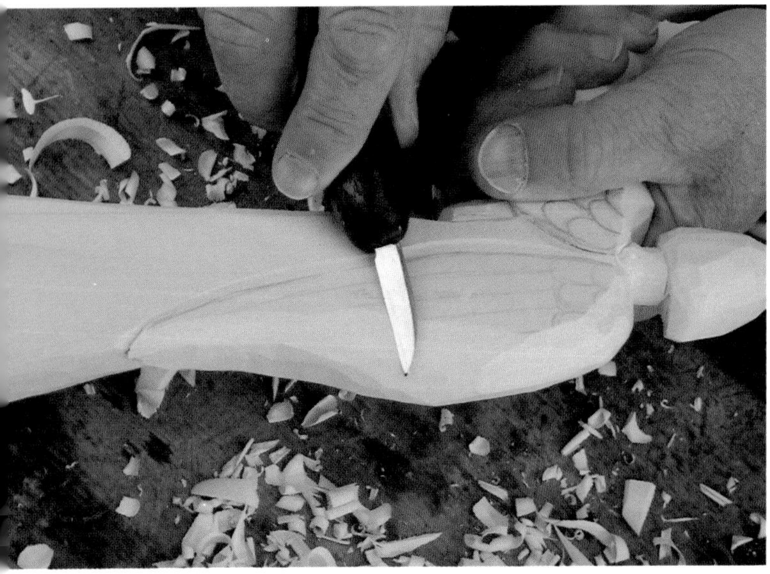

The rounded wing.

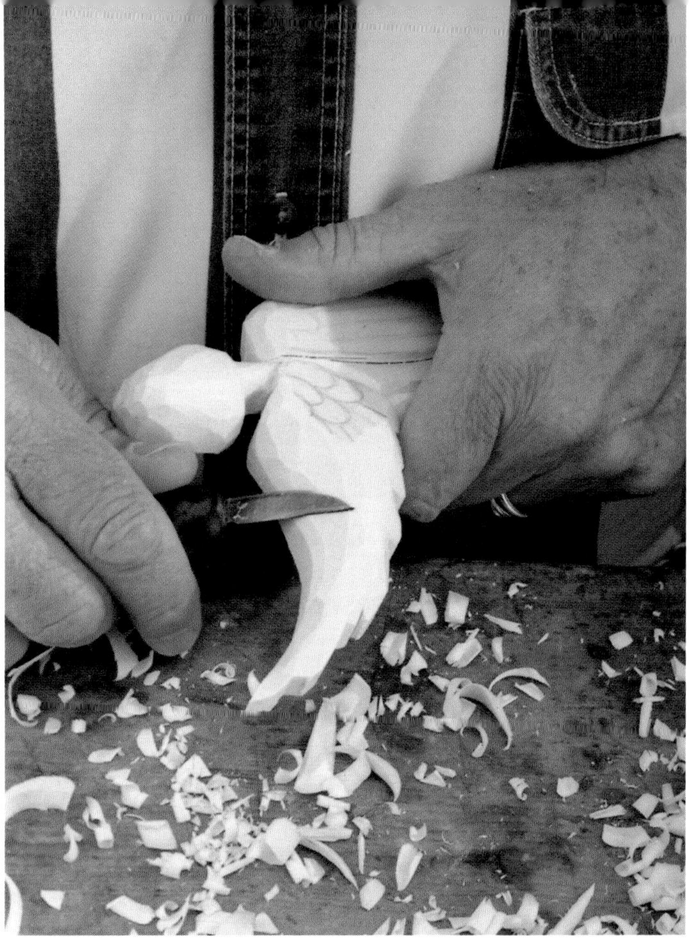

Rounding the extended wing, top and bottom. Be careful, your wood is getting thin here and it would be very easy to slip and ruin this piece.

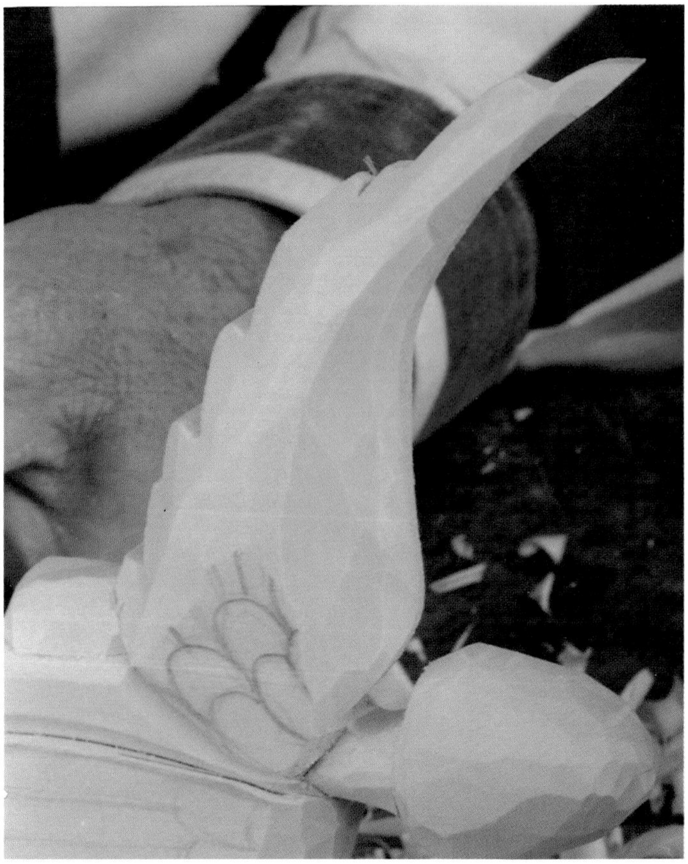

Continue rounding.

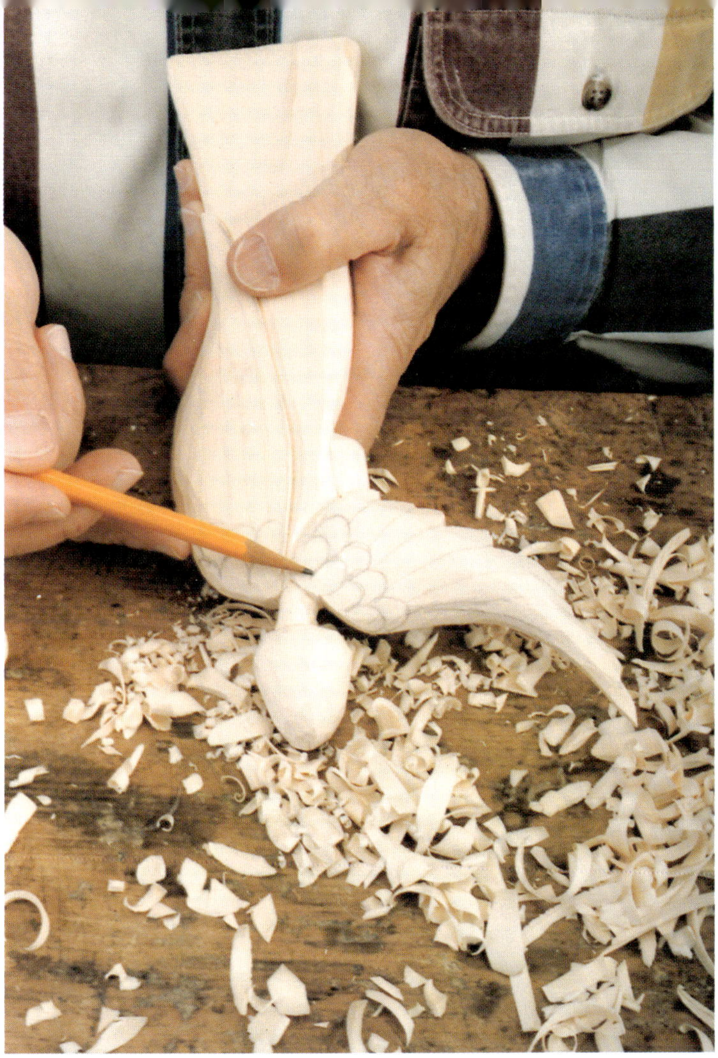

I have drawn the lines back in now that I have the wings shaped.

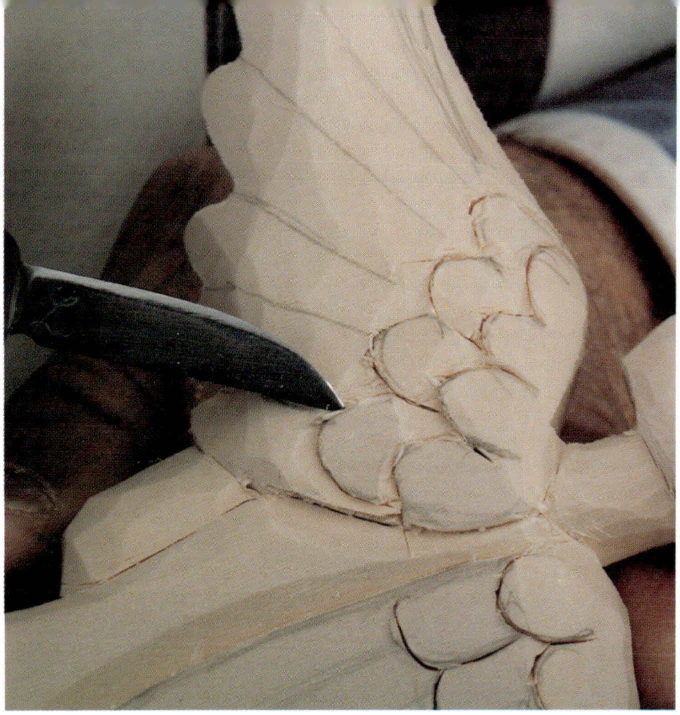

After incising, come back with your knife at an angle and gently cut away underneath the feathers.

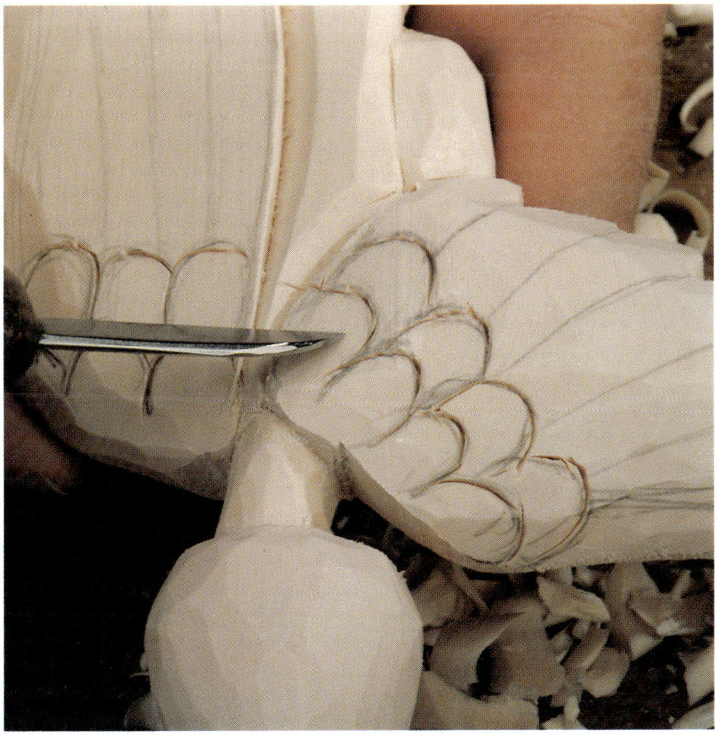

I have incised the feathers at the top of the wing on both sides now.

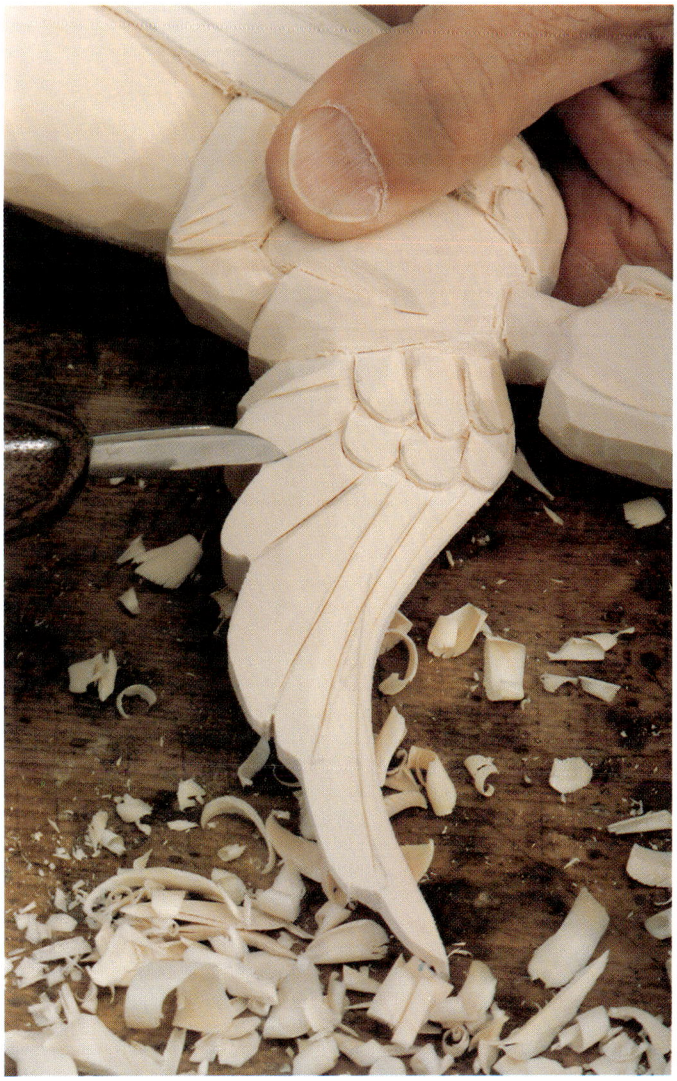

Incise each long feather along the wing.

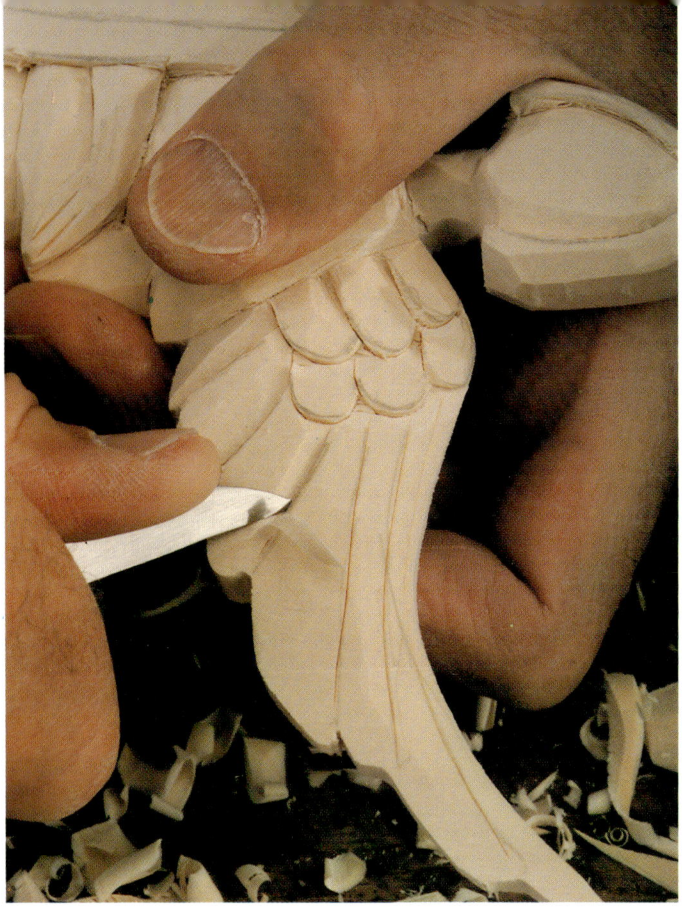

Cut back at an angle to undercut the feathers.

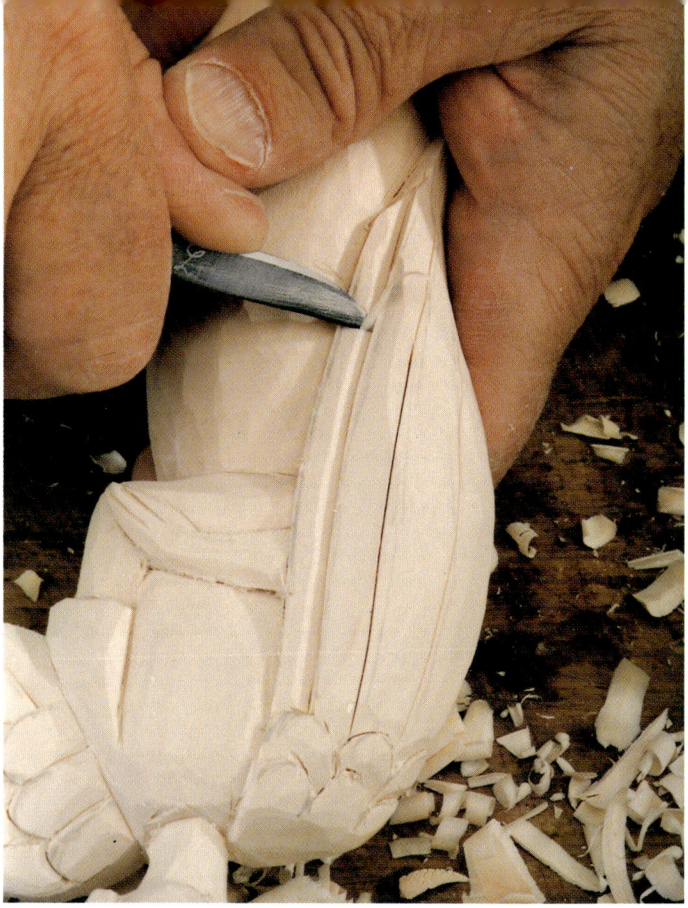

Go back and undercut along the long feathers of the draped wing.

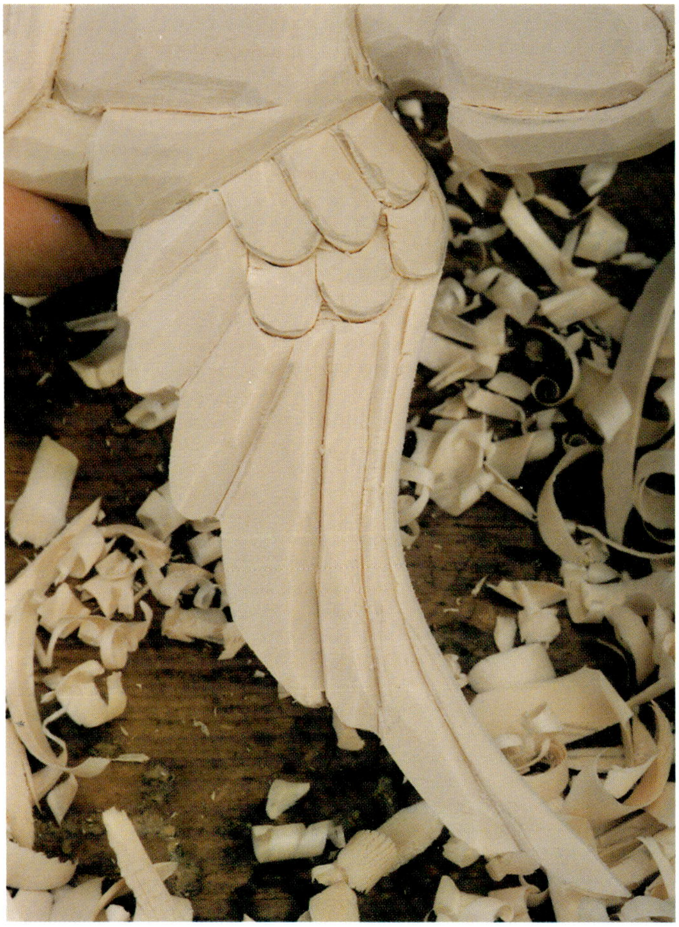

The incised wing. Repeat this process on the other wing.

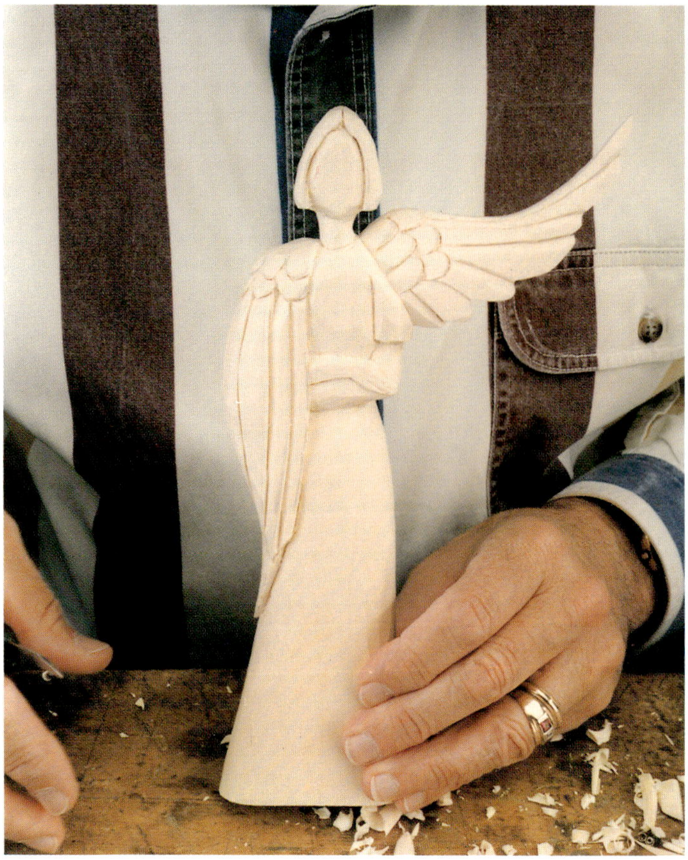

This angel is basically complete. I'll go back and check for some "fuzzies." I may use a little sandpaper, although I prefer to avoid it. I still may need to do a little sanding before I paint.

Angel Two

This is a good size and can be painted subtly or boldly.

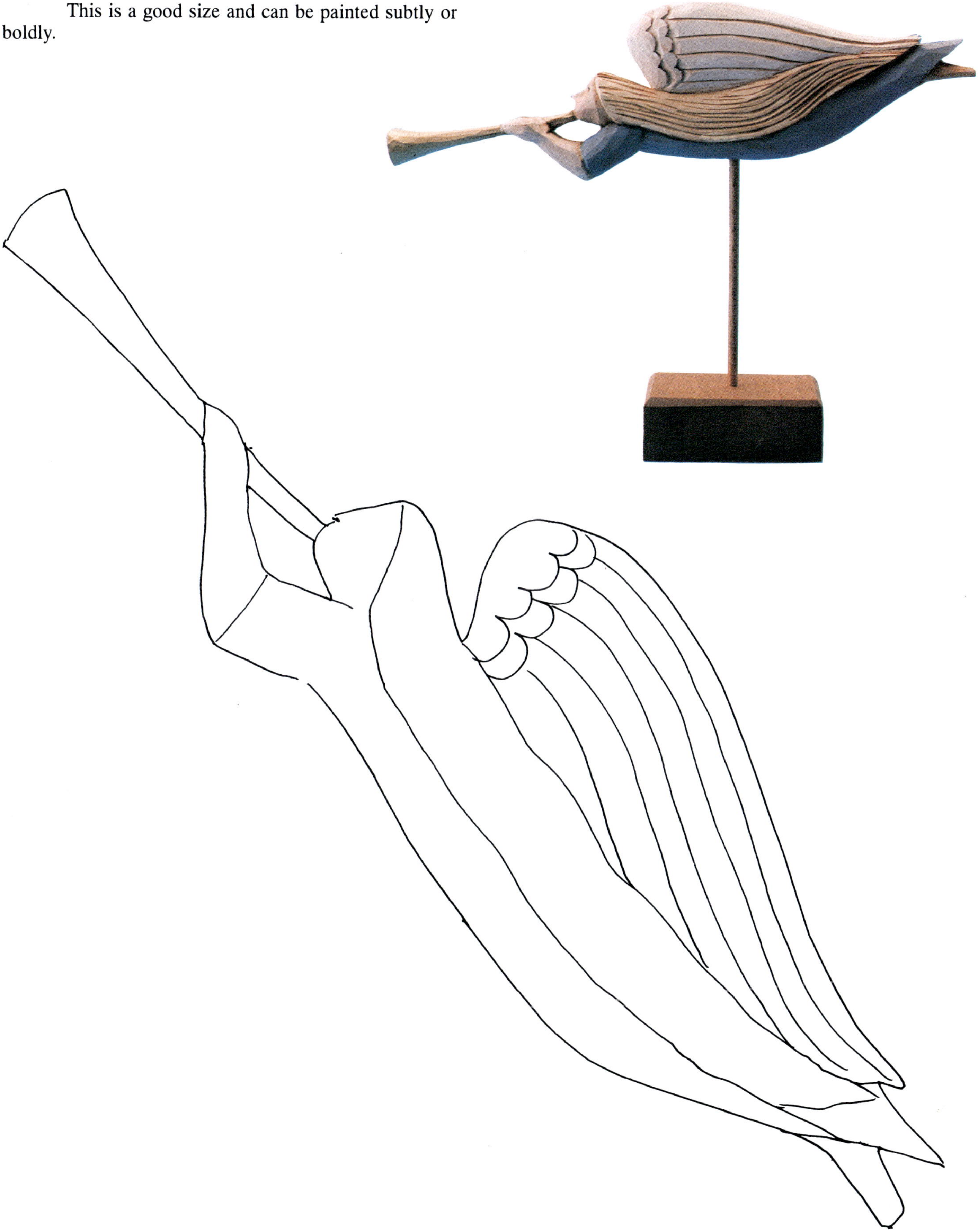

The rough of the winged angel with trumpet.

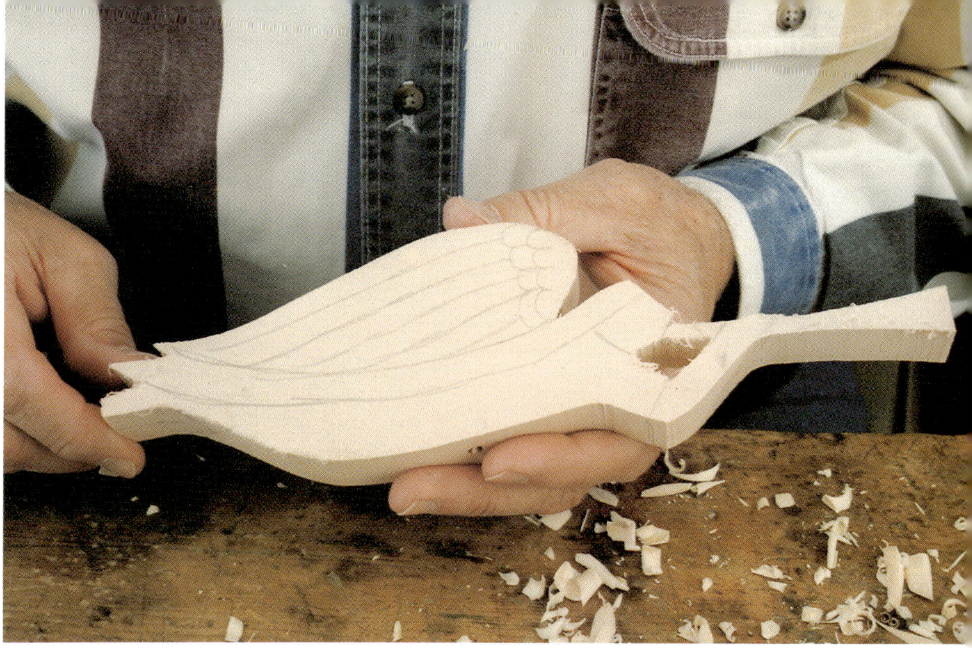

Incising the hair lines to start with.

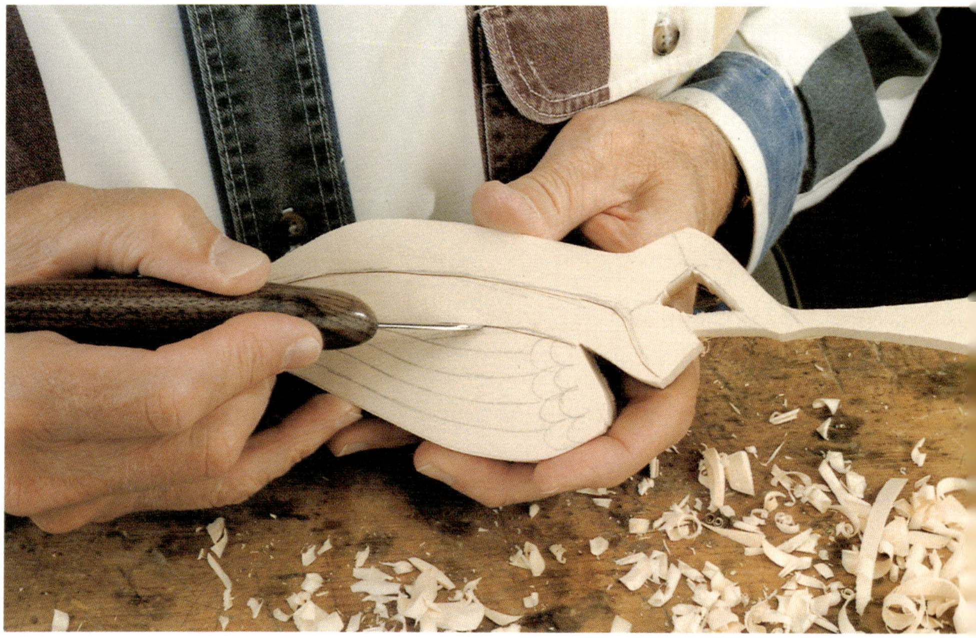

As this is a small piece, a center line is helpful. Draw in your center line to keep your carving in proportion on both sides of the line.

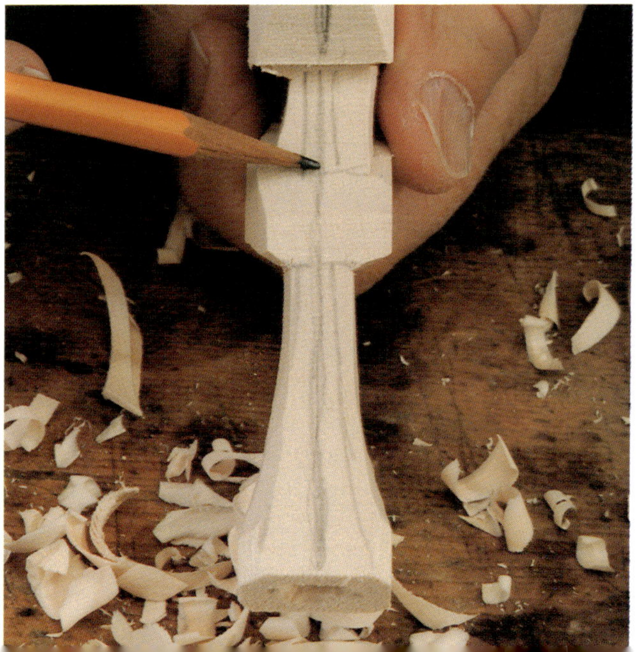

Use a gouge before you thin down the trumpet too much and take a little piece out of the front. You can also drill out this area.

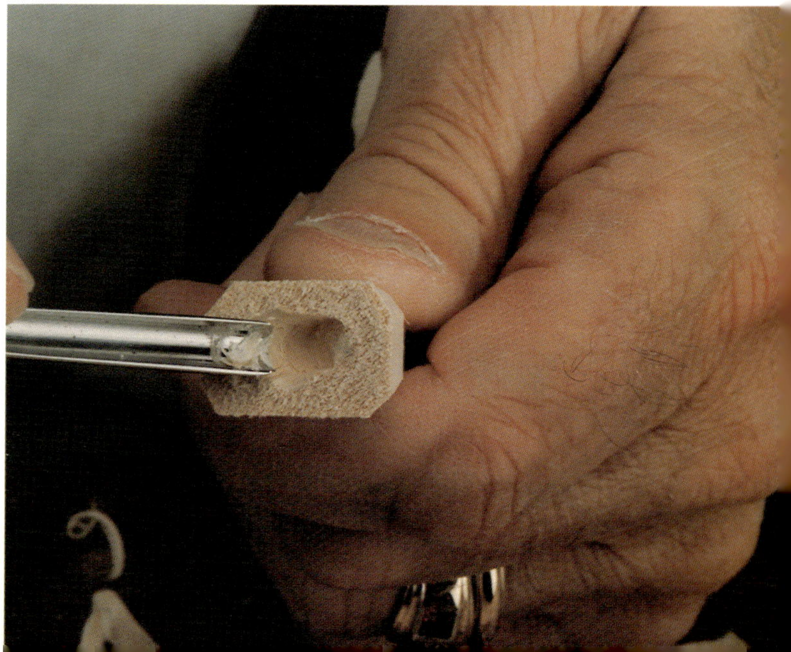

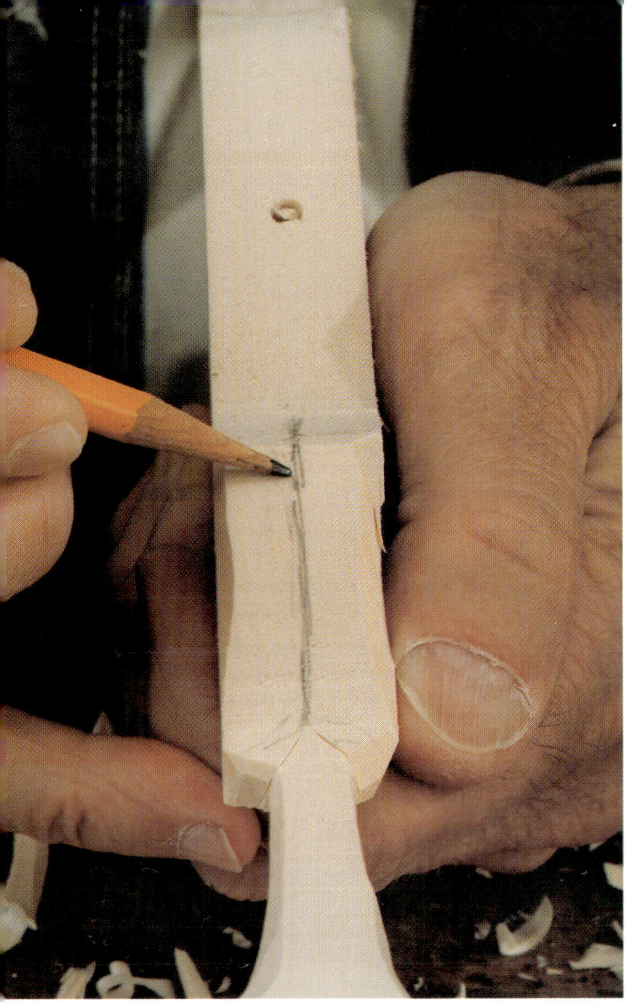

Draw a pencil line to divide the arms.

Make a deep incision between the two arms.

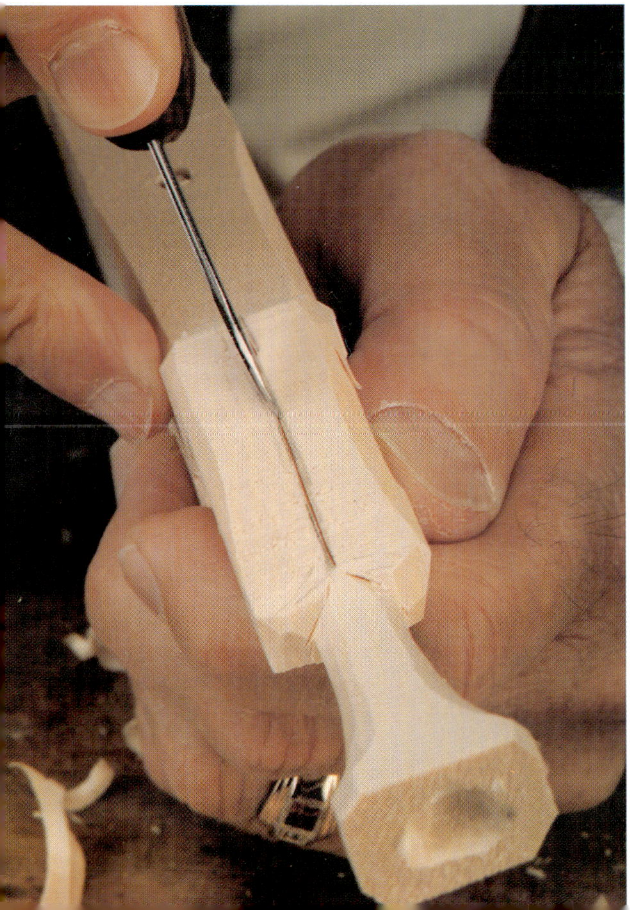

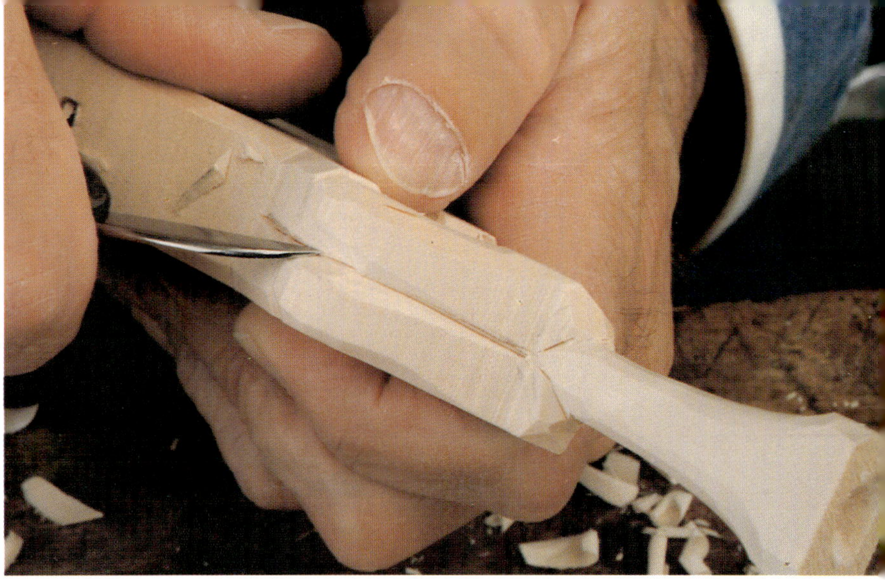

Come back and make a nice deep V cut to separate the arms.

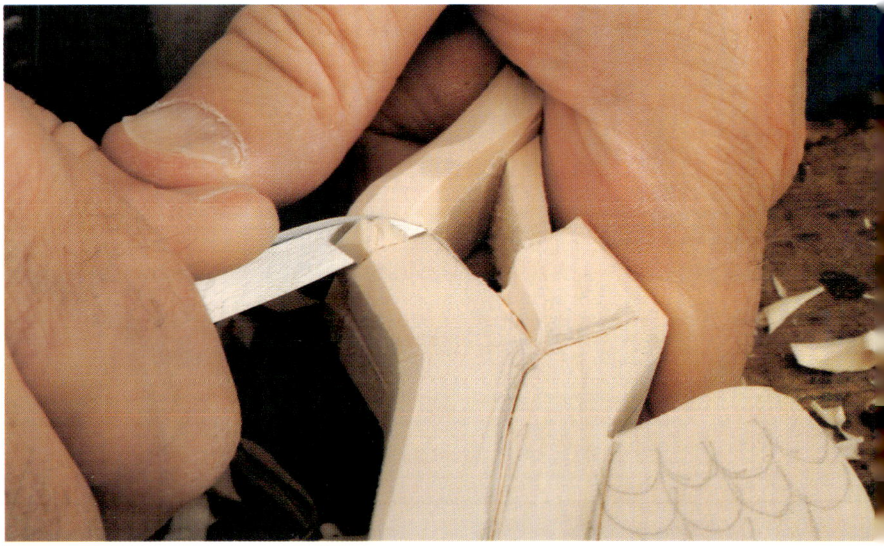

Cut the arms back into the sleeves of the robe.

Putting some shape in the arms where the arms and the hands come together.

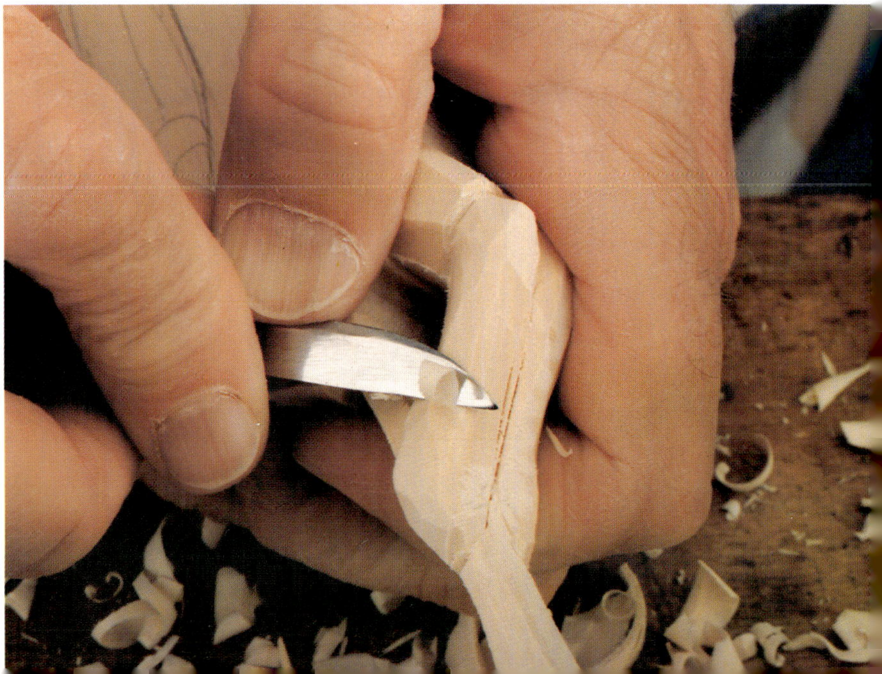

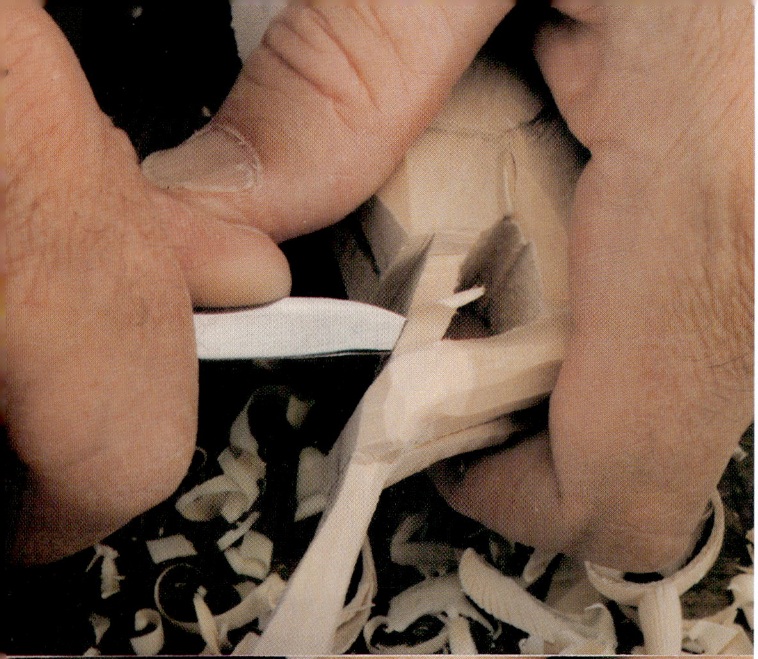

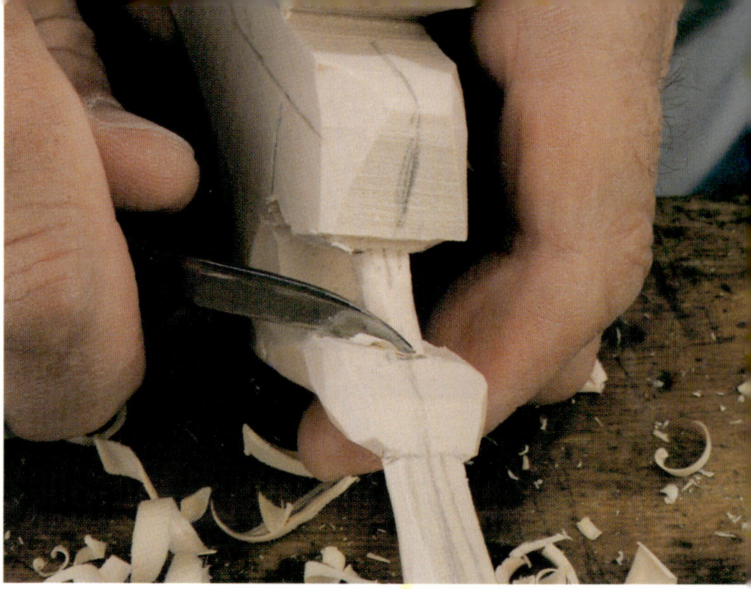

Cut away the lines, rounding the trumpet between the mouth and hands.

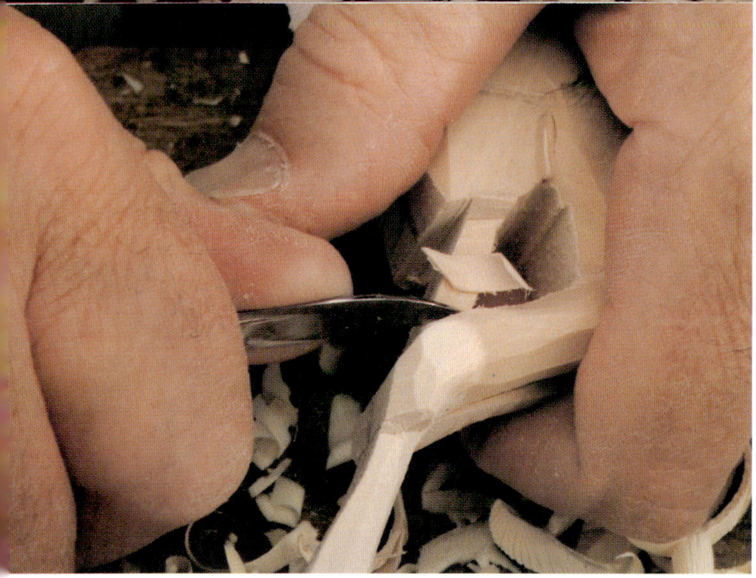

Cut along the length of the trumpet from the mouth toward the hands and cut off the wood chip at the hand.

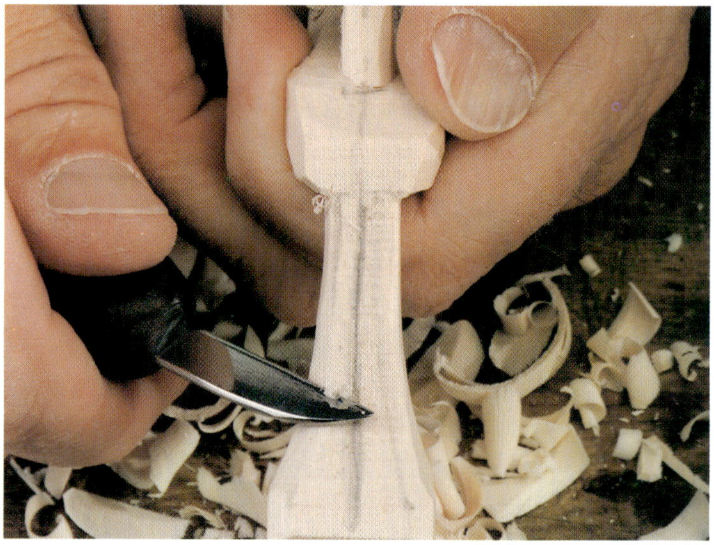

Using the center line of your trumpet as a guide, continue rounding the trumpet beyond the hands.

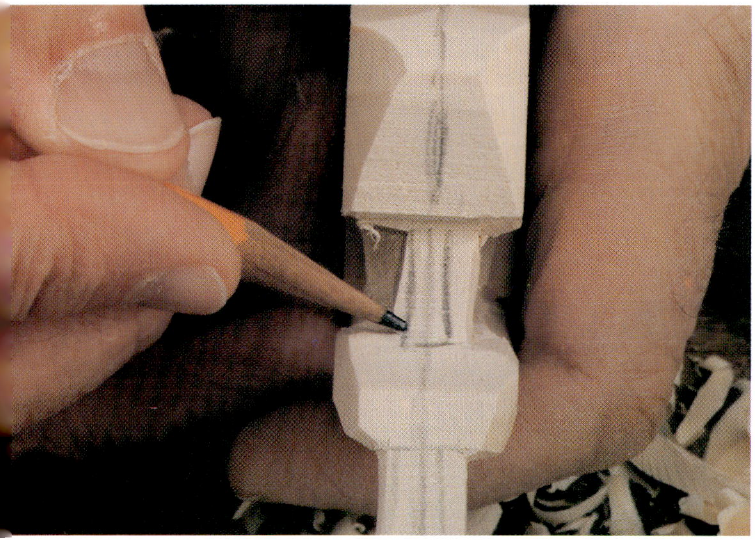

Continue to trim back to the trumpet pattern lines between the mouth and the hands.

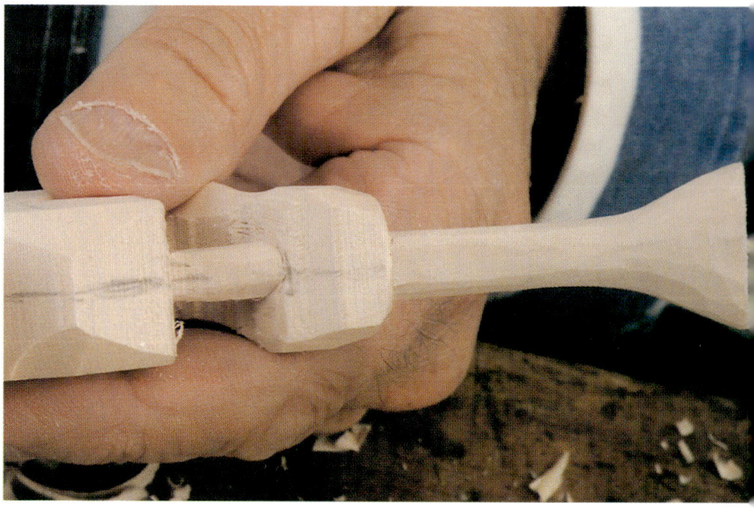

The reason I carve the trumpet first is that if I foul up the bell end, I can change the shape and make my angel a clarinet player. The trumpet is now rounded pretty much like I want it.

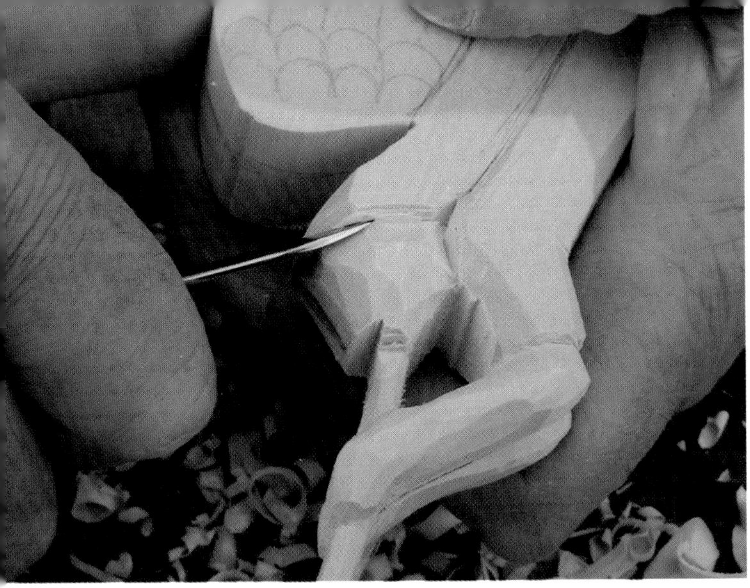

Cutting the face into the hair.

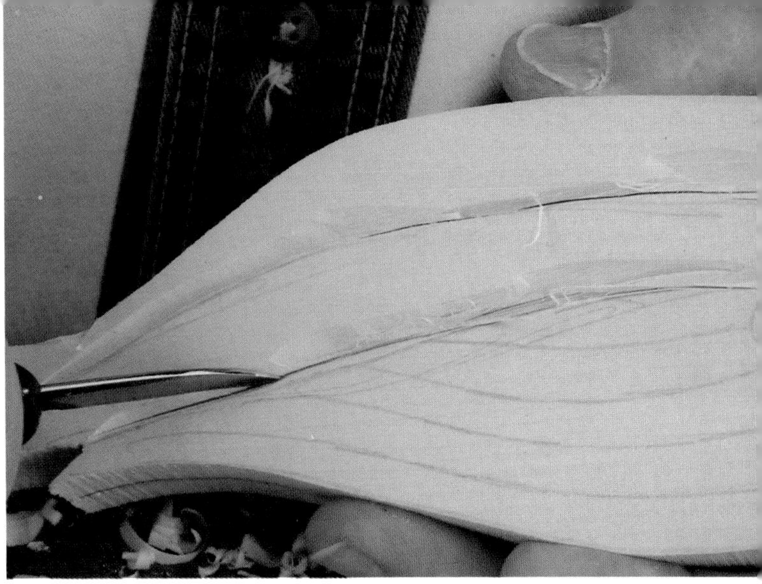

Undercut the top of the flowing hair into the bottom of the wing.

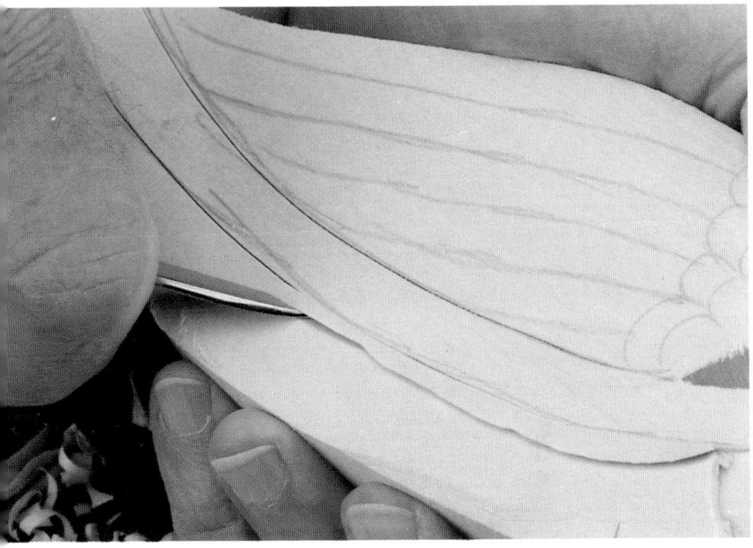

Undercut the robe into the long hair line.

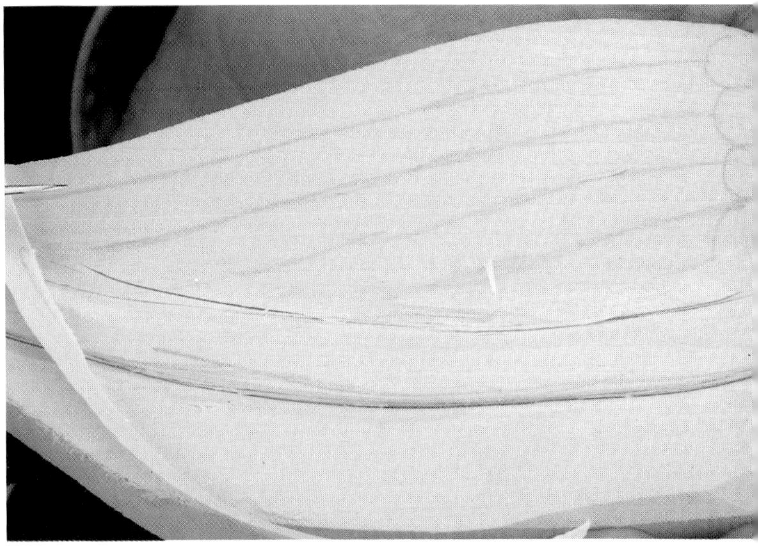

Repeat this process on the other side.

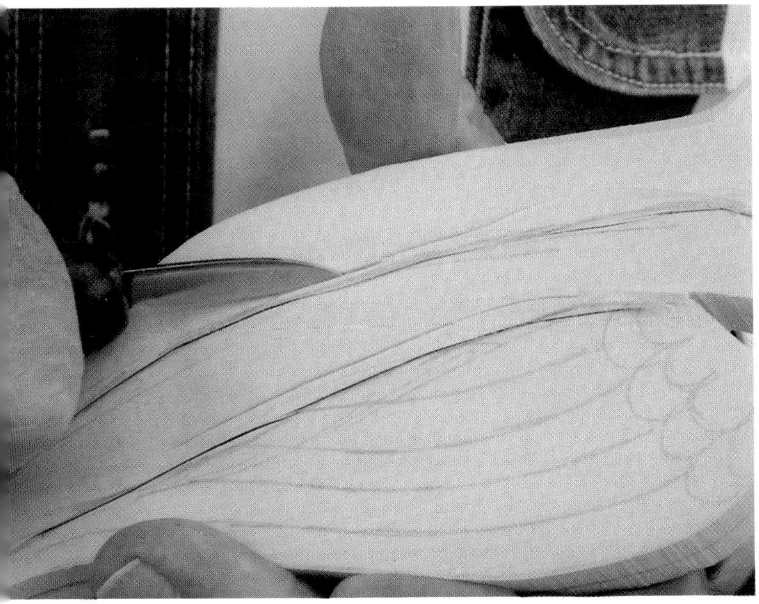

Repeat this undercutting on the other side.

Add a center line down the bottom of the angel. This line will give you something to carve to when you start rounding. You want each side to be roughly the same.

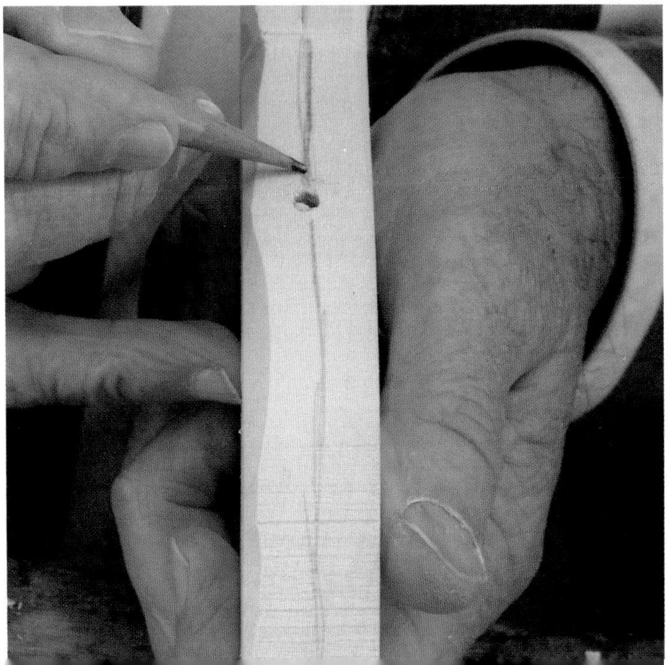

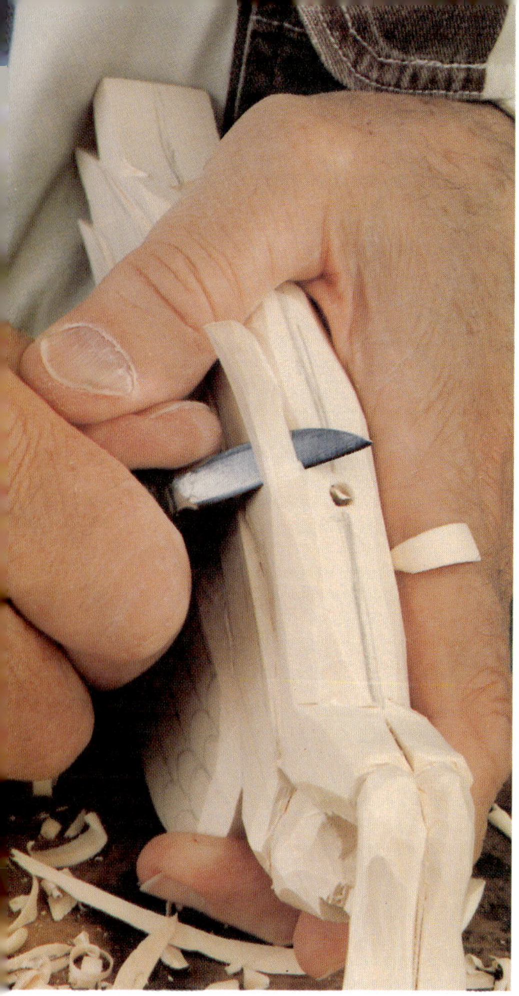

I've started to round the bottom side of the robe.

Incising and cutting a line to separate the two feet.

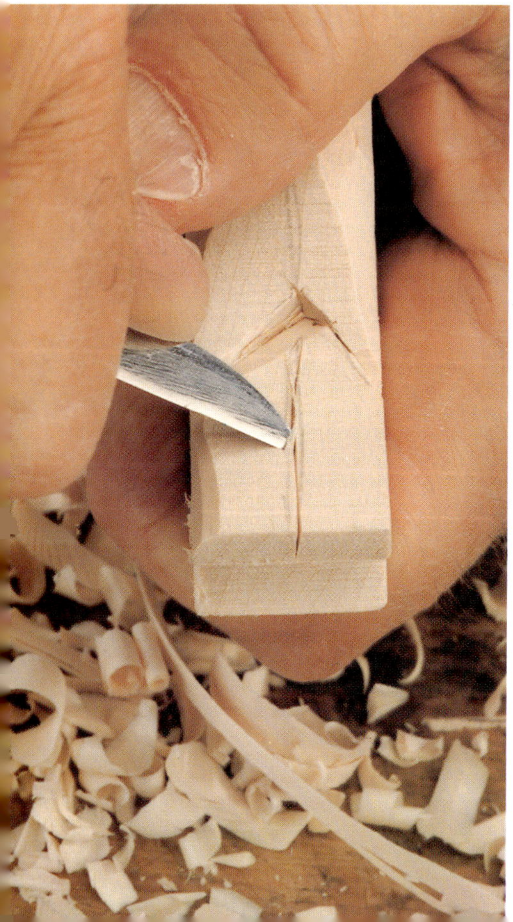

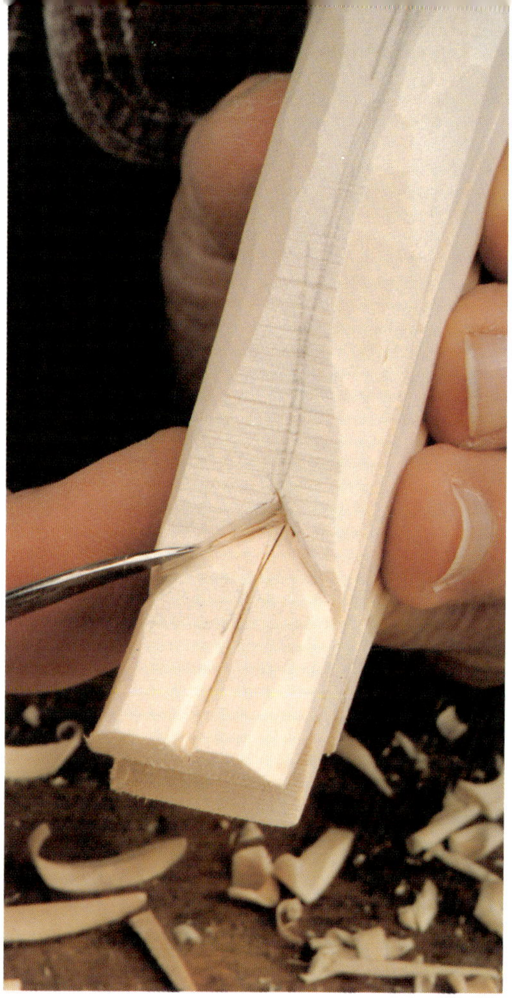

Cut out a little V shape where the feet go into the robe.

As I round the bottom, I go from side-to-side to be sure that the bottom remains symmetrical.

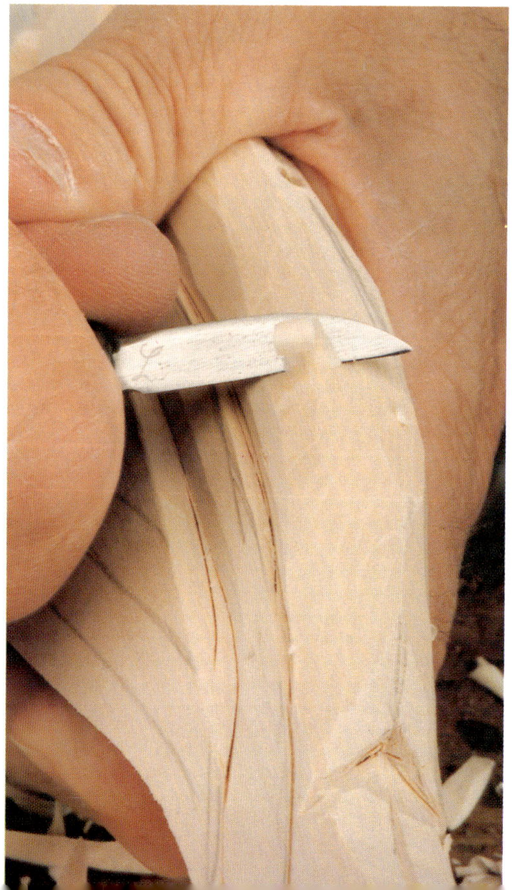

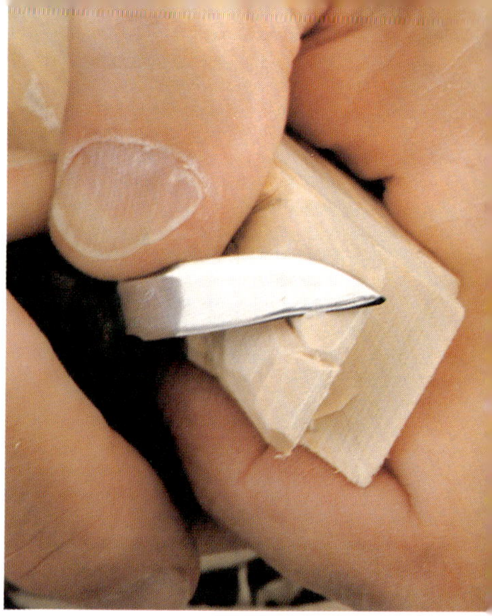

This angel is going to have bare feet. Start shaping the feet.

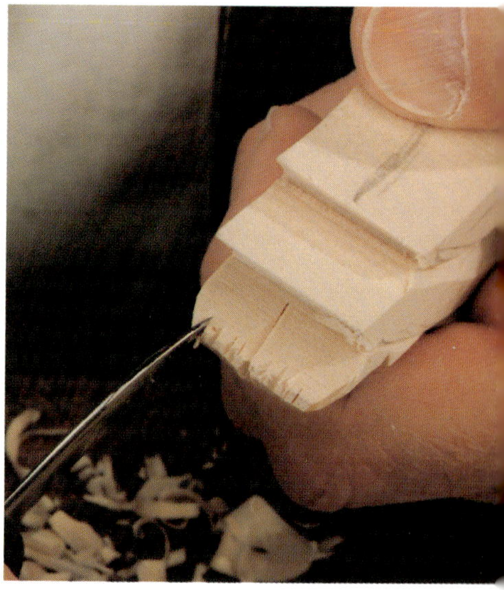

Make small indentations with your knife and carefully trim out the spaces between the toes. An antiquing process used later will bring out the details of the toes.

Repeat on the other side of the toes. If you have trouble with the toes, make slippers.

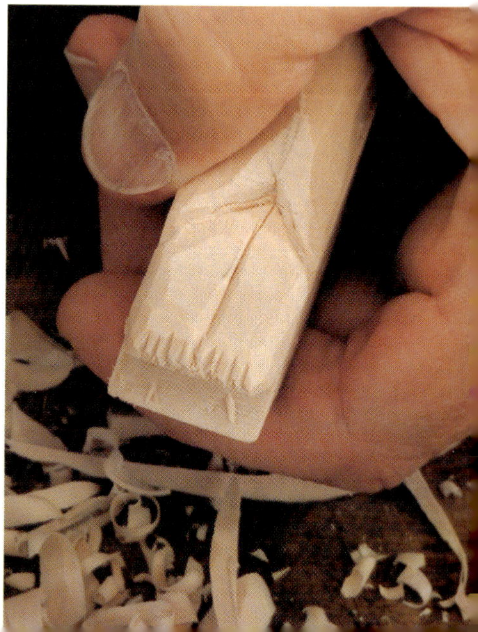

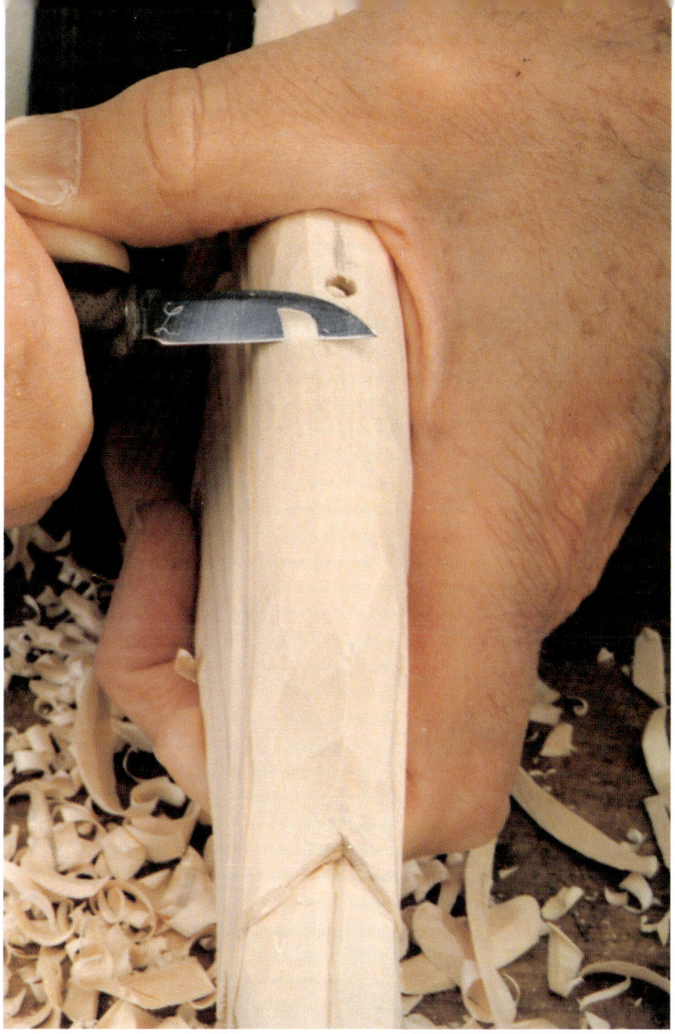

Turning the carving from side-to-side and continuing to take off the rougher places.

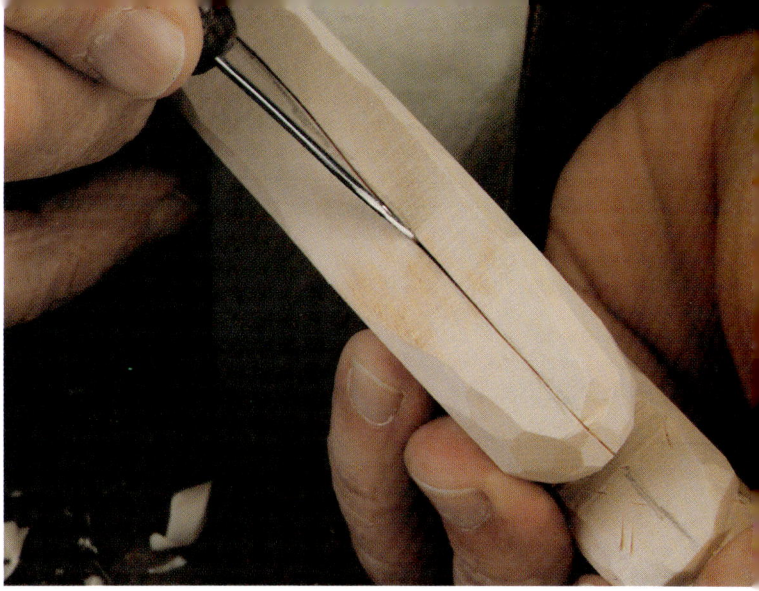

Cut a deep line down the center of the wings.

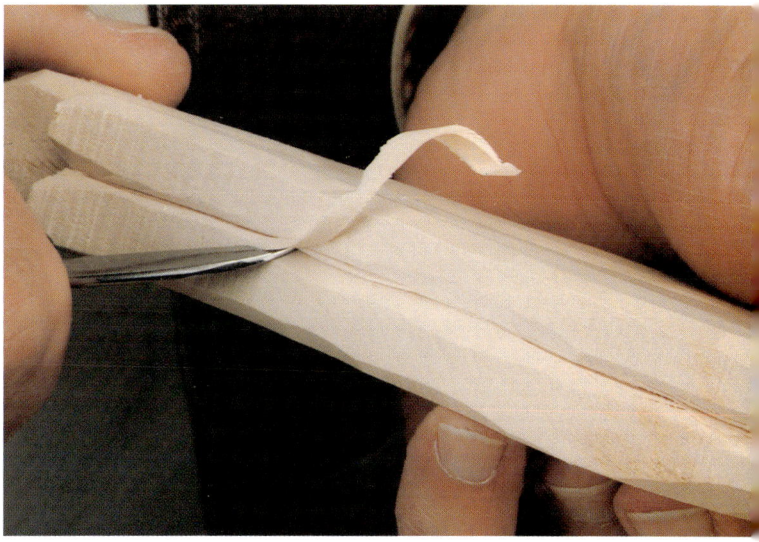

Cut a pretty deep V between the wings, cutting from side-to-side.

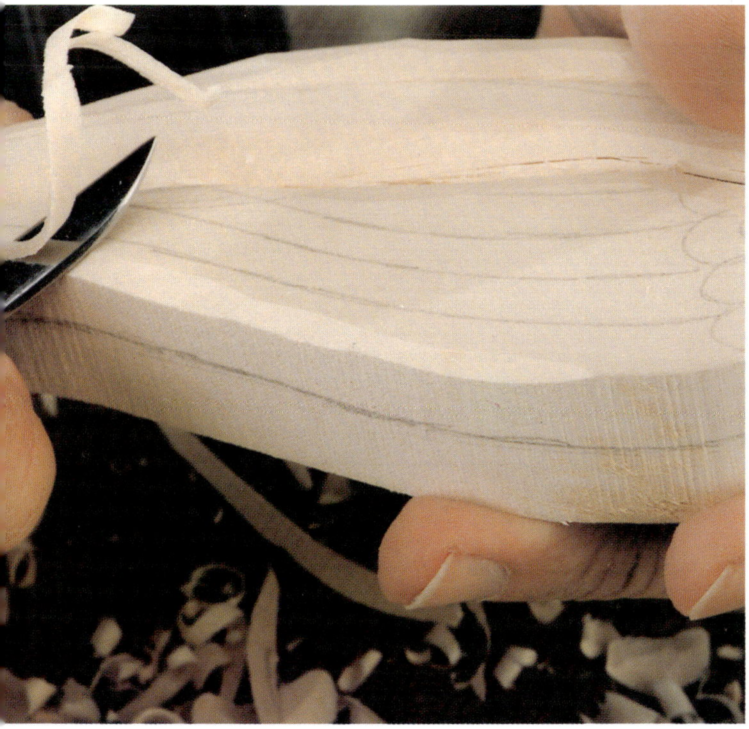

Before we carve details on the wings, I'm rounding them a bit.

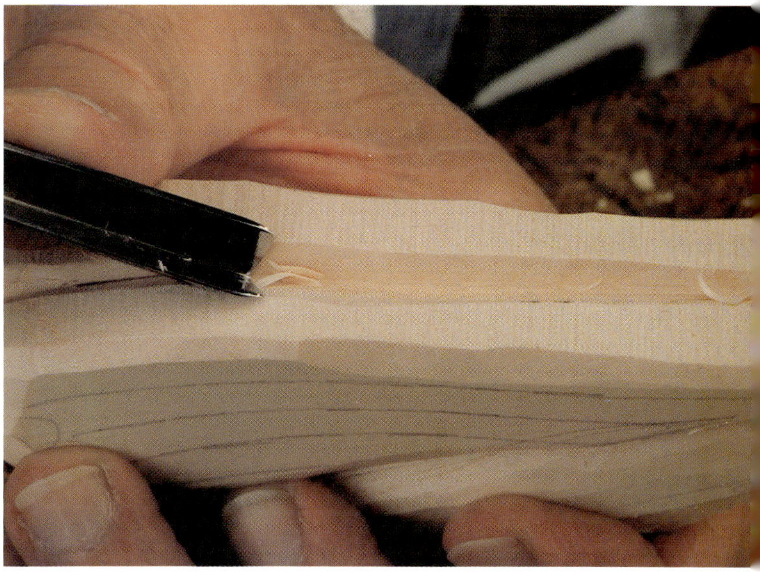

You can continue doing this with a knife, going down both sides. If you have a large V gouge, you can use it as well.

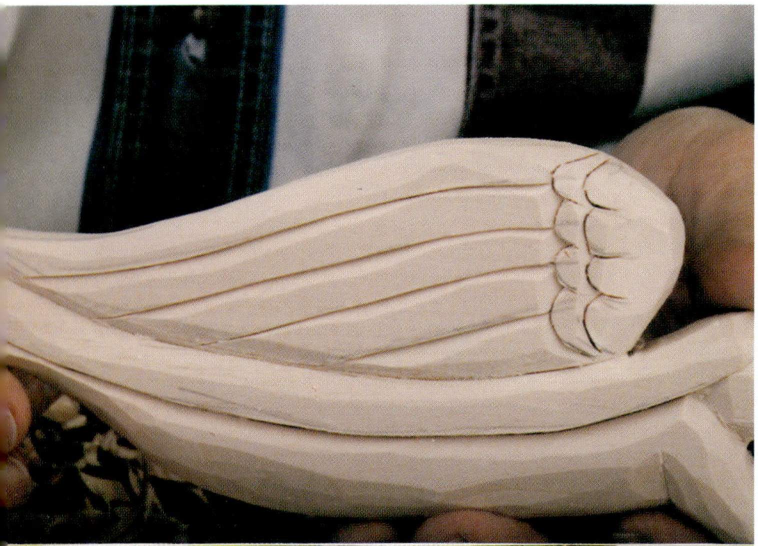

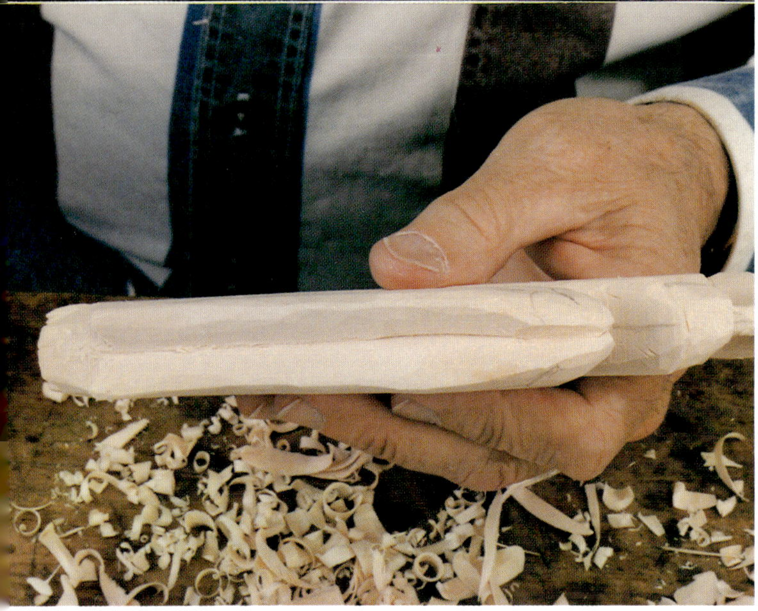

I have the wings shaped pretty much like I want them and I have drawn in the details.

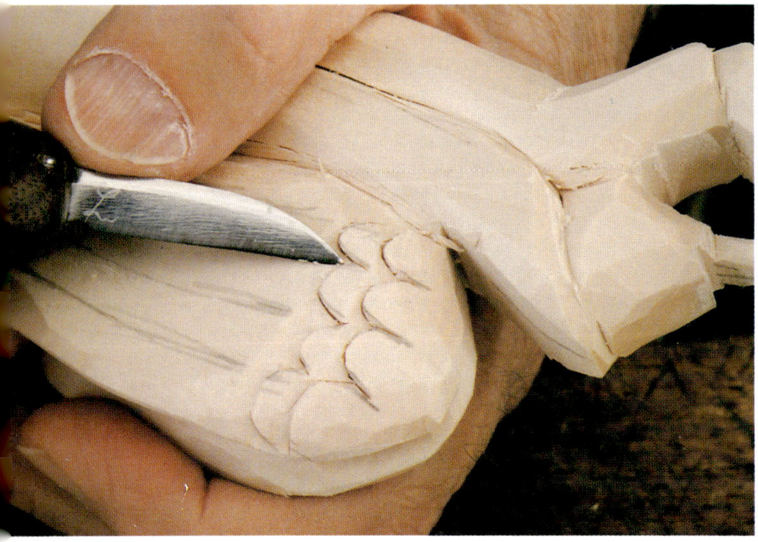

I have added another row of small feathers and have trimmed the small feathers in for detail.

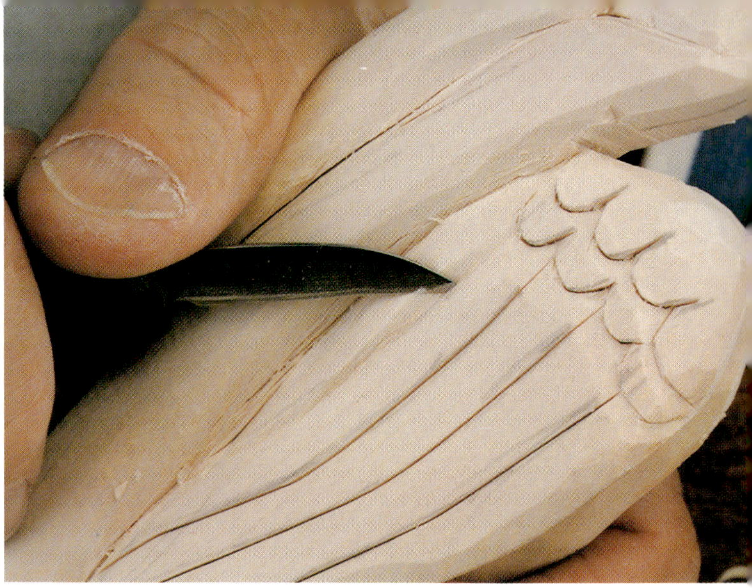

I have incised each of the long lines along the wings. I am undercutting each at an angle for detail. Do the same on the other side.

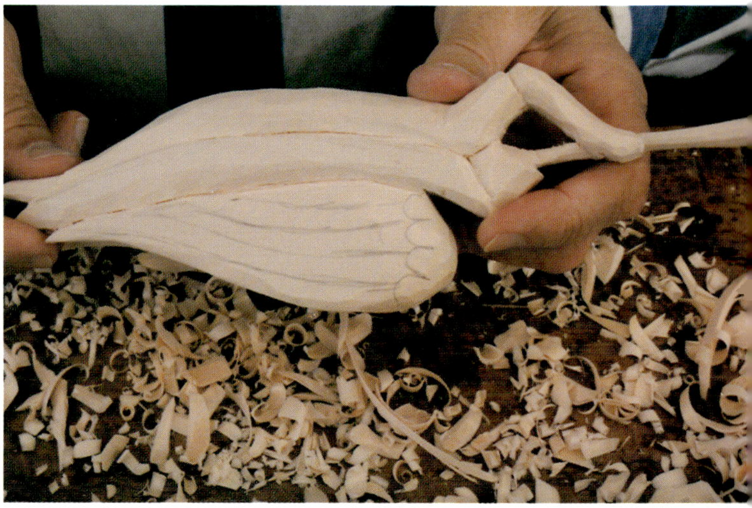

The finished wing.

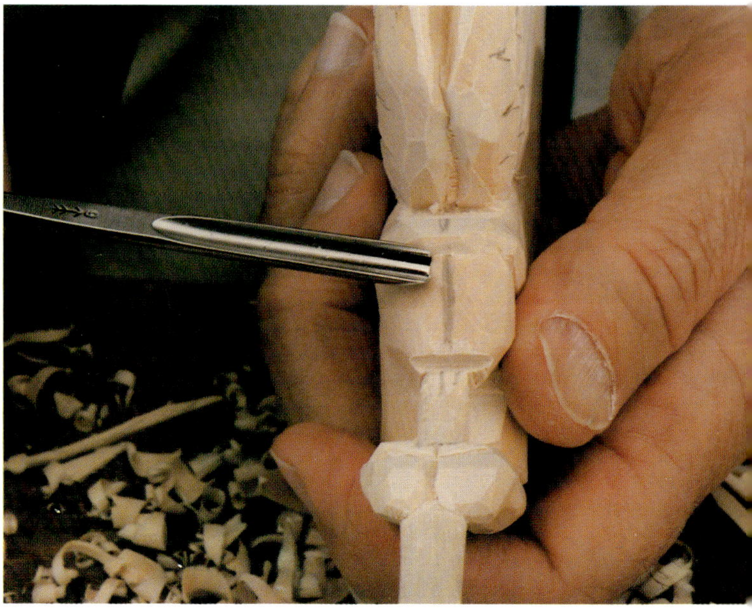

It is a good idea now to draw a line down the center of the angel's face.

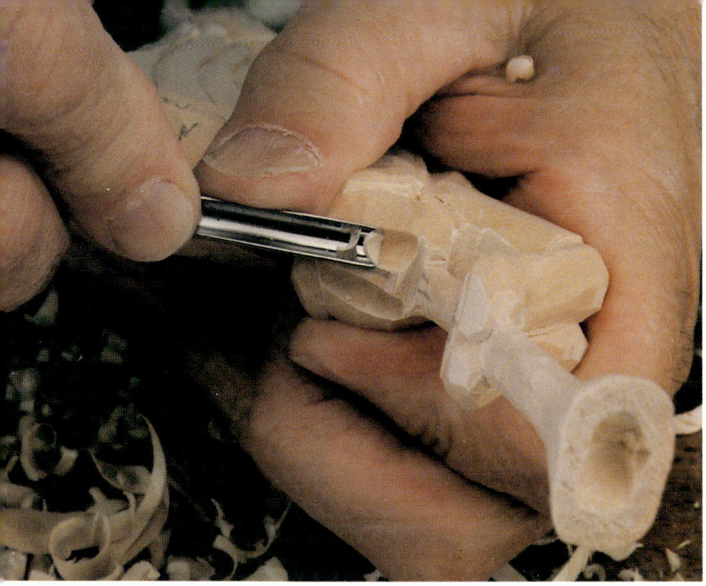

Take out a little piece along each side of the nose with a gouge.

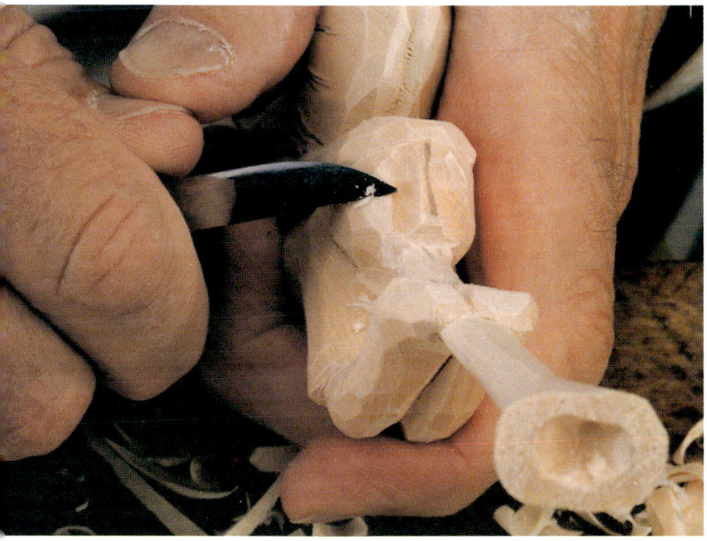

Take away the sharp lines where the gouge cut into the face.

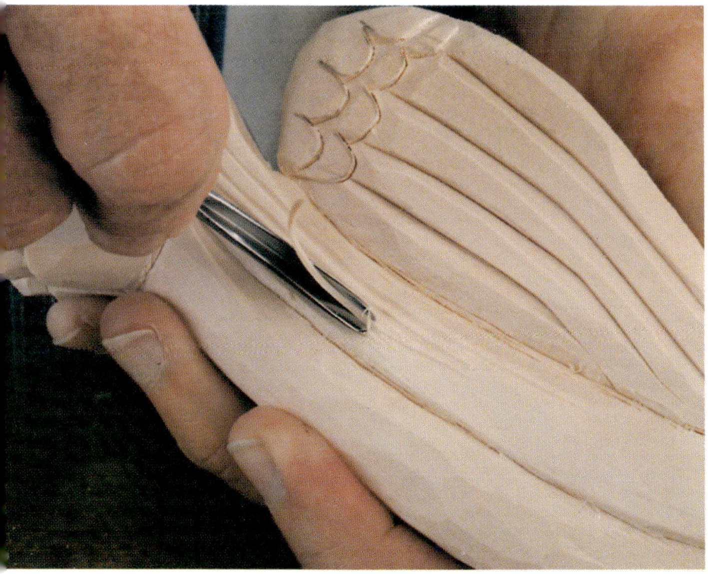

Take a small V gouge and make some hair lines. This can be done with your knife, but the V gouge makes it easier.

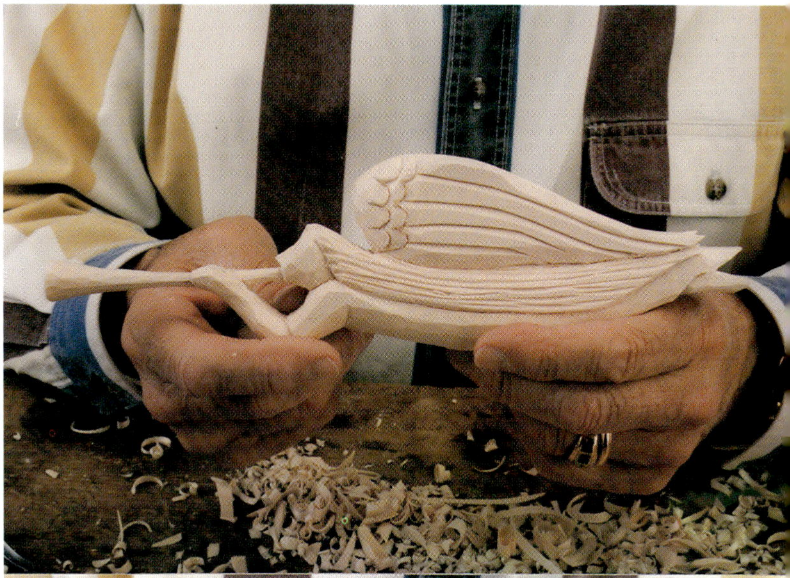

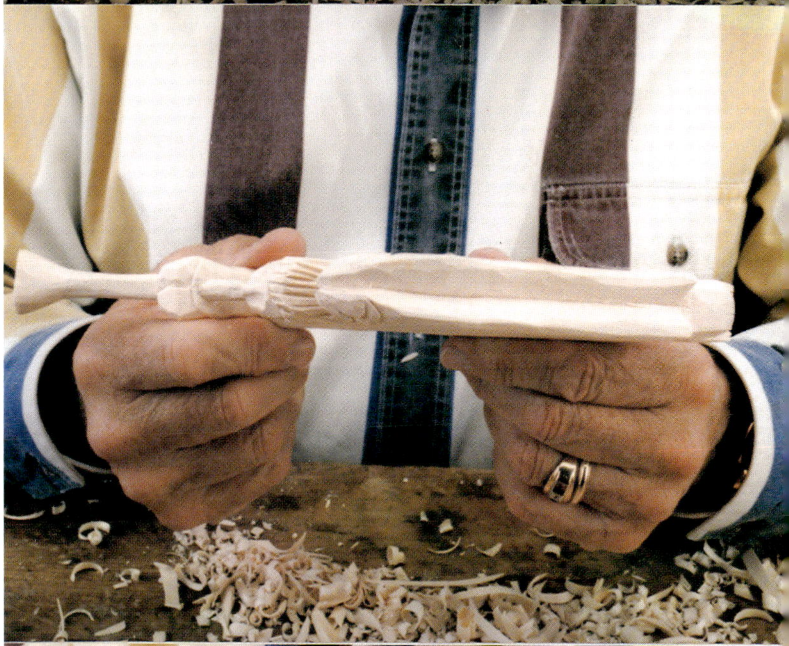

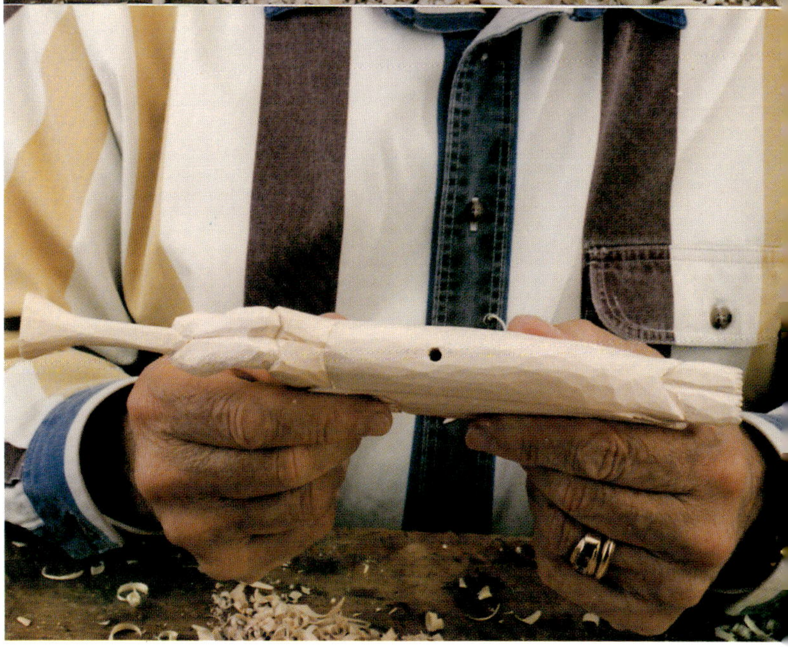

Ready to paint.

Angel Three

This angel lends itself to different painting styles. I chose the patriotic one which is very popular. This pattern can be doubled in size; in the gallery section I show it in two sizes.

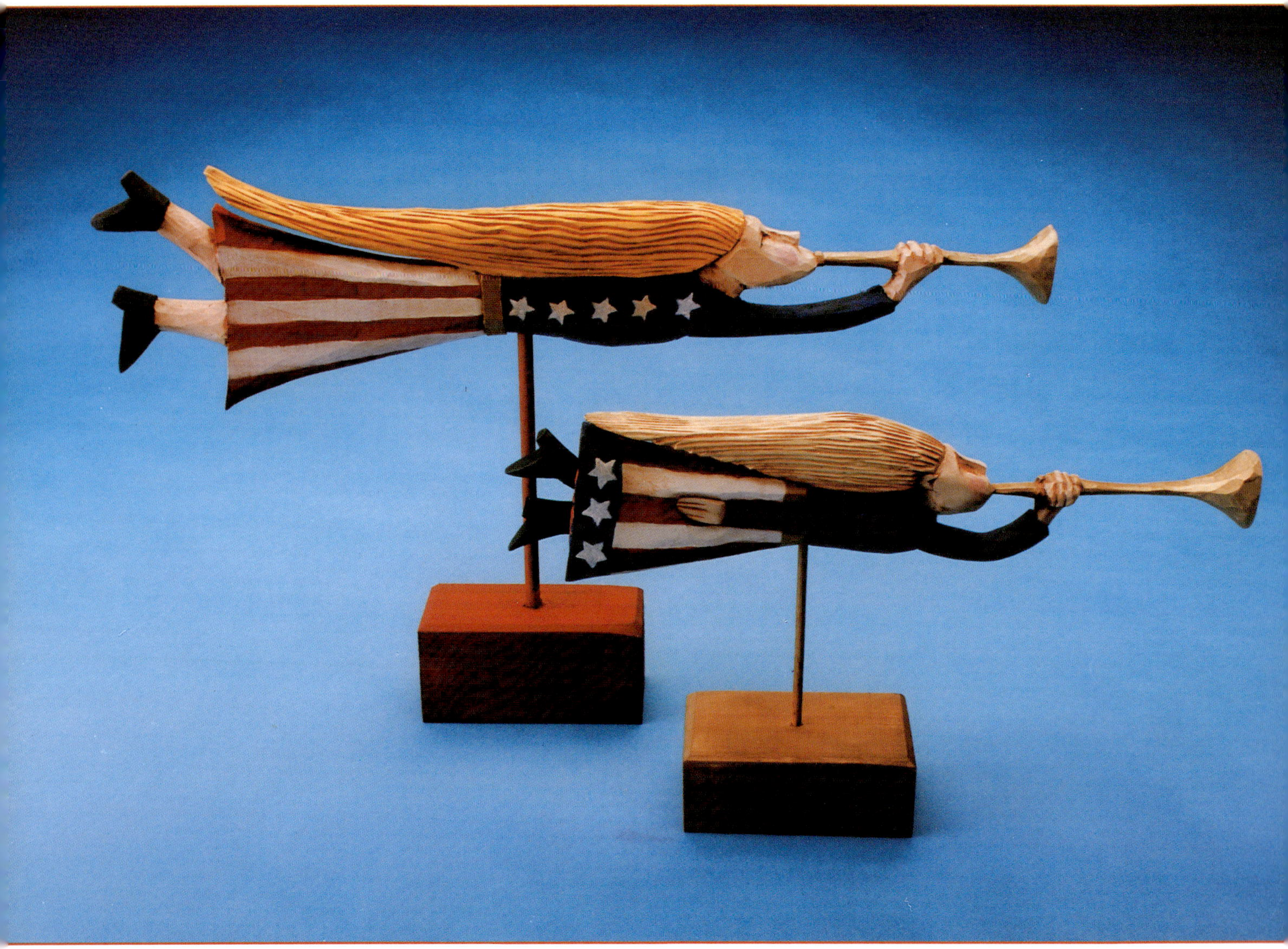

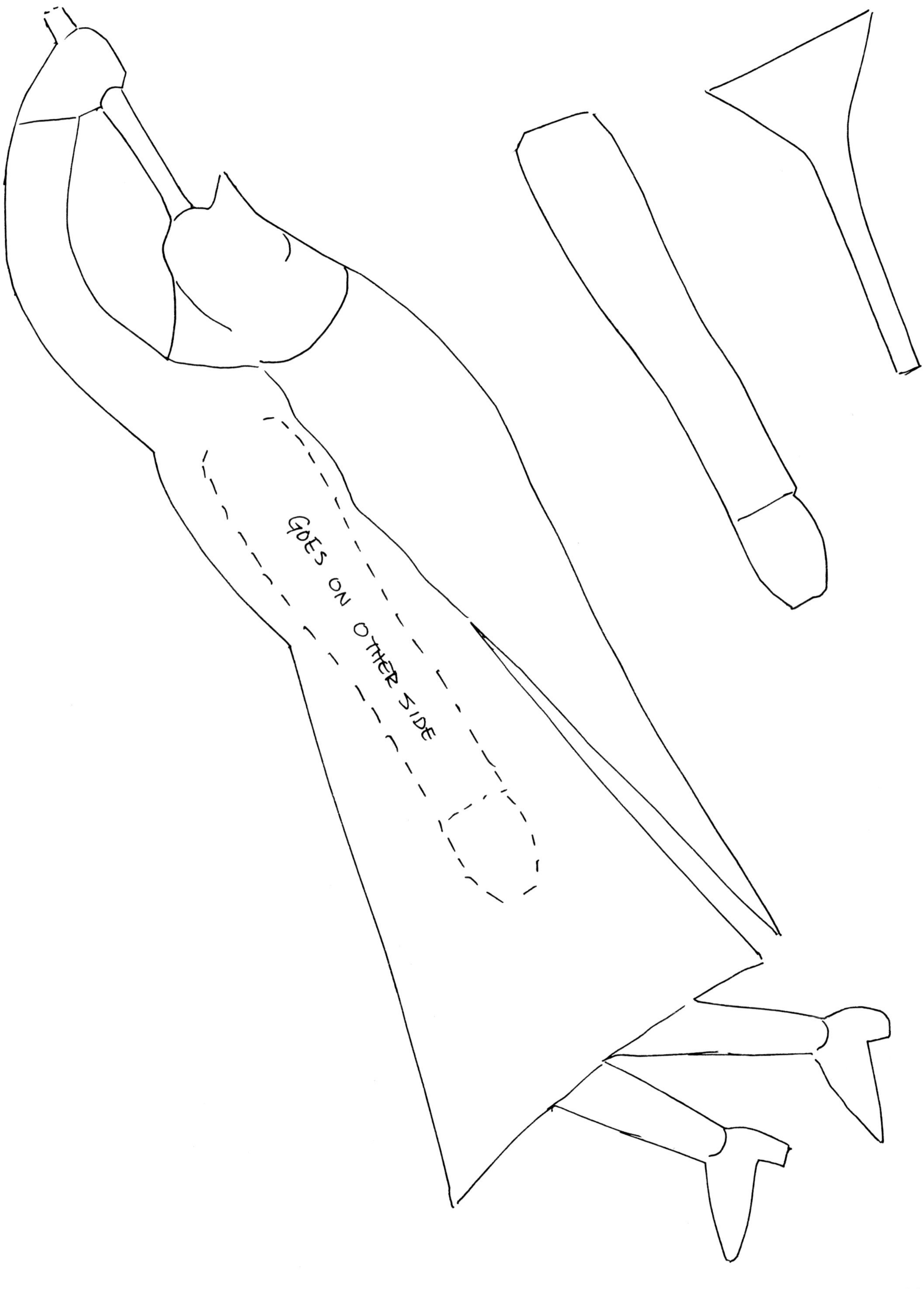
GOES ON OTHER SIDE

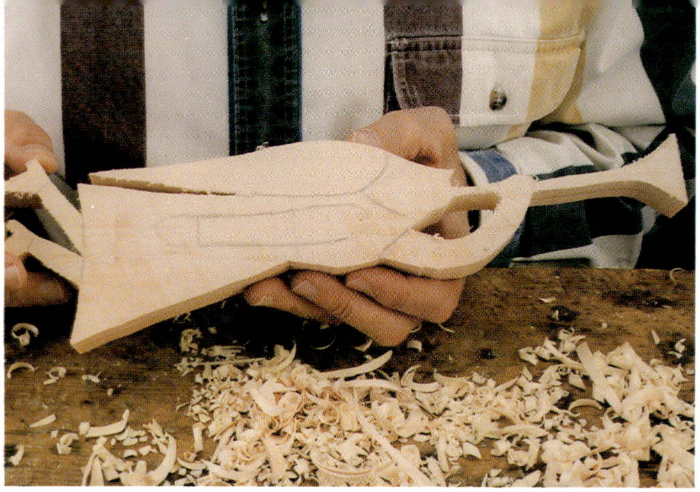

This angel will be a little bit different, with one arm going down the side and no wings.

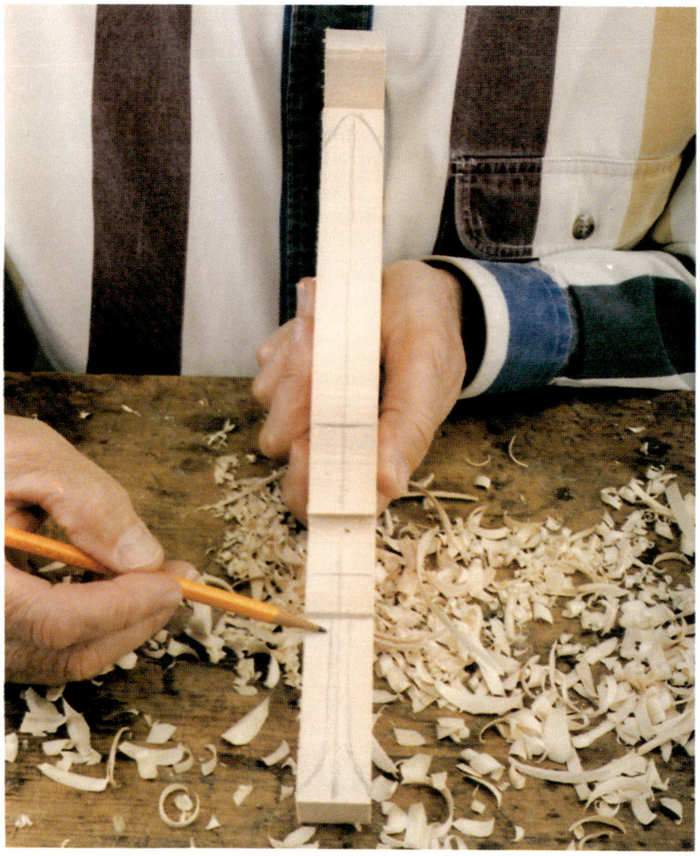

You'll notice that on the top and bottom I've made a center line and provided the outline for the trumpet.

As with the previous angel, I make a hole in the end of the trumpet with a gouge now before the wood gets too thin. You may also use a drill if you prefer.

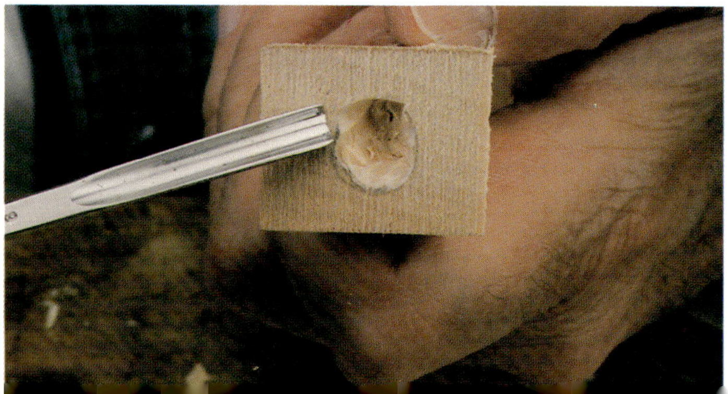

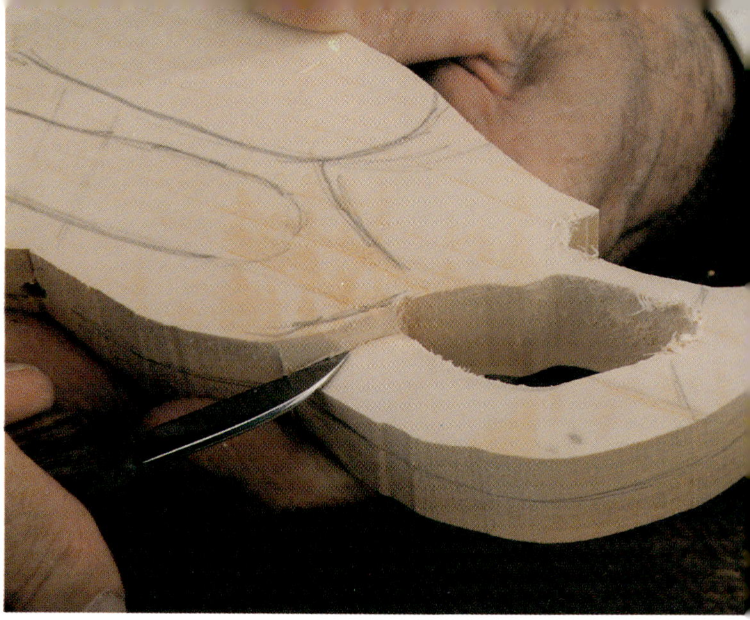

Cut away the excess wood from the arm holding the trumpet. You will have to cut away a good deal since the arm is on the left-hand side of the body.

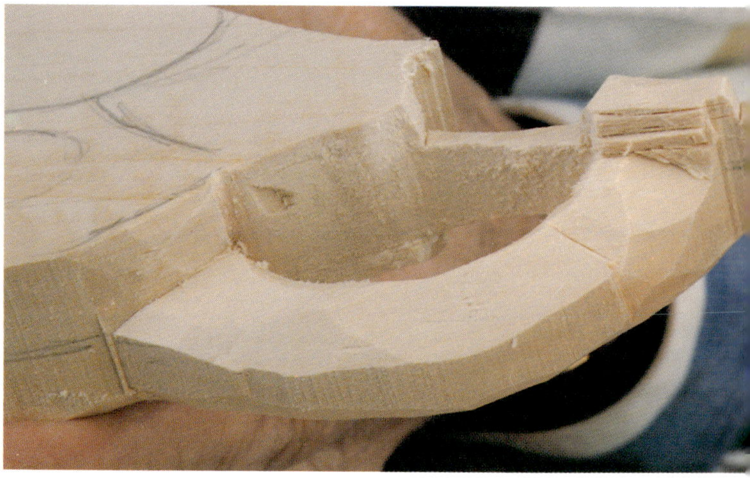

The arm has to go quite far over as it is not two arms joined together. The arm must appear to be coming from the far shoulder.

Start working on the area where the holding hand and the trumpet meet.

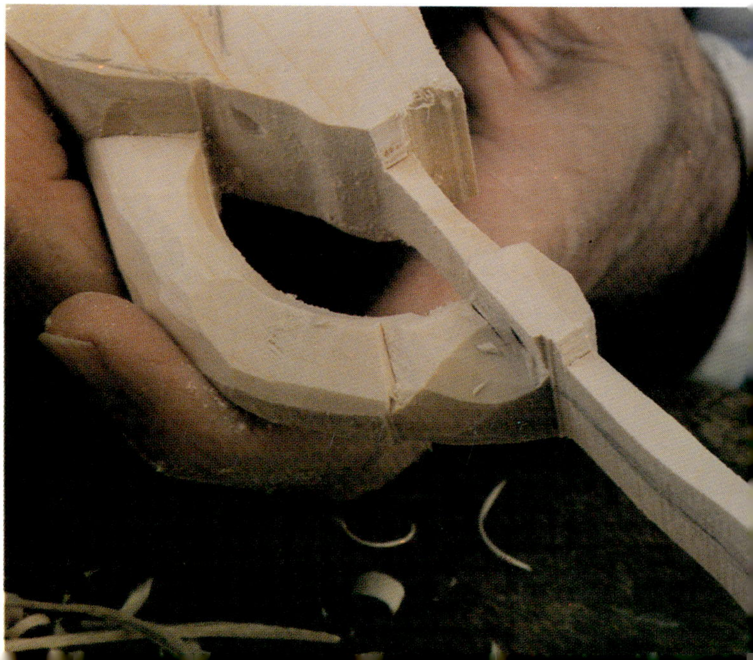

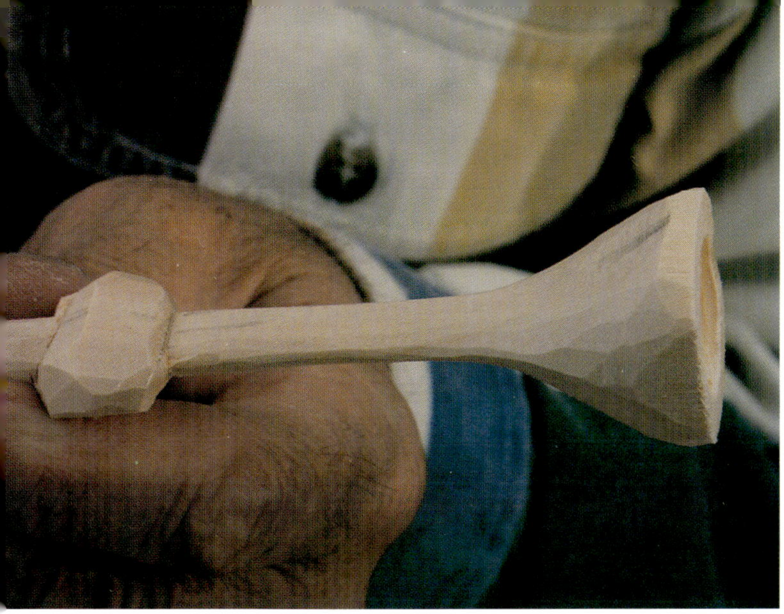

I have shaped and will continue to shape the trumpet as I go. Be extremely careful as the trumpet is long and narrow. It can be easily broken.

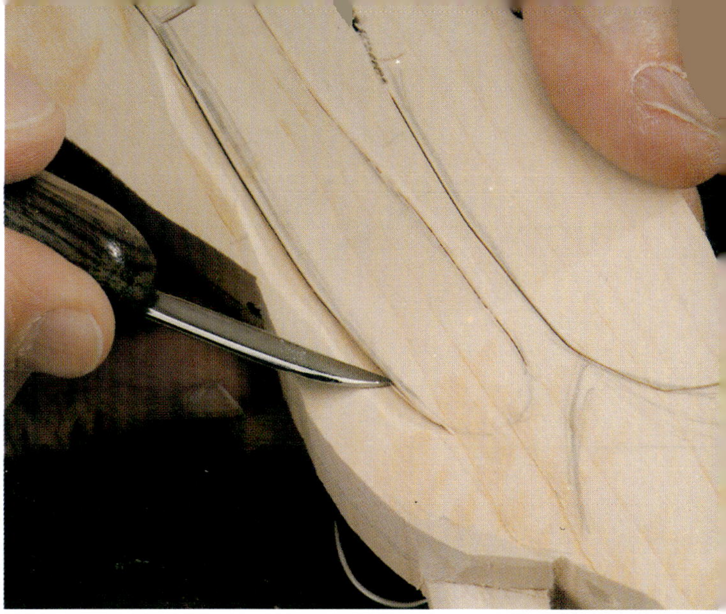

Lay the knife out at an angle to the incised line and remove a strip, separating the arm from the body.

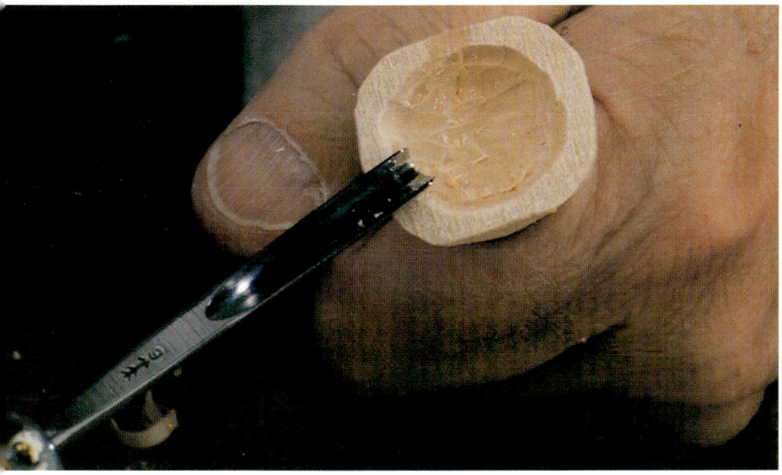

I have continued to clean out the end of the trumpet. You will probably spend as much time on this trumpet as on any other part of this angel.

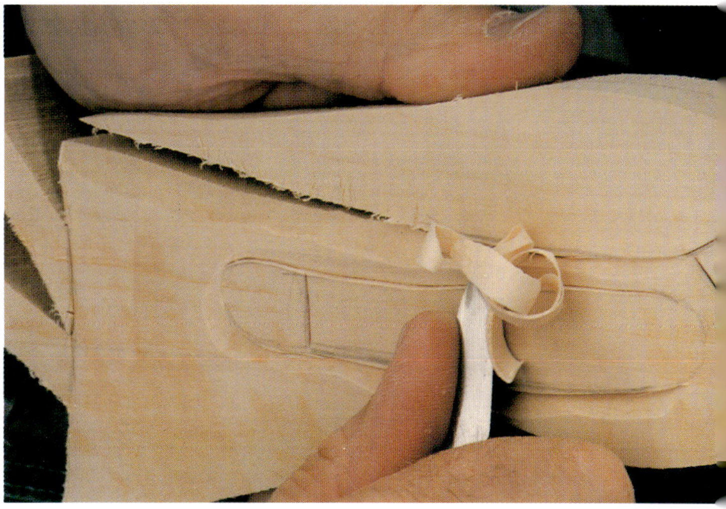

Start rounding the dress into the bottom of the hair.

I have incised along the right arm and hand beside the body.

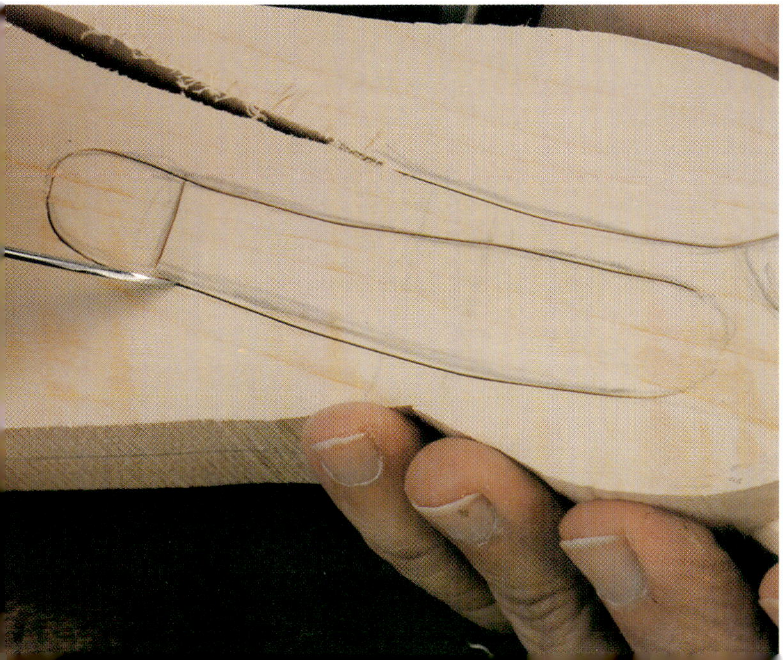

I've drawn a line down the center along the bottom of the angel to provide a reference point for rounding.

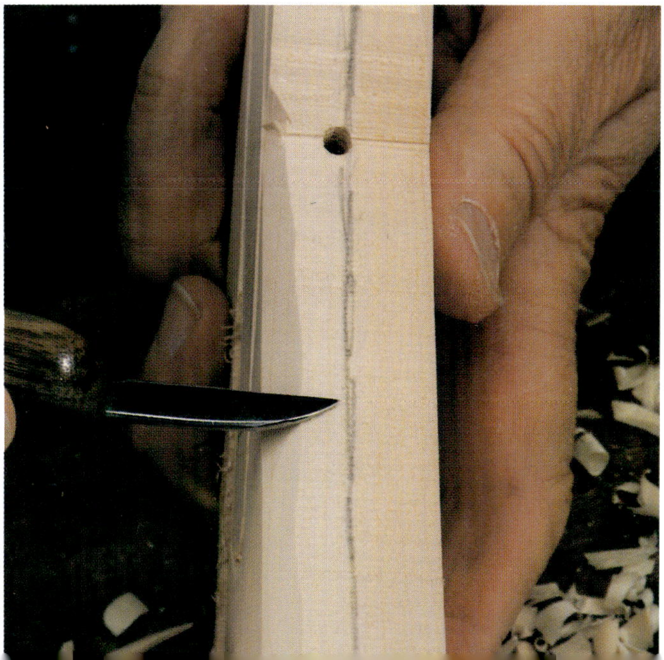

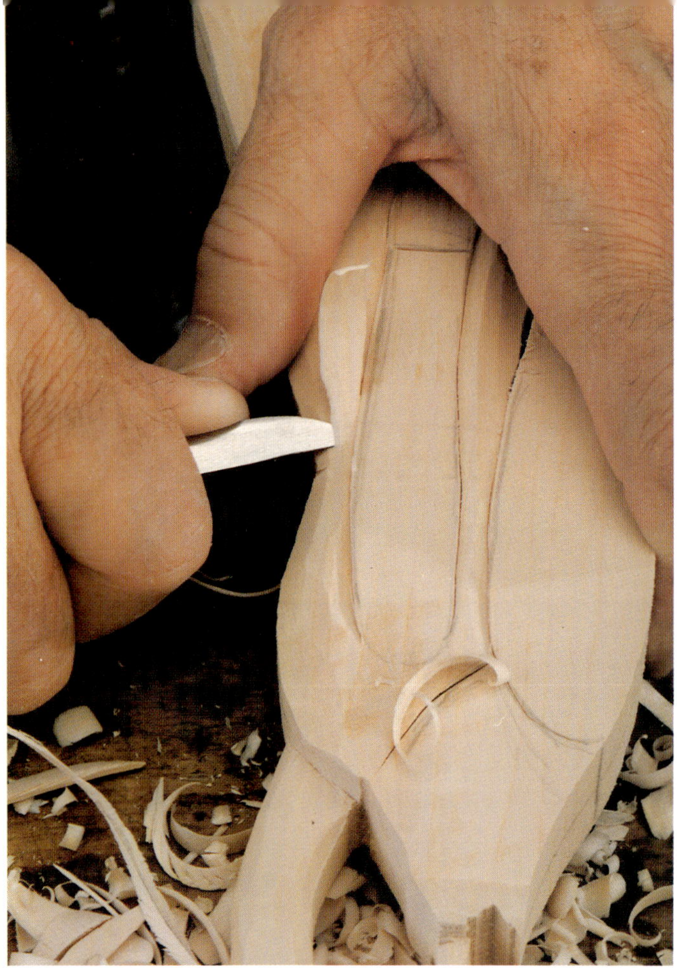

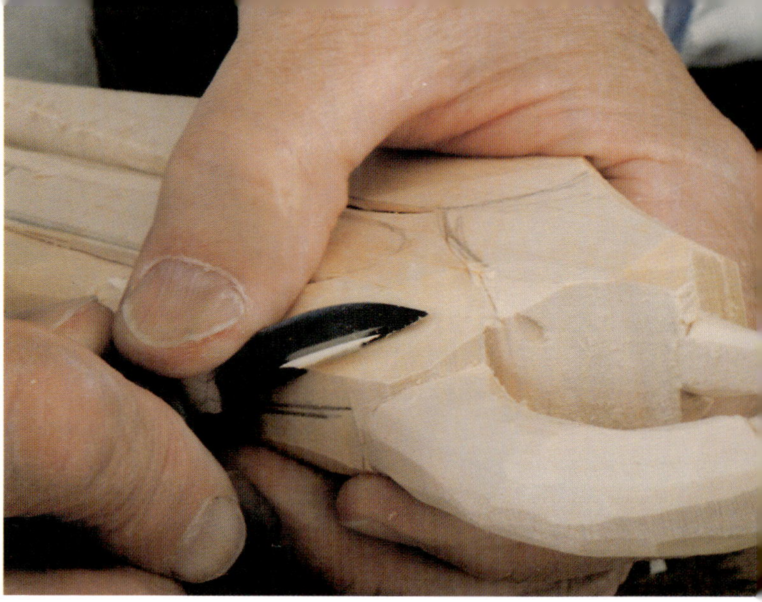

Rounding the chest into the left arm.

As you round away the bottom of the dress, the arm will take shape.

Rounding up to the bottom center line on each side of the dress.

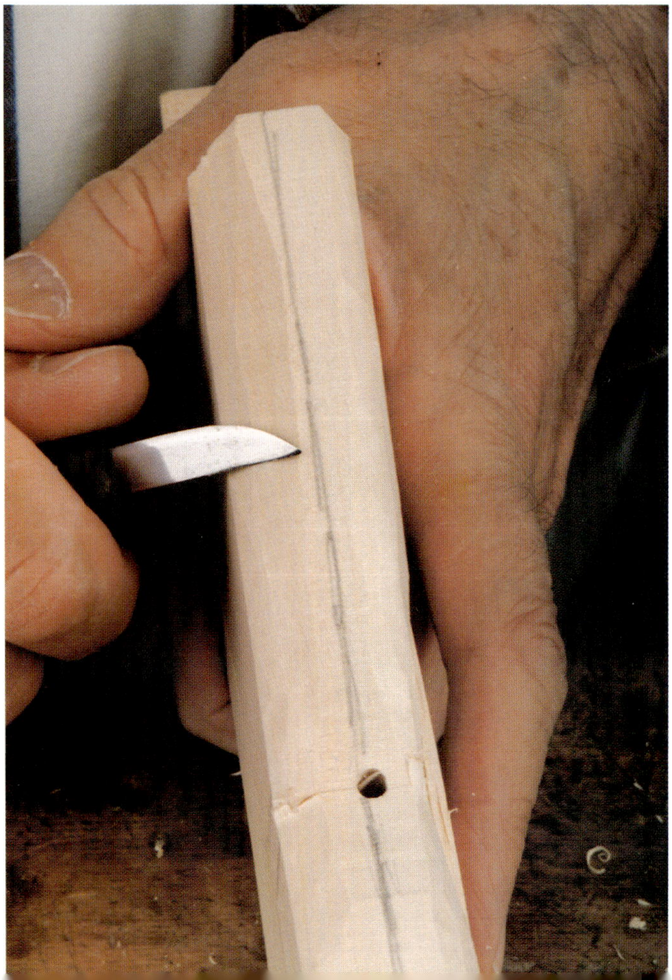

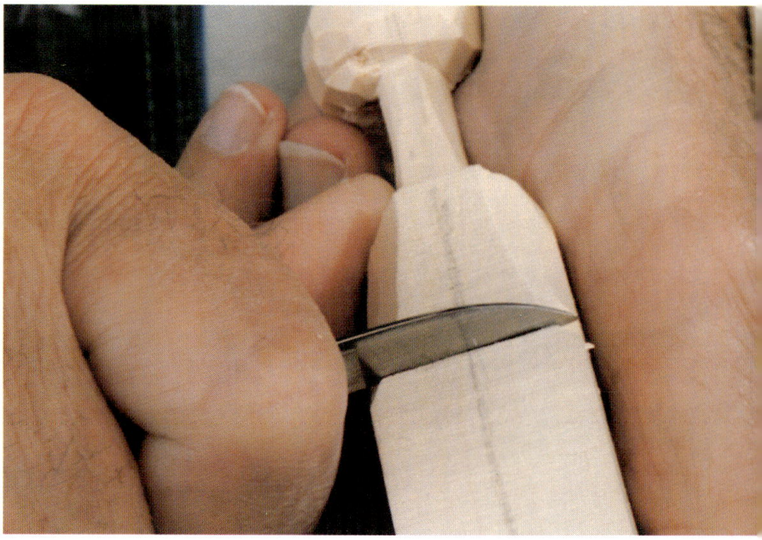

Lay the knife blade along the line where the hair meets the forehead and rock the blade to incise that line.

Rounding the dress under the flying hair.

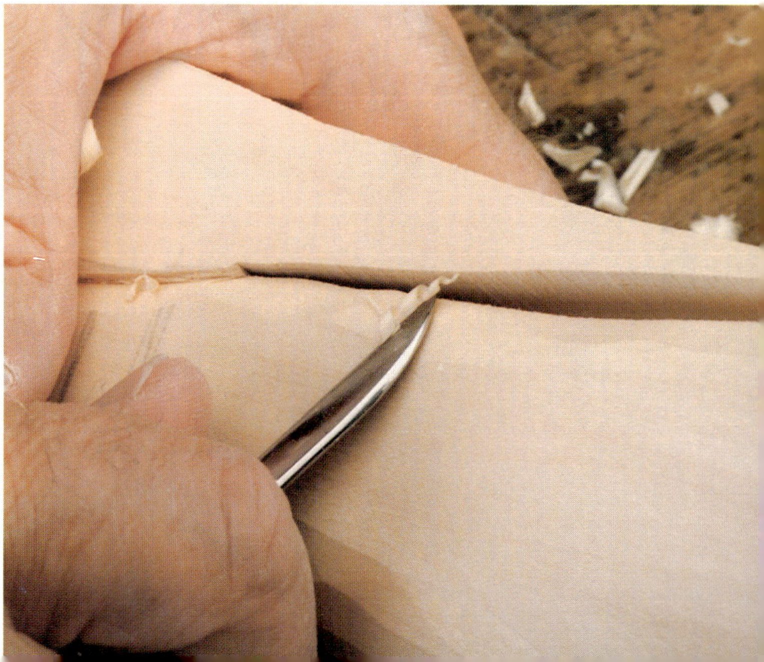

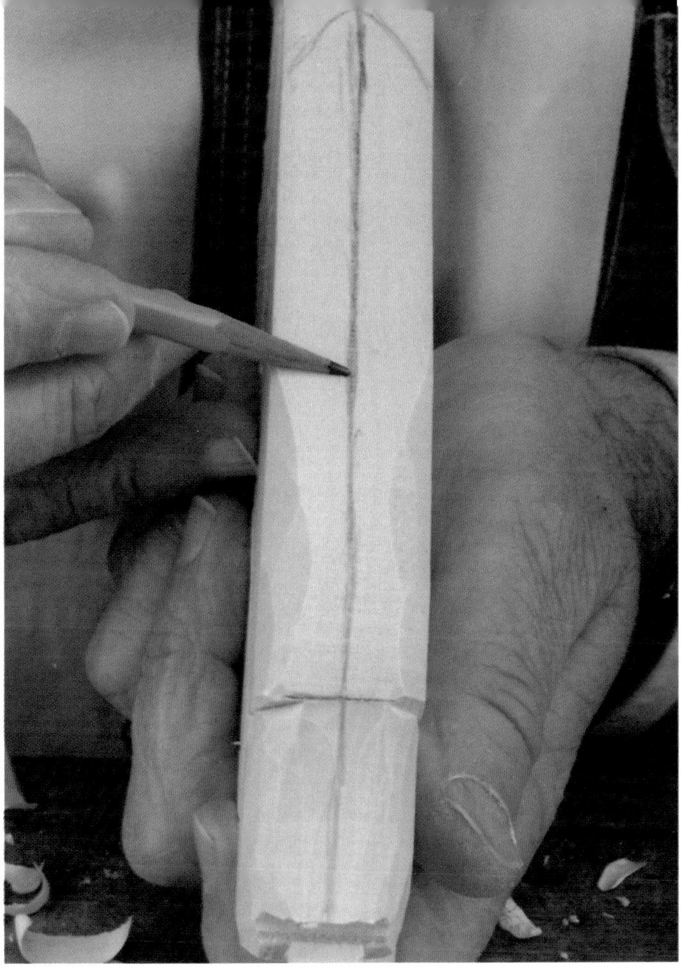

Draw a center line down the hair so that it will not be carved lopsided.

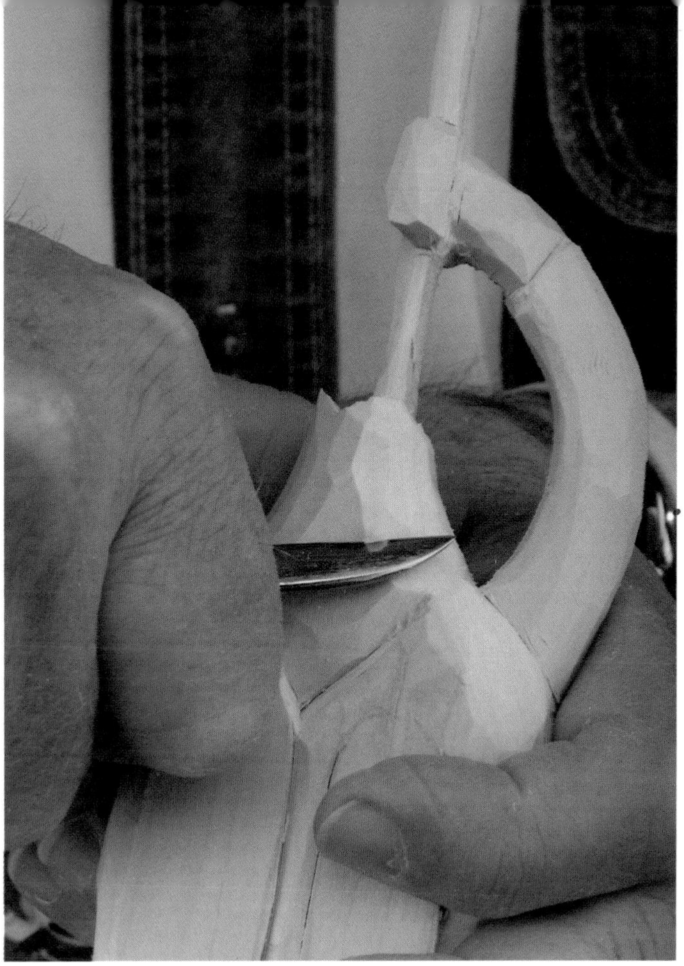

Rounding the neck and the jawline.

Rounding the hair.

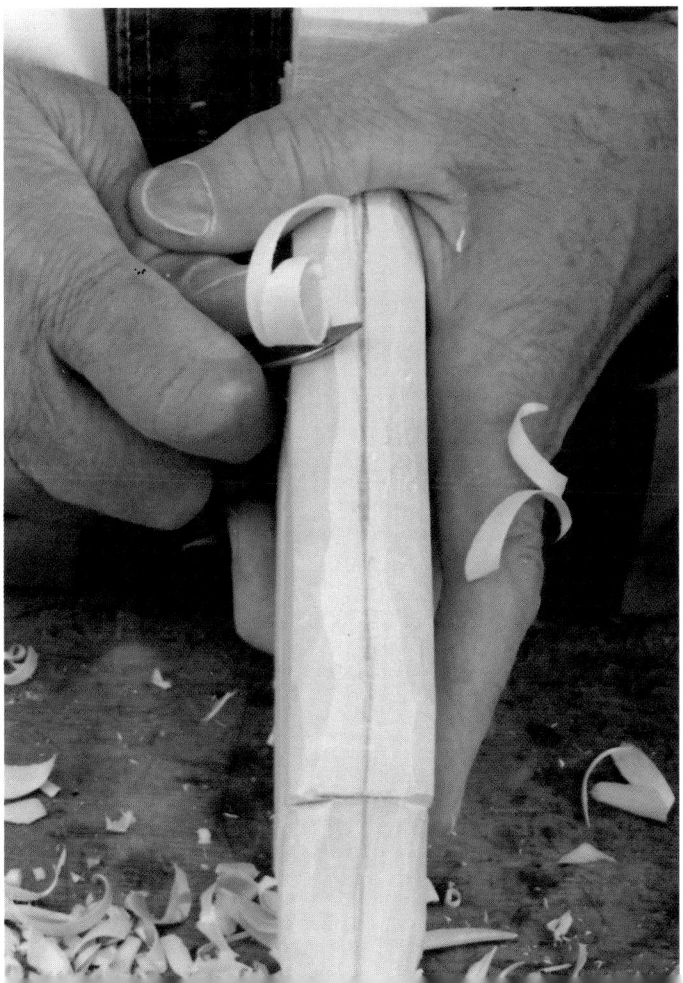

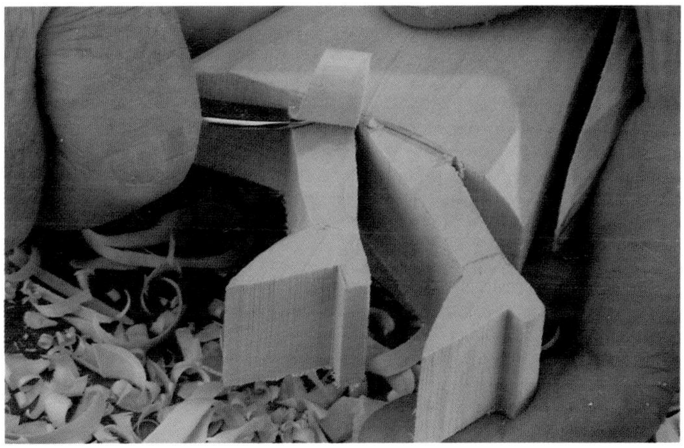

Start shaping these rather large legs down to size.

This gouge is very handy for removing wood from a tight place.

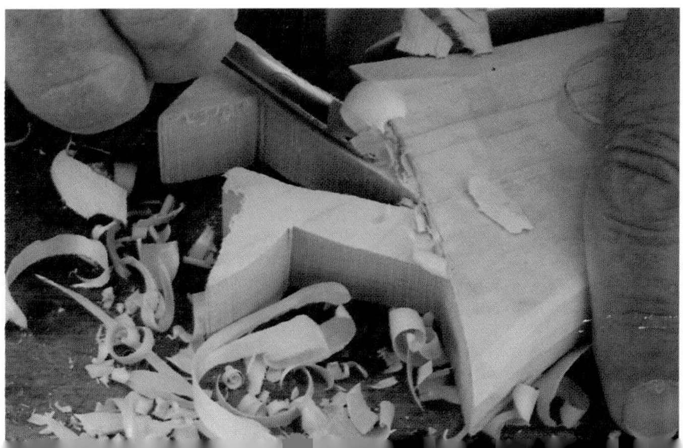

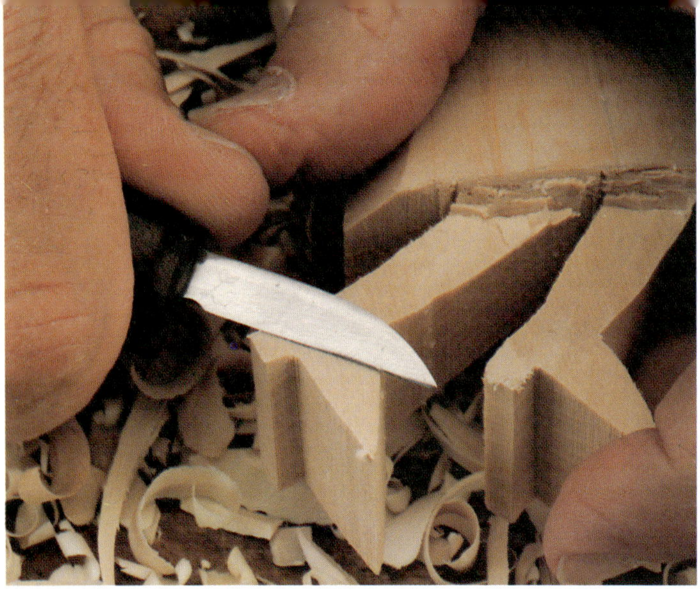

Now I can go back to the knife.

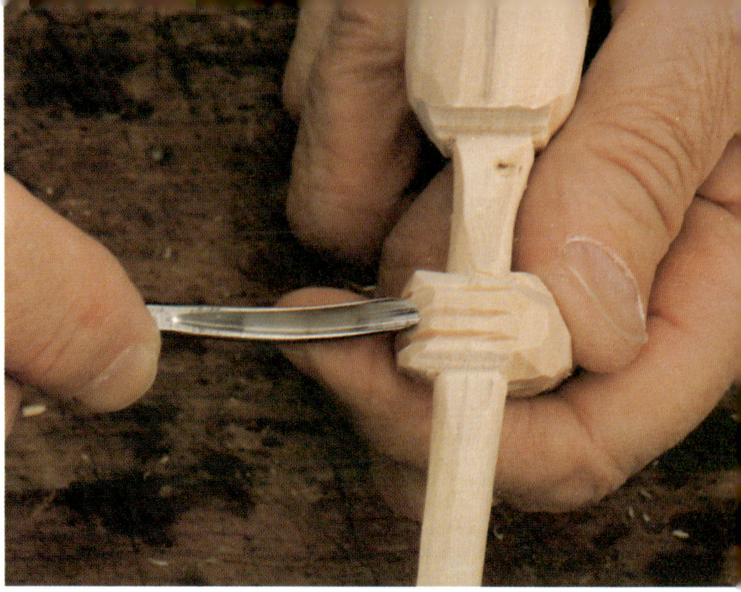

I have added some fingers to the left hand with my trusty little V gouge. While this can be done with a knife, it is easier with the gouge.

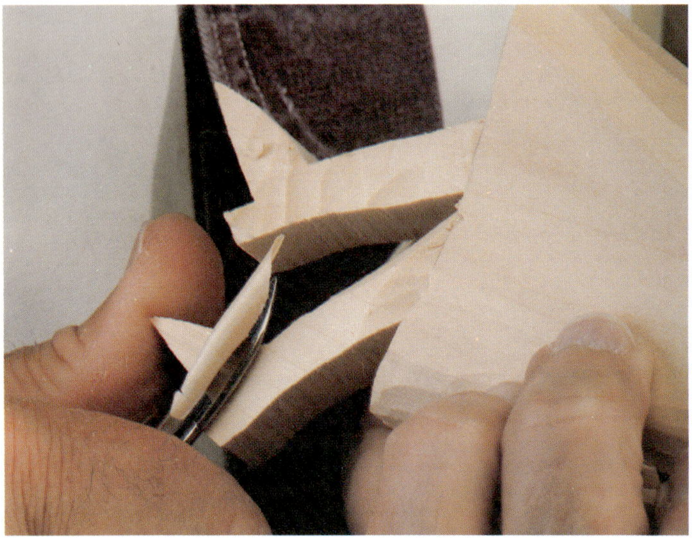

Sometimes you have to cut toward yourself. If your thumb is not as tough as mine, you'll want to wear a protective glove.

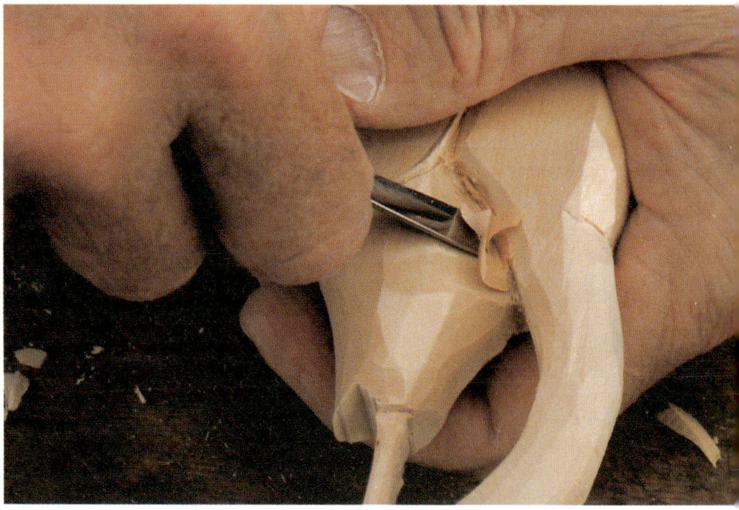

Using a #5, 8mm gouge, clean out around the neck and cheek line on either side of the head.

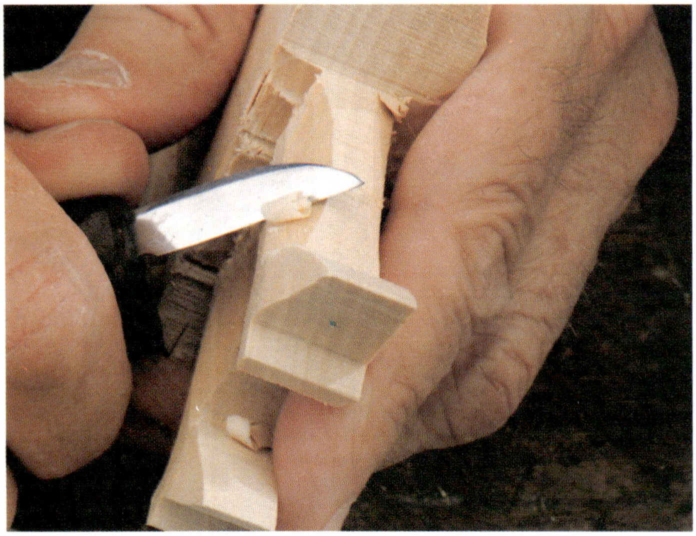

Now I have the legs down to the thickness I want and I will start to shape them.

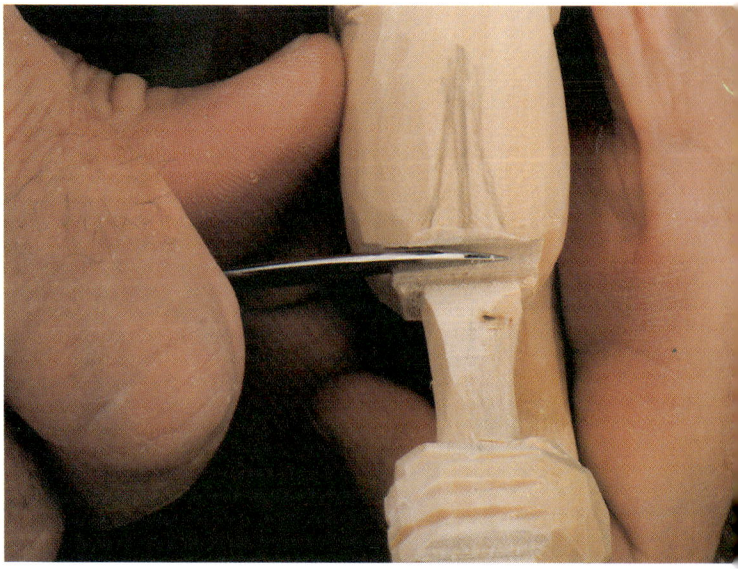

This nose was a little sharp, so I cut off a bit of the tip with my knife.

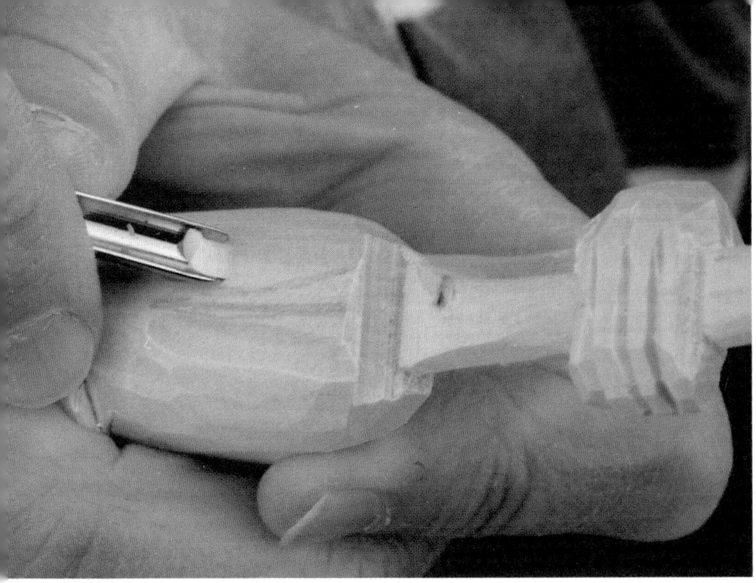

Going down each side of the nose with a #9, 5mm spoon gouge.

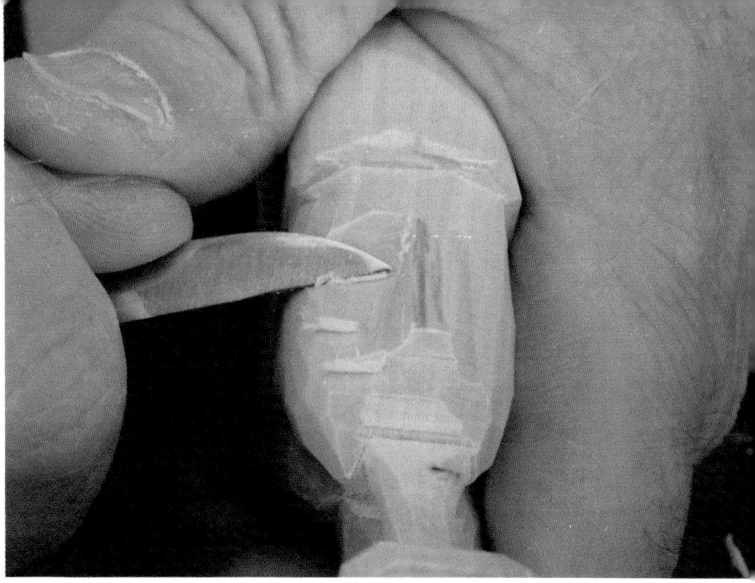

Take the knife and smooth out a small indentation where we will paint the closed eye.

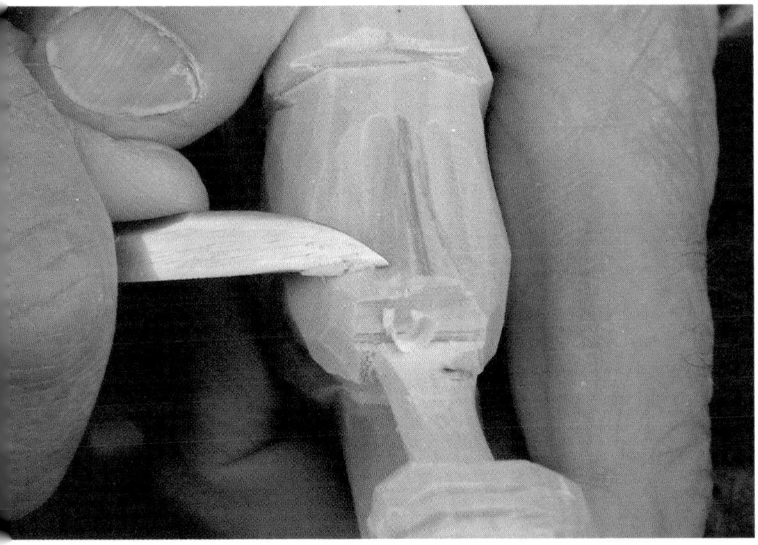

Trim down the sharp outer edge of the gouge line along the side of the cheek.

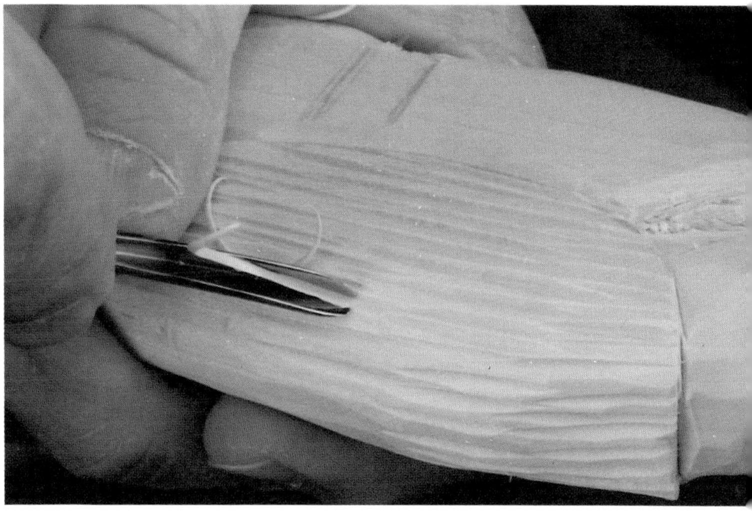

Put in some hair detail with a small V tool.

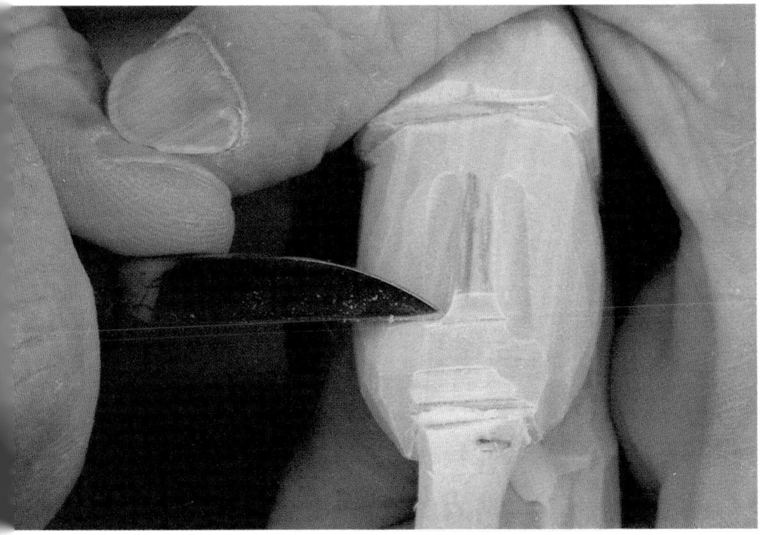

I decided the nose was a little too long, so I've shortened it with the knife.

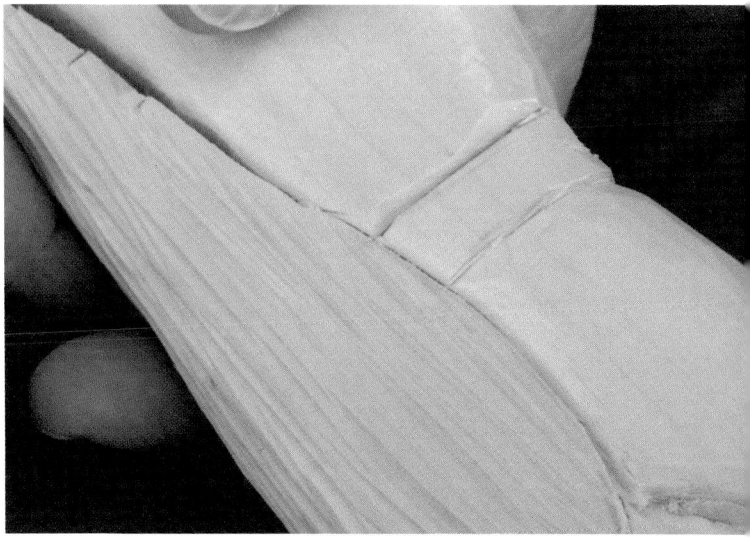

Draw in a belt all the way around the dress, incise the lines, and undercut it into place. You can also avoid carving in the belt and simply paint it in later.

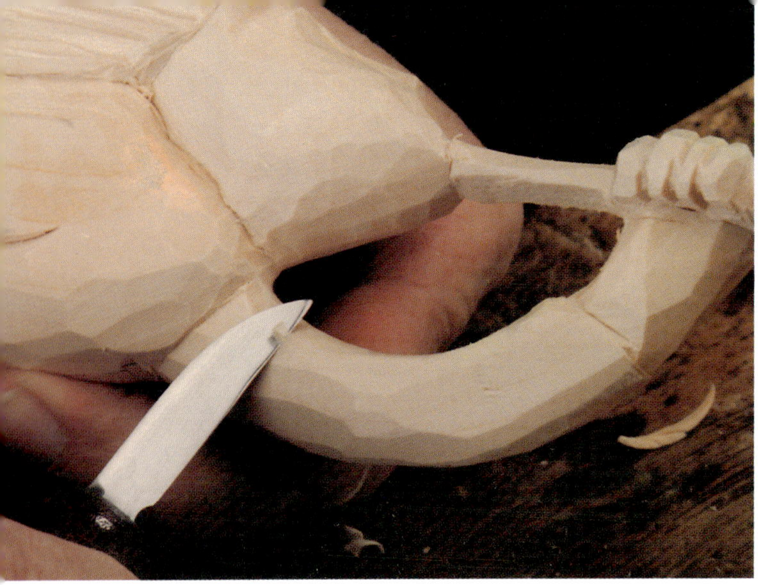

Take your knife and work your way around the angel, removing rough spots.

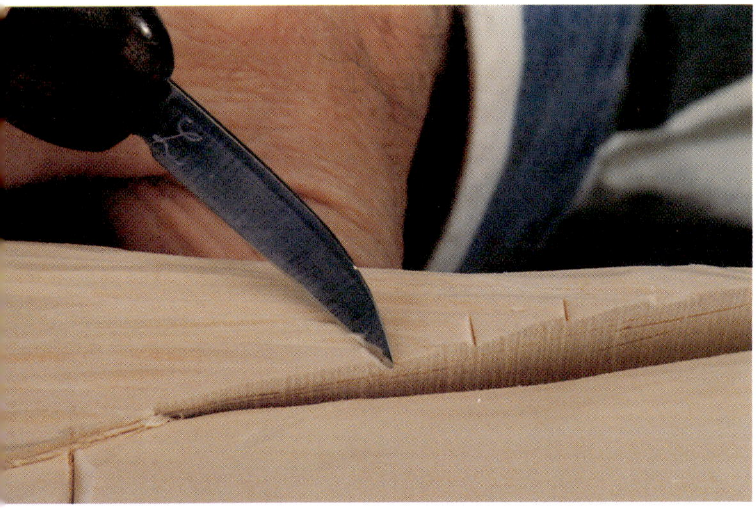

Make several notches along the hairline on both sides to show where different lengths of hair end.

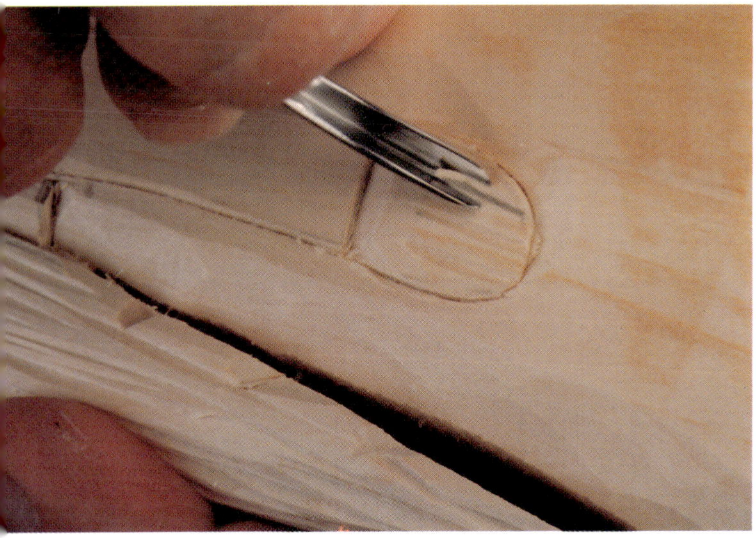

I've added fingers to the other hand with the V gouge. You only need four fingers here. The thumb is hidden behind the hand.

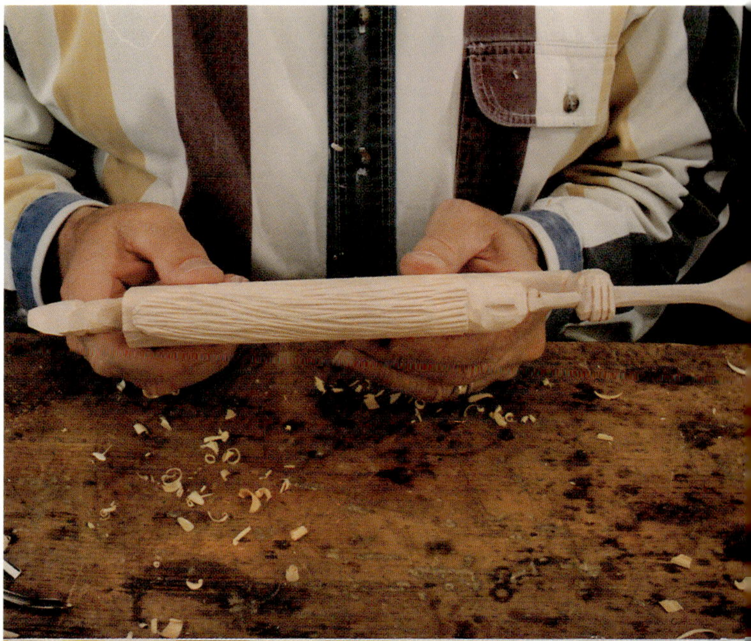

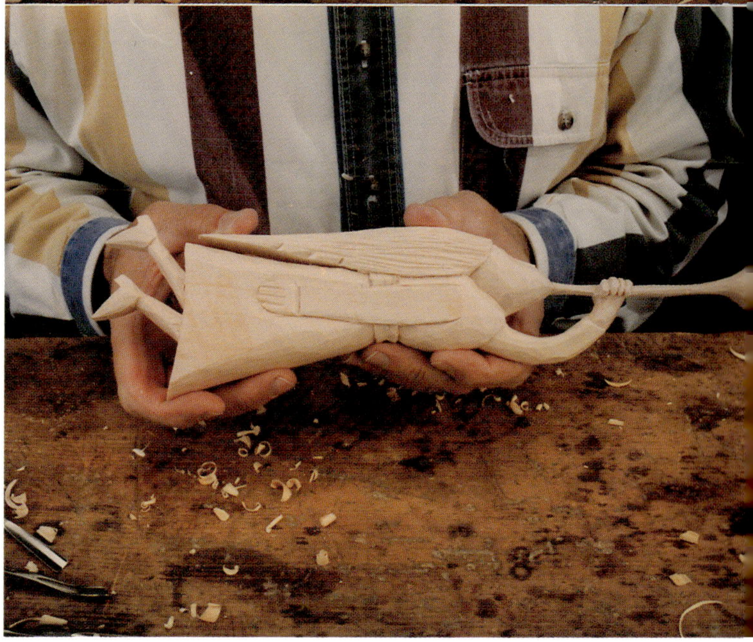

The carving is finished.

Angel Four

Those of us who play golf for fun would never call on our guardian angel to assist with a long shot over water or a knee-knocking putt to win a match. However, I would wager golfers approaching the amen corner at the Master's in Augusta, Georgia throw up many a prayer.

Have some fun with this one. It's another guaranteed seller.

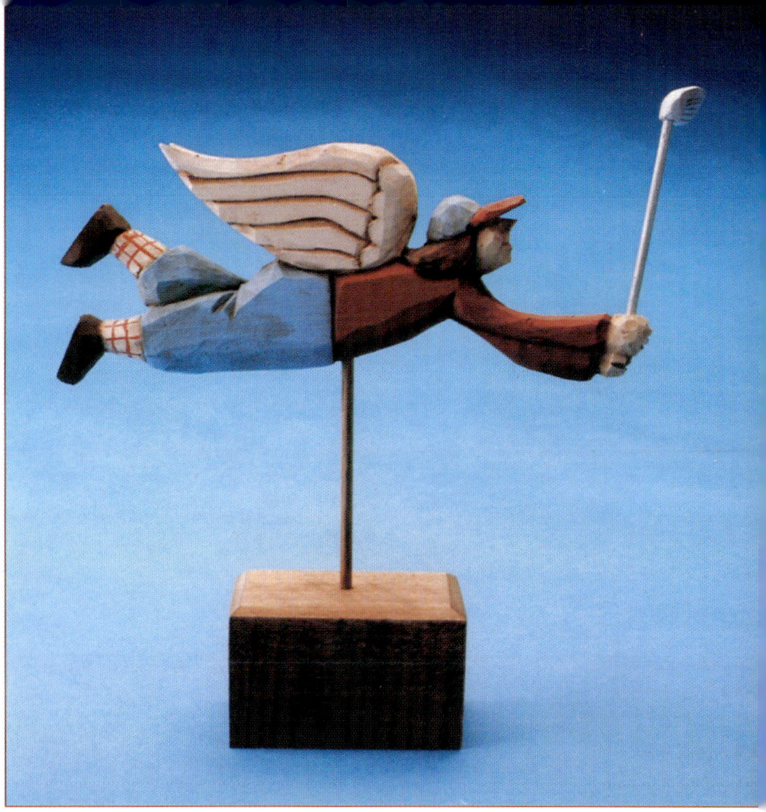

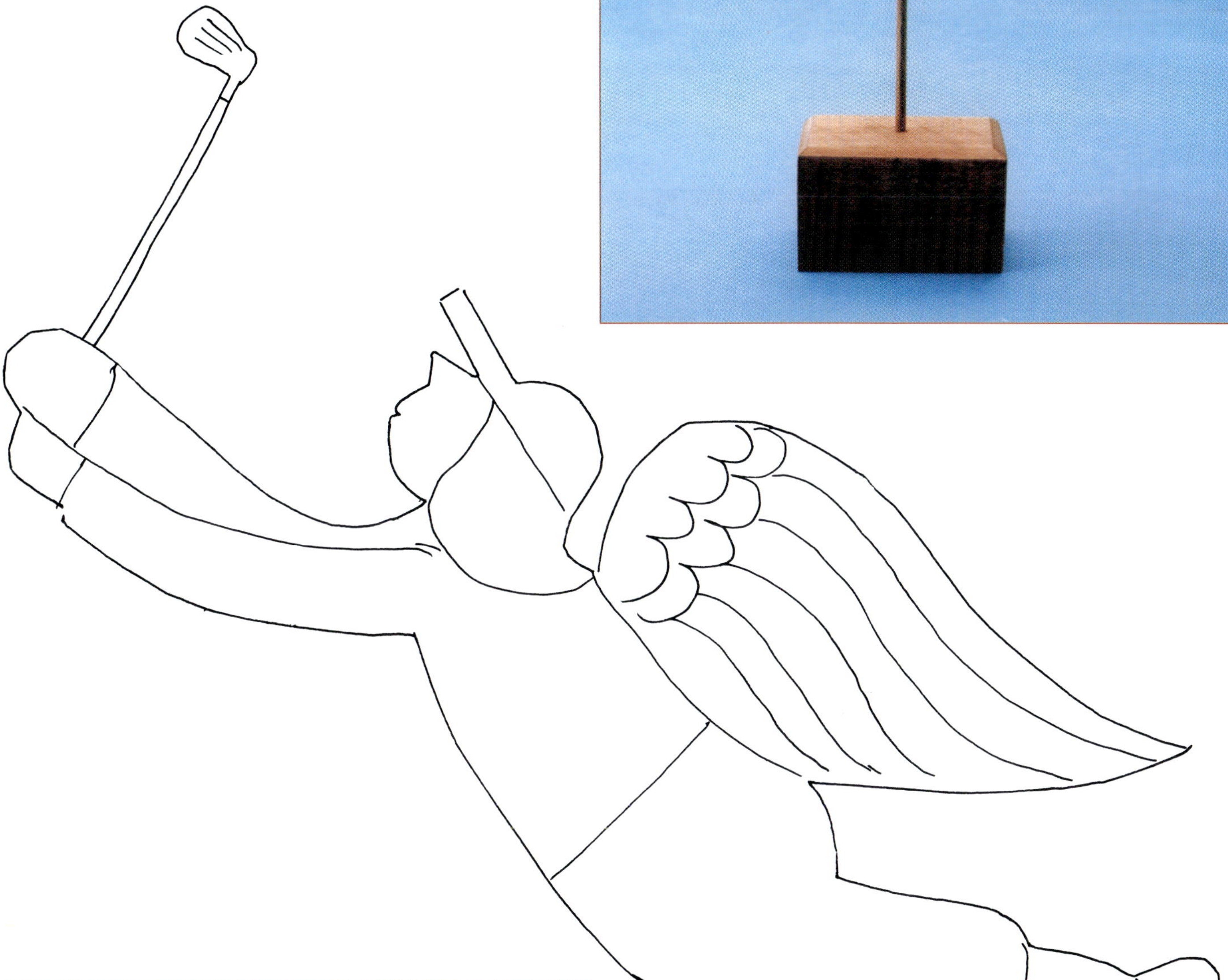

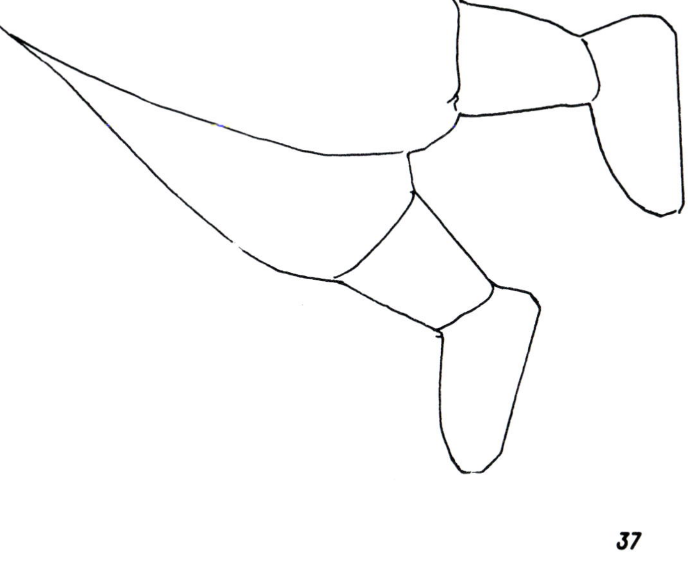

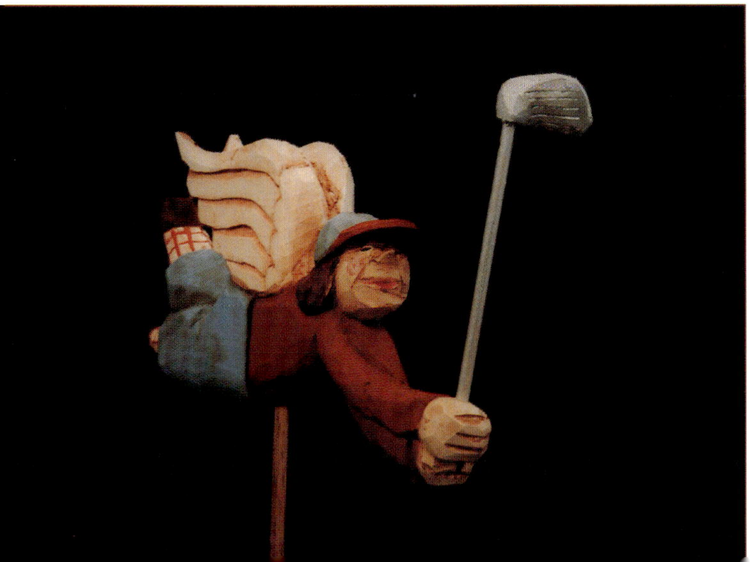

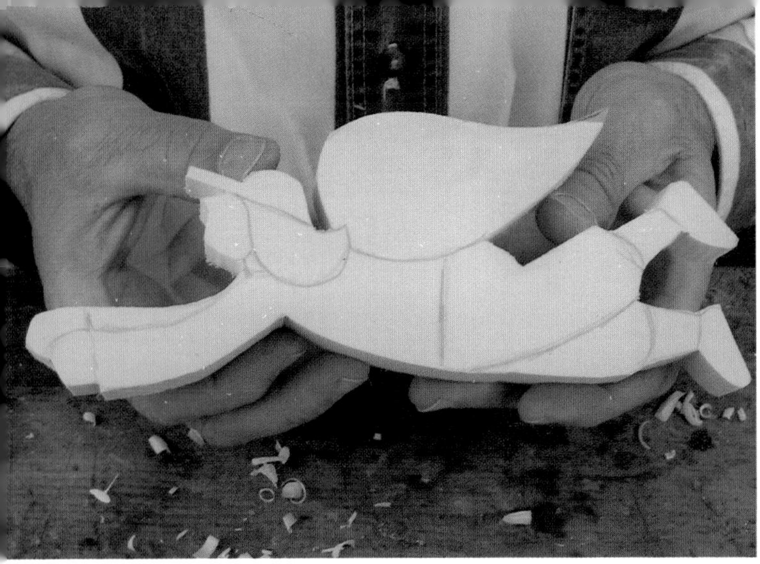

Angel to the golfers.

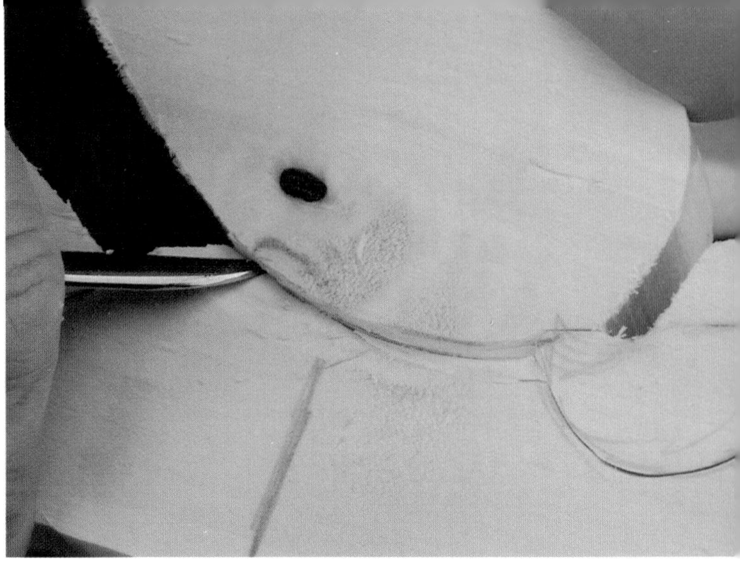

Undercut the wing.

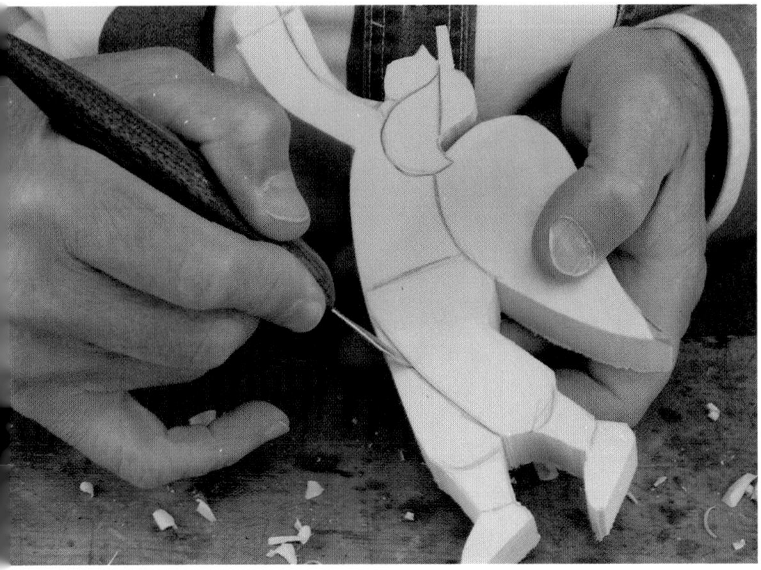

Incise all of the lines on each side with your knife first.

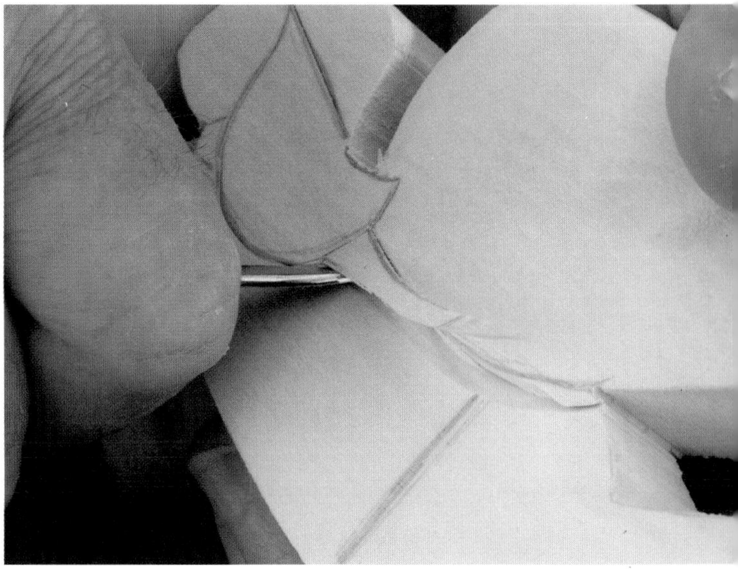

Undercut the other wing as well.

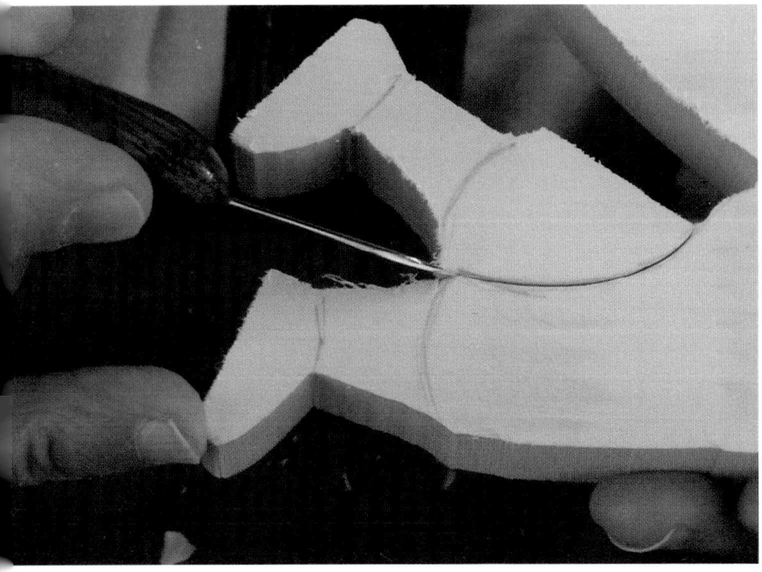

Score along the dividing line between the straightened right and bent left legs.

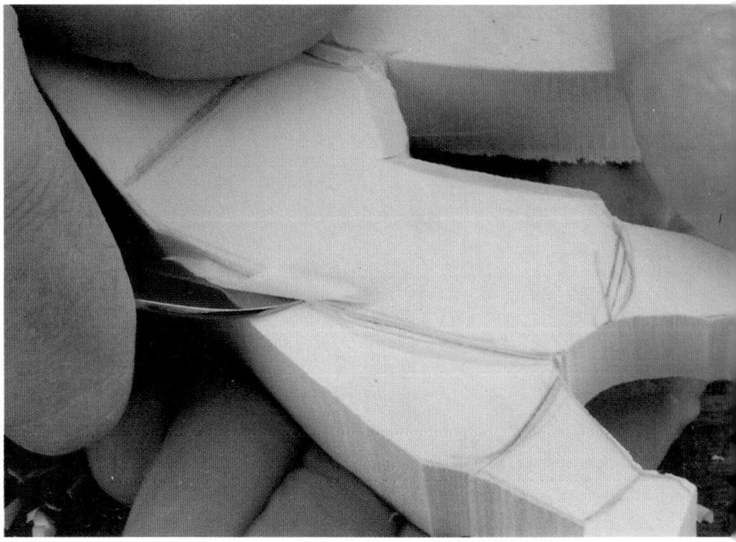

Because these figures are so small, I frequently shift from one area to another. Here I am removing the extra wood from the inside of the left leg.

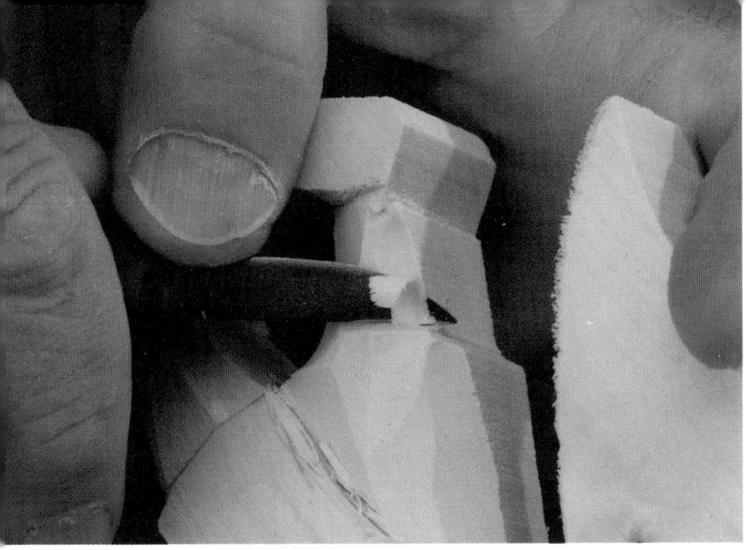

Shape where the socks go into the knickers.

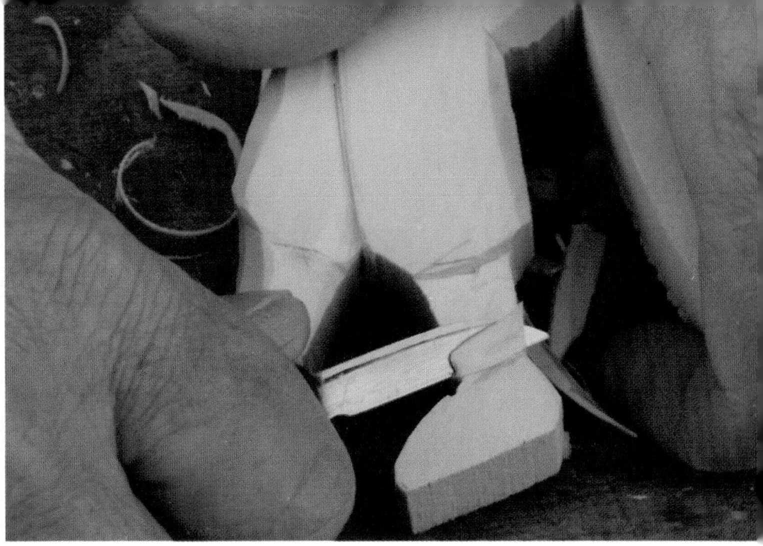

Repeat on the left sock.

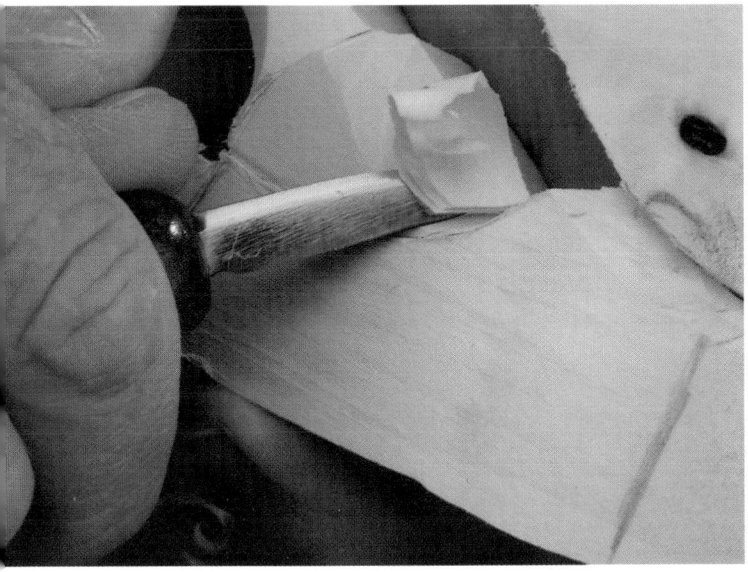

Separate the right and left legs, undercutting along this line.

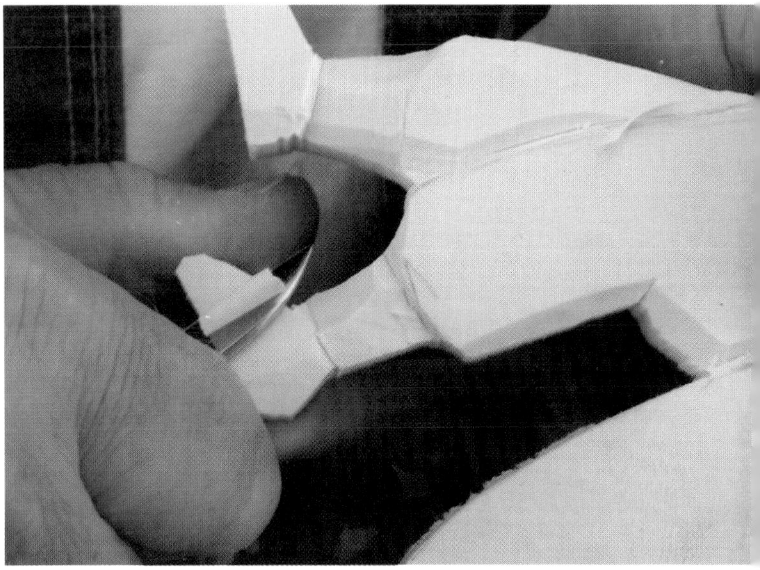

The shoes are too big, start reducing them with your knife.

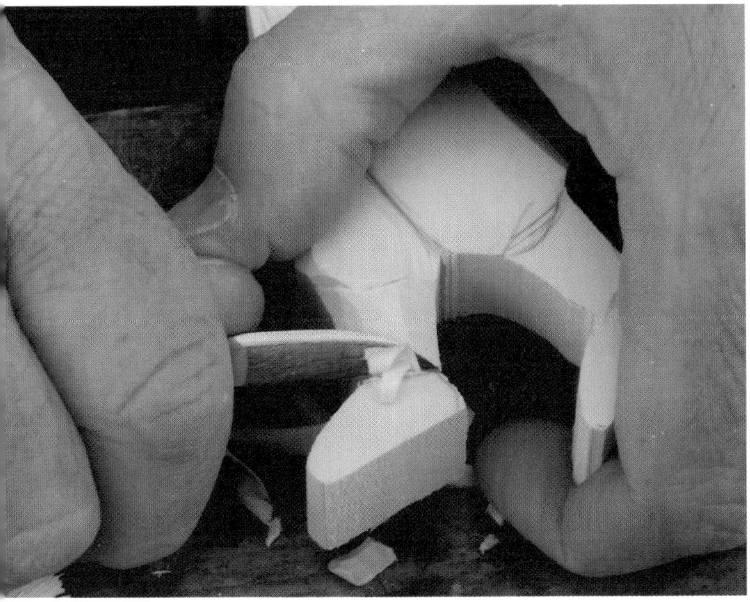

Separate the sock from the knickers and from the top of the shoe.

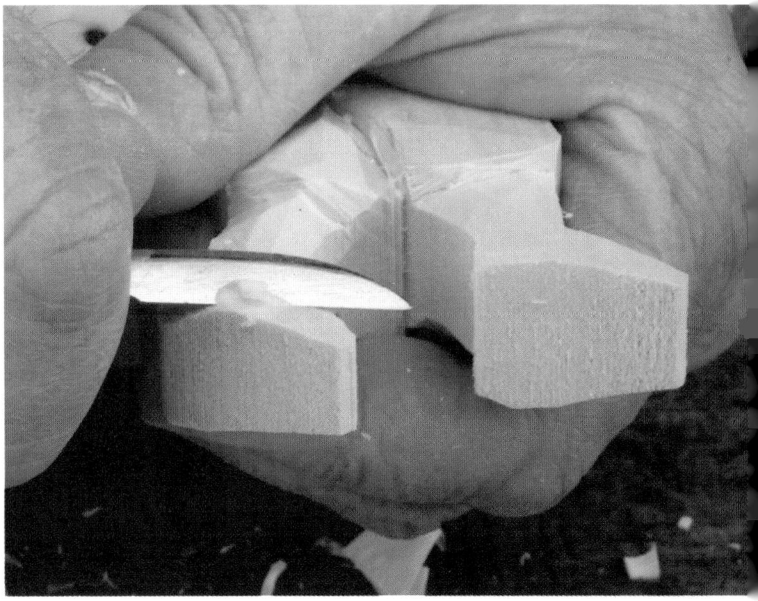

Continue trimming the shoes.

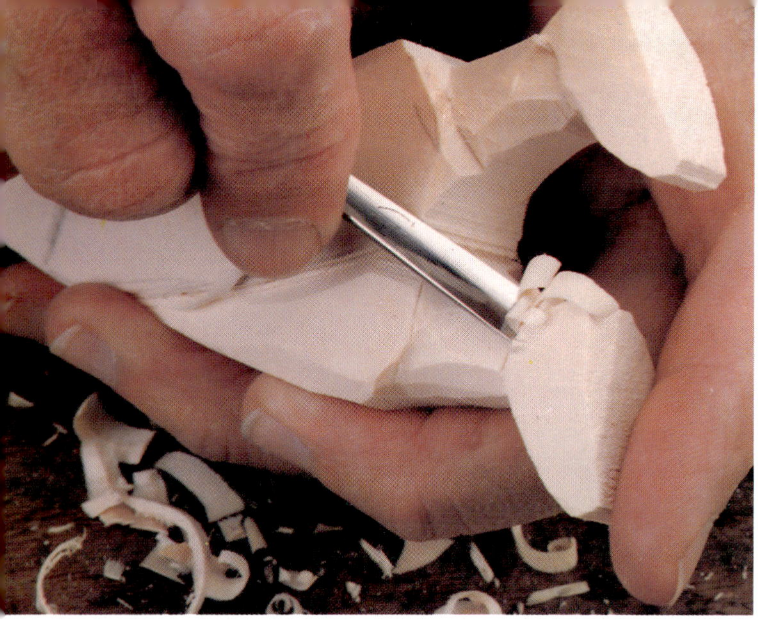

This #5, 8mm gouge is very good for getting into tight spaces.

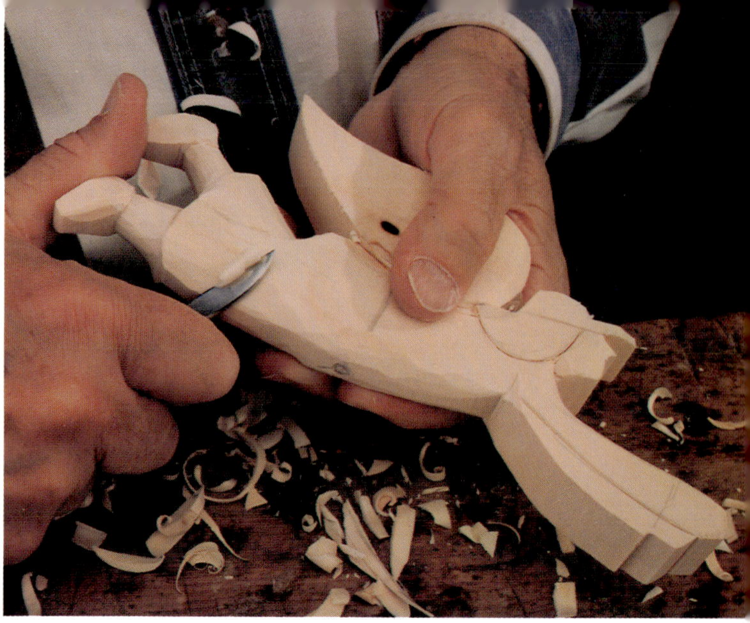

Continue to round and shape.

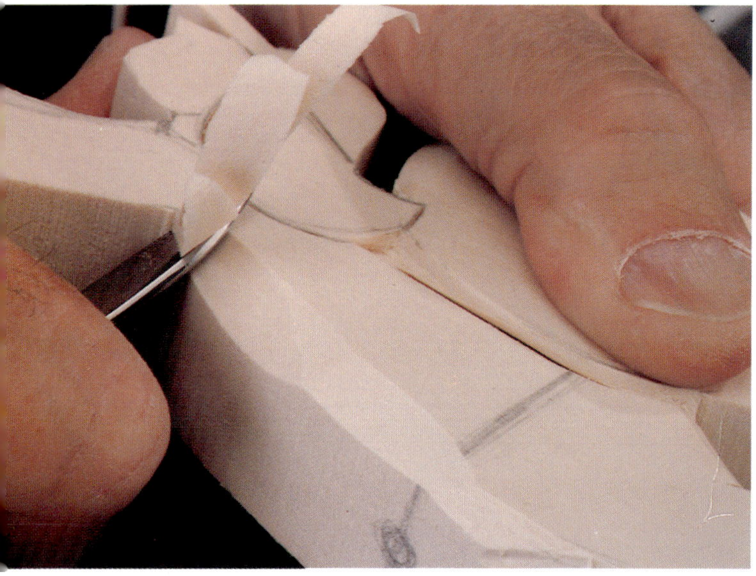

Begin rounding the chest and stomach areas.

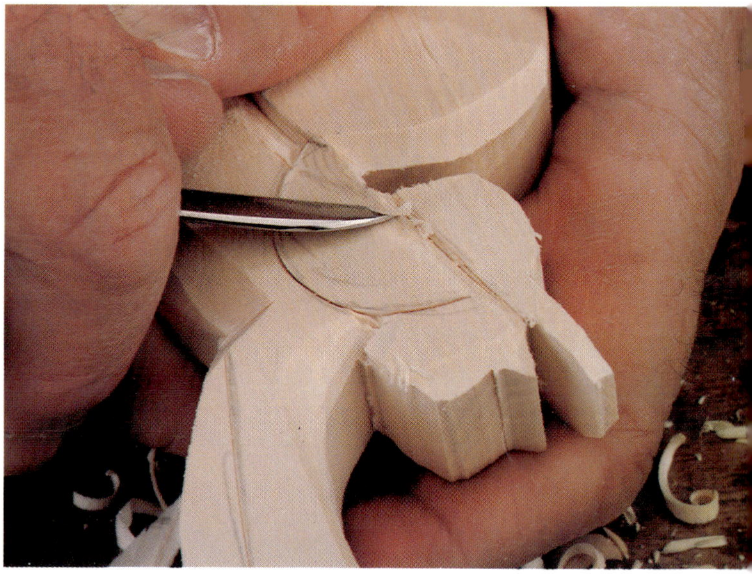

Shaping the golf cap into the head.

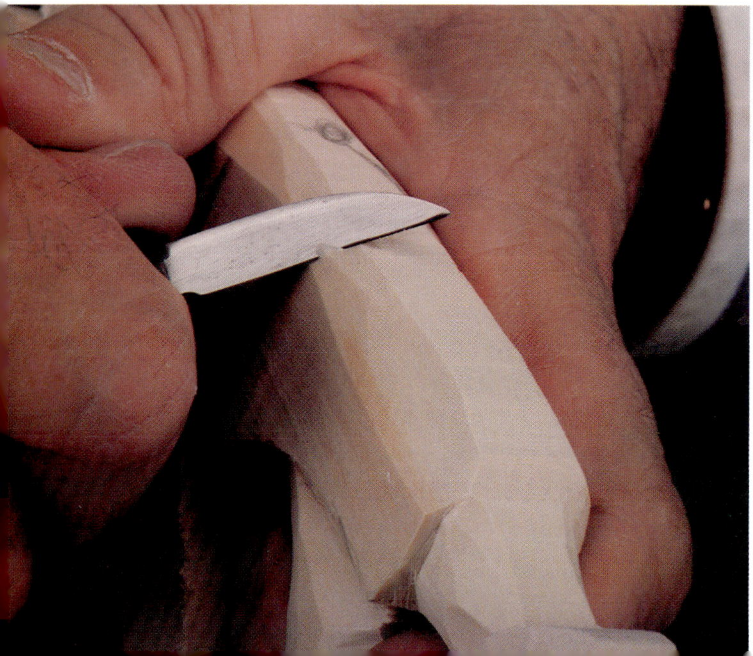

Round the knickers.

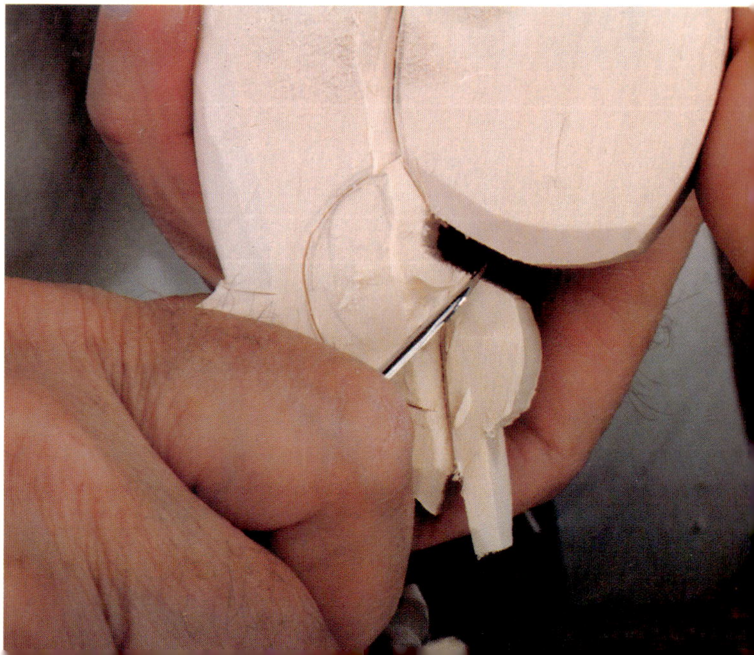

Rounding the back of the golf cap.

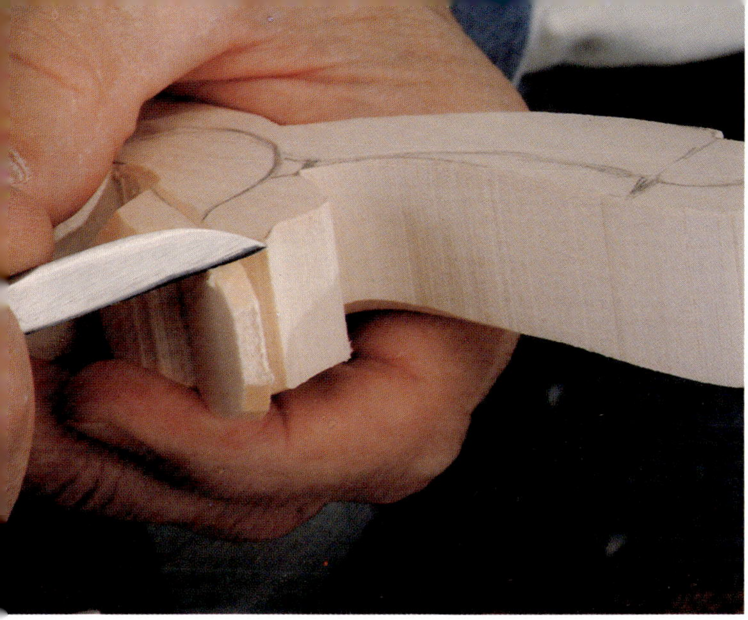

The cap bill is a very thin piece. Round the bill carefully.

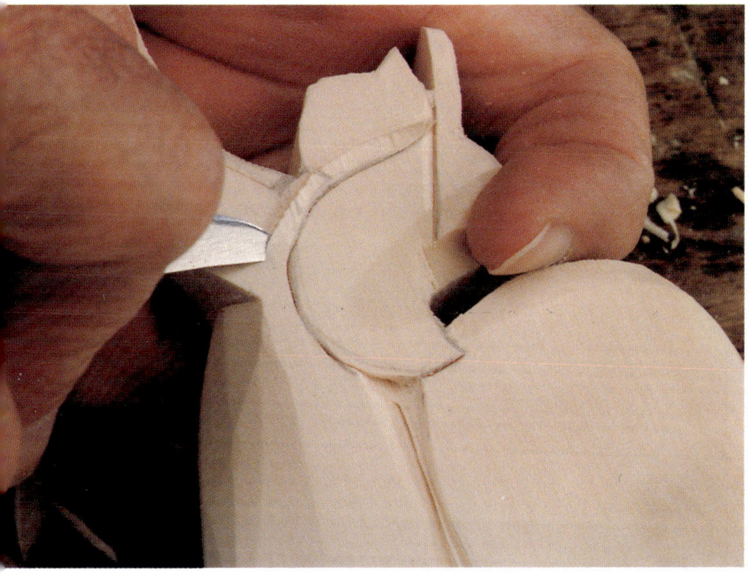

Separate the hair from the rest of the body.

Repeat on the other side.

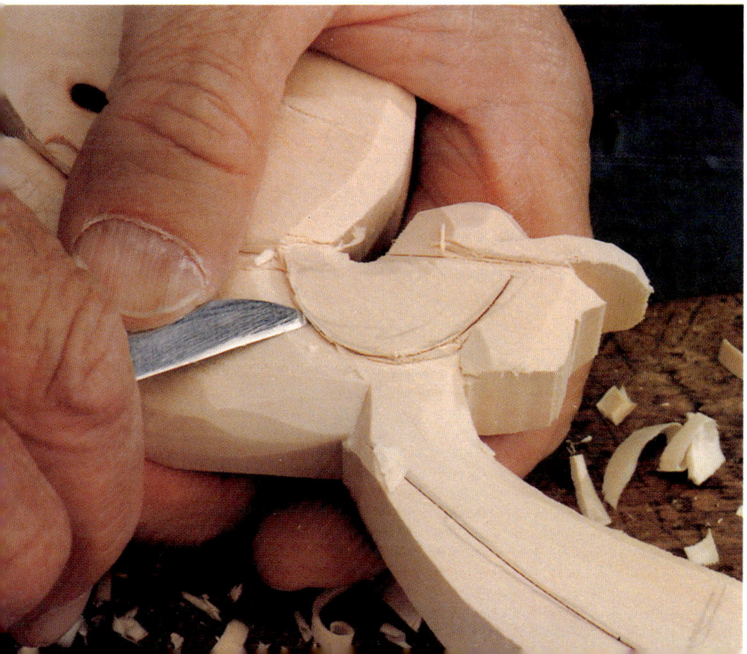

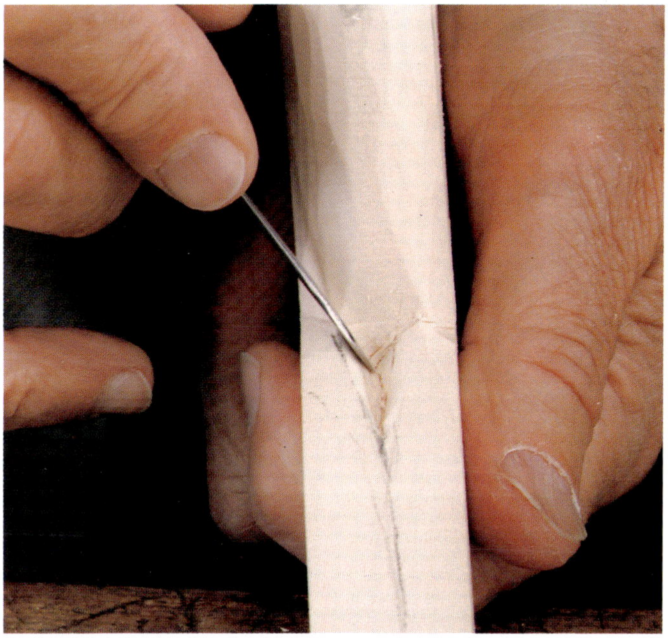

Take out a little triangular cut here at the base of the arms.

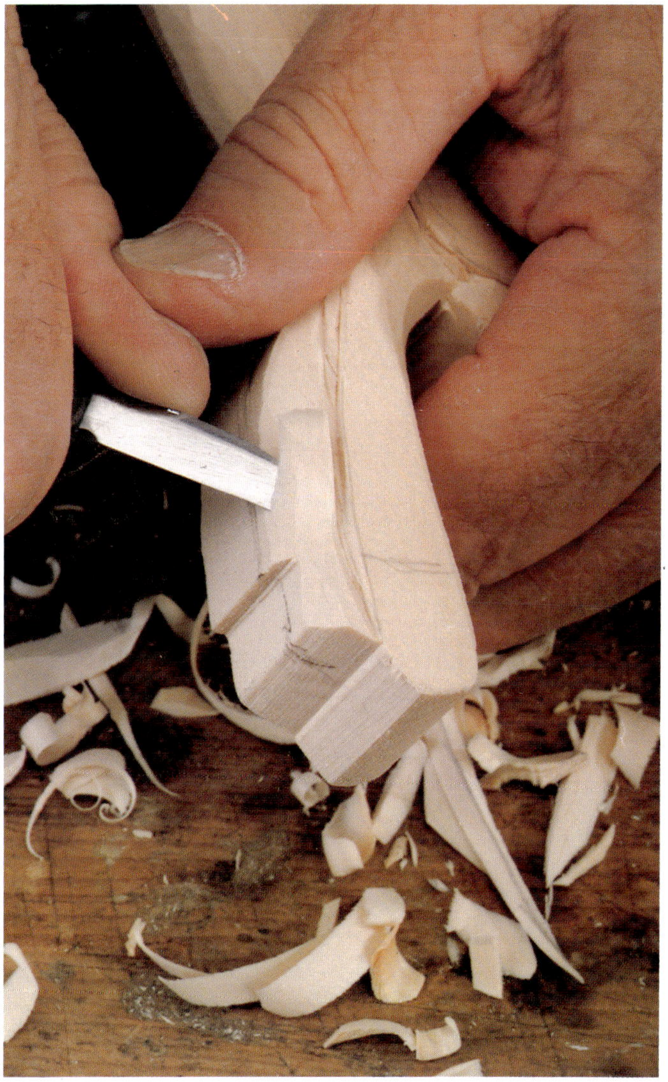

Take away the waste from the lower arm.

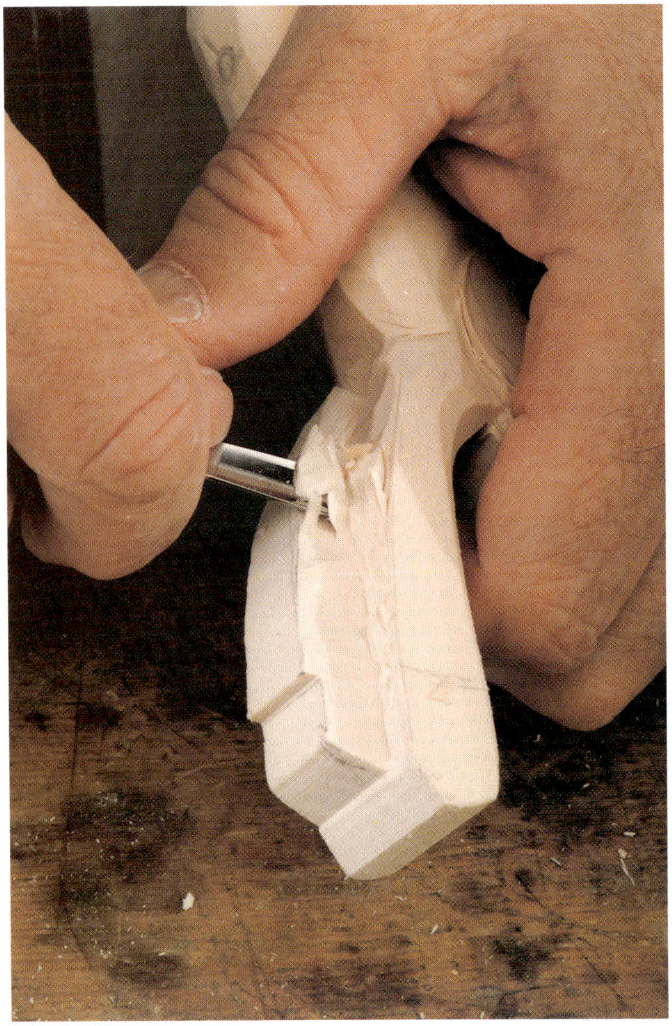

The #5 gouge is very handy for removing this wood waste.

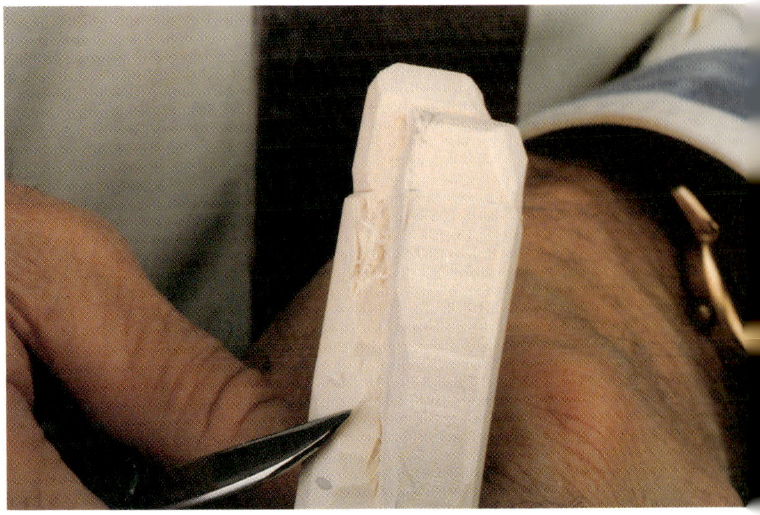

I've begun to shape the hands a little bit.

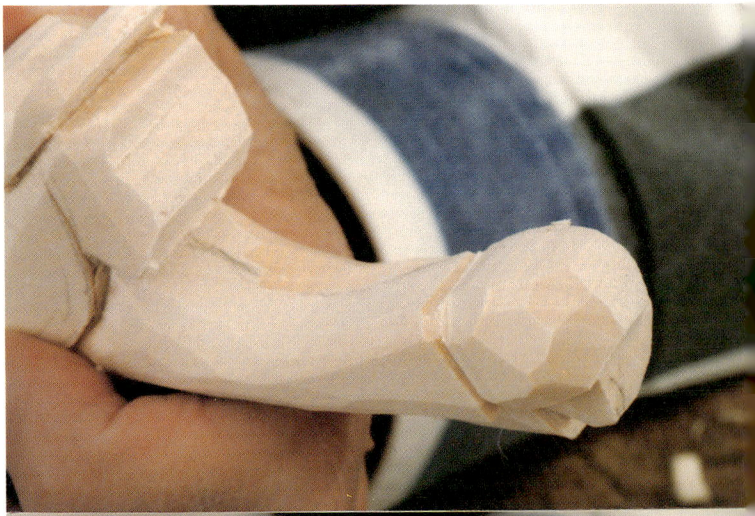

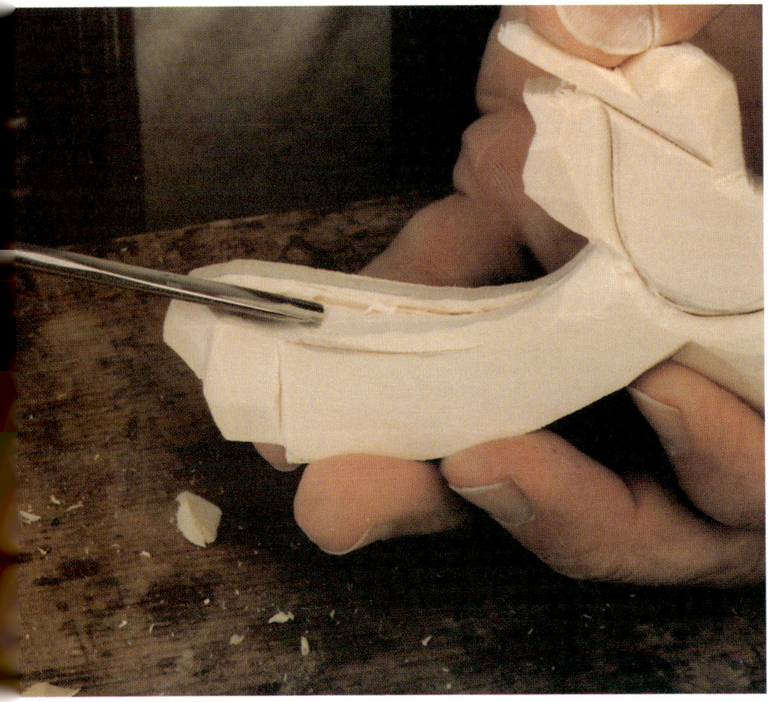

Taking away some of the waste between the arms.

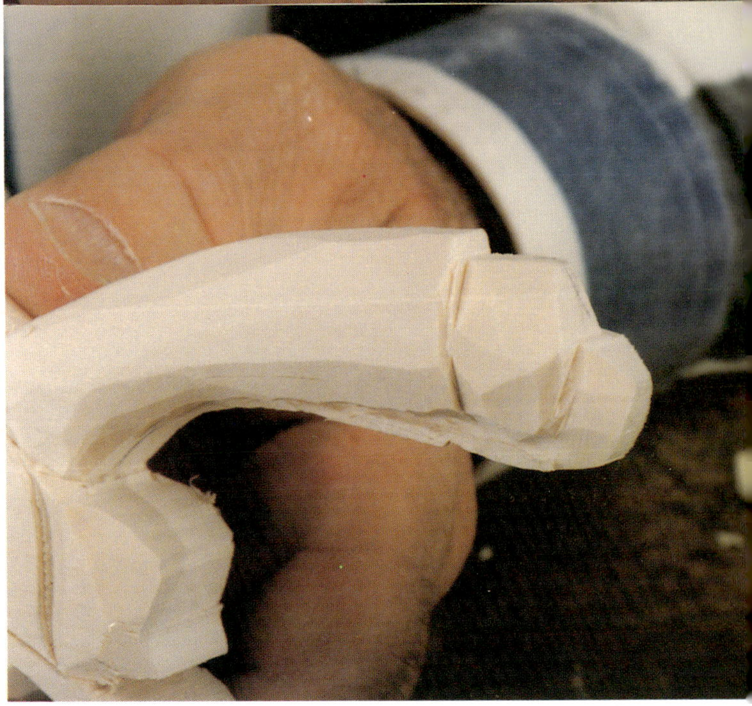

Shaping the hands.

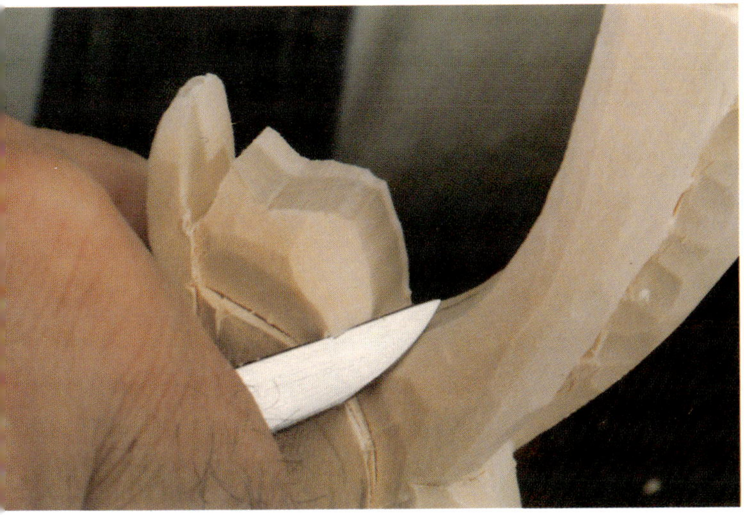

Thinning the face.

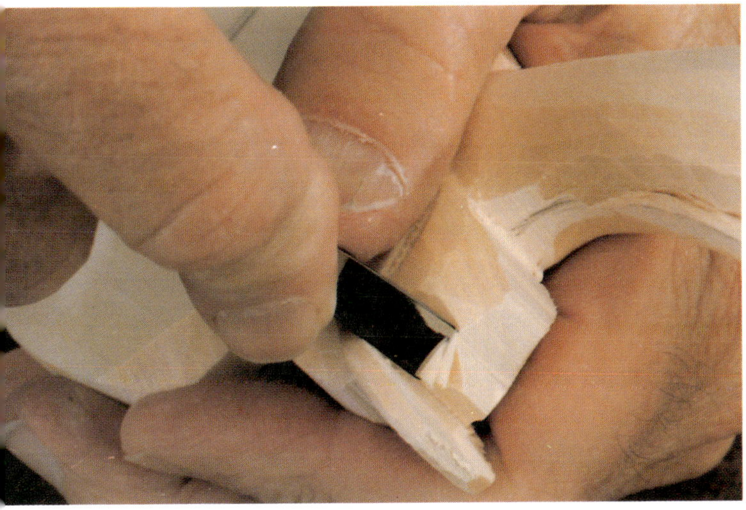

Take the #5 gouge and shape the nose. I can't shape it in the same way I did the others. The cap is in the way.

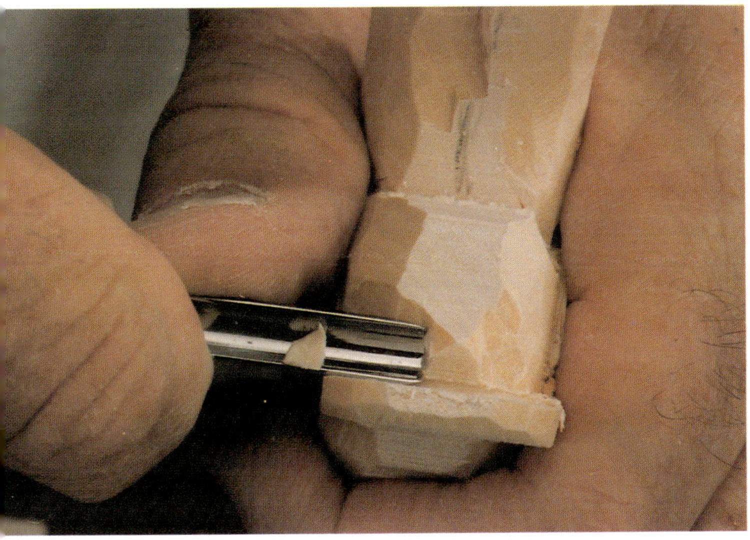

Take the #9, V shaped gouge and work it in from both sides to clean out where the eyes and nose meet.

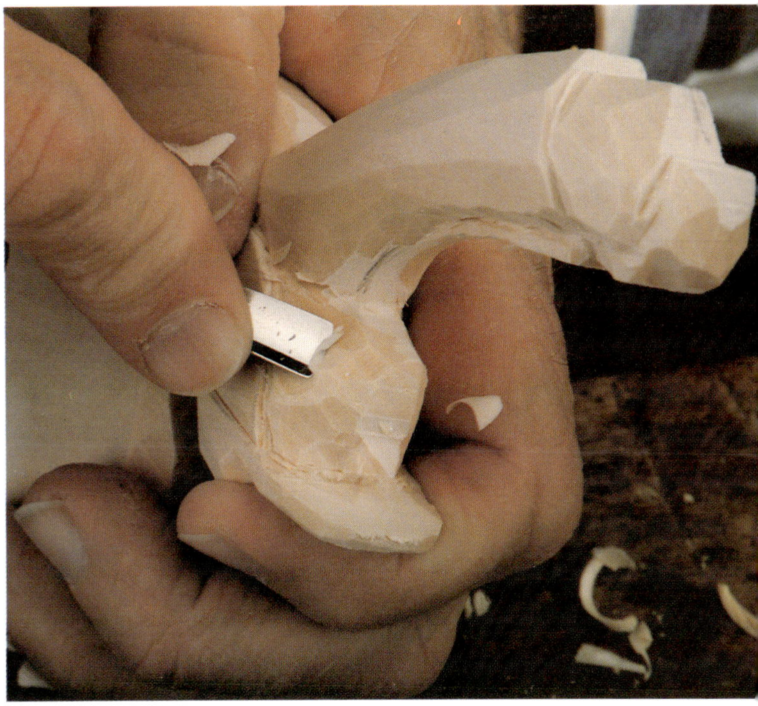

Remove some of the extra wood from around the chin with the #5 gouge.

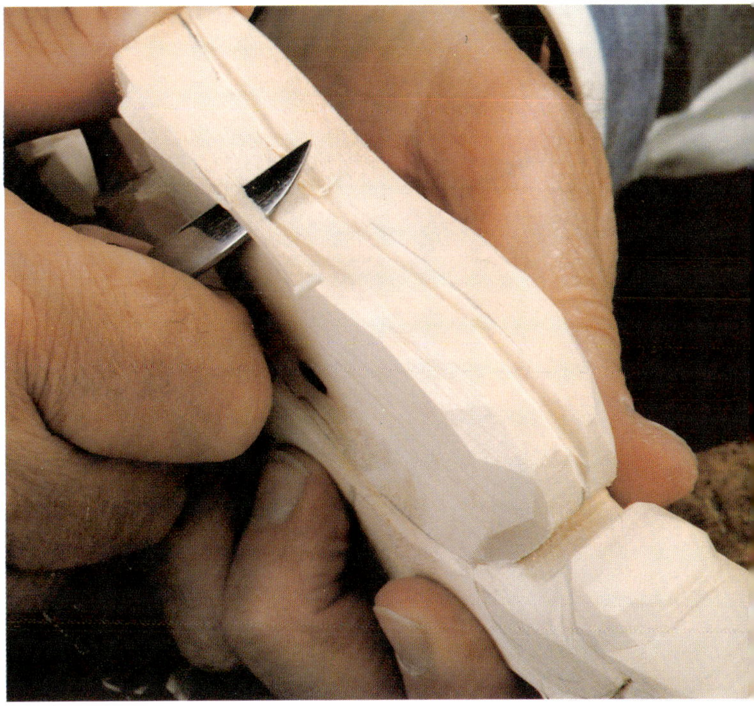

Round the top of the wings with your knife.

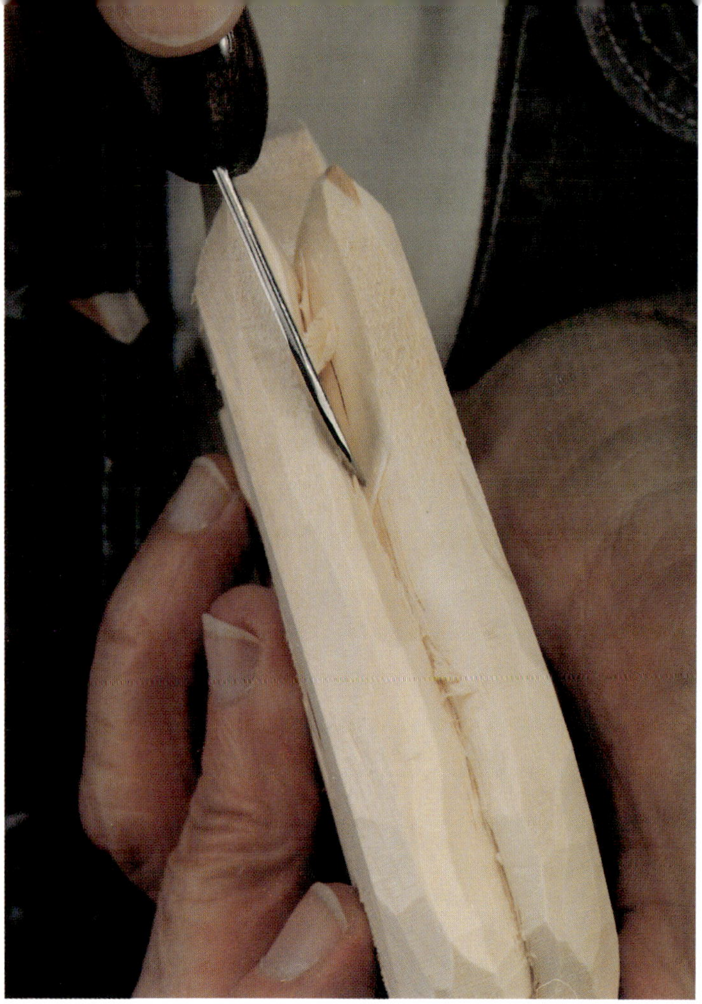

Cleaning out between the wings.

We need to do some more rounding of the wings down near the back of the golf cap.

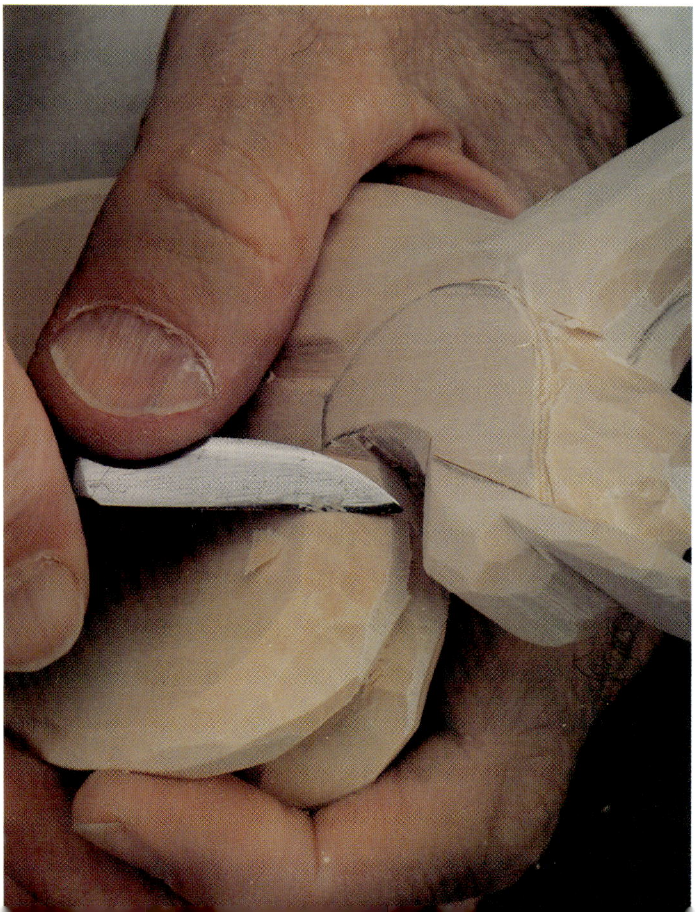

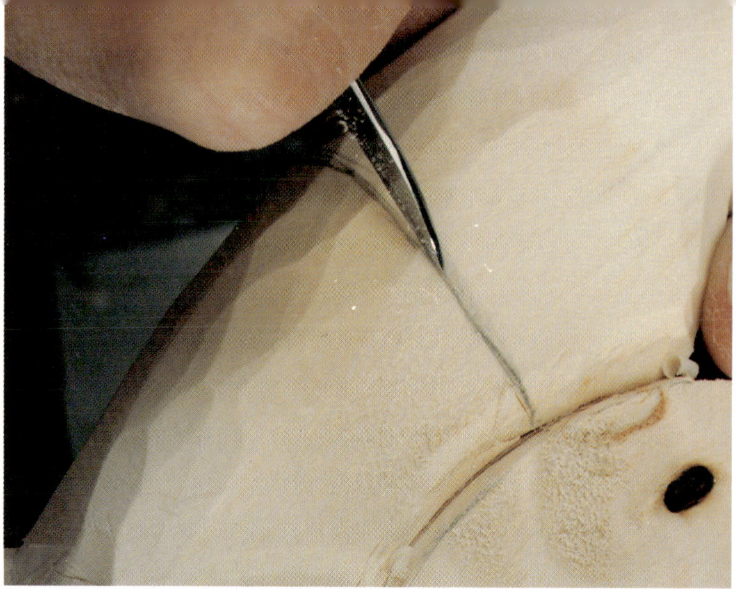

Draw and incise a line separating the knickers from the shirt.

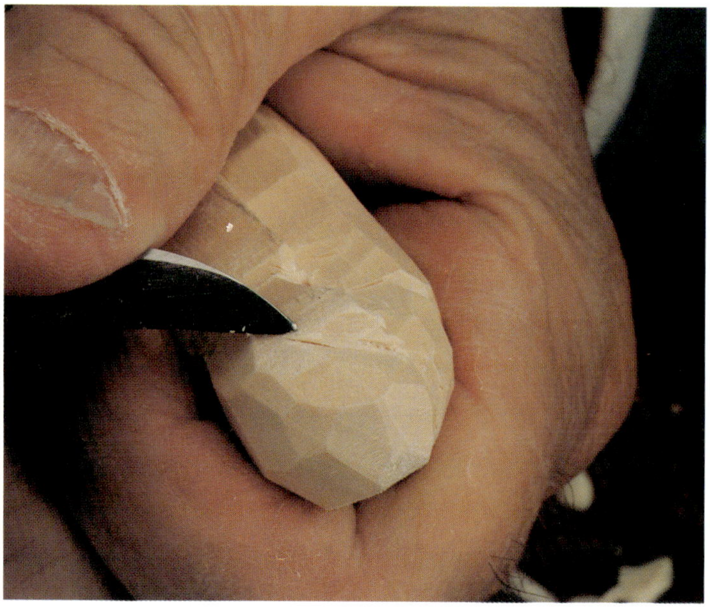

I'm putting in a little V between the thumb and the forefinger where the hole will be drilled to fit the golf club.

I have drawn in the fingers on the right hand.

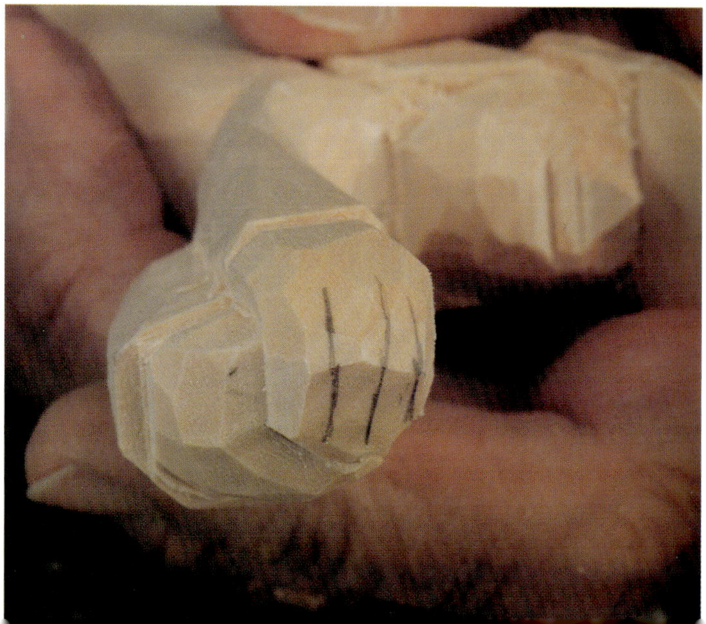

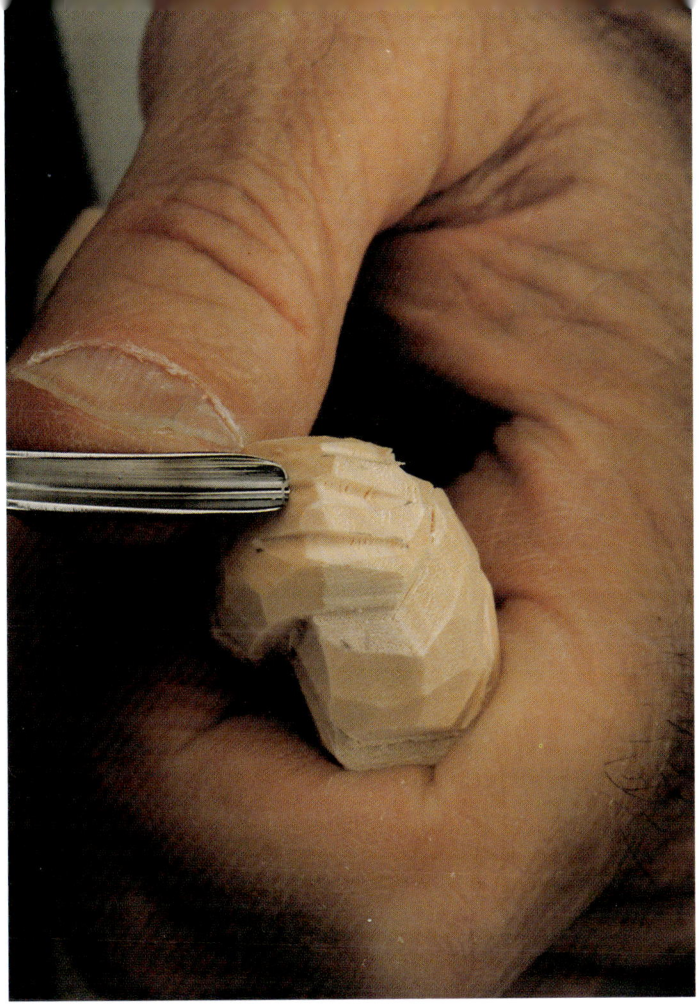

Using the gouge, follow the lines and make some fingers.

I have also cut in some fingers on the left hand.

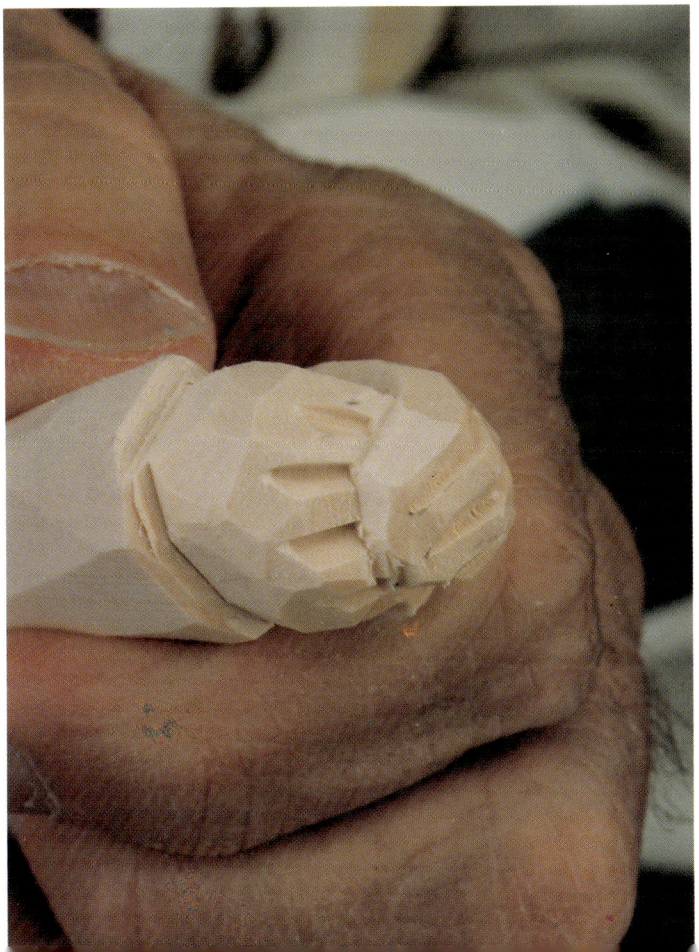

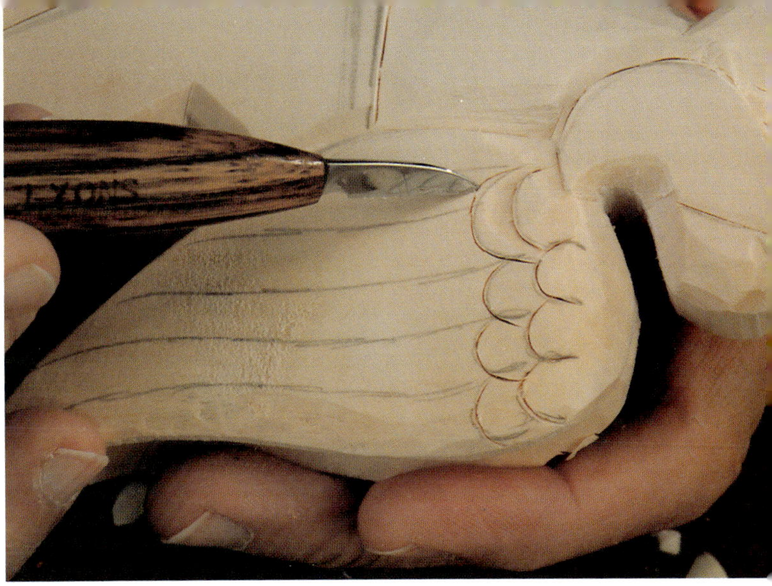

I have drawn in the wing details and have begun to incise them.

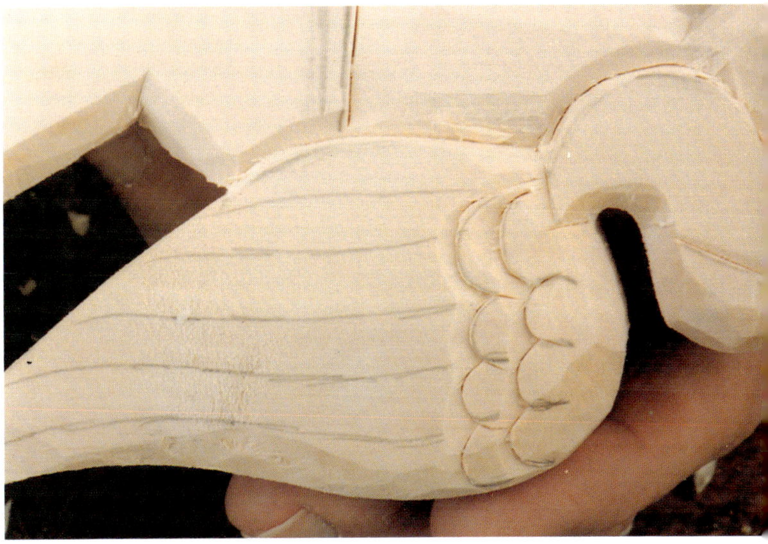

The incised and undercut upper wings.

I have incised the rest of the wing feathers with a V gouge although it can be done easily with a knife.

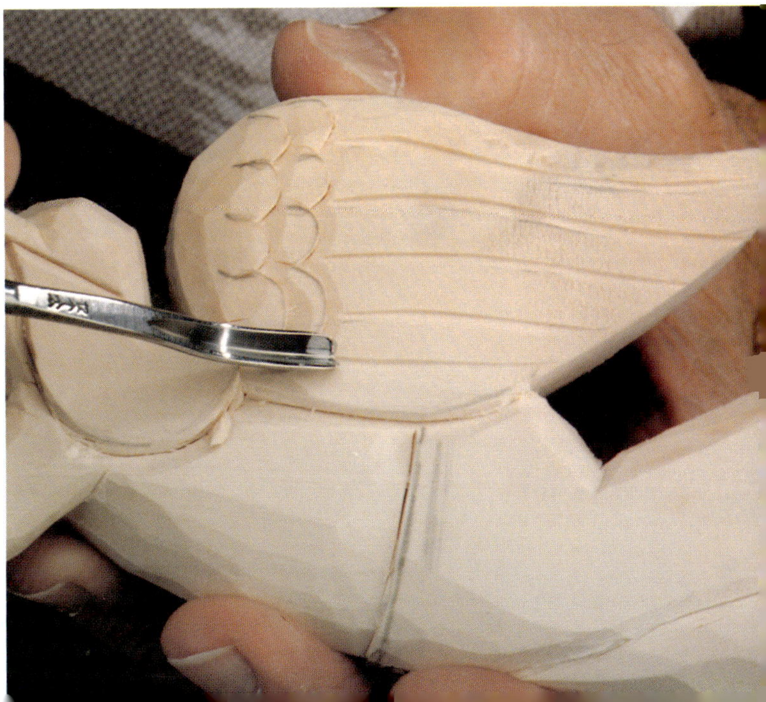

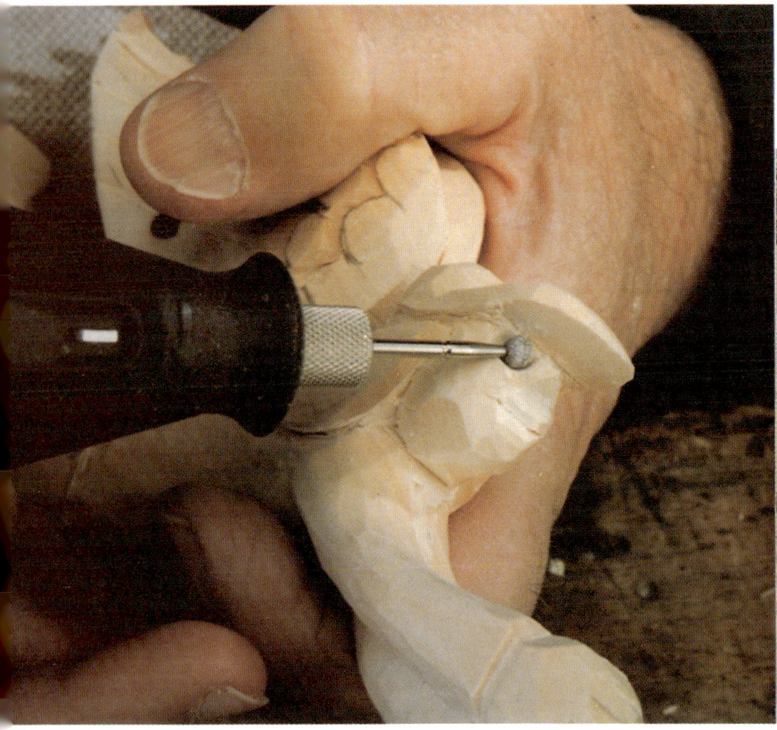

Due to the bill of the cap, it was easier to get this Dremel MINIMITE with a ball bit in for some detail in the eyes.

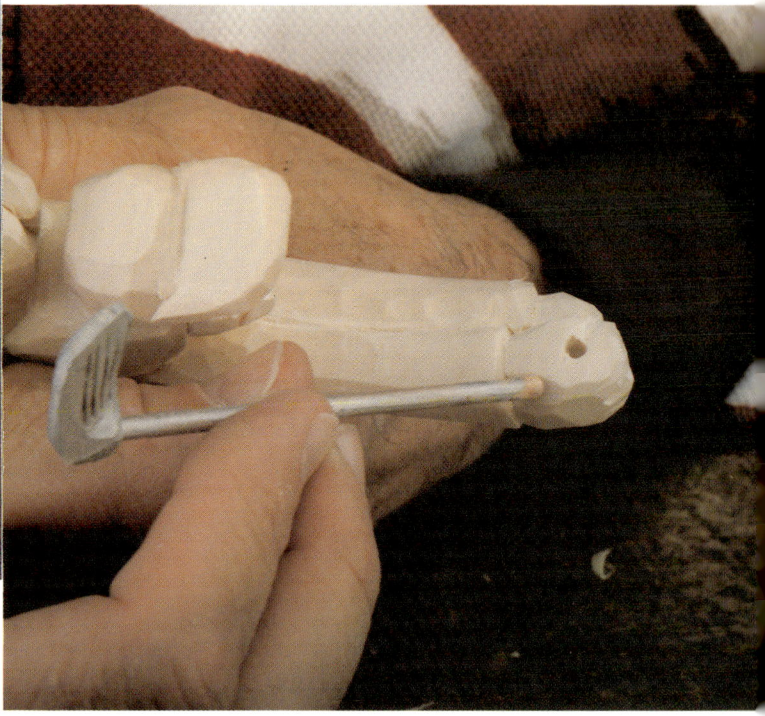

Drill a hole through the hands to fit the golf club. The shaft of the club is a dowel rod and the club head is just a small piece of bass wood. Bore a hole in the club head for the dowel before carving the head of the golf club.

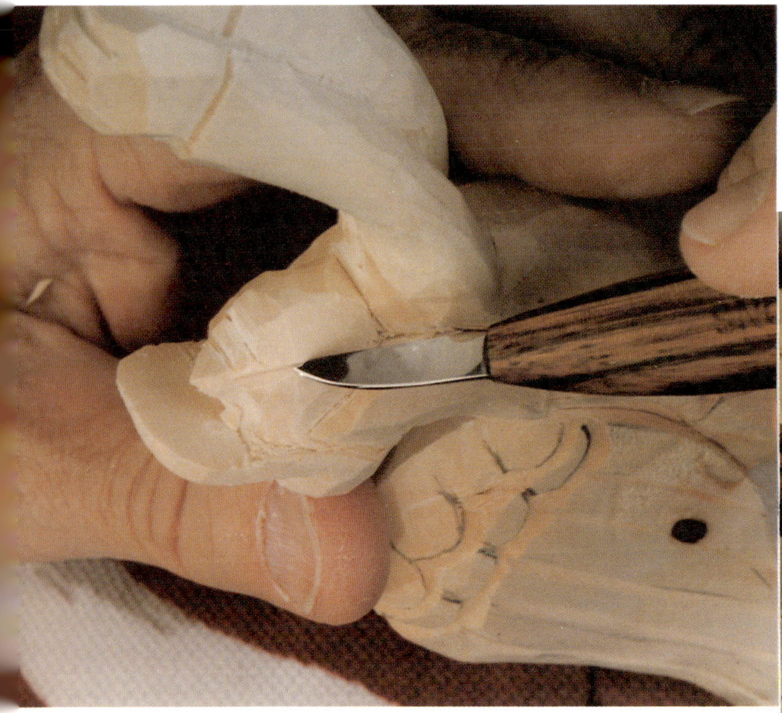

I've extended the line from the nose to the mouth with my knife.

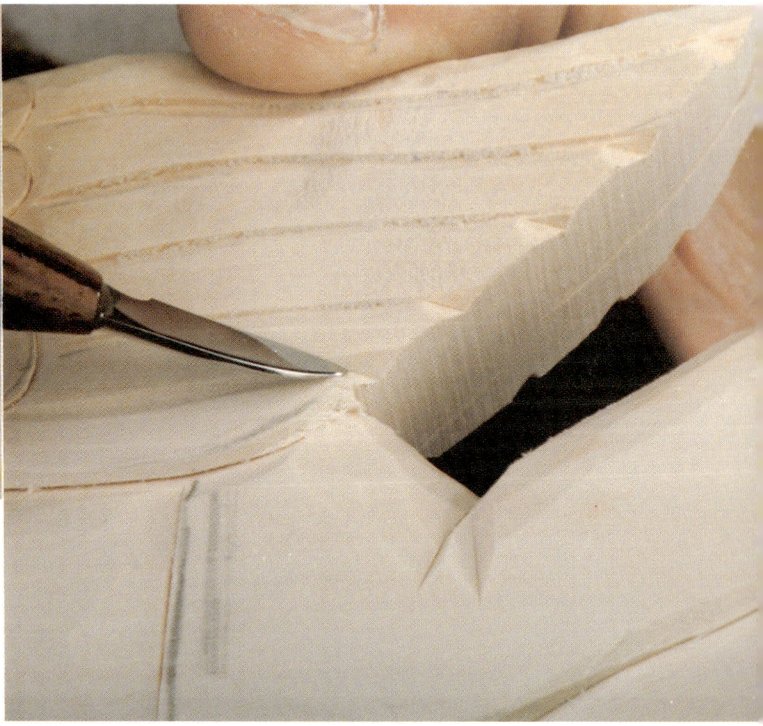

Notch the end of each feather as it gives a little more detail to the wings.

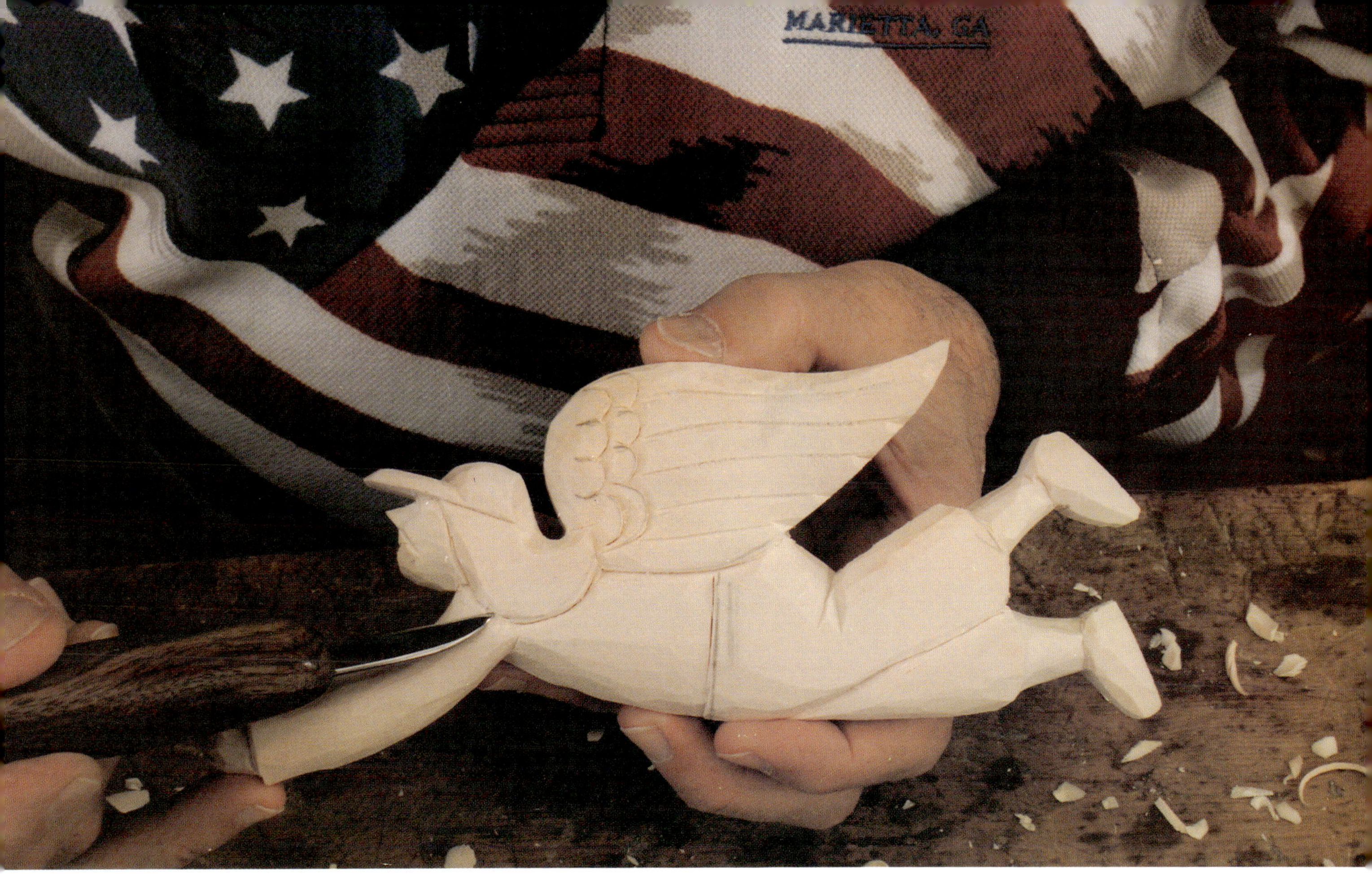

Go back now and check for "fuzzies" or any other areas you think need to be cleaned up.

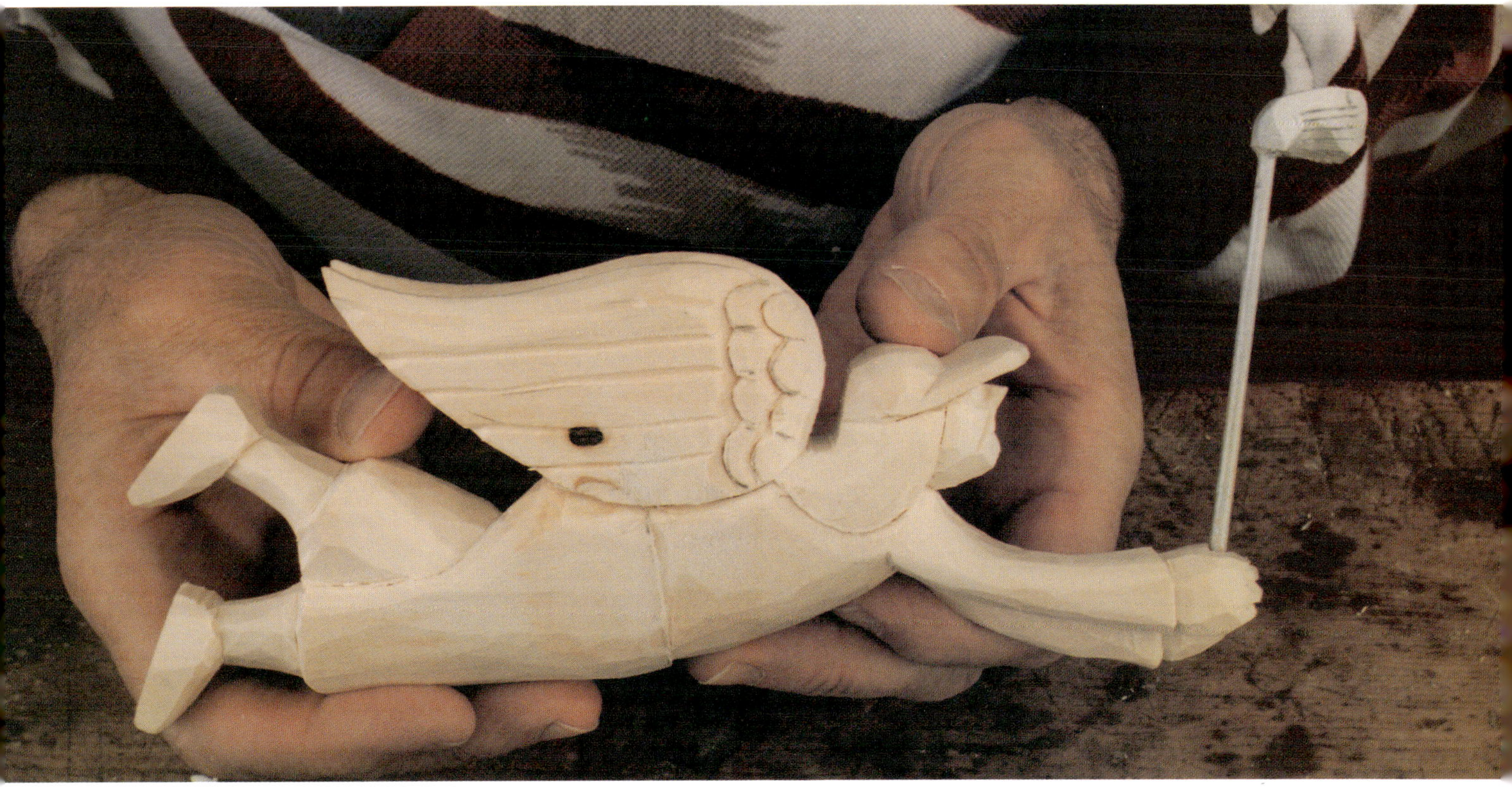

The angel with the club in place. The knot in the wing will be covered during painting.

Painting The Angels

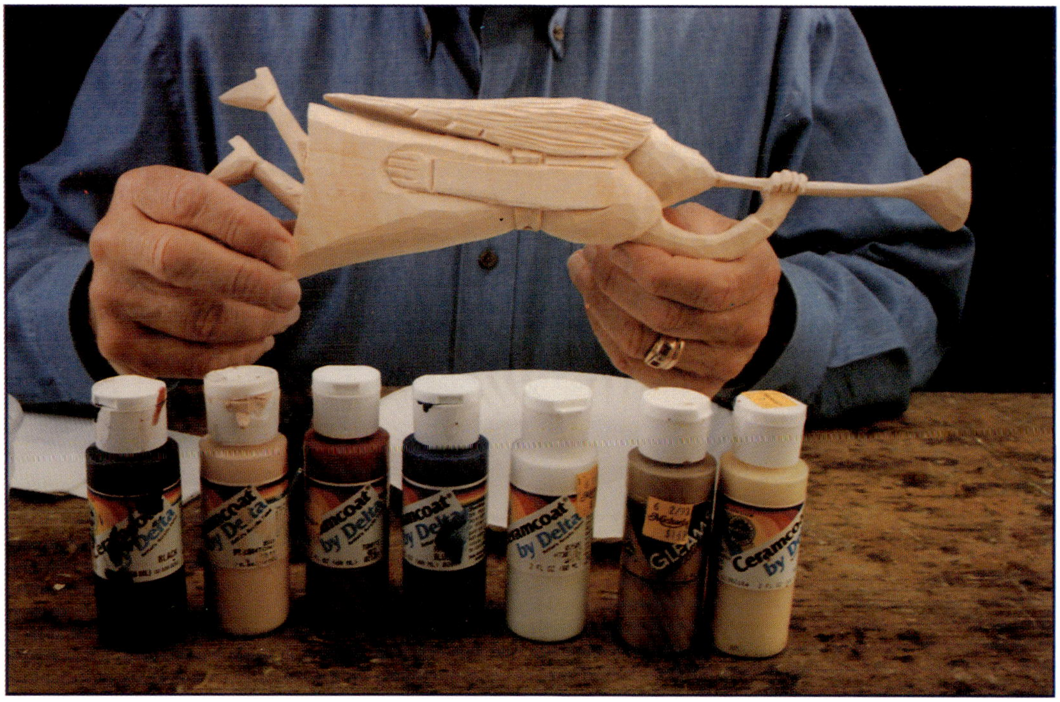

This is the angel with the long trumpet and the flying hair. These are the colors we will use to paint her. They are Ceramcoat by Delta.

The first color used is Navy Blue. Paint the blouse and the arms. I like to paint the largest areas first.

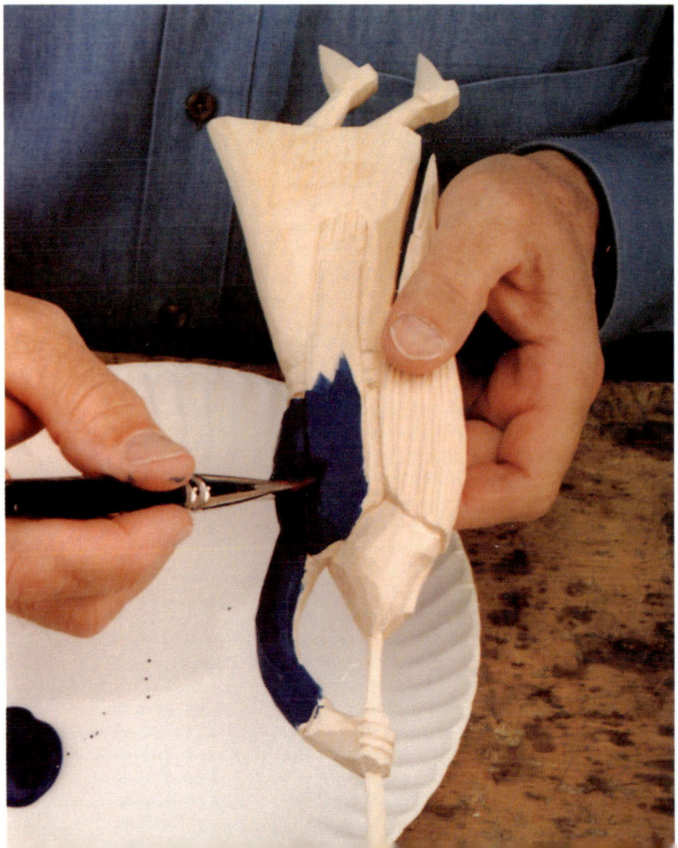

Like so.

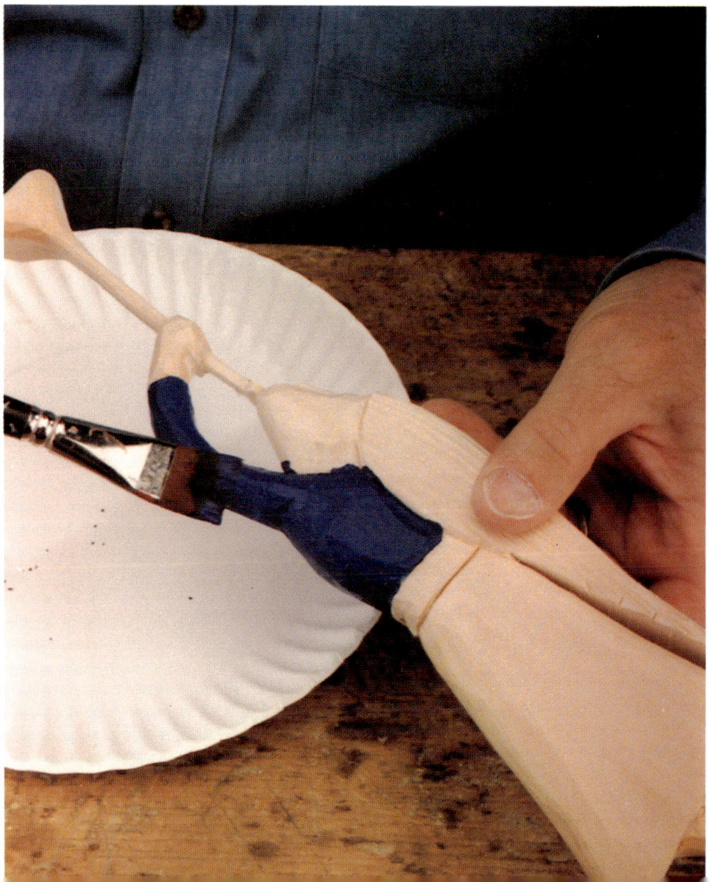

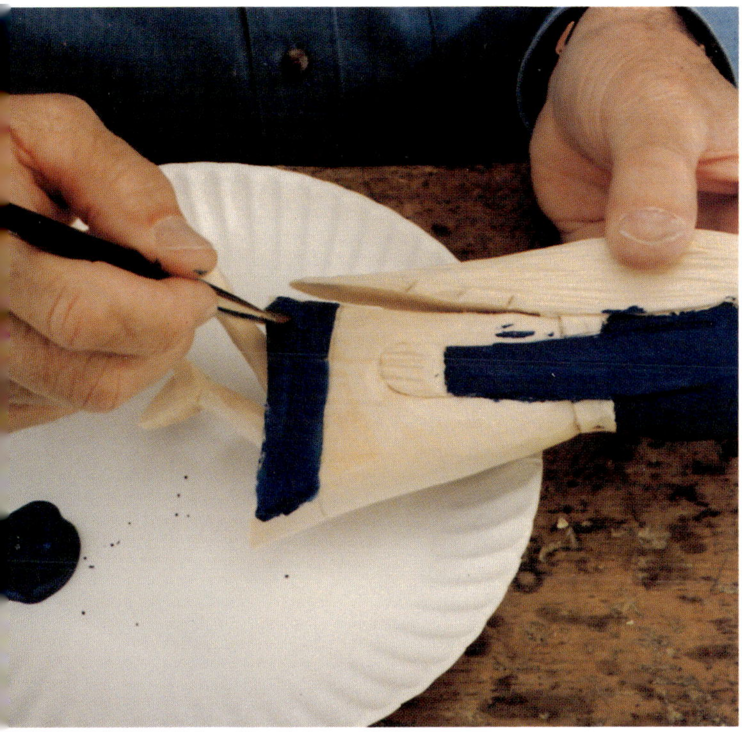

Paint a wide Navy Blue stripe around the bottom of the skirt. We will add some stars there later.

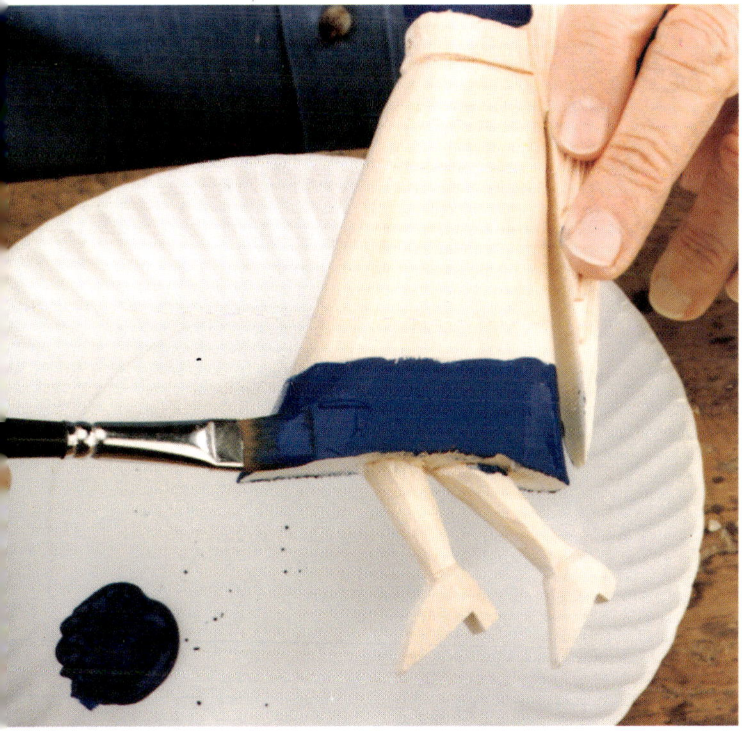

Paint the stripe on both sides.

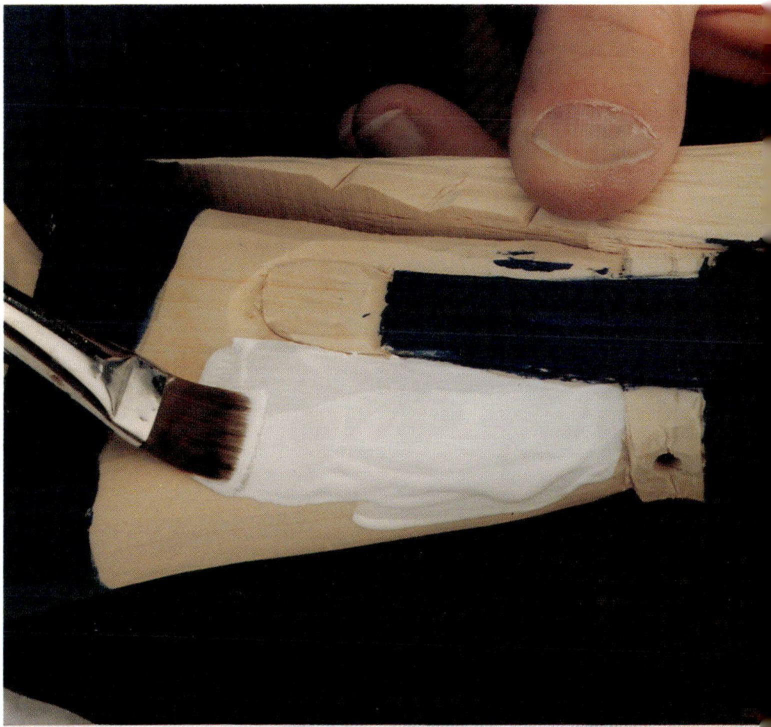

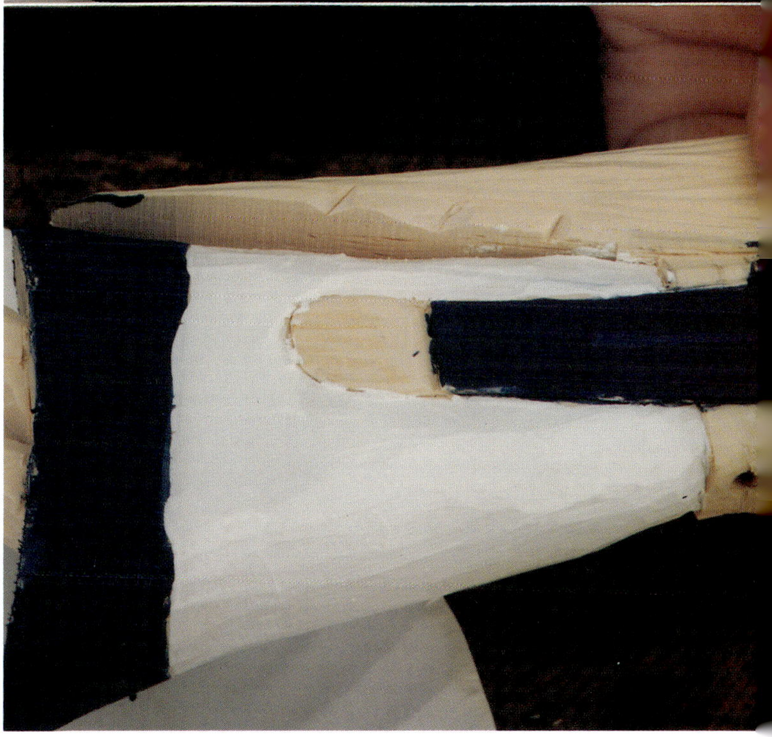

I am going to paint the rest of the skirt white.

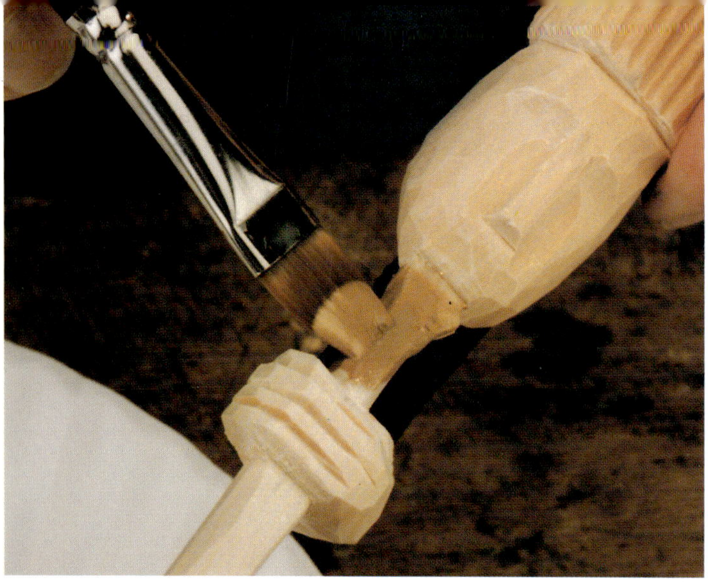

Begin painting the trumpet Kim Gold.

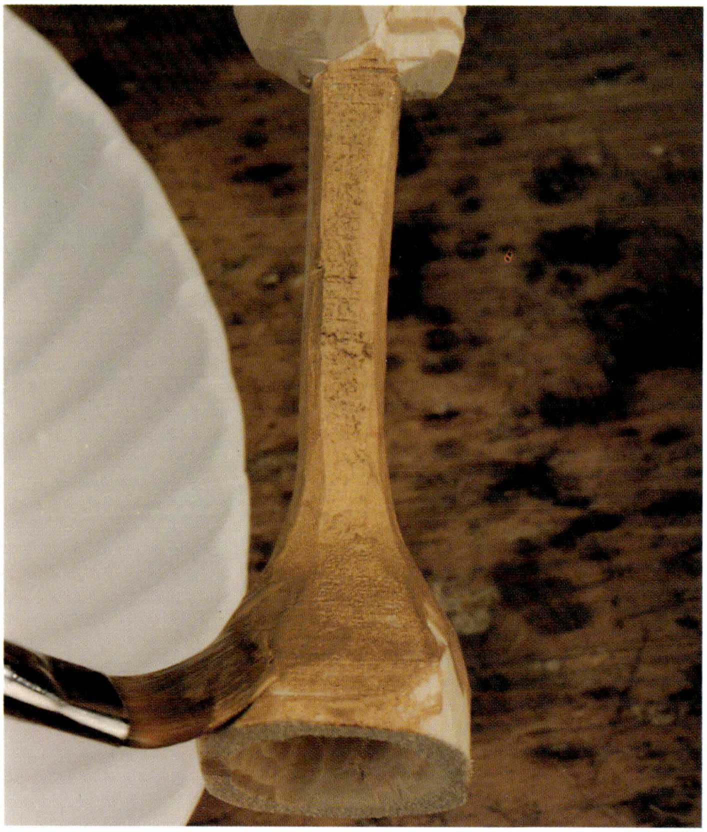

Continue painting the trumpet.

Paint the belt Kim Gold as well.

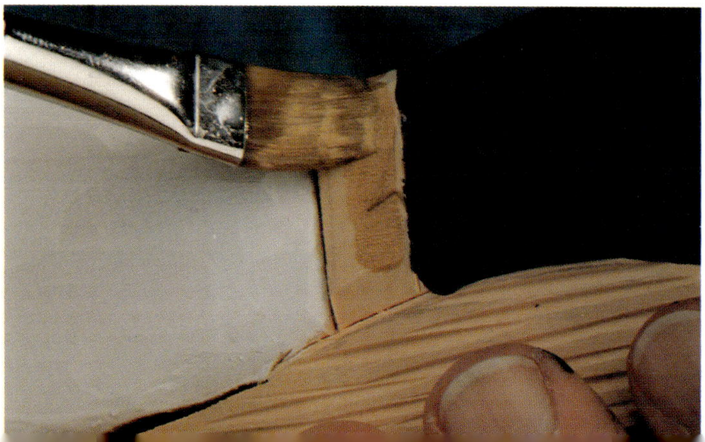

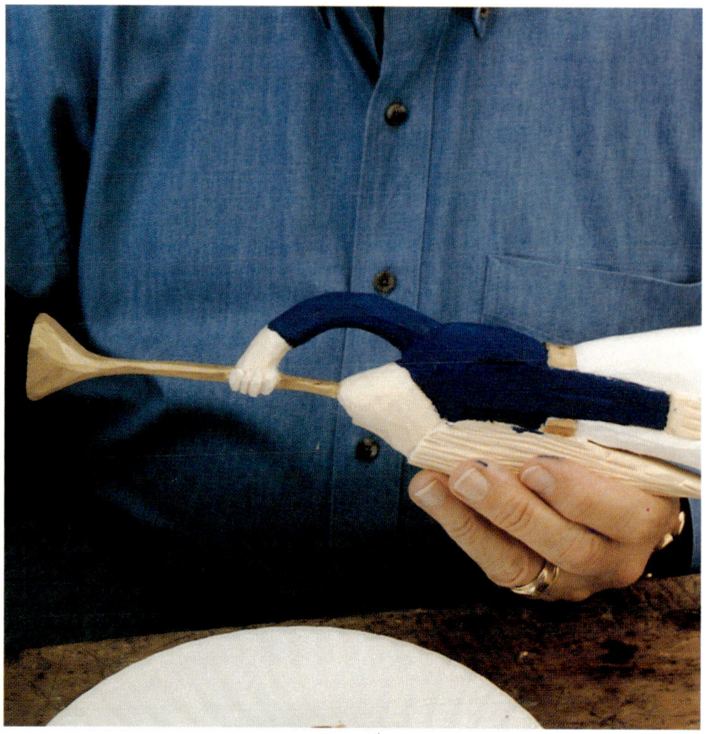

The gold belt and trumpet.

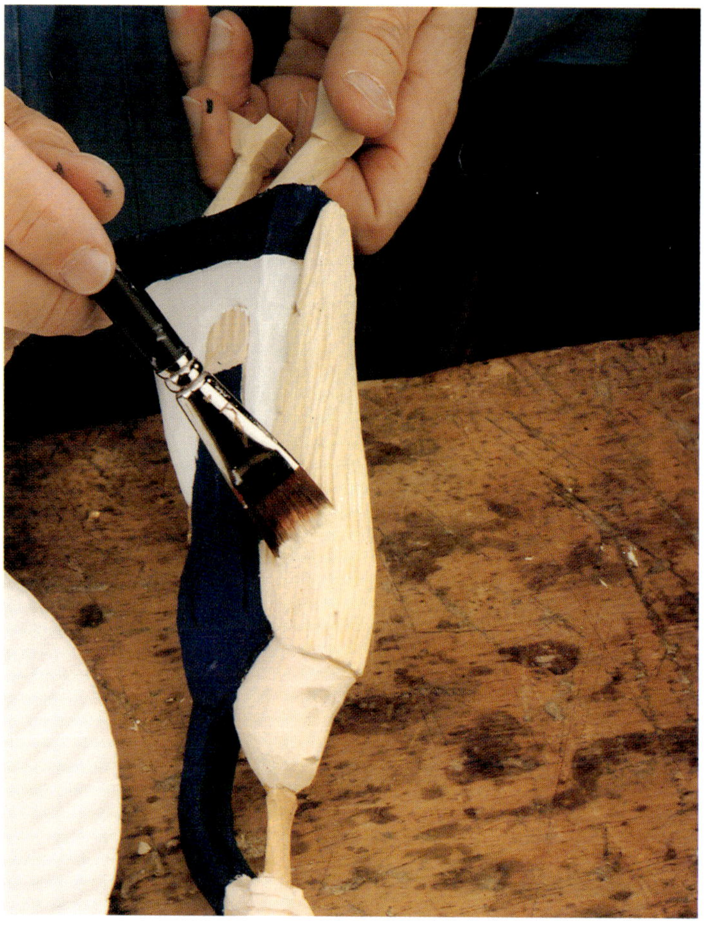

I'm painting the hair with Old Parchment.

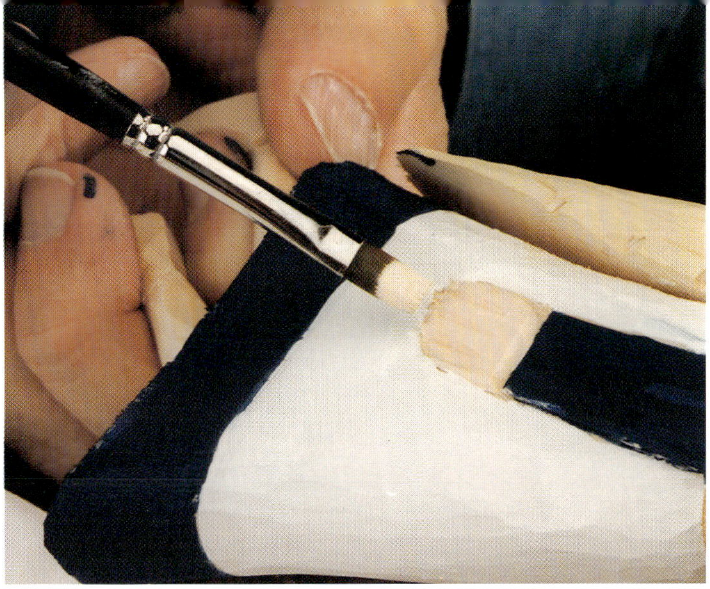

Paint the hands in Flesh Tone.

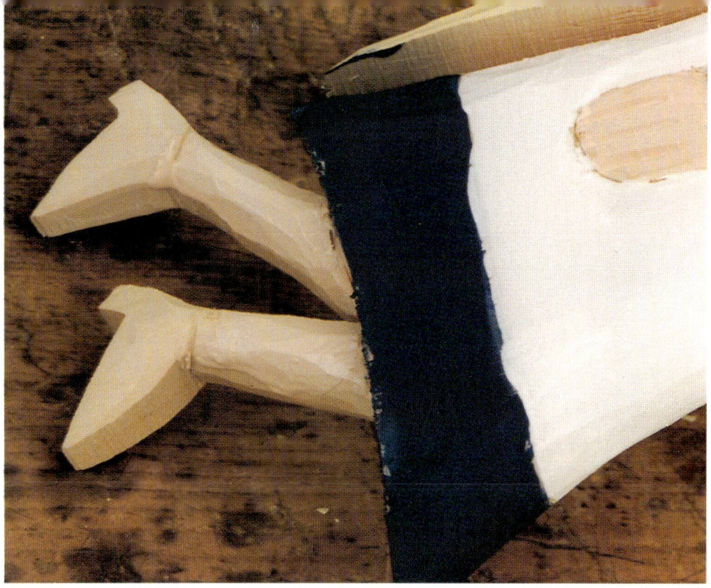

Don't forget to paint the legs in Flesh Tone.

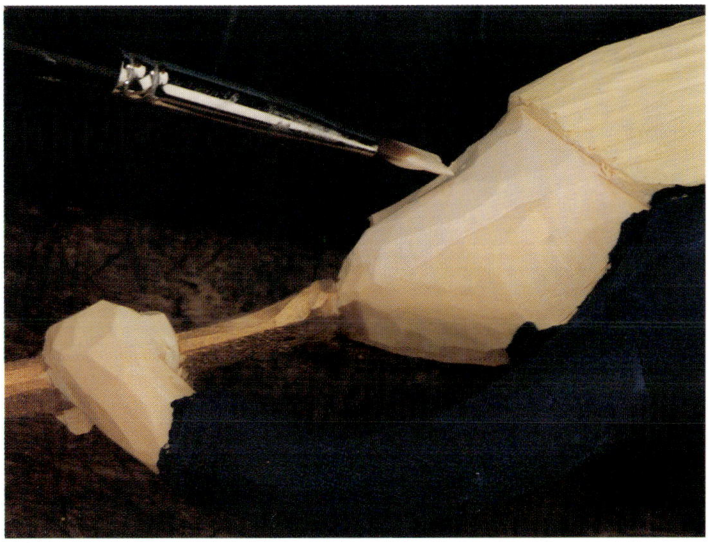

Paint the face in Flesh Tone as well. Be extremely careful when painting flesh on bass wood. The two colors are very close. If you should leave a bare spot and then antique the figure, that spot will turn dark.

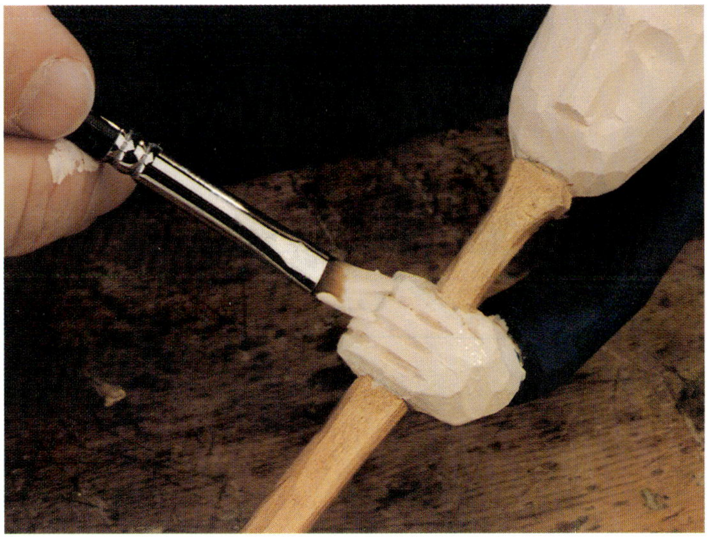

Paint the hand holding the trumpet as well.

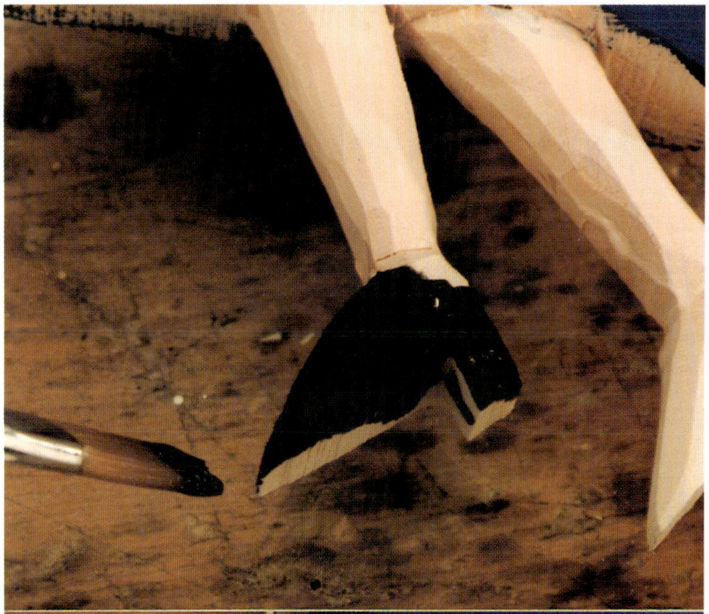

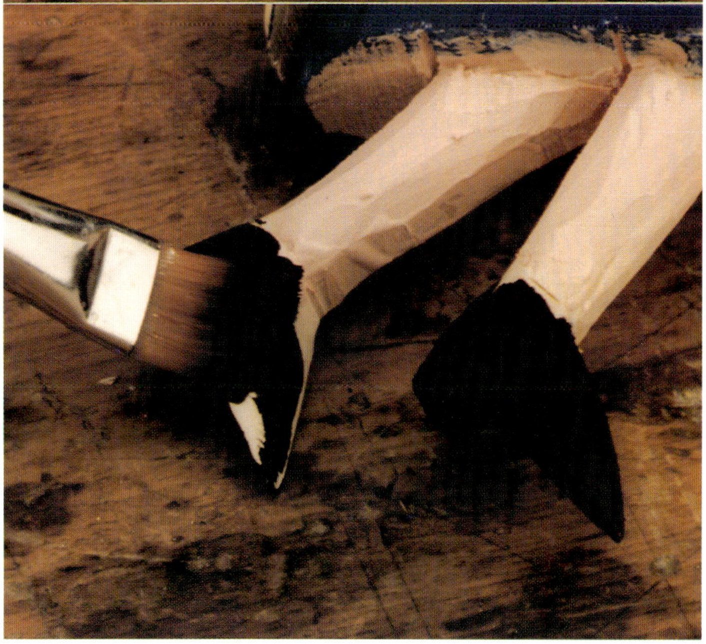

Paint the shoes black.

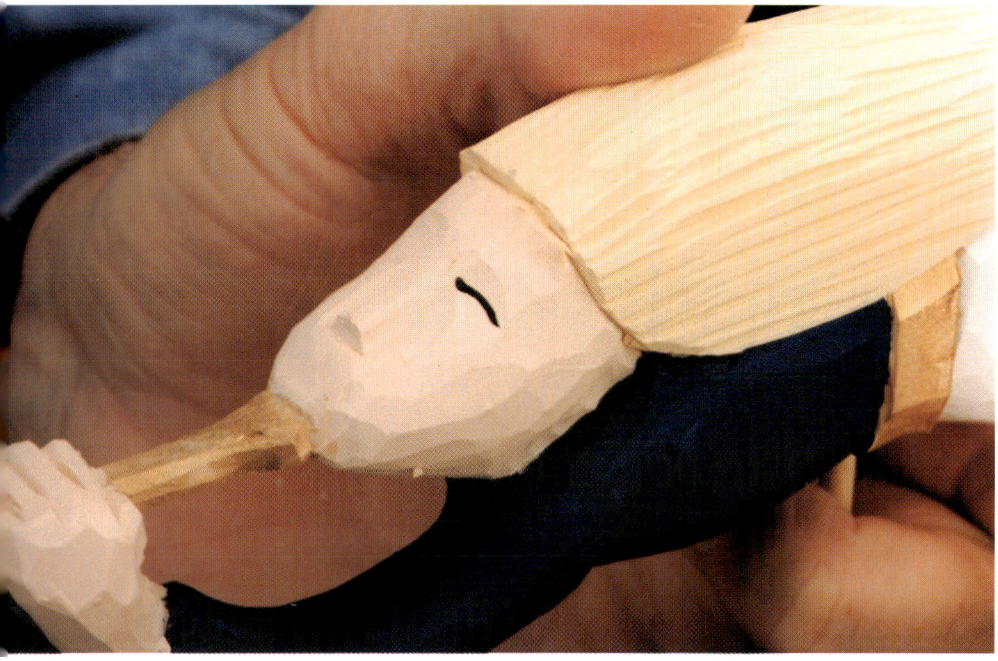

While you have out the black paint, put in the closed eyes.

The closed eyes.

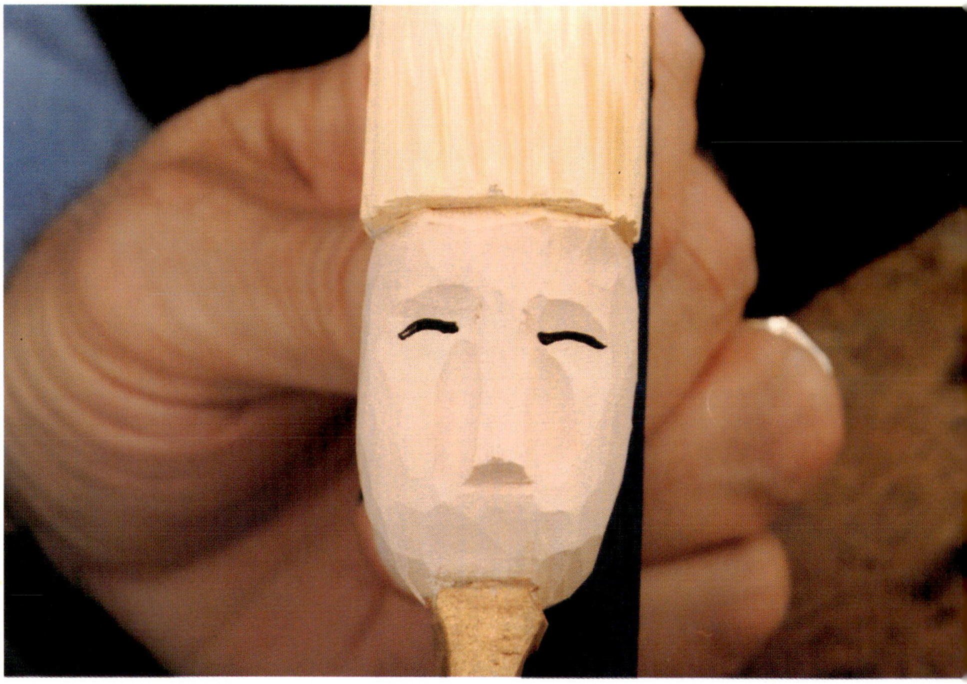

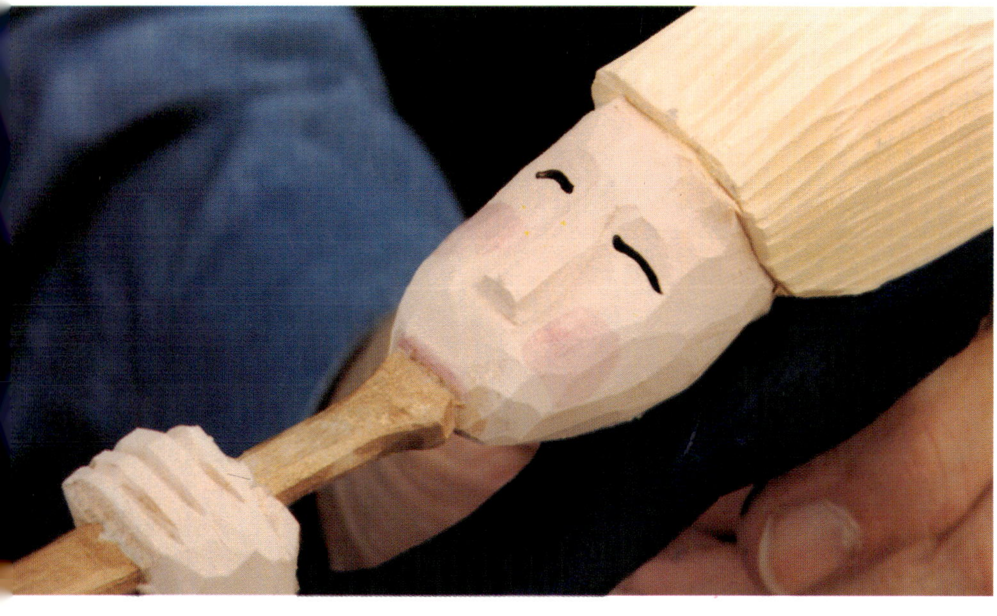

While the cheeks are still a little wet, I'm going to make pink cheeks by mixing a little red and skin tone. Apply a little bit to the cheeks and upper lip too.

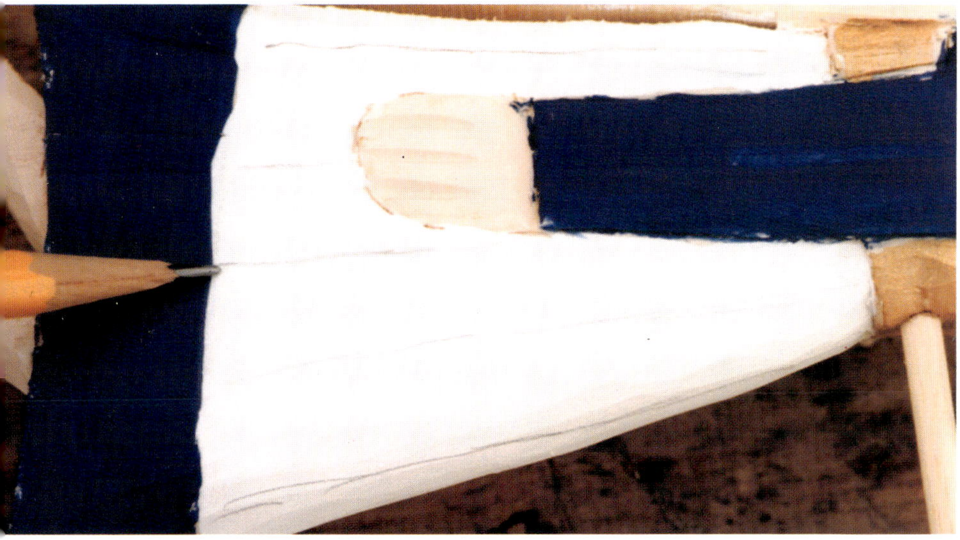

It may help to pencil in where you are going to put in the red stripes.

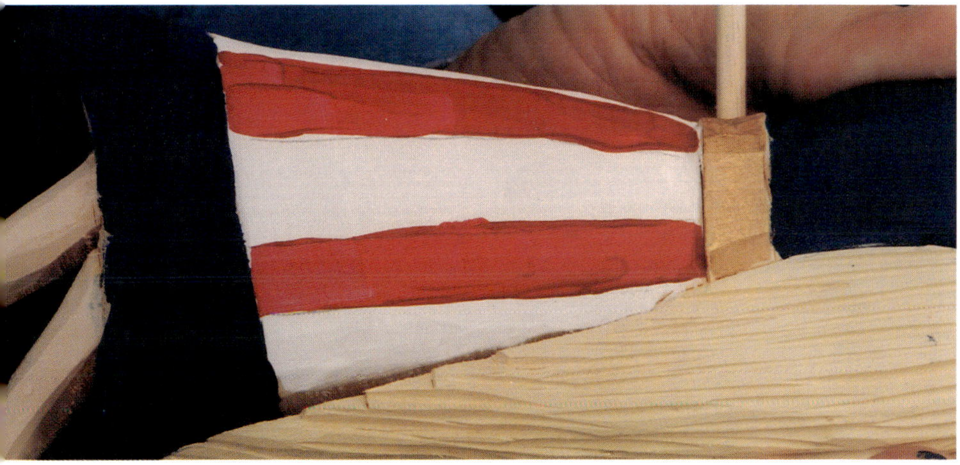

I'm painting the red stripes over the white skirt. I will probably have to apply two coats to get the red as dark as I want it to be.

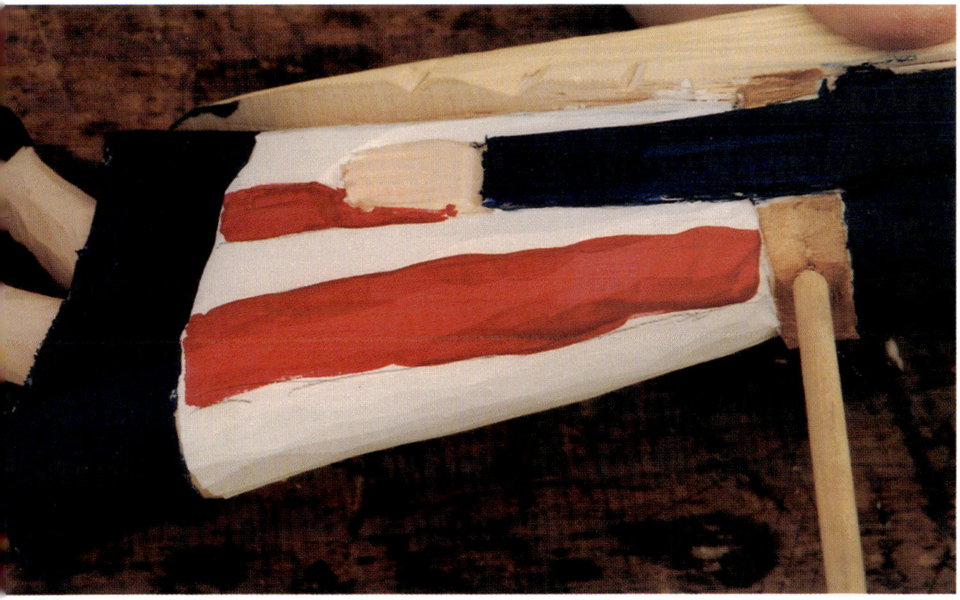

Continuing around with the stripes.

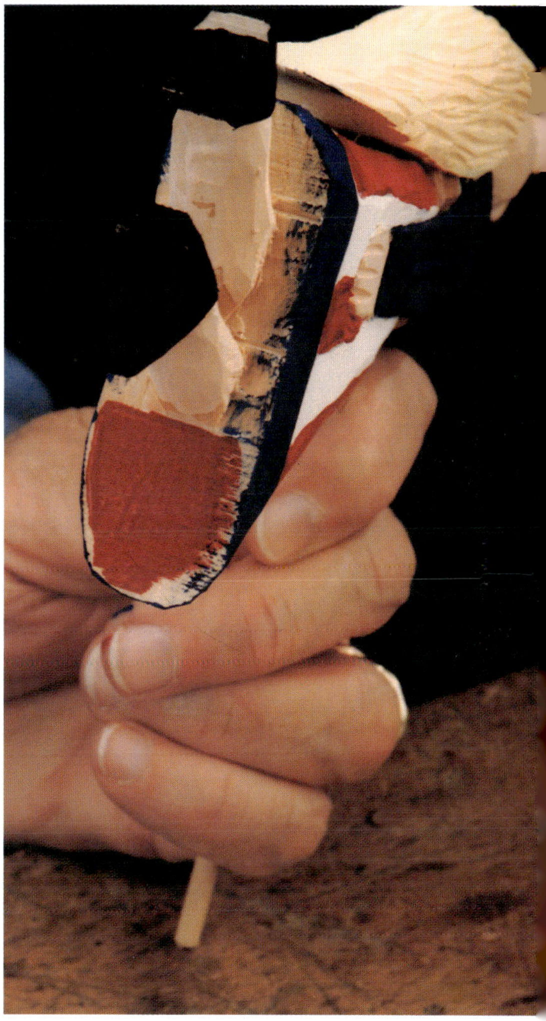

Painting the underside of the skirt red.

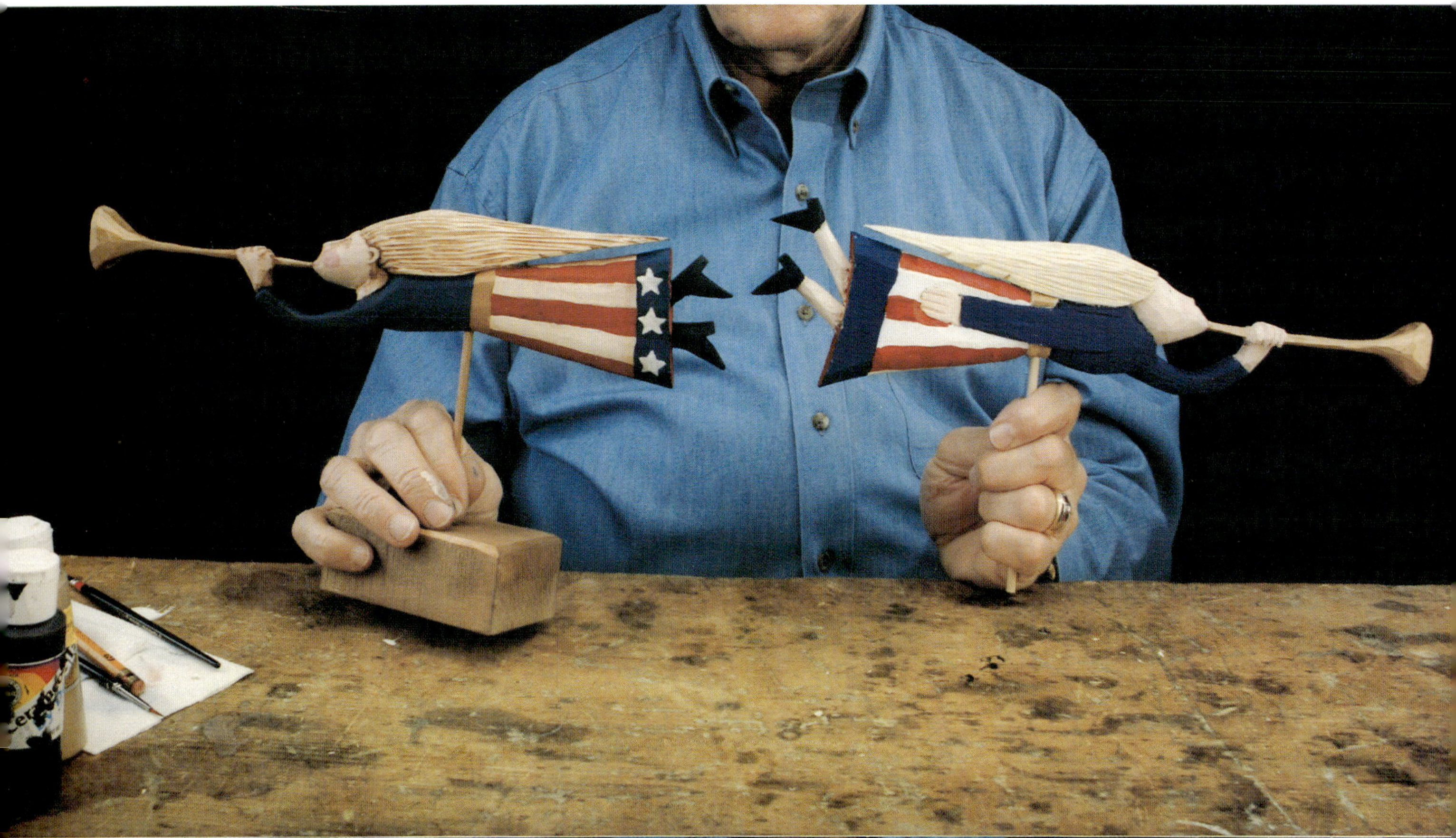

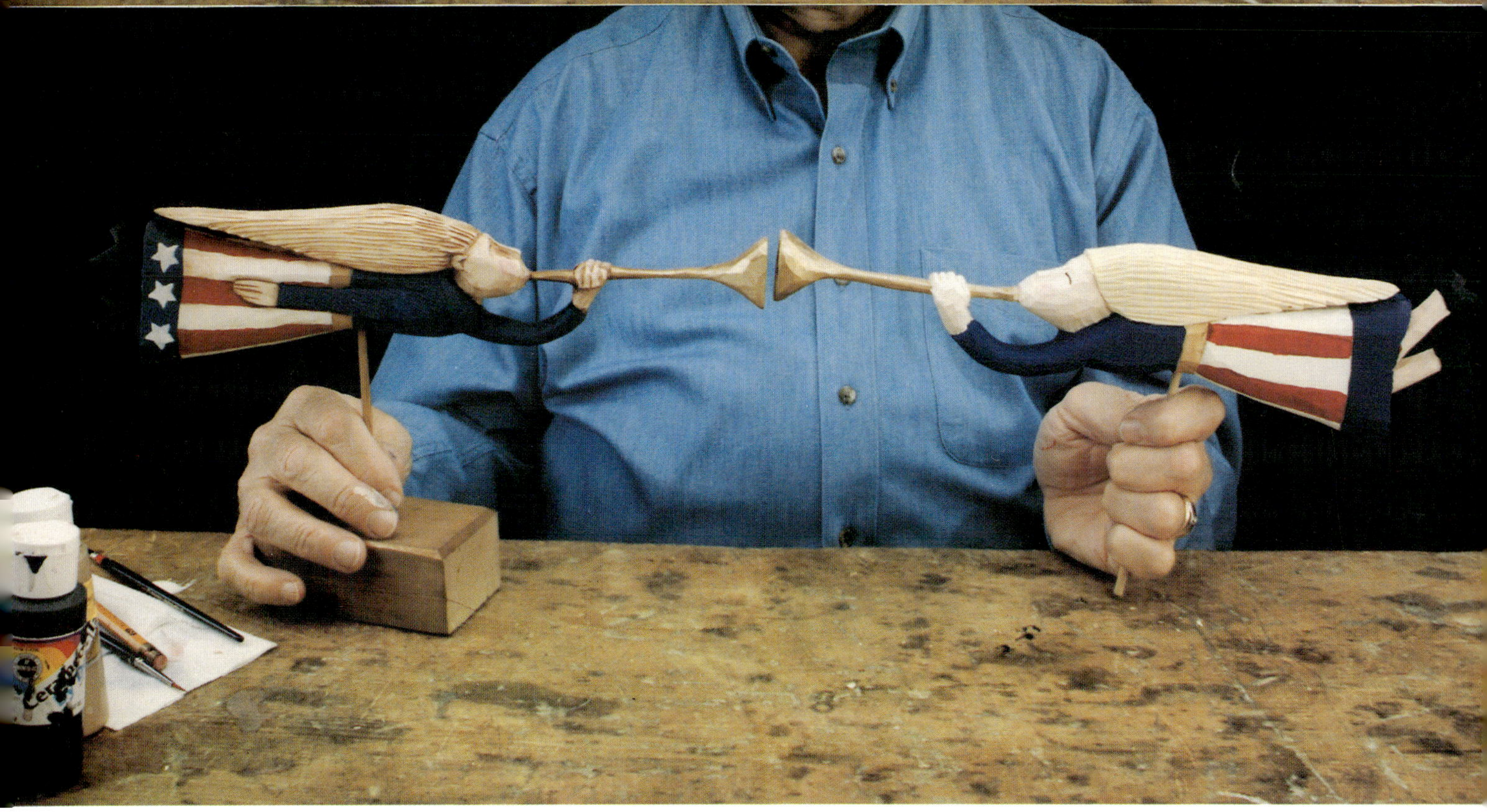

I made stencils for the stars on the lower skirt band as seen on the finished angel on the left.

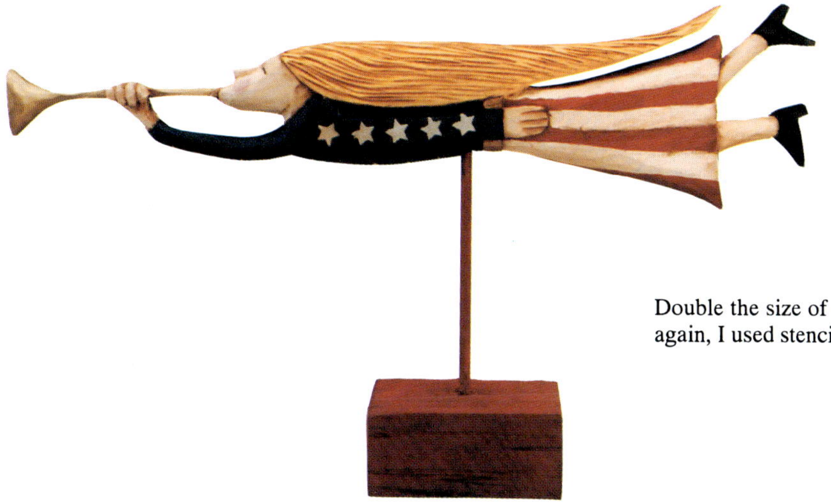

Double the size of the pattern to produce this trumpeting angel. Once again, I used stencils for the stars.

The angel with trumpet and wings. The arms, face and feet are Flesh Tone, the trumpet is Kim Gold, the robe is Cape Cod, the hair is Old Parchment, and the wings are White.

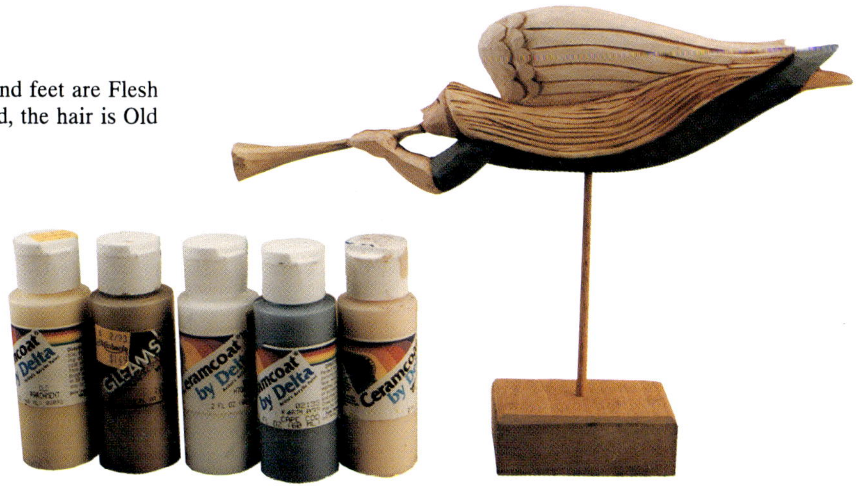

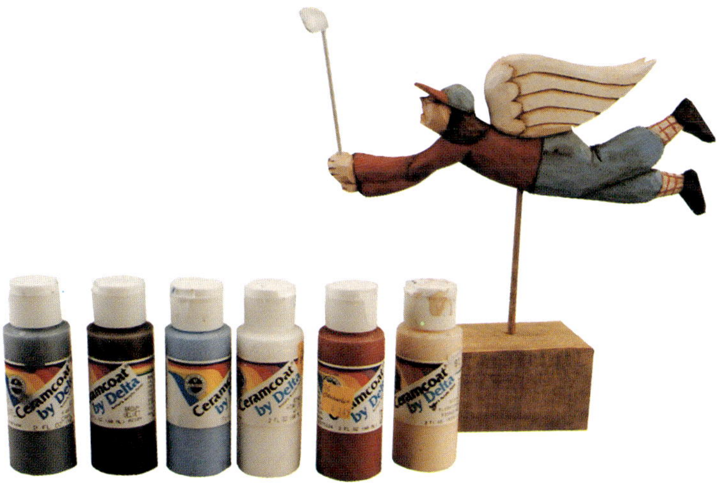

These are the colors for the golfing angel. Tompte Red was used on the shirt and the cap bill. The rest of the cap and trousers were painted in Blue Jay. The shoes and hair are Brown Velvet, the wings are painted White, and the golf club is Silver.

The skin of the angel with the folded wing is Flesh Tone, the hair is Brown Velvet, the robe is Cape Cod, and the wings are White.

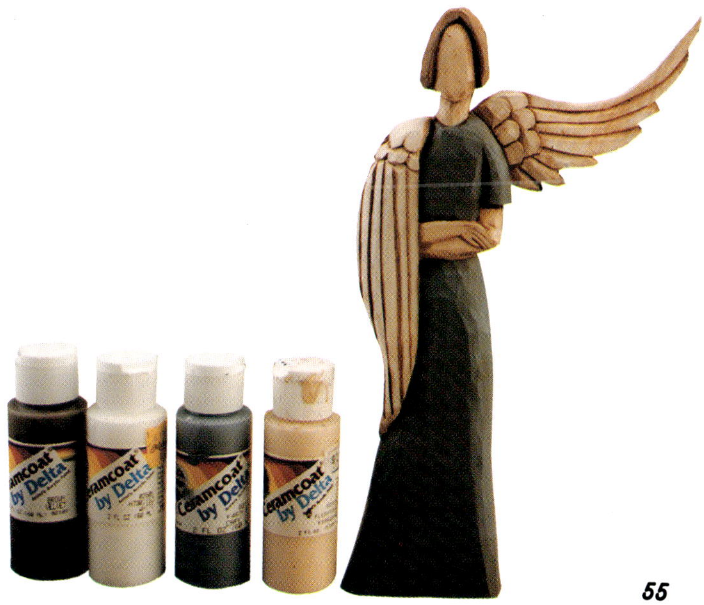

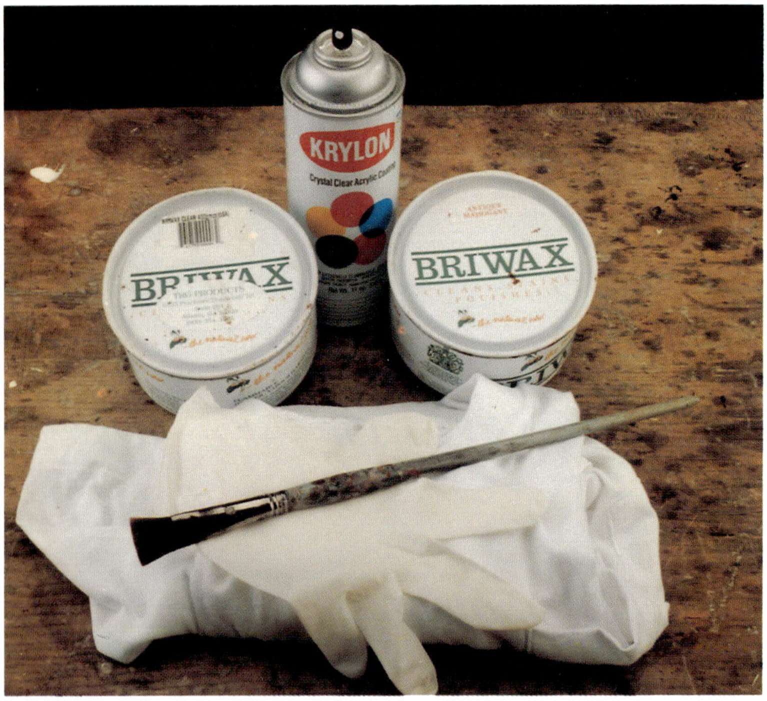

These are the products I use to "antique." If you have some other method, continue to use it.

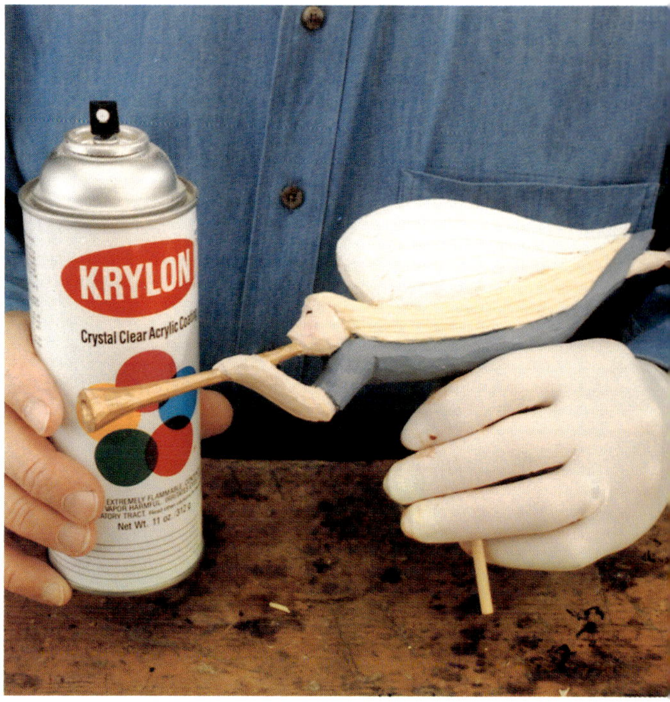

It is important to spray your painted, dry carving with Krylon 1301 acrylic coating.

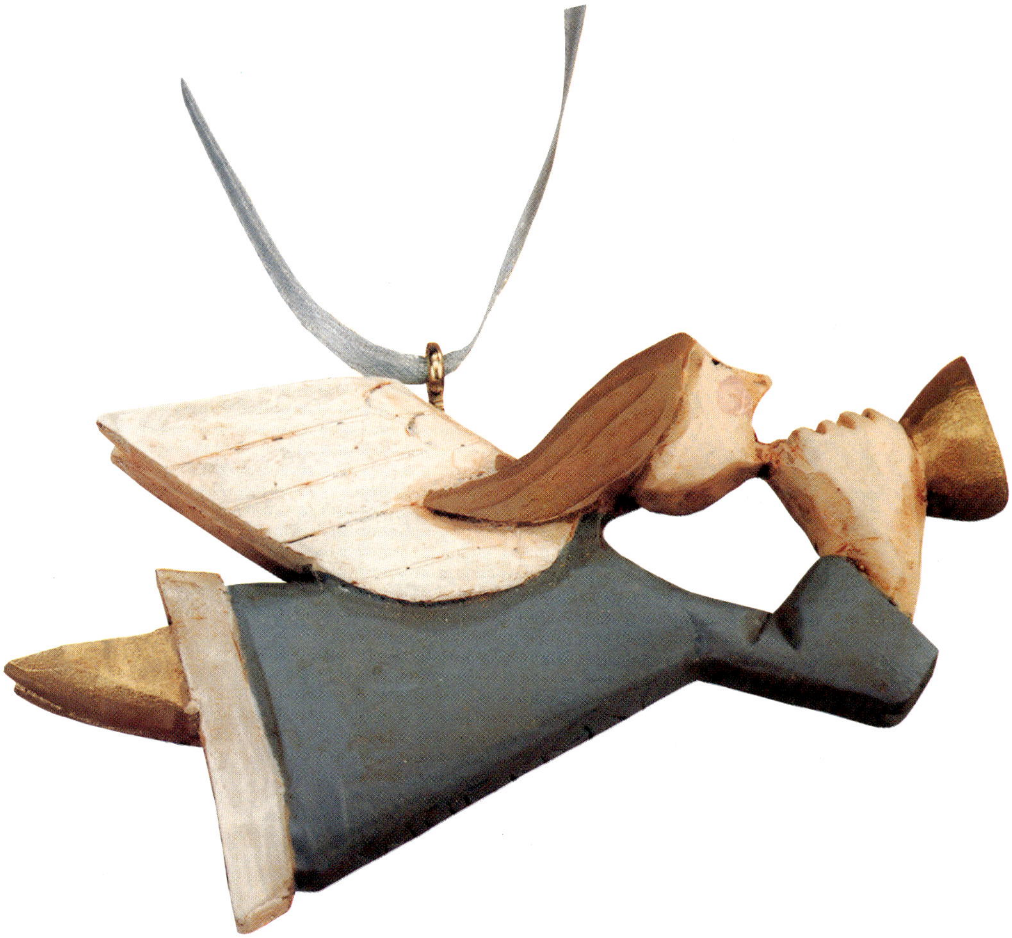

This design was in my book *Angel Carving and Other Favorites.* It was so popular I could not keep up. I had it cast in Pecan Shell Resin.

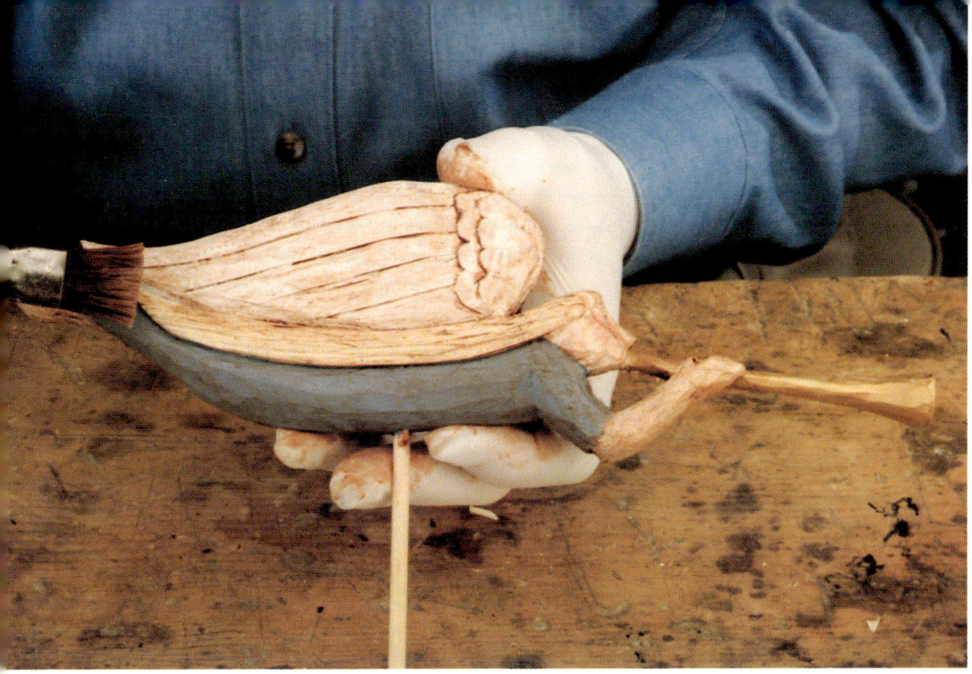

Cover the piece with a coating of Antique Mahogany Briwax. P.S. I am not dead! I am wearing a rubber glove to protect my hand.

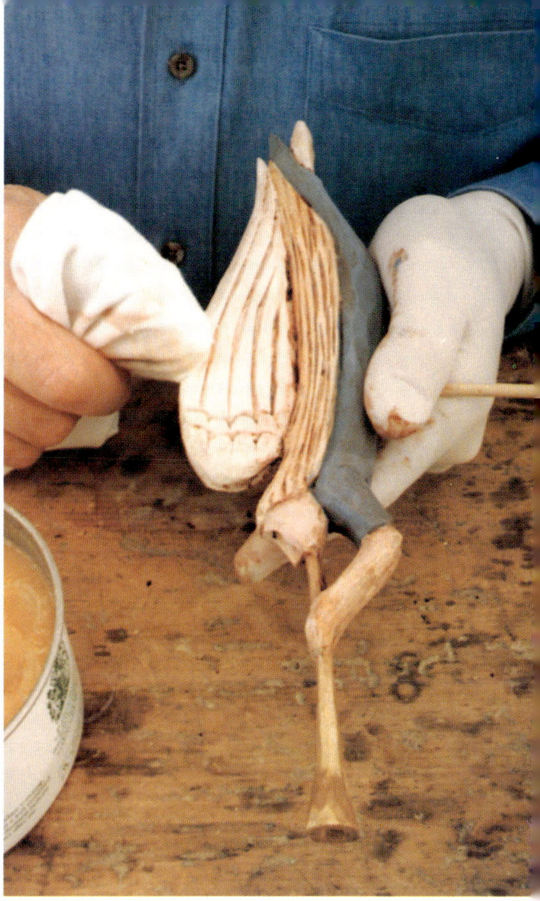

Take a soft cloth T-shirt or a cloth diaper and wipe off with neutral Briwax polish.

The finished piece with a nice antique patina.

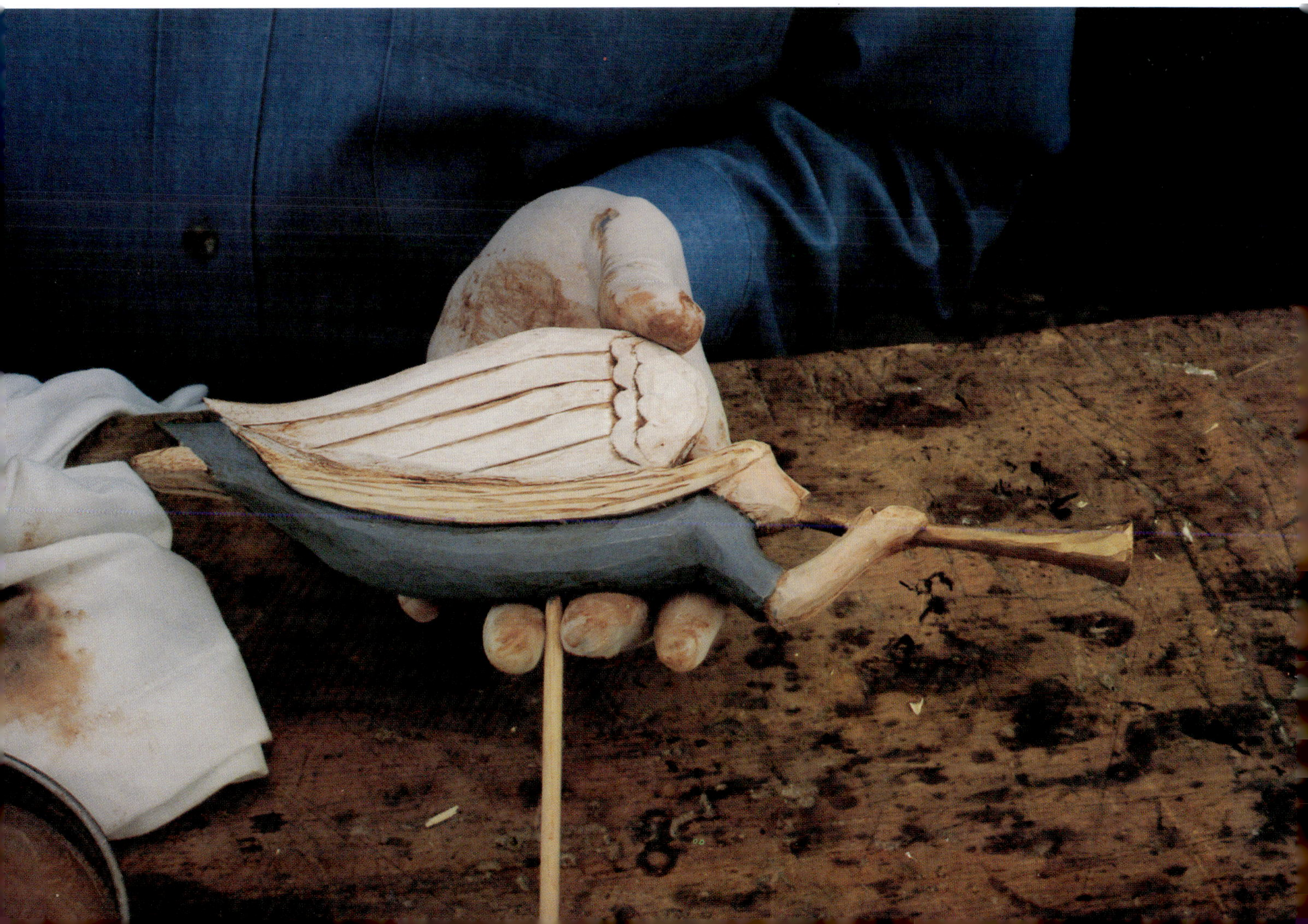

The Gallery

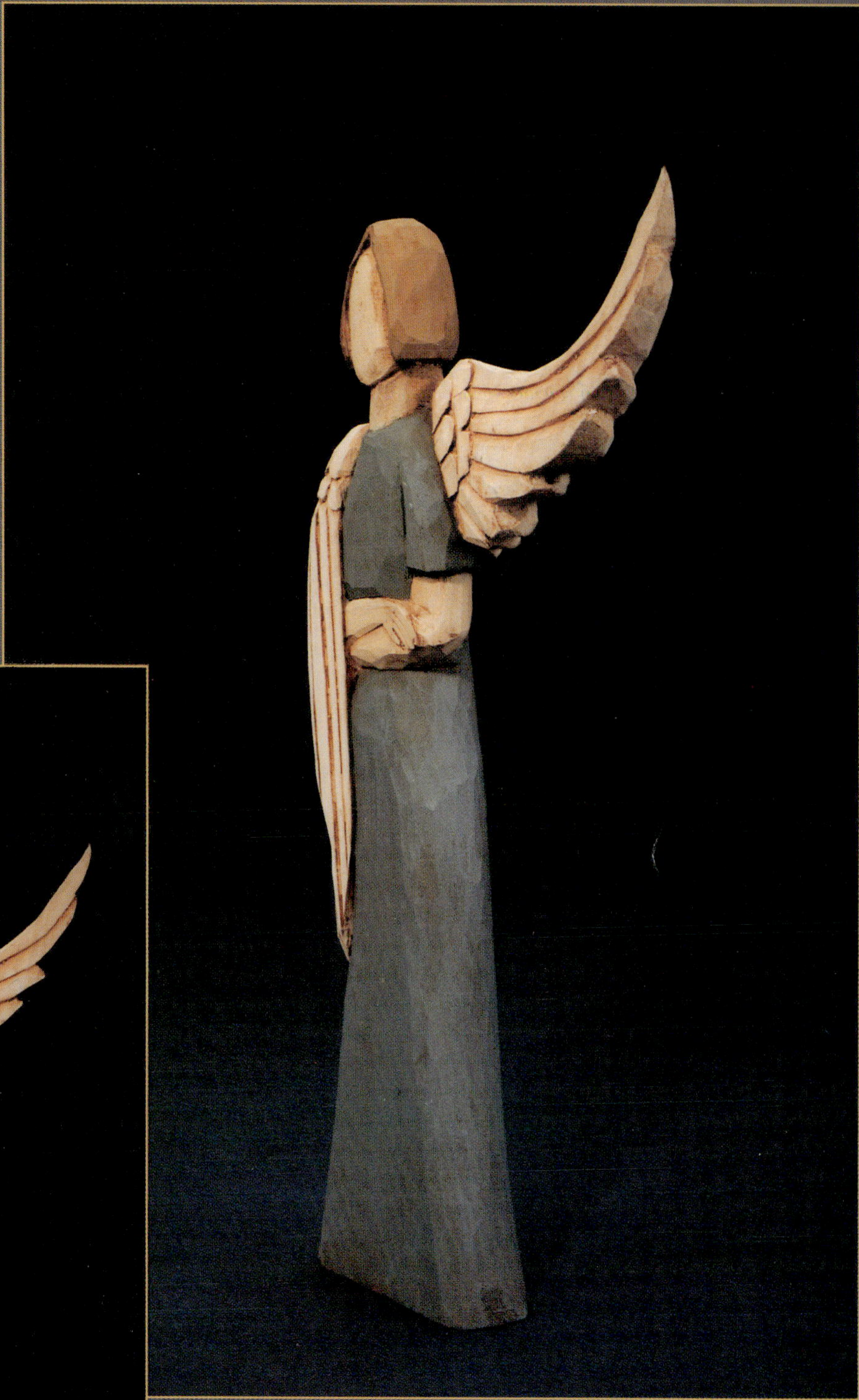

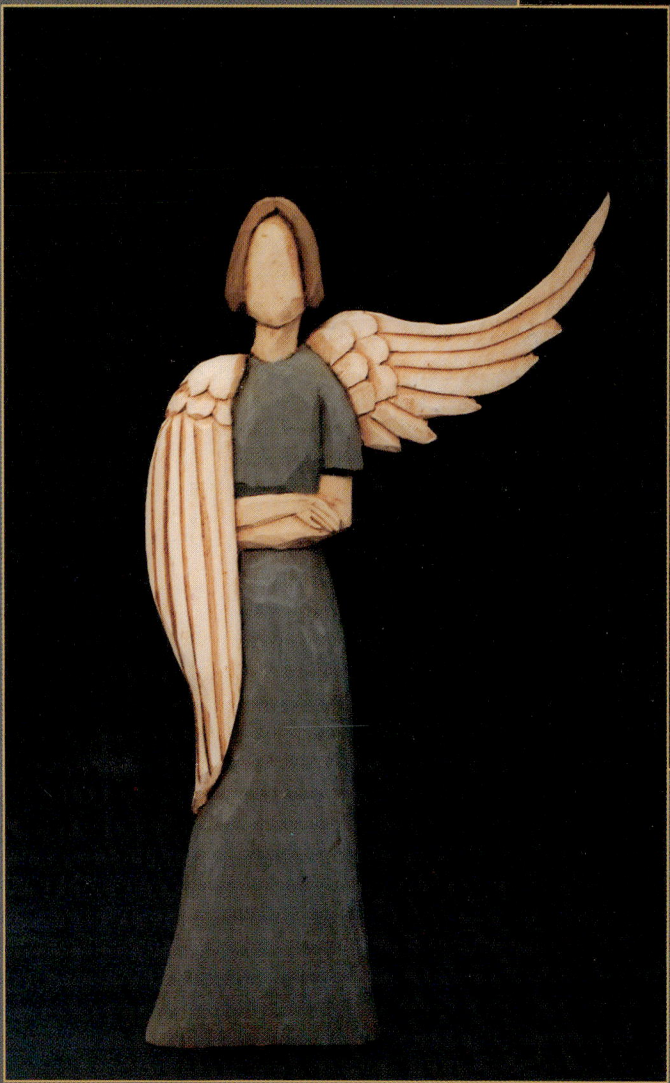

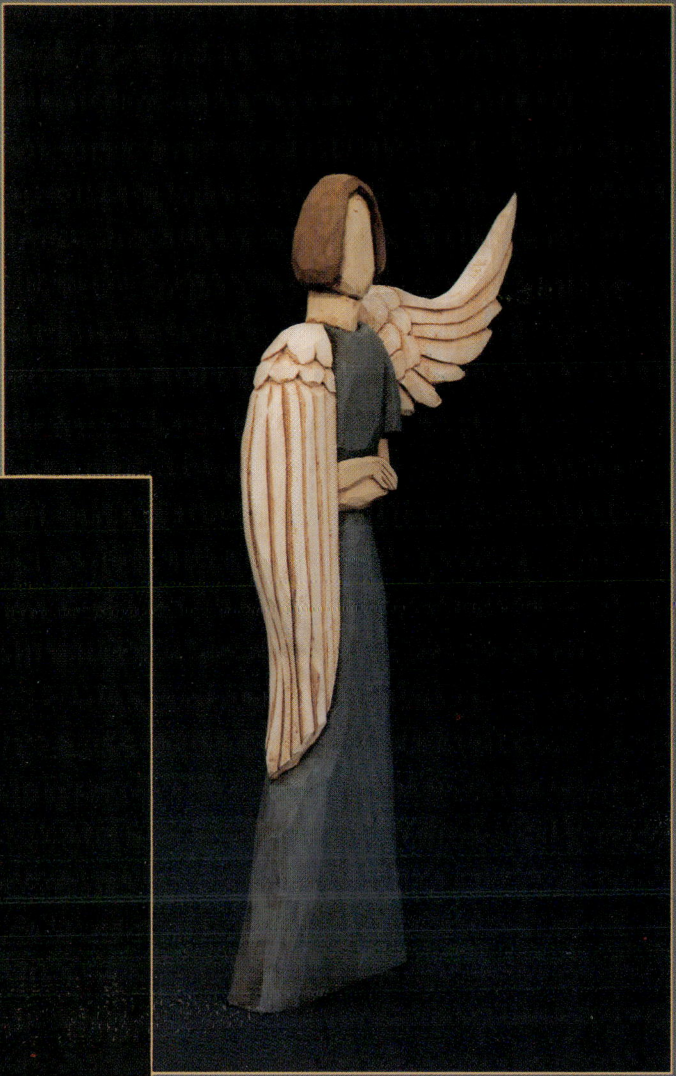

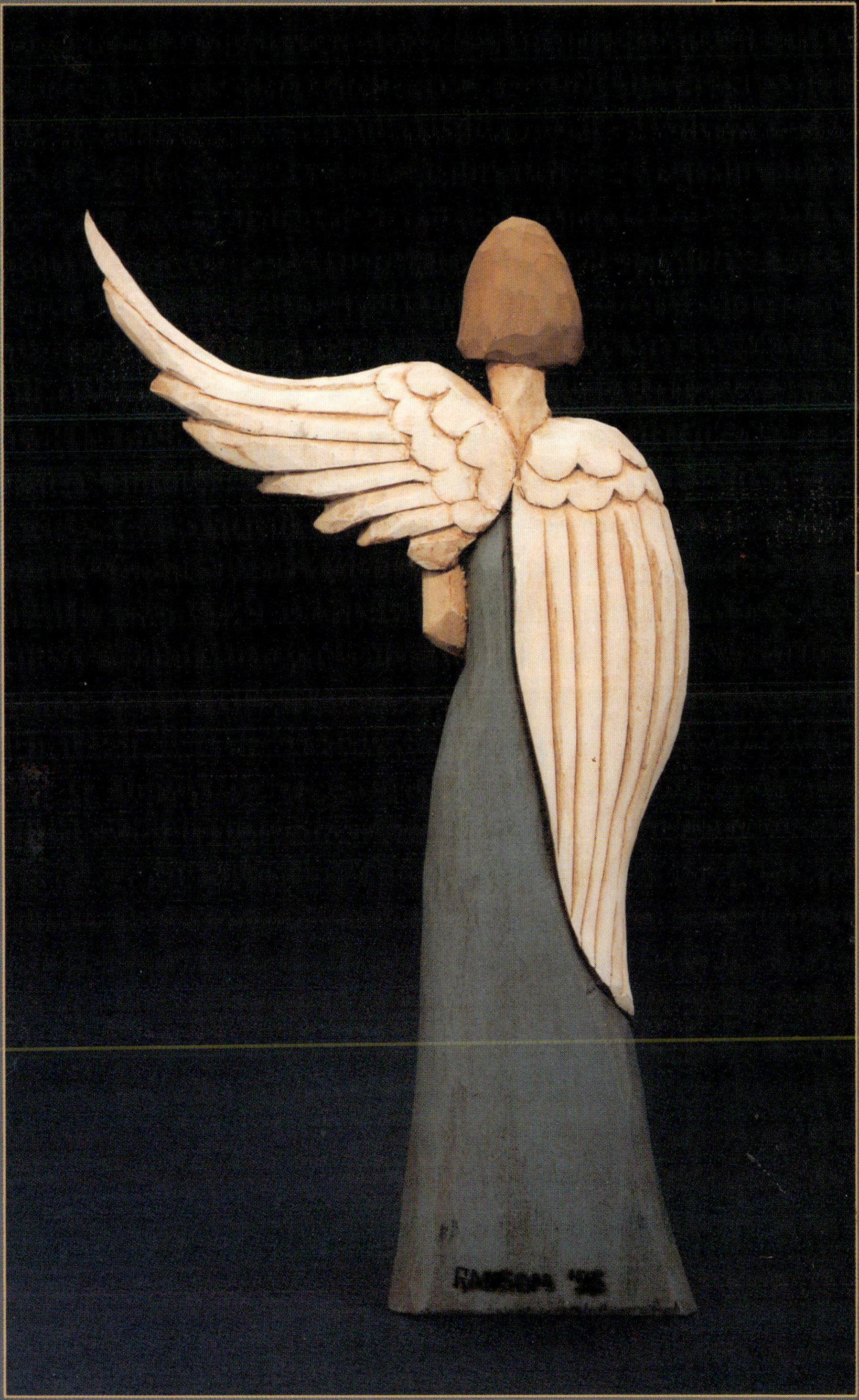

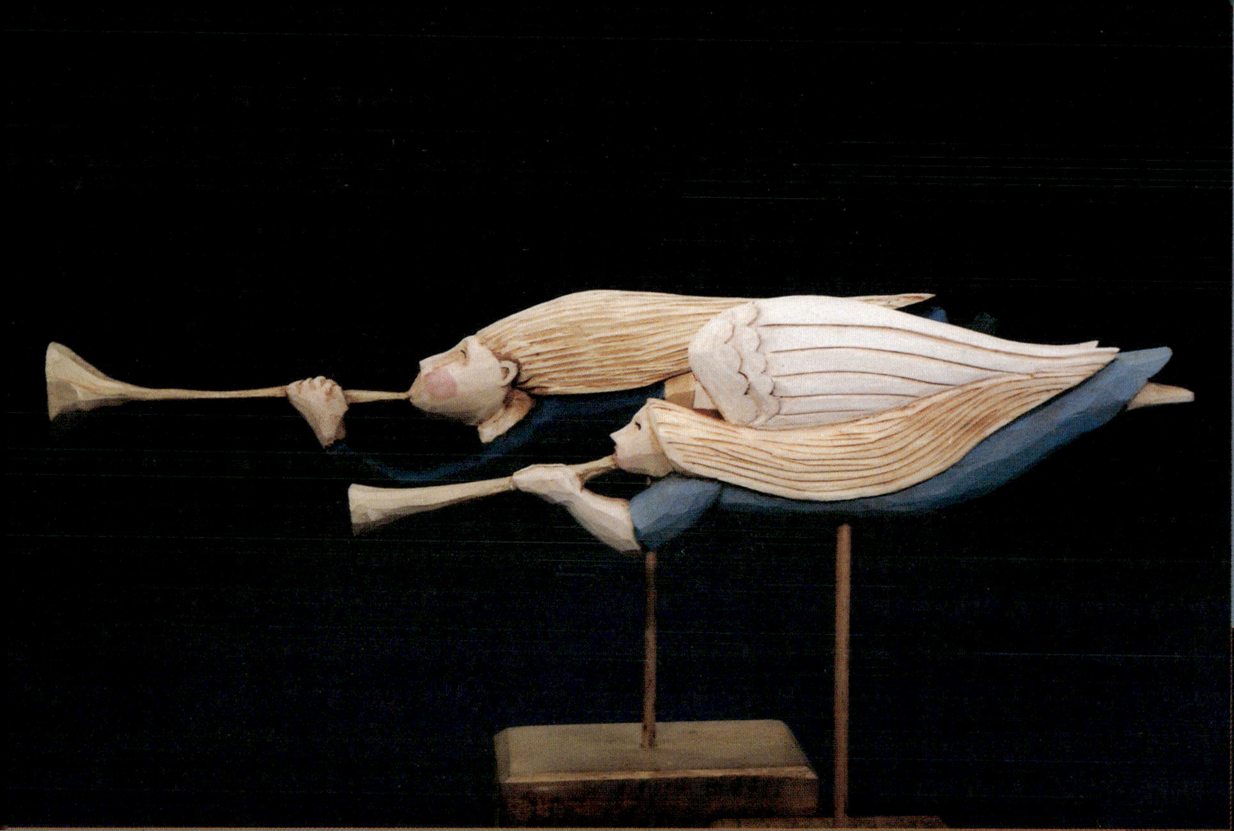

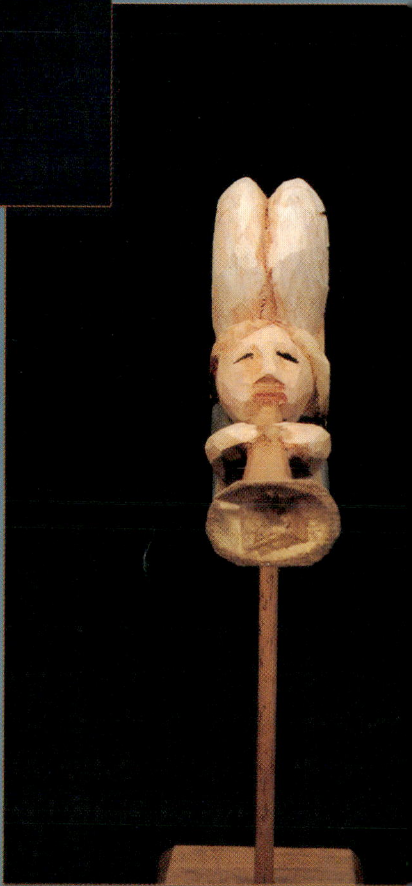

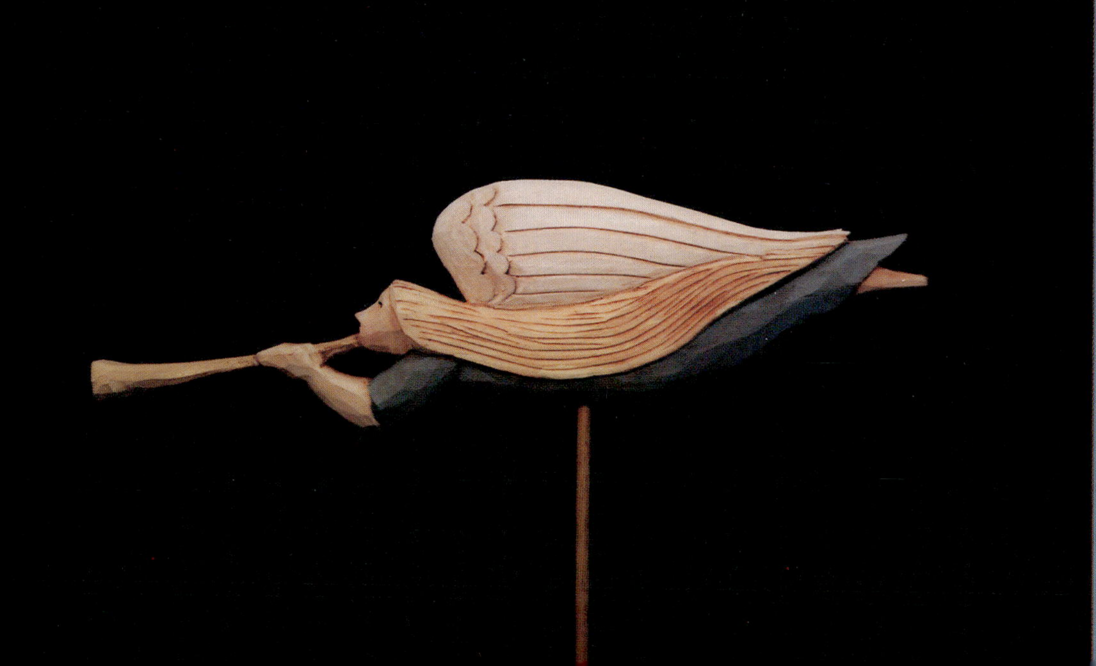

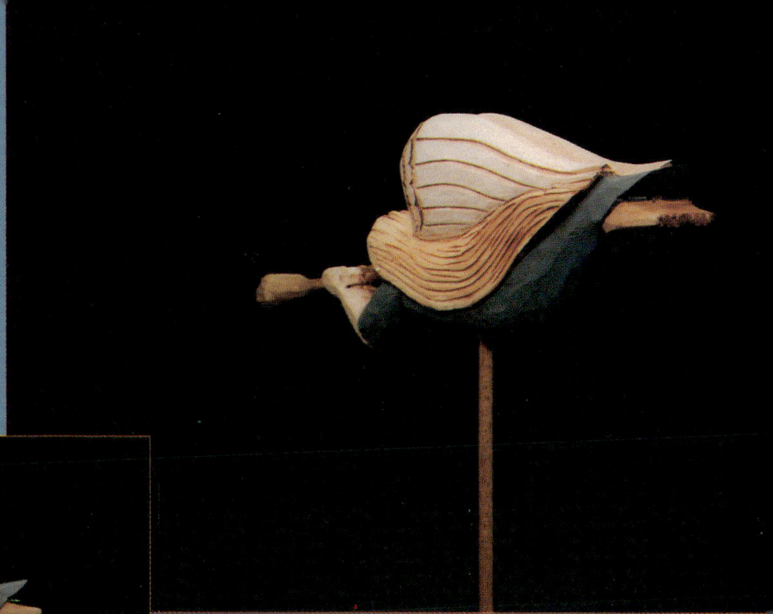

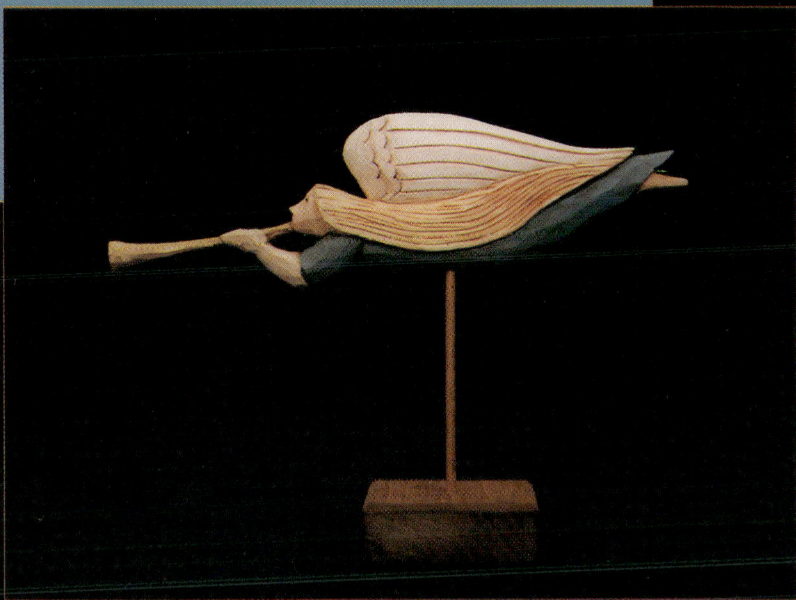

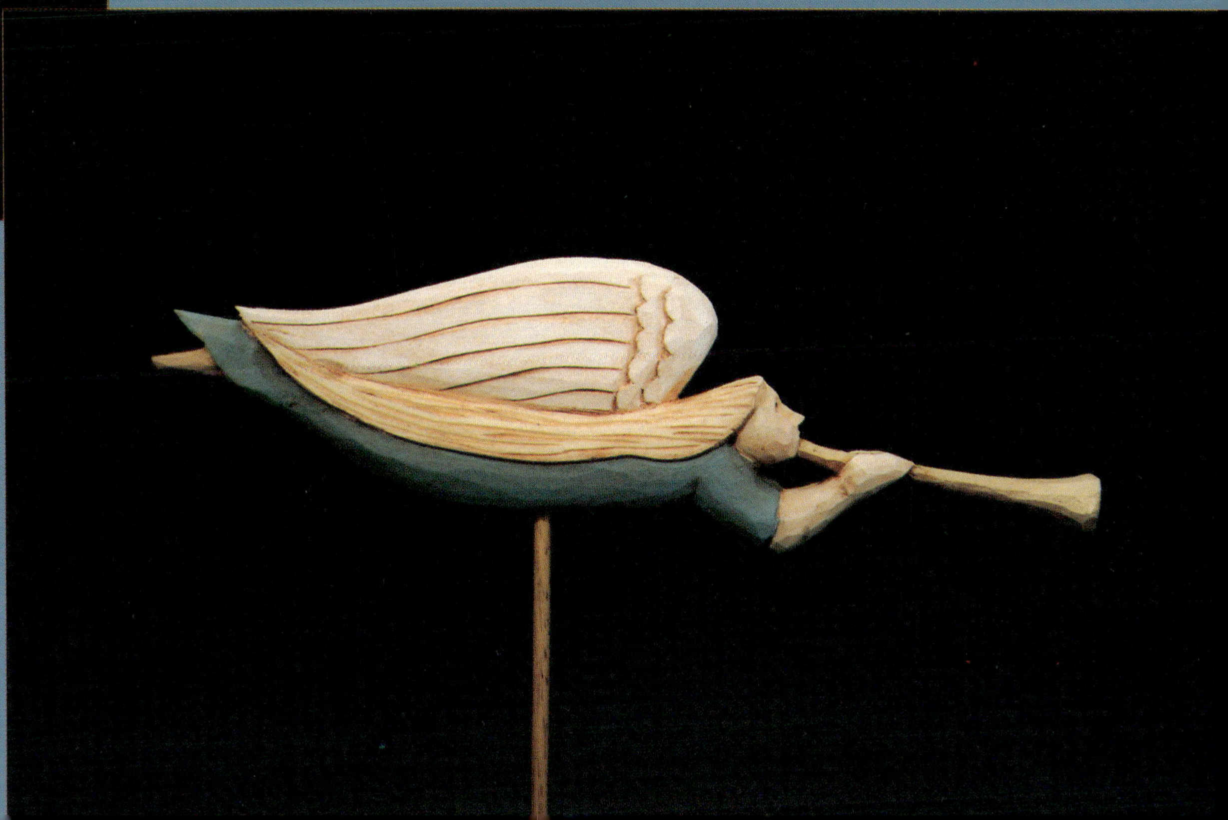

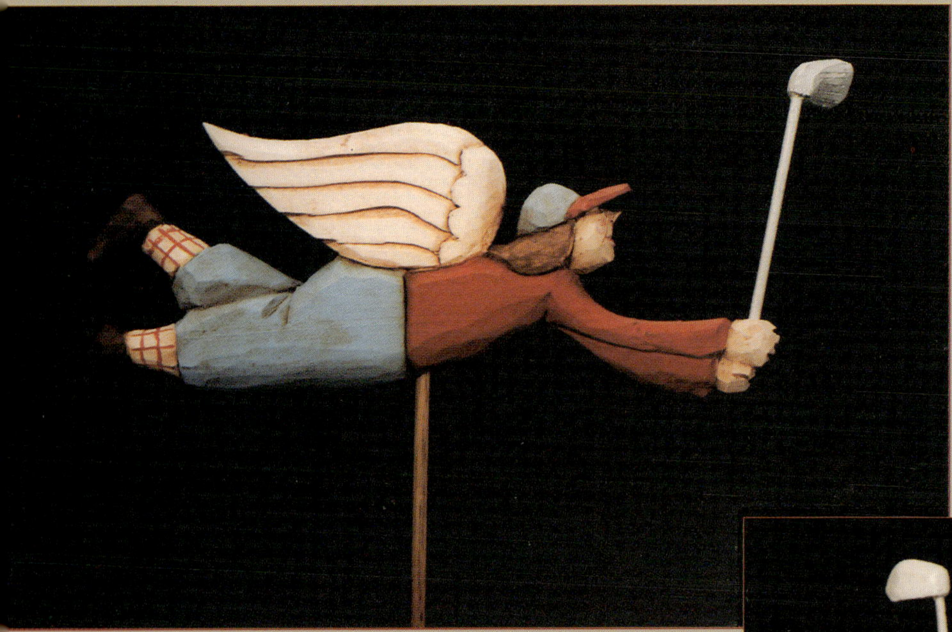

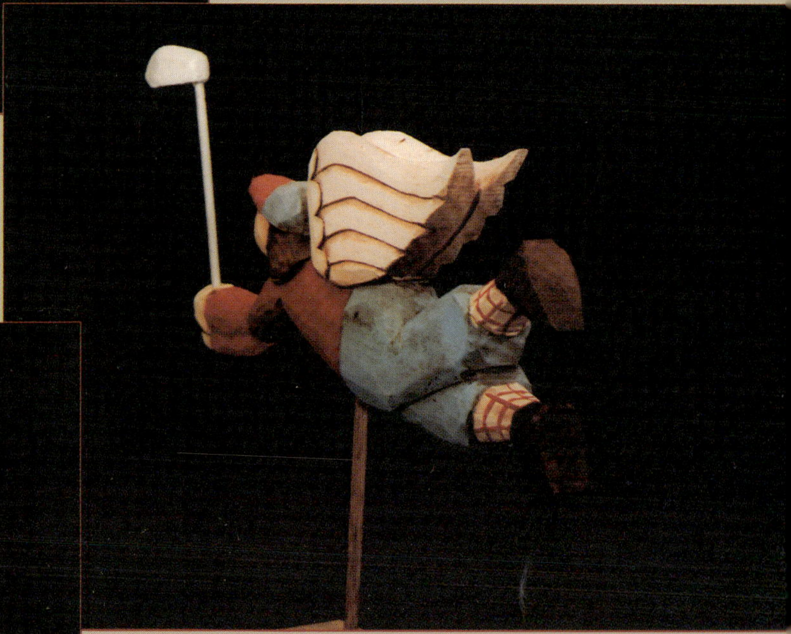

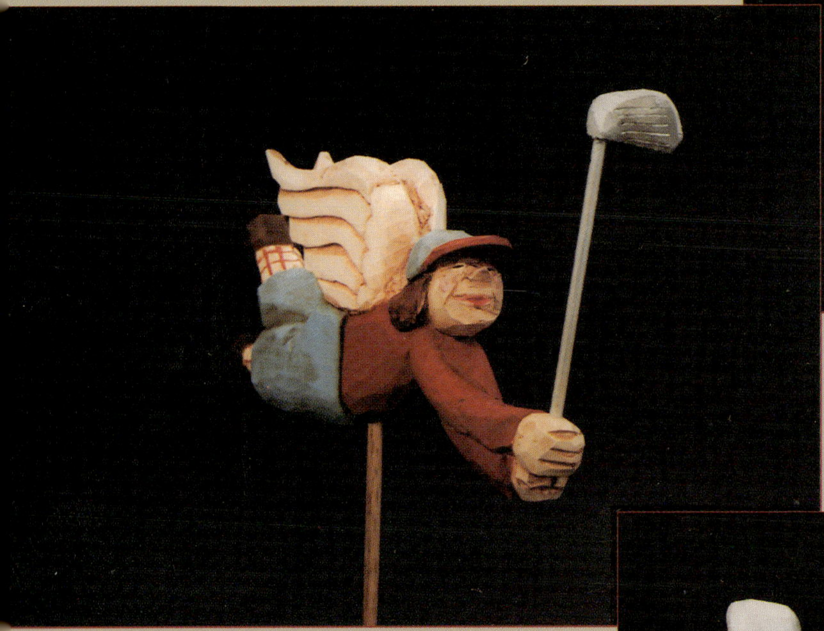

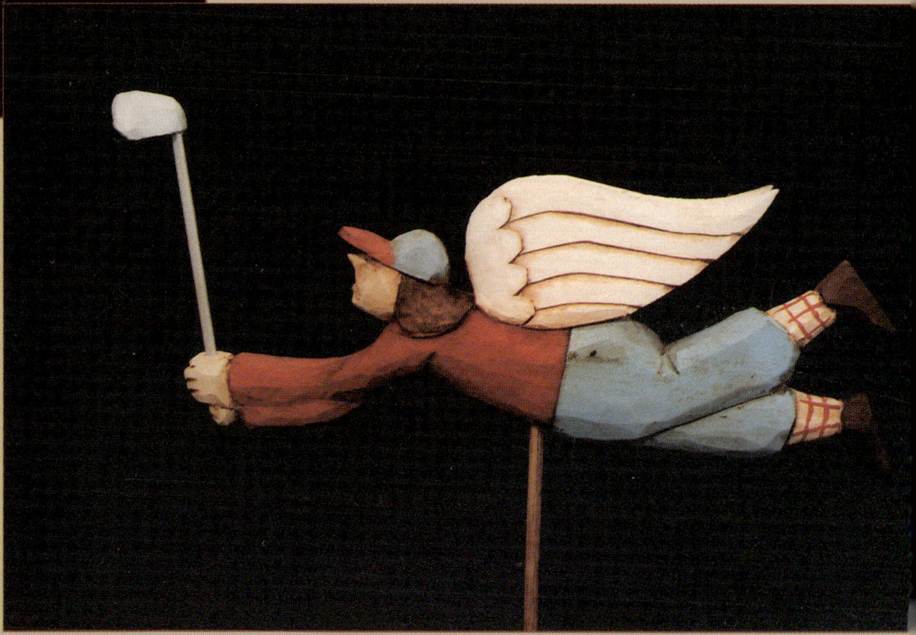

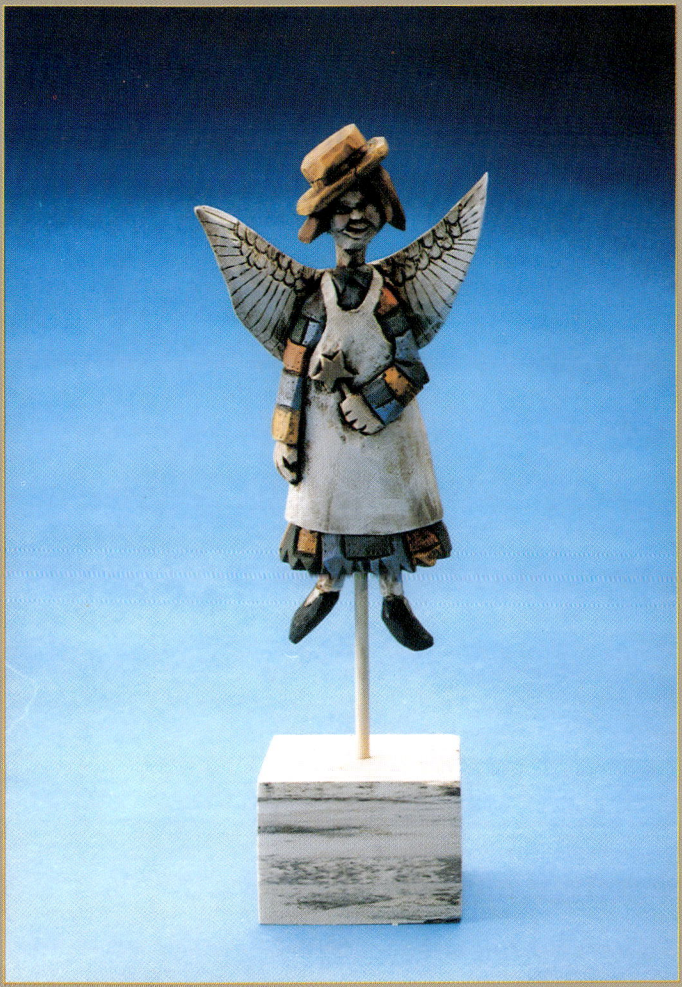
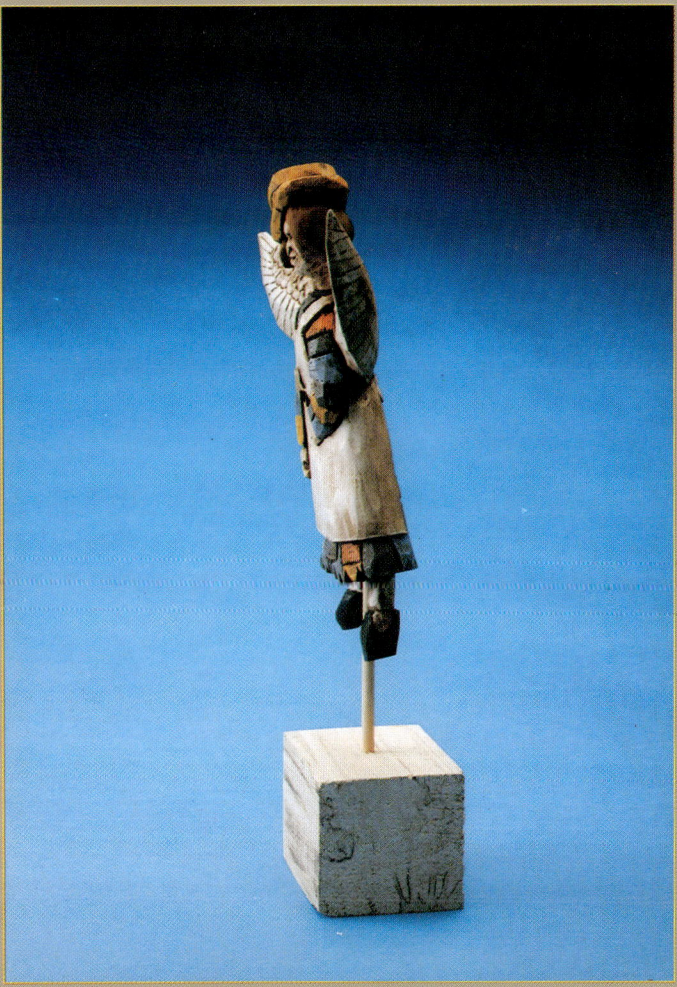
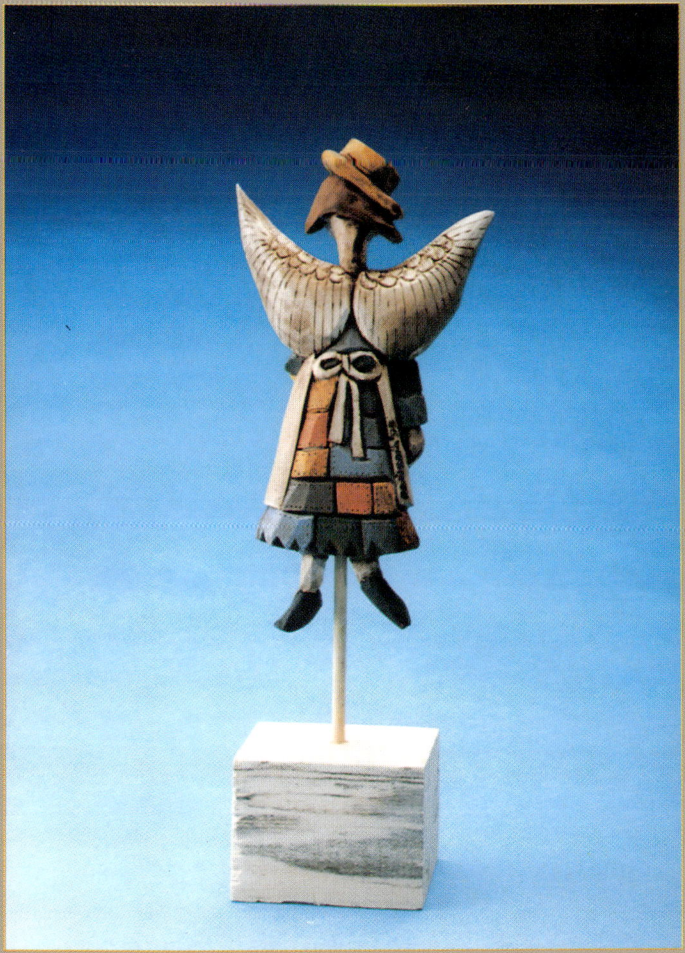
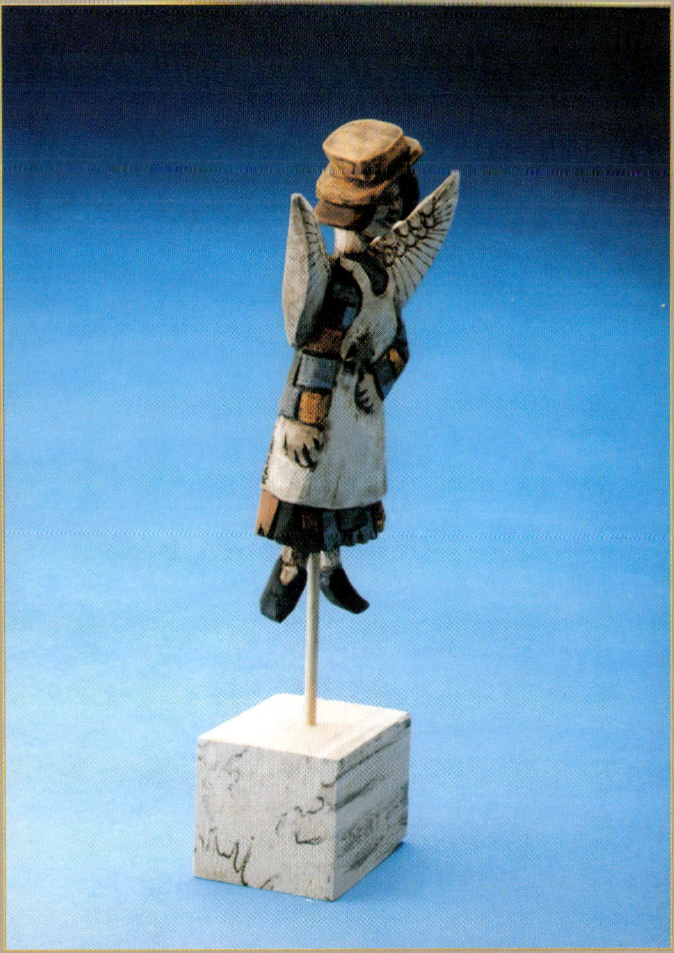

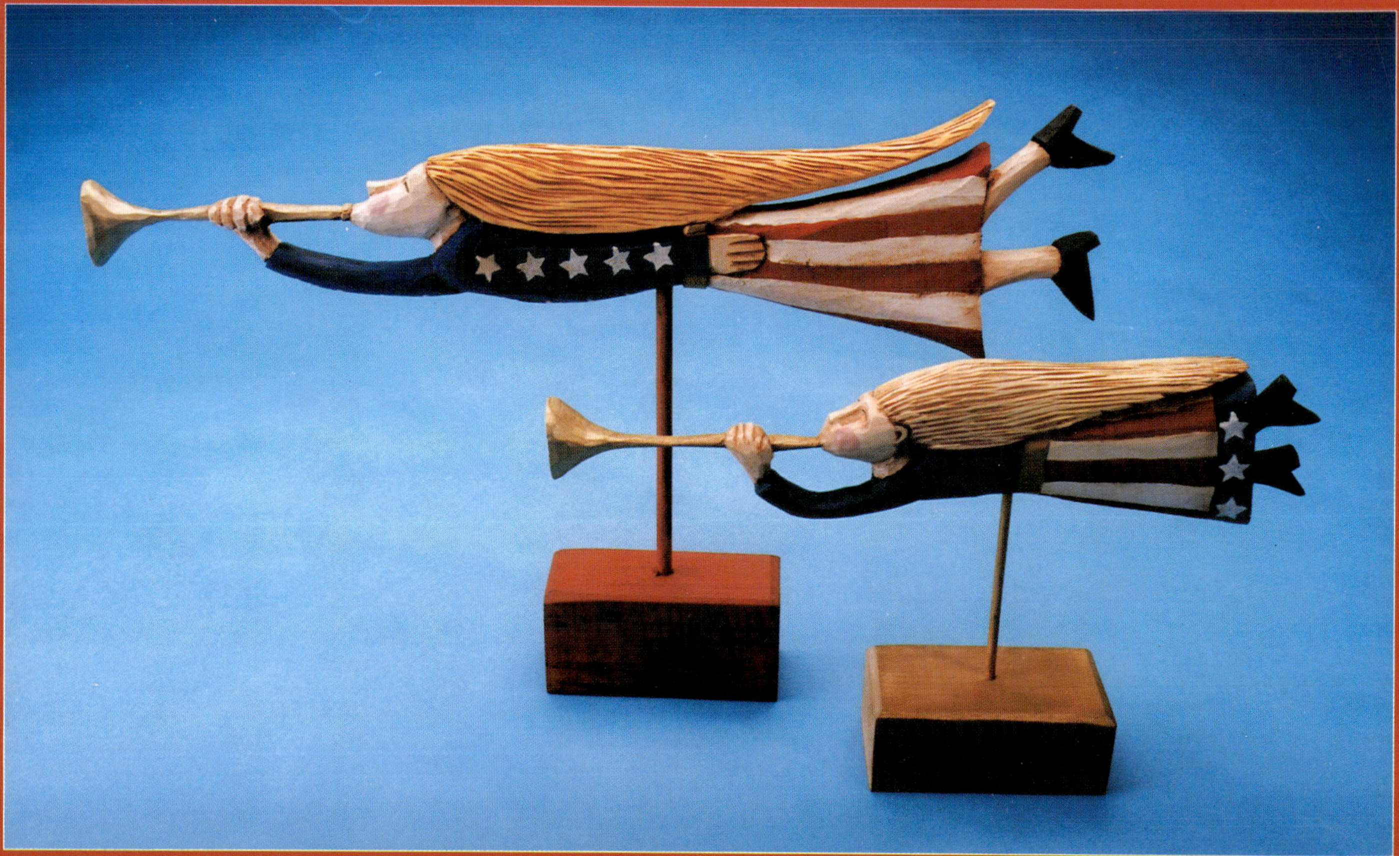

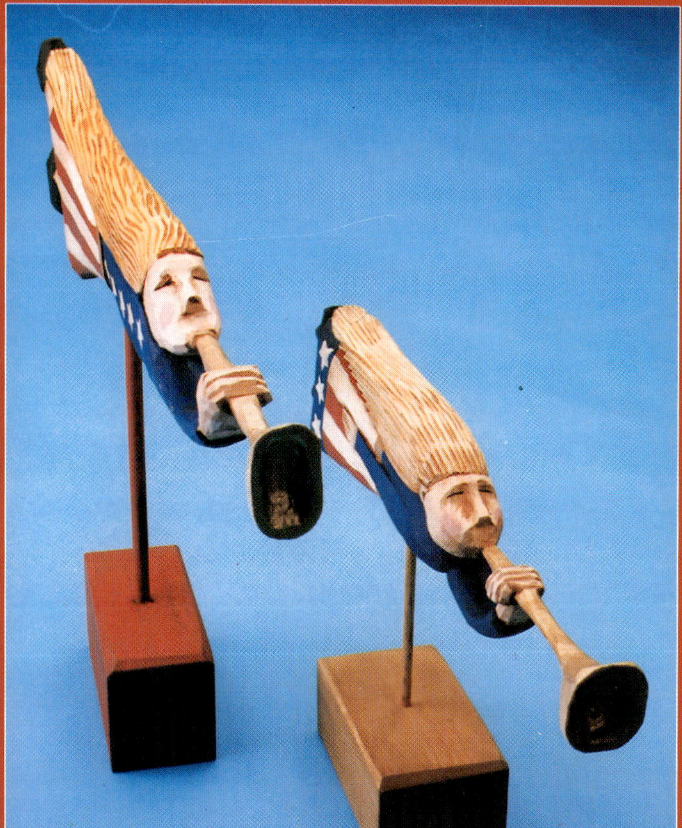

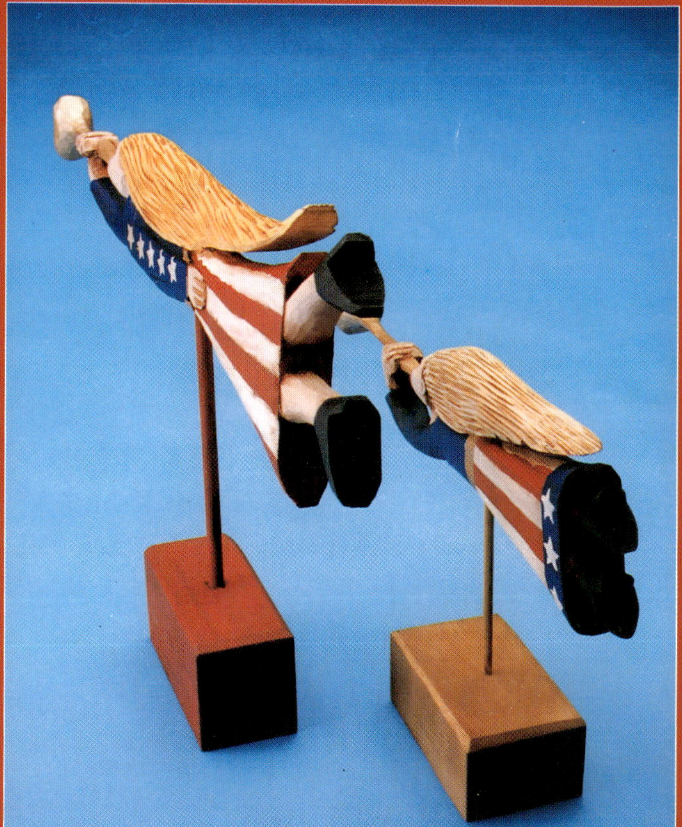